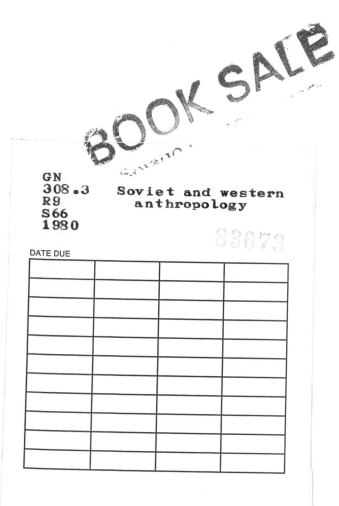

Soviet and Western Anthropology

Soviet and Western Anthropology

edited by
ERNEST GELLNER

with an introduction by
MEYER FORTES

Columbia University Press   New York   1980

Published in 1980 in
the United States of America by
Columbia University Press

Library of Congress Cataloging in Publication Data
Main entry under title:

Soviet and western anthropology.
    Includes bibliographical references and index.
    1. Ethnology–Russia–Addresses, essays, lectures.
    2. Communism and anthropology–Addresses, essays,
    lectures. 3. Anthropology–Russia–Addresses,
    essays, lectures. I. Gellner, Ernest.
    GN308.3.R9S66   1980   301'.947   80–11676
    ISBN 0–231–05120–4

Printed in Great Britain

CONTENTS

List of Contributors

S. Arutyonov, Institute of Ethnography, Academy of Sciences of the USSR, Moscow

V. Basilov, Institute of Ethnography, Academy of Sciences of the USSR, Moscow.

Yu. Bromley, Institute of Ethnography, Academy of Sciences of the USSR, Moscow.

T. Dragadze, Sociology Department, University of Leeds.

L. Drobizheva, Institute of Ethnography, Academy of Sciences of the USSR, Moscow.

Meyer Fortes, King's College, University of Cambridge.

E. Gellner, Philosophy Department, London School of Economics.

M. Godelier, Laboratoire d'Anthropologie Sociale, Collège de France, Paris.

J. Goody, St John's College, University of Cambridge.

C. Humphrey, King's College, University of Cambridge.

I. Kon, Institute of Ethnography, Academy of Sciences of the USSR, Leningrad.

V. Kozlov, Institute of Ethnography, Academy of Sciences of the USSR, Moscow.

L. Krader, Institut für Ethnologie, Freie Universität Berlin.

A. Pershits, Institute of Ethnography, Academy of Sciences of the USSR, Moscow.

Yu. Petrova-Averkieva, Institute of Ethnography, Academy of Sciences of the USSR, Moscow; Editor of *Sovietskaia Etnografia*.

J. Pouillon, Laboratoire d'Anthropologie Sociale, Collège de France, Paris; Editor of *L'Homme*.

Yu. Semenov, Moscow Physical-Technical Institute.

T. Shanin, Sociology Department, University of Manchester.

J. Woodburn, Social Anthropology Department, London School of Economics.

Preface

Meyer Fortes' Introduction deals most effectively with the relevance of Soviet social anthropology for its western counterparts. But the interest of the scholarly and intellectual activities which take place in the Soviet Union under the title of *etnografia*, and which can be treated as the approximate equivalent of social or cultural anthropology in the West, is not exhausted by its relevance for anthropologists, important though this is.

Soviet *etnografia* is also profoundly significant in other ways. It reflects or expresses the manner in which the intellectuals of the Soviet Union think about some of the deepest problems within their own society, and about its place in the scheme of things and in world history. The handling of such issues can only be described as fundamental social thought. Such thought is neither absent nor monolithic within the Soviet Union. The ideas expressed by members of the Soviet delegation to the small conference at Burg Wartenstein in 1976 constitute a sample of it. Precisely how representative the sample was, is a question which will no doubt be answered variously by different experts in the cultural life of the USSR, in the light of their assessment of Soviet intellectual trends. But there is no doubt in my mind whatever but that it is an important sample. So is the set of contributions by the western participants: but I do not comment on these. Articulated as they are in an idiom to which the reader is well habituated, they are more than able to convey their meaning without risk of misunderstanding.

It is my impression that the best fundamental social thought in the USSR is to be found in social anthropology and in history; and that there is rather more of it in these areas than in some other disciplines. If this impression is justified, there may be various explanations for it. It may be that philosophy is too abstract, and sociology too concrete and empirical, to provide an idiom for the discussion of the issues in social thought which really matter: such a supposition would not always be out of place in the West, and it may apply in the Soviet Union. Something similar may be true of the other human sciences, such as psychology or linguistics. But problems in the history of social structure may be specific enough to be discussed with less constraint than other issues, and yet general enough in their implications to be of very great interest. On the positive side it may be that the intimate links which exist between anthropology and history have been of great help in endowing Soviet anthropology with a certain sense of reality. As a number of contributors (e.g. Averkieva, Kozlov and Basilov) insist, in diverse ways, Soviet anthropology is 'historicist'. They might have added that a sense of historic depth and continuity is not merely a corollary of Marxism, but also a deeply-entrenched Russian intellectual tradition. In the West, or at any rate in Britain, anthropology took pride in its autonomy from history, and there even emerged the notion of the 'ethnographic present', the methodological fiction of a social structure or culture existing without a date. It is ironic that at the very moment at which anthropology in the West is finding its way back to history, not without difficulty, Soviet anthropology is in part practicing a mild detachment from it. The strategy of research into contemporary culture and ethnicity (as described for instance by Bromley, Drobizheva and Kon) involves, as a matter of inter-disciplinary division of labour though not as a matter of social theory, a concentration on contemporary and cultural phenomena, and a corresponding turning away from both the archaic and the structural.

Nevertheless, the intimate nexus between Soviet anthropology and history is striking and important. The kind of absolutely fundamental issue about the typology of human societies and historical periodicisation (discussed for instance by Semenov and Pershits and less directly by Kozlov and Arutyonov), can be found, in the very same idiom and as part of one continuous debate, amongst both historians and anthropologists.

This is the appropriate point at which to warn the reader about terminological and conceptual non-equivalences, which on occasion make translation difficult and which involve the risk of misunderstandings. It has already been stressed that *etnografia* means the science as a whole, including its theoretical parts, and is not, like western *ethnography*, the purely descriptive account of given ethnic groups. Given that Soviet theory is generally historicist in type, this of course explains the close links with history; and at this point, conceptual adjustment ceases to be a mere matter of substituting one word for another, and comes to require genuine intellectual imagination. It may be necessary to enter into a state of mind in which the tacit background assumption, the null hypothesis as it were, is not stability, but change, and moreover change of a certain general kind.

Or again, it is a relatively easy matter to remember that 'anthropology', without qualification, means physical anthropology in Soviet parlance. A difficulty arises for the reader from the fact that either the author or the translator, aware of the normal terminological expectations of the western reader, adjusts his phrasing to these expectations, and as it were compensates for the semantic drift between the two linguistic shores. The difficulty about this is that whilst it is quite impossible not to make such adjustments sometimes (when it is easy and is simply a matter of substituting one expression for another), it is also quite impossible to do so consistently and in all cases. The reason is that in the complex cases, where what is at issue is not just the use of one phrase rather than another, but of a whole complex of meanings and theoretical assumptions which are contained or implied in the phrase, any rephrasing would mean a profound re-writing and re-thinking of the position of the author who is being translated. The translation would then slide too far and impertinently into exegesis.

Thus, for instance, I have allowed myself to change 'anthropology' into 'physical anthropology': for the Russian-speaker, this would seem in these contexts to constitute merely an innocuous pleonasm, whilst it may save the western reader from misconstruing the sense. On the other hand, the habit of referring to the entire subject as 'ethnography', though quite easy to translate as 'anthropology' if one wishes, is somehow so much part of the whole atmosphere of Russian discussions – it is enshrined in the name of the Soviet journal devoted to the subject – that it seems better to leave it as it stands, just as one would, in the context of Russian affairs, refer to muzhiks and refrain from translating the term as 'peasants'. A translator from the Russian must on occasion be allowed to sport a fur cap for local colour. (It should perhaps be stated that the Russian papers were originally translated by official Moscow translators, who are not always familiar with *etnografia*, let alone with *anthropology*, nor unduly respectful of English word order or idiom. The Editor has taken the liberty of tinkering with these translations, without completely re-writing them, whilst doing his utmost to remain faithful to the meanings and intentions of the originals. The one exception is Semenov's paper, for the translation of which the Editor assumes complete responsibility.)

Amongst interesting differences of idiom are the following: when a Soviet author prefixes the term 'ethno' to another word, as in 'ethnogenesis', this generally means, I believe, that ethnos is an *object* of inquiry. 'Ethnogenesis' refers to genesis *of* an ethnic group. There is a fairly recent western usage in which the prefix 'ethno' implies not that an ethnos is being investigated, but that *something else* is being seen *through* the eyes, or rather through the concepts, of that ethnos. In such usage, 'ethno-botany' means the effort to see botany through the ideas and classifications of some given ethnic group and its language. It does not mean a direct study of the ethnos *through* botany, but seeing botany 'ethnically'. It is only a study *of* the ethnos indirectly, by an attempt to assume *its* subjectivity instead of one's own customary viewpoint, and thus understanding it 'from the inside'. As far as I can see, this usage has not yet spread to the Soviet Union, and the quite different ideas underlying the two uses of the same term may easily lead to misunderstanding. (I have made no attempt to tinker with the Soviet usage in this case.)

A philosophically most interesting difference in usage, and one which can unwittingly lead to very serious misunderstanding, concerns the 'breadth' and 'narrowness' of *meaning*. It is my belief, which I have not attempted to check systematically, that when a western scholar refers to breadth and narrowness of meaning, he is referring to denotation, not connotation. He might say, for instance, 'the ethnos in the broader sense includes any ethnic group with a distinctive language or culture', and go to say, 'an ethnos in the narrower sense only includes those groups which *also* possess their own socio-political institutions'. In other words, the 'narrowness' of the latter meanings refers to the fact that there are *fewer* examples of cultural groups with socio-political institutions, than there are of cultural groups *sans phrase*. The former is a *sub*-class of the latter.

Some Russian scholars at any rate use this distinction in the opposite way, which of course is just as legitimate. 'Cultural groups endowed with socio-political institutions' is referred to as the *broader* concept; of course it is richer in the sense that it contains a *greater* number of *traits* (though the number of *examples* falling under it is correspondingly *smaller*). As, generally speaking, connotation and denotation vary inversely – the richer a concept, the fewer the concrete instances of it, and vice versa – the misunderstandings which can arise here may lead to the total inversion of the intended sense.

At the same time, the philosophical doctrine I have invoked to explain how the different meanings are related – the doctrine about the inverse relationship of connotation and denotation – is philosophically contentious. (Cf. R. M. Eaton, *General Logic*, New York, 1931, 1959, pp. 265f. F. H. Bradley, *The Principles of Logic*, Oxford, 2nd ed., 1922, p. 170.) Hegelian logicians deny it, and perhaps Marxist ones do so too. It is possible that such a denial is implicit in what seems to me Semenov's logical 'realism' in his contribution to this volume. 'Modes of Production', which for him are, on the one hand, real entities, causally operative in history, and yet also are only exemplified in individual named societies and can never exist on their own, have *precisely* those characteristics which led the Anglo-Hegelians to speak of the 'concrete universal' and, in its name, to deny the inverse relation of connotation and denotation. Some modern logicians, e.g. Quine, who are not, at least on the surface, conspicuously Hegelian, also deny the usefulness of a notion of 'sense' or meaning, as distinct from denotation, from the actual set of objects covered, and repudiate it as a hangover from Aristotelian essentialism. (Perhaps they are open to the suspicion that they use the notion without avowing it.) But Semenov's position, if I understand it correctly, is overtly and proudly essentialist or Realist in the mediaeval sense: socio-economic formations are not abstractions for him, but names of real entities, which are causally responsible for the more diversified concrete and individual societies located in historical time.

Given the complexity and contentiousness of the issues involved, it would have been scholastic, pedantic and impertinently intrusive to insert some kind of explanatory footnote in Bromley's text. Moreover, a discussion of connotation and denotation would be totally tangential to his topic and preoccupations. At the same time, to leave his terminology as it stood would have almost certainly led to misunderstanding. Under the circumstances, I adopted the solution of translating him into western idiom, whilst indicating here that I have done so.

One of the points at which identical terminology (or terms habitually translated between the Russian and English languages as if they were equivalent) hides profoundly significant differences in connotation, which can lead to total misunderstanding, concerns the phrases 'primitive society' and similar expressions. In western anthropology, this is a negative and residual category, endowed with a very minimum of theoretical content. A primitive society is simply one which is small, and devoid of writing or of any powerful technology. A person employing the expression is not thereby committed to any views whatever about its internal organisation, historic role, or similarity to any other societies also so labelled. By contrast, in Soviet usage, which is very well explained by Pershits, the expression which can be translated in this way (*p'ervobytnoe obshchestvo*), and which I would prefer to translate as 'primordial community', is not merely a theory-loaded term; the theory it incorporates is absolutely central to the explanatory strategy, and perhaps also to the entire moral vision, of Soviet Marxism. The 'primordial community' is an explanatory concept co-ordinate with 'feudalism' or 'slave society'; and primordial communities, notwithstanding differences which are allowed to exist within the general category, are expected to share certain traits and a certain historic role. Amongst those traits, state-lessness and class-lessness are the most important, the two being intimately linked. The well-diffused custom of western anthropologists of distinguishing between state-less ('acephalous') and state-endowed tribal primitive societies, simply contains a contradiction if projected into the customary definitions operating within Soviet *etnografia*.

My main contention is that Soviet etnografia is of importance not merely on merit, as anthropology or as historical sociology, but for the light it throws on Soviet thought and the manner in which social and philosophical problems are conceptualised in the Soviet Union. What are these issues? No doubt there are many: but four of them leap to my eye.

1. The relationship of the economy to the polity, of production to coercion. Marxist doctrine has been interpreted in diverse ways on this point. I suppose it depends on whether one concentrates on the idea that the mode of production and reproduction is in the last analysis fundamental, or whether one stresses the idea that *only* capitalism has really pushed the separation of economic activity from other spheres to an extreme point. As such a separation does not obtain in other social

forms, it is not entirely clear what meaning should be attributed to statements about the relationship of the 'base' and 'superstructure'. Maurice Godelier's interesting re-formulations of Marxism endeavour to make use of this very non-separation, and it is for others to judge whether his view, whatever its other merits, can still claim to be 'Marxist'. Do the forces of coercion have an independent historic role alongside the forces of production? Do political organisation or culture constitute independent historical factors? Can something which could not be isolated (('relations of production') yet be said meaningfully to determine other kinds of relation, even if 'in the last analysis' it cannot be abstracted from them?

However, this is not the place to attempt to handle the problem of the relationship of economy and power. What it is important to say is that it is not simply a question of theoretical interest. It is absolutely central to the self-understanding and proper management of industrial society. (In my view a very great deal of western thought on this topic contains most abominable confusions.) All this being so, what Soviet thinkers have to say about it – even, or especially, through the prism of ethnography and whilst interpreting other and historical societies – is of the utmost possible interest.

2. There is the closely related problem of the typology and evaluation of human societies. The great philosophies of history, including Marxism, were elaborated in the late-eighteenth and nineteenth centuries. Much has happened since then. This question really amounts to asking – who are we and where are we going?

Western sociology nowadays, if it has any pattern underlying its eclecticism at all, is Weberian. I have long assumed that the difference between western Weberian vision and Soviet Marxism is basically the difference between the gate-keeper and the Hegelian acorn-to-oak-tree theories of history. On the former model, industrial society was born of an unique combination of circumstances, and it was never the universal shared potential of every and any human society, due to come to fruition sooner or later, whatever happened. It only became universal through diffusion.

Even philosophies of 'development', which have been accused of being an upside-down Marxism, such as W. W. Rostow's, merely offer a scheme of what happens if and when economic development does occur, and contain no general theory of history which would entail that it must, some time or other, be initiated. In the Acorn vision, on the other hand, human society is a seed which contains the same ultimate potential wherever it may be found, and it can only be deprived of it by destruction. If not destroyed, its fulfilment may be delayed but not prevented.

Semenov's fascinating interpretation of Marxism, contained in this volume, is still acorn-like in its insistence on the law-bound and inescapable potential of the acorn and of its successive incarnations, prior to its final *épanouissement* in a glorious oak tree. But at the same time, through his insistence that these laws apply, in effect, but to a single case – human history as a whole – and not to a whole open category of cases (individual societies), his *Problemstellung* comes far closer to the unique Weberian gate-keeper, than to what he himself describes as the customary, uncritical (because unwitting and barely considered) and incorrect interpretations of Marxism. (Semenov's position has its severe critics within the Soviet Union. See, for instance, Nikiforov's *The East and World History*, Moscow, 1976.)

If the important laws of history are realised in but a single object – global history as a totality – then the logical difference between historicist and gate-keeper explanations is whittled down though not non-existent. The historicist still holds that the same pattern would necessarily obtain in other worlds – *if* they existed – which the Weberian denies; but the difference is about what *would* happen in other worlds, not so much about this real world. It is not easy to put it to the test.

No wonder that in the course of the Wartenstein discussions, Maurice Godelier called Yuri Semenov a Hegelian. (There is nothing that academics will refrain from saying to each other in the heat of debate.) What is true about Semenov at this point seems to me equally true of the brilliant English neo-Marxist Perry Anderson, whose *Lineages of the Absolute State* implicitly adopts a Weberian, gate-keeper *Fragestellung*. However anti-Weberian Anderson's specific conclusion, the manner of posing the question is automatically, almost unconsciously Weberian. Such a position assumes that the unique gate could only be opened by a rare combination of circumstances, which on Anderson's interpretation actually included the ideological retention of the memory of an earlier and lapsed social form. Whether this can really still usefully be called 'Marxist', is something I must leave to those who feel themselves qualified to confer or withhold this label.

3. Less closely connected with the previous two sets of issues, there is the supremely important – theoretically and practically – question of the nature and role of *ethnicity*, both throughout human history, and in contemporary industrial society in particular. Bromley's insistence, echoed by some of the other Soviet participants, on the definition of *etnografia* in terms of the study of the *ethnos*, provides a charter for the study of this topic, both in the past and in the present. Semenov's schema contains a definite answer to the question of why it was quite essential for humanity to be organised in diverse ethnic groups – quite apart from the accident of dispersal and distance. In his version of Marxism, ethnicity becomes historically necessary, instead of contingent. Other theoreticians have invoked 'uneven development' to explain the politicisation of ethnicity; his theory requires both uneven development *and* its political and ethnic expression, to explain how history can, at certain crucial points, move on to 'higher stages'.

But leaving history and general theory aside, this definition of etnografia provides a warrant for investigating ethnicity and culture in the contemporary Soviet Union, and as described by Bromley, Drobizheva and others, this idea is in fact being vigorously pursued. Nationality is crucial in East and West. Soviet ethnography now becomes one of our main sources of information about its manifestation – and the manner in which it is being handled – in the Soviet Union.

4. As Bromley, Drobizheva and others stress, ethnicity increasingly manifests itself through *culture* (what Russians call 'spiritual culture'), i.e. roughly leisure activities and intellectual idiom and identification, rather than in the organisational infrastructure of society. In this way, by pre-empting the ethnos, Soviet anthropologists have also laid their hand on and staked their claim to the study and interpretation of Soviet *culture*, and we shall need to study them for information and ideas about this topic.

The infrastructure of this volume, which springs from a Conference at Burg Wartenstein in 1976, was generously assured by the Wenner-Gren Foundation for Anthropological Research. Burg Wartenstein fuses the décor of the feudal mode of production with the conveniences of late monopoly capitalism, a combination which has a very great deal to commend it. Hence profound gratitude is due to the Foundation, its Director of Studies, Dr Lisa Osmundsen, and her entire staff. Sir Raymond Firth must also be cited for the generosity with which he supported and encouraged the project from its inception.

Amongst the Russophone western participants who helped with administrative problems and various meetings before and after the Conference itself, Tamara Dragadze and Caroline Humphrey deserve special thanks. Tamara Dragadze also devoted a great deal of time to interpreting the Russian parts of the tape-recording of the Conference for Meyer Fortes, and thus must have made a most valuable contribution to his Introduction. Caroline Humphrey interpreted admirably during a follow-up lecture by Yulian Bromley at the Royal Anthropological Institute.

During the actual meetings at Wartenstein, in addition to the charming official interpreter, prodigies of simultaneous translations in Russian, French and English were performed by the brilliant and polymathic Sergei Arutyonov, who combined sensitivity to nuance in three languages with a mastery of the underlying subject of discussion. But the height of his performance as interpreter was reached when he continued, calm, impassive and poker-faced, to interpret whilst two other participants – the present editor one of them – indulged in a stand-up procedural row and shouting match.

> O, who can hold a fire in his hand,
> By thinking on the frosty Caucasus?
> *(Richard II)*

But for his Caucasian background, one would be strongly inclined to speak of *le Russe avec son sangfroid habituel.*

This row – the Russians referred to it as the *skandalchik* – was my fault. I am told that it has been erased from the tape-recordings of the Conference by a person or persons unknown, which if so may confirm the Soviets in any preconceptions they may have about Nixon-like habits in the West. But I do not mention this episode – which I cannot remember without embarrassment, nor can forget – from any Dostoievskian yearning for public self-abasement, a sentiment which is not highly developed in my breast. I mention it for a different reason. There are problems involved in scholarly exchanges between men of diverse ideological and political background. Whether or to what extent we explored these problems, and how deeply we probed, is something which the reader will assess for himself on the basis of the papers provided. How far one should probe when communication is first established, and whether crude or subtle styles of communication are best, are questions which will no doubt be answered by each reader for himself. But it shows that one charge, at any rate, would not be warranted: these meetings were serious, and were not any kind of smooth Public Relations exercise. I have never yet been accused of mounting a P.R. operation, and do not intend to begin such a career in my old age.

In the editing of the volume, I have been very greatly assisted by my secretary, Margaret Kosowicz, and by Deborah Blake. The final preparation of the MS for publication was carried out whilst I held a research post at the Centre de Recherches et d'Etudes sur les Sociétés Méditerranéennes, at Aix-en-Provence, and I am indebted to this Centre and its Director, Maurice Flory, for enabling me to do so.

E. G.

MEYER FORTES

Introduction

As I look back on the conference of which this book is a record, three episodes stand out in my mind. The first is the concise clarification of his concepts of 'ethnos' and 'ethnicos' with which Bromley responded to a question I raised; the second is the far-reaching exchange between Semenov and Godelier on the definition and functions of relations and modes of production; and lastly there is Basilov's wise and penetrating commentary on the hypothesis adducing the 'Oedipus complex' which I advanced in my paper.

It hardly needs saying that my principal interest in the conference was to learn something more than the literature we have access to provides of the theoretical guidelines and research activities of Soviet social and cultural anthropologists. And these three episodes, between them, seemed to me to epitomise the mutual understandings our conference achieved.

To begin with, they brought sharply into focus a feature of Soviet ethnography – as they call it – which I had not anticipated. There is clearly no such thing as a unified, let alone monolithic, system of theory or practice in Soviet ethnography. To be sure, there is a basic framework of, loosely speaking, Marxist orientation. But in terms of what they actually do, their problems and procedures of research, Soviet ethnographers, linguists, demographers and sociologists are as diverse in their interests and in their approaches as are anthropologists the world over. If it seems odd to make a point of this, let the blame be laid at the door of the ignorance of Soviet anthropological scholarship which is still widespread in the West. It was chastening to find how well informed in contrast to most of the 'western' participants the Soviet participants in our conference were about international anthropological scholarship in English, French, and other 'western' languages. Happily, the gap is closing fast, as this conference reminded us. For apart from Krader, so long dedicated to bringing together Soviet and 'western' theory and research in the anthropological sciences, there were four 'western' participants (Gellner, Dragadze, Humphrey, and Woodburn) who are fully at home with Soviet anthropological scholarship and have been acquainting us with this literature.[1] But for my part, this face-to-face association in a week of unconstrained and forthright argument and discussion was incomparably more valuable in advancing mutual understanding of our points of view and our work than was the previous circulation of publications.

As our discussions developed, it became clear to all of us, I think, that the 'objects' of our studies (to paraphrase Bromley) were fundamentally the same and that the different approaches represented overlapped and converged. There were times when the 'western' emphasis on synchronic analysis seemed to run counter to the Soviet method of diachronic contextualisation. But implicitly, if not in every case explicitly, there was the common ground that all our studies rest upon the basis of empirical research among living peoples and societies. Even when historical and archival records are drawn upon for descriptive material or for adding the dimension of extension in time to a study, the final test of an hypothesis was seen to be empirical observations among living peoples. I would not exclude from this claim even the typological and evolutionist models proposed mainly by the Soviet participants. What, for example, the discussion between Pershits and Woodburn came down to in the end was the relevance of empirically observable (i.e. ethnographically validated) modes of livelihood and of social organisation for the reconstruction of prehistoric 'social formations'.

If I lay special stress on this, it is because of the fact noted by Dragadze[2] that the Soviet participants adhered scrupulously to the terms of reference of the conference, that is, submitted papers that define the place of anthropology in relation to such other human sciences as linguistics, demography, psychology, etc., whereas the 'western' participants for the most part submitted papers on anthropological themes of special interest to themselves. Thus, it turned out that the Soviet contributions, being concerned with general principles, in contrast to the particularistic contributions of the 'western' participants, set the main lines of our discussions. At the same time, we were constantly made aware of the extensive field experience that lay behind the Soviet concern with general principles. Having myself been engaged in a review of demographic anthropology in Africa just before the conference, I was particularly struck by the wealth of field experience – and, of course, the elegance of the theoretical analysis – presented in Kozlov's paper and amplified in the discussion.

To return to the three episodes I have referred to, as they are admirably reported by Dragadze[3] I need not go into details. It is their general import that is of main interest to me, for they focussed graphically on the central issues of our discussions. It was inevitable that the dominant theme was the elucidation of the concepts of 'ethnos' and 'ethnicos'. Could 'ethnos', in the sense of 'a people', be equated with the concept of 'society', and 'ethnicos' with the more general concept of 'culture', as a parameter of human social life that is not subject to spatial or temporal limitations? Since neither 'ethnos' nor 'ethnicos' is tied to specific territorial or economic or political community, to equate either with the concept of 'society', for example in a Durkheimian sense, would not seem correct. However, the principal issue is, I suppose, how Bromley's concepts of 'ethnos' and 'ethnicos', with their undertones of 'national consciousness' are related to the 'western' concept of 'ethnicity' as represented, for instance, in the work of Barth and of Cohen.[4] In the discussion with Bromley I have referred to, it was made clear that, unlike 'ethnicity' as Barth, Cohen, *et al.* represent it, 'ethnos' is not a function of opposition between ethnically or culturally different groups in a pluralist territorial or political community. It appeared that the essential cultural continuity over time, and specificity at a given time, of 'ethnos' and 'ethnicos' are perceived as embodied objectively in the distinctive customs, beliefs, and practices of the members and subjectively, for them, in their self-awareness, their sense of identity, as the carriers and transmitters of their 'ethnos' or 'ethnicos'. This is not a function of opposition to other groups, for 'ethnos' is as characteristic of small, isolated, technologically backward pre-industrial communities of, for instance, hunters and gatherers (e.g. Eskimo) as of modern nation states. 'Ethnos' pertains to the internal life of a people, regardless of class differences or territory. Is this a more sophisticated version of the one-time Boasian theory that every culture is, at bottom, unique and can only be properly understood from within, that is, in terms of its own distinctive contents and forms of existence? Does this amount to a form of cultural relativism which rules out cross-cultural comparison with the aim of reaching generalisations of pan-human validity? And what are the institutions and mechanisms (e.g. endogamy, family structure and the associated child-rearing practices, ritual and religion) that maintain the closure and continuity of 'ethnos' and 'ethnicos'? How at another level does 'ethnos' in particular relate to the patterns of political nationalism and evolution which Gellner and Krader examined? These and related questions, notably in connection with defining precisely the 'self-awareness' postulated in the delineation of 'ethnos' and its connection with the factors of 'national character' examined in Kon's paper, came up several times. My conclusion is that a vital parameter of human social existence at all levels and stages of social life is adumbrated in Bromley's concepts. But I venture to suggest that we are only at the beginning of the researches that are needed in linguistics, ethnology, sociology and psychology to bring out their full theoretical implications. It would be particularly rewarding, in my view, to develop parallel research by Soviet ethnographers and 'western' ethnographers to distinguish more clearly in what ways 'ethnos' and 'ethnicos' overlap with (if at all) or (more likely) contrast with the externally oriented ethnicity by opposition and differentiation that is attracting so much attention now among 'western' anthropologists.

As an unreconstructed structural-functionalist, I found the exchange between Semenov and Godelier especially congenial and stimulating. A brief comment on this episode is all I can permit myself here. With all due respect, it seemed to me that Semenov's model of what I might perhaps designate as the paradigmatic human society was fundamentally a structural-functionalist one and that, if modified in the direction of Godelier's insistence on the relative autonomy of kinship institutions, it could easily accommodate such classics of British ethnography as Evans-Pritchard's *The Nuer*, Forde's *Yakö Studies*, A.I. Richards' *Land, Labour and Diet*, and Firth's *Primitive Polynesian Economy*. Critical as Semenov is of 'western' economic anthropology, he gives the impression of being more sympathetic to the 'substantivist' than to the 'formalist' analyses of pre-capitalist economies; and this brings his views closer, as I read him, to those of the descriptive ethnographers of pre-capitalist economies I have mentioned than to the more ambitious theoretical works, even those that are framed in Marxist language that command attention in 'western' anthropological circles.[5]

Semenov's exposition of his Marxist frame of analysis was at a level of generality or abstraction that made discussion difficult, even after Godelier had introduced particular ethnographic examples from his own and others' field work. Godelier brought out eloquently the conceptual difficulties and empirical obstacles to understanding the distinction between 'base' and 'superstructure' and the implications of such dicta as (to quote Semenov) 'relations of production are primary, fundamental, while all the rest are secondary, derivative' that figure so prominently in Marxist anthropological writings. Like Godelier, I claim that the evidence is incontrovertible that kinship, ritual, and political institutions constitute relatively autonomous domains of social structure and can by no means be reduced to emanations of the 'relations of production' *sensu stricto*. It is significant that Semenov allows for 'special interests', for 'ownership relations determined by morality' and for special rules that determine 'which circle [? of pre-existing social relations] a newly born person may enter', which, as I see it, is nothing less than an admission of the autonomy of kinship relations and contradicts his assertion that 'kinship relations have no content, but are simply formal connections'. That this, curiously enough, aligns Semenov with the distinctly non- if not anti-Marxist kinship – formalists such as Beattie, Needham, Leach and Schneider did not escape Godelier's attention. The point is clear when we consider particular cases, as was elegantly exemplified by Pouillon and expounded by Godelier. The autonomy, relative to the actual processes of producing, distributing, and consuming the necessities of life and the services required to maintain a society, of the juridical, political, and ideological 'superstructures', above all of kinship institutions and their reflexive power of organising the 'productive forces', then becomes abundantly clear. Just how 'relations of production' can, as Semenov argued, both mobilise 'volition' and yet be independent of 'the will and consciousness of people' also remains unclear to me.

Much Marxist discussion of 'modes of production', 'socio-economic formation' and other such formulae strikes me as essentially a verbal reformulation or general rubric for observations and interpretations that are commonplace in structural-functional ethnography. The evolutionist implications of this language, as regards the pre-capitalist, or better stated, pre-industrial economies anthropologists normally study, do not help me in my analytical and explanatory tasks. In this field too we need much more research and, above all, discussion. Semenov's grandiose scheme of social evolution in the framework of world history could not fail to win the admiration of all participants for its sweep and erudition, but I doubt if any of us was able to see how it could be applied to the humdrum tasks of empirical ethnographic research.

'Ethnos' and 'systems of productive relations' seem to reflect very different emphases in Soviet ethnography and point to different but equally important areas of theoretical concern for all anthropological studies – the more so as, to my mind, they direct attention to the necessity for more empirical research in a synchronic context. This was brought out, it seemed to me, in Drobizheva's 'ethno-sociological' studies in urban settings, and in Arutyonov's brilliant account of Soviet linguistic science.

Basilov's presentation of Soviet theory and research in the ethnography of religion and magic had, at times, a classical Frazerian tone. While emphasising the wide range of social interests and needs, sometimes tied to class differences, subserved by religious institutions, he referred also to 'archaic' forms of magical ritual surviving among some Christian and Moslem sects; and in commenting on Humphrey's account of Soviet studies of shamanism, he suggested, at one point, a 'polydaemonistic origin' presumably in an evolutionist sense, for these beliefs and practices. However, when presenting his own point of view, a distinctly structural-functionalist interpretation, so it seemed to me, could be read into his analysis. A point of importance was his drawing attention to the principle that a shaman is powerless to choose the role for himself – he must, it is accepted, be chosen for the role by the spirits with whom he will later commune. Whether it is considered to conform to definitions of religion or not, shamanism is an institutionalised cult geared to social needs, not a manifestation of individual idiosyncracy.

This emphasis on the social implications of religious and other forms of ritual beliefs and practices was the keynote of Basilov's incisive and perceptive comment on my paper. The argument he put forward, and the general discussion it stimulated, especially impressed on me the extent to which both the descriptive objectives and the theoretical aims of 'western' and Soviet anthropology coincide. His remarks are well summarised in Dragadze's previously quoted review. Matching the empirical basis I claimed for my case with his own observations, he contended that the evidence pointed to an alternative interpretation of the data to the one I offered. It was, he argued, at best superfluous, at worst gratuitous, to adduce an underlying 'oedipal' conflict to explain the opposition of successive generations of parents and children. He agreed, in common with most ethnographic observers, that there is a general tendency for successive generations, e.g. fathers and sons, to be mutually antagonistic. But, he insisted, the sexual rivalry presupposed in the hypothesis of the 'Oedipus complex' to which I had had recourse, is not empirically demonstrable. It is certainly not relevant at the time when sons reach the social and economic maturity to come into conflict with fathers. What is at stake, then, is not sexual access to the mother but rights of inheritance and succession, rights to property, authority and other cultural assets. The conflict can be fully accounted for by social reasons that do justice to the ethnographical facts. Why, then, drag in the 'Oedipus complex'?

This bare summary does scant justice to the elegance and persuasiveness of his argument. What is significant is that it was supported, not only by other Soviet participants, but by so authoritative a 'western' colleague as Professor Goody and was followed up by Pouillon with a balanced suggestion for reconciling the two views.

Conceding the force of Basilov's argument (and encouraged by some remarks of Bromley) I, nevertheless, defended my standpoint on two grounds. Firstly, there is the problem of explaining why the opposition between successive generations is, among many peoples, objectified in rules of ritual or moral avoidance that operate from the earliest infancy of the filial generation and are connected, by the actors themselves, with the incest taboos. Thus, it seems that the conflict has its roots in the early relations of parents and children within the parental family. And secondly, I argued that the social institutions and relations to which Basilov referred must be thought of as built up upon such 'elementary particles' of social life as the propensities postulated in the notion of the Oedipus complex. Retrospectively, I would draw attention to the fact that the transmission of property, office and power from generation to generation is usually regulated by juridical custom and need not, therefore, engender conflict.

There is much more to be said on this topic, and I do not suppose that my defence of my hypothesis convinced Basilov or those who agreed with him. The important thing, for me, was that we were able to present and consider the alternatives with complete mutual understanding, and in the light of the available empirical evidence.

I must refrain from enlarging further on the discussions that were held during our meeting. Certainly, there emerged important and critical differences between the ways Soviet ethnographers on the one hand and British, American, and French social anthropologists on the other see their empirical tasks and their theoretical objectives. This was brought out with impressive eloquence and skill by Godelier when, presenting some of his own field data on initiation rituals among the Baruya of New Guinea, he questioned the objectivity and the uniqueness of the 'ethnos' as a property of a cultural system over and above the details of economic, political, and national custom. And I do not suppose that Bromley's response, drawing attention to the different levels of 'ethnic' identification open to a person who at once is a Cossack, a Russian, and a Soviet citizen, answered Godelier's criticism to his satisfaction. Debates of this type were the order of the day throughout the conference. Yet, at the end, I venture to assert, the conviction emerged for all the participants that our fundamental scientific tasks and objectives are the same and that there is more overlap and convergence between our several theoretical positions than there is irreconcilable divergence. A foundation has, I believe, been truly laid for much future cooperation.

NOTES

1 E.g. see Gellner's articles in *European Journal of Sociology*, 1977, vol. 18.

2 T. Dragadze, in *Current Anthropology*, 1978, vol. 20.

3 Ibid.

4 Fredrik Barth, *Ethnic Groups and Boundaries: The Social Organisation of Culture Difference*, London, 1969. R. Cohen, Preface to R. Naroll and R. Cohen (eds) *Handbook of Method in Cultural Anthropology*, New York, 1973.

5 See, for instance, his paper 'Marxism and primitive society', *Philosophy and the Social Sciences*, 1975, 5, 201-13.

PART I

Marxism, anthropology, history

MAURICE GODELIER

The emergence and development of Marxism in anthropology in France

Marxism only made its appearance in anthropological research in France some time around the 1960s. Before this, the mainstream of anthropological thinking had grown out of the work of Durkheim, Lévy-Bruhl, Mauss and others; this current had not only influenced French anthropology, but also Anglo-Saxon sociology and anthropology. Fieldwork was far less thorough, less 'monographic' than that of Anglo-Saxon anthropologists, who drew their inspiration from Malinowski and Boas. However, monographs by Maurice Leenhardt and Marcel Griaule stood out quite sharply, the main thrust of their analyses centring around representations and religious practices. Still in the minority at that time, though about to achieve predominance, the structuralists were developing powerfully through the writings of Claude Lévi-Strauss. Louis Dumont had adopted the structuralist method in order to analyse the caste system in India, but his analysis was openly idealist and anti-Marxist in tone, contrary to Lévi-Strauss, who insisted that his studies of systems of kinship and of systems of mythical representations were materialist and even, to a certain extent, 'Marxist'.

Around 1960, quite independently of each other, Claude Meillassoux and I became anthropologists, the former having been a sociologist, the latter starting out from a grounding in philosophy and subsequently in economics. Both of us had reached the conclusion that it was time to analyse, from a Marxist point of view, the findings and theories accumulated by anthropologists since the beginning of the century. But our ways soon parted over the question of what a 'Marxist point of view' might be. Our differences arose over three main points, and since that time these differences have never been settled: 'Marxist' anthropology in France henceforth adopted two sharply distinct and opposing paths and forms. The three points are:

1. How are we to understand the distinction between infrastructure

and superstructure in precapitalist societies? What does the central hypothesis of historical materialism, namely the determinant role of the infrastructure 'in the last instance' signify in societies where kinship or politico-religious relations appear to dominate the functioning and the reproduction of these societies?

2. What should our attitude be towards functionalist and structuralist theses and methods? What elements may we reject or adopt critically with a view to developing them within a Marxist approach, while still developing a Marxist approach in anthropology? The question of what attitude to adopt with regard to Lévi-Strauss's work in the fields of kinship and of myths was crucial in this respect and, right from the outset, it gave rise to a fundamental divergence between the two currents.

3. Finally, what should be our political attitude, what kind of radical militant praxis ought we to adopt in order to act upon and within French society? And, as anthropologists, what kind of militant action could we engage in against colonial oppression in Vietnam, Algeria, West Africa, Polynesia and so on? This determination not to confine ourselves to the realm of ideas or of scientific practice but to go beyond this, to become involved in the broader struggles of the working class and of other exploited categories of society, marked us off from Lévi-Strauss who, though taking materialism and Marxism as his references all the while, has *in practice* always abstained from seeking to act upon his society.

Naturally, we both thought that the first task of a Marxist was to focus his attention upon the study of the 'economic' structures of primitive societies, and we found ourselves grappling with the problems of 'economic anthropology' at a moment when the debate between formalists and substantivists was at its height. Broadly speaking, we both tended to side with Polanyi against the formalists, while stating our belief in the need to go much further. But the moment we tried to go further, the disagreements concerning the three points outlined above once more rose to the surface.

1. For Meillassoux, kinship was only a superstructure, 'masking' the essence of the 'reality' of social relations, namely economic relations. These themselves he reduced to various forms of the labour process encountered in a given society: hunting, fishing, farming, and so forth, and analysis of these labour processes was somehow supposed directly to provide the key to interpretation of superstructures. In his book *Anthropologie économique des Gouro de Côte d'Ivoire* he devotes only twelve pages to the family and marriage, and none to religion, representations of nature, power, lineage, etc. He more or less reduces the Gouro to their economic infrastructures.

2. Under the influence of a current that is very powerful among French Africanists, one that is hostile to structuralism, Meillassoux

denied all scientific value to Lévi-Strauss's work and to the method known as structuralist analysis. For him, this method reduced all reality to abstractions and was fundamentally 'idealist'.

3. On the third question, that of political commitment and militant action, the opposition between us was radical from the start. Meillassoux was active in Trotskyist circles whereas I was a militant in the Communist Party. In 1968, a Maoist current formed around Terray and Rey. These two joined up with Meillassoux, re-reading the latter's book in the 'light' of the theses of Louis Althusser, a philosopher and Communist Party member. While adopting Althusser's theoretical positions, however, Terray and Rey joined forces with Meillassoux in the political sphere in the fight against Althusser's own party.

Such, briefly, were the circumstances and the reasons for the emergence of Marxism in anthropology in France, and for the existence of two so profoundly distinct and opposing currents within it. In what follows I shall try to show how I now see the following problems:

1. Determination in the last instance;
2. The oppositions between functionalism, structuralism and Marxism;
3. The 'ideological' and the analysis of religious representation practices, which is particularly tricky for a Marxist.

The distinction between infrastructure and superstructure

Marx's crucial discovery was the role of transformations of the material base of society in understanding the logic of forms of social life and of their evolution. After Book I of *Capital* was published Engels, in June 1877, wrote a brief 'Introduction to Marx' for the benefit of readers of the *Volkskalender* of Brunswick, in which he said:

> Of the many important discoveries with which Marx has inscribed his name in the annals of science, we may pause here to consider two only: the first is the revolution which he wrought in the entire conception of world history. History was for the first time set upon its rightful basis. Marx's second important discovery was the final elucidation of the relationship between capital and labour, in other words the demonstration of the process whereby, in present-day society and in the existing capitalist mode of production, the worker is exploited by capital. Modern scientific socialism is founded upon these two important facts.

Later, in his famous speech at Marx's tomb on March 17, 1883, Engels took up this theme again, calling the former discovery a 'general law' and the latter a 'specific law' of historical materialism.

What then do we mean by infrastructure? By infrastructure or the material base of society we refer to a complex combination of:

1. the ecological and geographical conditions within and from which society extracts its material means of existence;

2. the productive forces, i.e. the material and intellectual means which man invents and employs in different labour processes in order to act upon nature and to extract therefrom his means of existence, to transform nature into 'socialised' nature;

3. relations of production, i.e. all social relations whatsoever, which serve a threefold function: first to determine social access to and control of resources and the means of production; secondly to redistribute the social labour force among the different labour processes, and to organise these processes; and thirdly to determine the social distribution of the product of labour.

'Mode of production' refers to a specific combination of determinate productive forces and of determinate social relations constituting both material and social conditions, and the internal material and social structures through which society acts upon its natural environment in order to extract from it a series of socially useful goods.

I should like to dwell a moment on these definitions in order to draw attention to a major point that is rarely subjected to thoroughgoing theoretical analysis. Among the productive forces (and hence forming part of the infrastructure) are representations of the nature that society exploits, representations of tools, of their rules of manufacture and use. These representations exist socially and are thus capable of being communicated. So we have to include among the productive forces both these representations and the linguistic means required to express them and to hand them down from generation to generation within a given culture. Here, thought and language function as productive forces and hence as components of the infrastructure. The distinction between infrastructure and superstructure, therefore, is not between material and immaterial; as we shall see, it is a distinction that concerns functions and not institutions. This becomes clearer when one turns from productive forces to look at the social relations of production. The three examples which follow should make the point.

If we take hunting-gathering societies such as the Australian aborigines we can see that the social relations between groups and among individuals, which serve as social conditions of access to natural resources and as a framework for the organisation of the labour process and the redistribution of products, are in fact social relations of kinship; these, moreover, govern marriages, matrimonial alliances between different groups, and descent – this being the explicit and universal function of kinship relations. The relevance of this example lies in the fact that it shows us the same institutions, namely kinship relations, functioning both as infrastructure and as superstructure. So the distinction is no longer between institutions, but between functions within a given institution.

If we now consider a Greek city, such as Athens in the fifth century B.C., we find that, this time, it was political relations which functioned from within as relations of production. Citizenship carried with it an exclusive right to use the city's land and, conversely, only landowners could be citizens. To be a citizen, that is, a free man, was simultaneously to be a landowner, to have full access to public office and political responsibilities, and to have exclusive rights to participation in the religious life of the city, and to the protection of its gods. Men who, though free, were foreign, were barred from ownership of land and from agricultural activities, from public office and from the city's temples and shrines. A first division of labour flowed from this, since such men were restricted to handicrafts, trade and banking. At the same time, however, free men, whether citizens or aliens, were at liberty to run their affairs themselves or else to rely on slaves to run them. This was the second division of labour in the Greek city. Such were the specific features of the Greek economy. To grasp this fully it is essential to understand that it was not these forms of division of labour which resulted in political relations functioning both as relations of production and as superstructures. On the contrary, it was the fact that politics functioned simultaneously as a relation of production which gave rise to these forms of division of labour within a hierarchy of statuses.

I come now to my last example. Oppenheim's study of Assur in ancient Mesopotamia shows that most of the city's land was regarded as the property of the god Assur. A temple standing in the middle of the city was the dwelling place of the god and the priests. The economy functioned as a vast centralised system within which village communities and individuals were placed under the authority of the priests and the temple, to which they owed a portion of their labour and their output. Here, it was religious relations – religion – which functioned as social relations of production.

We can see then that the 'economic factor' does not occupy a constant locus throughout history and that, consequently, it assumes different forms and that its mode of development varies. By mode of development I mean two things: short and long-term conditions of reproduction, and the effects on material and intellectual forces of production, enabling a society to provide for its material means of existence. From an epistemological point of view, I would stress the importance of not defining infrastructure and superstructure as institutions, but as functions. This is the first condition for breaking out of the spontaneous ethnocentrism characteristic of our conception of relationships between economy and society. Both Marxists and non-Marxists alike spontaneously share this ethnocentric prejudice. In other words, they apprehend ancient or exotic economies through the form taken by the social relations of production in our society, where indeed they do appear as a series of separate institutions of kinship, relations of production and religious

relations. The theoretical question, then, if we are to study the history
of modes of production scientifically, requires that we seek to discover
the reasons and conditions which have resulted in changes in the locus
of relations of production in the course of history, and which have
caused these relations of production to change form and effect in changing their locus. Needless to say, any such history cannot be the fruit of a
single, partial discipline, as it mobilises historians, anthropologists,
sociologists and economists together.

However, being a Marxist is not merely a question of identifying and
defining social relations of production at different epochs and in different societies. It also implies putting forward the hypothesis that the
over-arching logic of these societies depends on the nature of their
infrastructure. Empiricists, however, starting from the visible hierarchy of institutions, draw the conclusion that, with the exception of
capitalist societies, economy does not play a determinant role in the
last resort in human history but that, depending on the case in question, this role is played by kinship, politics or religion. To this end, they
even invoke the very examples I have just cited. This is the strategic
knot lying at the heart of the Marxist interpretation. The problem is
usually formulated as follows: how can a Marxist simultaneously
account for the determination, in the last resort, of economics, and for
the dominance of kinship, politics or religion? Determination and
dominance, the problem revolves around these two terms.

There are two currents of Marxist thought on this point. The more
usual interpretation, to be found in its most sophisticated form in
Althusser's thought, presents the economy's determination in the last
resort as a process of selection in a given society, by the economy, of one
superstructure from amongst possible ones, which is then somehow elevated into a dominant position. Whatever the terminology employed,
the causality of the economy is thought of as a relation between institutions and not between functions.

For others, including myself, if kinship functions in many societies as
a dominant relation, it is because it functions from within as a social relation of production, as the social relation within which man's action
upon nature, jointly with the social control of the means of production
and of products are organised. Similarly, where politics dominates
social life as a whole, this is because it acts from within as the social relations of production. On each occasion, what transpires through the
domination of one or another of these structures is the same hierarchy
of functions as exists in our own society, since we can see that in all
societies structures only play a dominant role if they function simultaneously as economic infrastructures. It is not adequate to say, as
empiricists do, that if relations of kinship are dominant in many primitive societies, this is because they assume several functions. It is not
enough for social relations to 'plurifunction' in order for them to dominate a society's logic, mode of development and system of collective
representations; they must, of necessity, assume the function of re-

lations of production. This, it seems to me, is the correct understanding of Marx's hypothesis concerning the mode of production's determinant role in the last resort.

This discovery arises from quite specific historical conditions which are in fact the reasons behind the epistemological rupture which gradually built up through Marx's thinking on the question of the capitalist mode of production. For it is only within the nineteenth-century capitalist mode of production that the distinct functions of infrastructure and superstructure existed in the form of distinct organisations. For the first time, the process of production has developed within institutions that are almost entirely separate from the family, from politics and from religion. However, separate here does not mean being devoid of any internal relations of correspondence. There is a working-class form of family and a bourgeois form corresponding to the new capitalist mode of production, and these forms evolve in step with the latter's development. The important point, though, is that it is not within the framework of political or family relations that the social process of production is organised. In this context, it became easy, for the first time, to recognise the role of the economy in the evolution of society; and here lies the origin of the epistemological rupture engineered by Marx. With the emergence of capitalist relations of production, it became possible to see in the history of Ancient Greece something other than what the Greeks themselves saw, and to see this history differently. But at the same time, it became harder to discover economics where it exists as a function of relations of kinship or of political relations. We are confronted with what can only be termed an 'epistemological chiasma'; the same social relations reveal something of the past and cause something of the past to vanish, but it is not the same thing. What Marx discovered was not only the role of economics in capitalist society but, through analysis of the capitalist mode of production, the existence of a hierarchy of structural functions and causalities which provide the conditions of reproduction of society – of any society – without prejudging the nature of the structures assuming these functions in any particular case or the number of functions that a structure may assume. And this is what Engels meant when he credited Marx with having discovered both a general and a specific law of historical development.

It should now be clear that in order to employ these hypotheses, Marxism requires an extremely complex methodology, one capable not only of isolating structures but also of throwing light on the effects structures have on each other within a given hierarchy of functions. It is here that Marxism competes with the methods of functionalist empiricism and structuralism.

Functionalism, structuralism and Marxism

Marxism, in the social sciences, involves analysis of social relations in terms of structure and the search for a hierarchy of causes determining the functioning and evolution of societies. This means that it is obliged to devise an extremely complex methodology for the analysis of social facts. As with functionalist empiricism, Marxism does not take individuals as its starting point, but their social relations, and it analyses these social relations not separately, but together, as systems. But unlike empiricism, Marxism does not confuse social structures with the social relations that are visible on the surface of society, and still less with the representations individuals may form of their social relations. Marx for example demonstrated that if one looks solely at the apparent relations in capitalist society, it looks as if the wage paid were equivalent to the value of the goods produced by the worker, and as if the added value, or capitalist profit, flowed from the capital itself and from the circulation and sale of commodities, not from their production. What visible relations, practical institutions such as wage-labour, hide is the crucial fact that the capitalist class's profit is unpaid social labour, a value added without any equivalent in exchange. The 'wage form, which only expresses the false appearances of wage labour, renders the *real relation* between capital and labour *invisible* and in fact demonstrates precisely the *opposite*; it is from these that all legal notions of the wage-earner and the capitalist, all the mystifications of capitalist production, are derived' (*Capital*, Book I, ch. 19). The economic categories of wage and profit, interest and so forth thus express the visible relations of the everyday practice of business and have a pragmatic utility as such, but they have no scientific value in themselves since they are confined to systematising the appearances of the production process and of the circulation of commodities. The scientific representation of economic and social reality does not emerge by 'abstraction' from the spontaneous or elaborated representations of individuals. It must, on the contrary, contest the evidence of these representations in order to uncover the hidden internal logic of social reality. For Marx, however, scientific knowledge of the content of a social relation will never, of itself, abolish the individual's own spontaneous representation of this relation. It modifies its effects and its importance in the practice of individuals and social groups but it does not suppress it.

Lévi-Strauss too refuses to take visible social relations for the only possible social reality, founding his structural analysis upon a rejection of all empiricist presuppositions. For Lévi-Strauss, too, structures also form part of reality:

> The ultimate proof of the molecular structure of matter is supplied by the electron microscope, which enables us to observe real molecules. But this exploit cannot alter the fact that molecules will not become visible to the naked eye in the future. Similarly, it is pointless to expect that a structural analysis will alter our perception of concrete social relations. It will merely explain them better. [C. Lévi-Strauss, 'On manipulated sociological models', *Bijdragen*, 1969, 6, p. 52]

Whatever the differences concerning the notion of structure between functionalism, structuralism and Marxism, all three approaches are agreed on a point of method, that is the priority accorded to analysis of structures over that of their origin and their evolution. Analysing the historic origin of a structure means analysing the conditions of the formation of its internal components and of the establishment of their interrelations. So we must identify these components and their relations beforehand, which means that this structure needs to be analysed theoretically before we can reconstitute its genesis and its evolution. One example given of this method in Marx is the way he deals with the process of the genesis of the capitalist mode of production in Book I of *Capital*. Only after having defined the content of value and the nature of surplus-value does Marx rapidly outline the historical process of the genesis of the radical separation of producers from the means of production and from money, this separation lying at the very foundation of the capitalist mode of production. He then goes on to discuss what classical economists called 'primitive accumulation of capital', this being an accumulation that occurred within the feudal economic order gradually leading to the dissolution of that order. Marxism is not a form of historicism; it proceeds along the lines of a constant to-and-fro between analysis of structures and analysis of historical events.

Despite their shared critique of empiricism, there is a radical difference between structuralism and Marxism. Although he does not deny history, Lévi-Strauss cannot really give an account of it owing to the fact that in his analysis of social structures he separates analysis of the form of social relations from analysis of their functions. Not that these functions are either ignored or denied; it is just that they are never explored as such. As a result, we can never properly analyse the way these social relations really hinge together within a hierarchy of functions. History appears as a *mélange* of chance and necessity – necessity internal to each structural level, and chance where relations between these levels are concerned. Hence, Lévi-Strauss's statement to the effect that he agrees with Marx's hypothesis regarding the '*primacy* of infrastructures' remains just that, having no impact upon his actual work, and devoid of meaning. For him, the notion of infrastructure remains an empirical one, not a scientifically reconstructed notion. When analysing the material infrastructure of Indian societies, for example, he falls back on empirical disciplines such as geography, technology, historical demography, botany, and so on. Each discipline contributes its specialised information, but no attempt is made to discover the internal components and the structural relations which define the social and material infrastructure of these societies. What is most striking is that Lévi-Strauss – while borrowing from Marx the notion of infrastructure and, further, while accepting his hypothesis of the primacy of infrastructure in the logic of the functioning of these societies – entirely ignores the concept of relations of production. He therefore adopts empirical definitions of the economy and contradicts, in discussing infrastructures, the principles and the methods he employs in analysing relations of kinship or myths and forms of religious thought. Some people, e.g. Lucien Sève, have accused Lévi-Strauss's method of being responsible for his failures to analyse history. One can certainly take him to task for having separated the study of the forms from that of the functions of social relations, although this separation was necessary in the first stage; but by extending it he ultimately made it impossible to account for the evolution of whole societies. This is not the main point, though, as it is not his method which brings Lévi-Strauss up against a wall; it is Lévi-Strauss himself who abruptly abandons his method precisely when he comes to analyse infrastructures. Over and beyond the writer's thought, there is the thinker himself, rooted in his personal and social context.

To be a Marxist in the social sciences therefore means to try to reconstruct, reproduce in thought, the logic of the processes which give rise to the visible order of facts and institutions and which determine their possible transformations. In order to carry this through, we need to be able to pinpoint the contradictions existing within societies, these being of two types: internal contradictions on a given structural level – such as the contradiction between capitalist and worker – and contradictions between structural levels – such as the contradiction between productive forces and relations of production. Far from being foreign to each other, moreover, the two types of contradiction are organically linked. While it is generally fairly easy to identify contradictions internal to a given structural level, it is far harder to uncover the contradictions that emerge between structural levels in a society's production process, for these are not contradictions between institutions or things, but between the properties of social relations; properties which limit their reproductive capacities to maintain themselves within certain limits. By moving in this direction we may hope to discover some of the laws of transformation of social relations, the laws of motion governing societies.

Obviously, though, this analysis of contradictions does not fit in with a Hegelian-type dialectical logic, for the latter rests, in the last analysis, upon a non-scientific, metaphysical principle, the principle of the identity of opposites in which the slave is both himself and his master, and his master at once himself and his slave. To be scientific, an analysis of the internal and external contradictions of societies must start out from the unity of opposites, a conflictive unity of partly opposing and contradictory properties; and from conflicts leading to the development of these contradictions.

The difference between Hegel's dialectic and that of Marx does not lie, as Althusser put it, in the fact that in the former's view contradictions are always simple, while being 'overdetermined' in the latter. The difference goes far deeper than that. It lies in the acceptance or rejection of a metaphysical, non-scientific, principle. On this point neither Mao-

Tse-Tung nor Lenin manage to be very clear, both of them slipping constantly and imperceptibly from the notion of the unity of opposites to that of their identity. Needless to say, both notions exist for Hegel, since the very fact that opposites are identical also makes them united. For him, the principle of the unity of opposites is a complementary principle derived from the initial principle of the identity of opposites. When Marx claims to have extracted the 'rational core' of Hegel's logic he strikes me as trying to say that he has managed to split Hegel's two principles, retaining one while casting aside the other.

In fact, Marxism reveals the existence of two levels of rationality. First, the intentional rationality of individuals and groups acting within determinate social relations and upon these social relations on the basis of their own representation of these relations and in pursuit of their ends. Beyond this, however, there is an unintentional rationality which consists of all the objective properties of these social relations and of their specific laws of transformation. If Marxists gradually manage to uncover these two levels of rationality they will transform Marxism into the most complex form of modern scientific practice, the most complex form of rationalism in the production of knowledge.

Towards a materialist theory of religion

The third problem, which we shall only touch on here, concerns the materialist explanation of social representations and more particularly of those ideals represented by gods and the symbolic practices employed in their worship. This is to raise the problem of a Marxist theory of ideologies.

I should like to begin by disposing of any conceptions in which ideology appears only at and as the surface of social relations, or, borrowing Althusser's vocabulary, as the superstructure of the superstructures. As I have already shown in listing the realities that go to make up the infrastructure of societies, there is no such thing as a purely material force of production. A tool has no social existence unless its rules of manufacture and use are known and communicated. These representations are also productive forces and constitute an internal element in the infrastructure. Generally speaking, a social relation cannot be reproduced unless people have a representation of this relation. And this representation, far from being a mere reflection of the relation, is one of its internal conditions of existence. Hence we find ideas and representations at every level of society not merely as one of its conditions of reproduction. Thus ideology cannot be seen as a specific level, as one instance separated from other instances.

Does this mean that the problem of such differences and contradictions as may exist between the representations people have of their social relations and the content of these social relations no longer exists? Does it mean that I have decided to take the illusions of a society or an epoch concerning itself for reality? Quite the reverse. This way of conceiving the distinction between infrastructure and superstructures as a distinction between functions within the process of social life, more than any others, enables us to throw light on the foundations and the machinery of the illusions each society creates about itself.

As an example, in a society where kinship relations function as a relation of production, hence dominating the over-arching logic of that society, all social relations necessarily appear to be so many aspects and effects of kinship relations. As a result, relations of production do not appear as the social conditions and forms of a material process of production, a process itself dependent upon a determinate level of productive forces, but mainly as aspects of a process of exchange of women and of descent. The very way in which relations of production appear causes their content partly to disappear. This appearance constitutes the point of departure for spontaneous representations which individuals and groups have of their own relations and of their relations with nature. For this reason, the relations which individuals have with each other and with nature are, spontaneously, partly illusory or imaginary.

Another example is that of the citizen in Ancient Greece, for whom all problems were basically political; or conversely, in order to be thought of as a problem, the matter in hand had to take on the appearance of a political problem, a problem for the city. This was because political relations dominated the functioning of society as a whole and were the conditions underlying the reproduction of the social whole. But we have already suggested that the reason why politics governed the reproduction of the city seems to be that it functioned from within as a social relation of production, as 'infrastructure' or, to put it another way, as a social relation which programmed the material base of their society. The thinkable and the unthinkable are therefore historically and structurally determined. And what was uppermost in determining them were the places occupied and the forms taken by social relations of production. It would appear, then, that all societies have illusions about themselves, but that these illusions are nevertheless involved with the realities themselves, since they are rooted in the places and forms of relations of production. By developing as an extension of the appearances of social relations, spontaneous social representations leave an essential portion of these relations of production opaque, namely their material content.

But the practical consequence of this partly illusory relation which spontaneously grows up between individuals and their material conditions of existence is a proliferation of illusory acts upon an imaginary reality. Thus the Greeks insisted many times on executing, after defeat at the hands of their enemies, the strategists they had appointed to lead their armies. For them, the defeat of Athens could not be anything but a political problem carrying with it the punishment provided for those who betray a political cause. What was unthinkable, non-representable in their way of thinking, was that there might have been other causes for the decadence of Athens and for the collapse of its imperial power. The whole theory of historical necessity begins to raise its head here, for causes are unceasingly active, even when men know nothing of them. And they operate all the more necessarily when men are unaware of them or ignore them.

On the basis of these two analyses it may be possible to sketch out a Marxist approach to religious phenomena. In primitive societies, the sacred is not merely a theoretical category but a practical device for acting upon the relations between a man and his fellows and between men and nature. Gods and supernatural powers represent imaginary conditions of reproduction of nature and society. But it is inadequate to say only that these ideals are 'illusory' representations of the conditions of reproduction of nature and society, if we want to produce a materialist theory of religion. We must also elaborate a theory of the conditions and the mechanisms governing the production of these idealities. Marx, in *Capital*, warned against a narrowly materialist conception – inherited from the abstract materialism of the natural sciences – when writing on the subject of religion: 'It is far easier to discover by analysis the earthly core of nebulous religious conceptions than to develop (*entwickeln*), conversely, these celestial forms, on each occasion, out of the real conditions of life' (*Das Kapital*, I, p. 389, n. 89). I have altered Roy's French translation, its revision by Marx notwithstanding, as he translated *entwickeln* by 'faire voir comment les conditions réelles de la vie *revêtent* peu à peu une forme éthérée' (to show how the real conditions of life gradually assume an ethereal form. *Editions Sociales*, I, t. 2, p. 59). Roy's translation suggests that the real conditions of life may exist before and in the absence of 'ethereal forms', i.e. religious representations, and that they gradually assume these in the process of historical development.

One would need to explain how the real conditions of life lead man to represent the invisible causes of the visible order of nature and history as the work of Powers conceived in man's image, intentionally governing the order of the universe. This theory is now beginning to emerge in the work of Vernant and Détienne, among others. If we want to take a global view of the diversity of religious phenomena and of the complex relations existing between economic infrastructure, political power and religious forms, we may say that in primitive hunter-gathering societies, tools are such that everyone can make them for himself and that technical knowledge is shared among everyone. But even here, imaginary knowledge regarding the gods, the masters of animals and plants, was unequally appropriated by different groups and individuals. The first monopoly could have been a monopoly of the imaginary rather than a monopoly of the material means of production. In the development of social inequality, with the appearance of early forms of classes and the state, it seems that we observe a qualitative change. The Inca, personifying the state, is no longer the representative of mankind dealing with the gods, but the representative of the gods among men. He is the son of the Sun, and on him depends the fertility of women and the fields, the reproduction of society as well as that of the cosmos. The development of class relations and that of the state would seem to be accompanied by a process of divinisation of a fraction of humanity, and of divinisation of the institutions manifesting that fraction's power. Religion is not merely the fantasmatic reflection of social relations, an ideology that legitimises existing relations of production after the event, as it were, but functions as one of the components of the internal framework of these relations of production, as one of the essential conditions of the relation in which an aristocracy controlling the powers of the state exploits the peasantry. The moment each individual and every community thought he or it owed his conditions of existence to the supernatural power of the Inca, each individual or community recognised an obligation to offer him labour and produce, both in order to celebrate his glory and his divine reality, and to render to the Inca a portion of what he (the Inca) had done for the reproduction and the prosperity of all. Religion here served as a source of violence-free constraint; in some ways it constitutes the greatest strength of the state and of the dominant class, since it obliges those dominated to consent to their domination from within.

The mistake here would be to confuse effects and reasons. Religion was not invented in order to force the dominated to consent to their domination, but it exists in such a way that it results in this consent. Seen thus, we may restate the problem of the origin of class relations within classless societies and that of the appearance of primitive forms of the State. But we are not really in a position to discuss that at this point.

*

To conclude, I should like to dwell for a moment on Marx's formula in which he speaks of the 'transparency of social relations' which will exist when class relations have disappeared. I do not believe 'transparency' can mean absolute knowledge, by each individual, of all that concerns him, but that it means non-alienation, i.e. the recognition that everything that happens is either human or natural in origin, without alien additives, without the intervention of human- and nature-transcending powers. The transparency of relations does not mean a state of knowledge, the impossible and metaphysical dream of some absolute knowledge, but a state of social relations in which men no longer consider each other and themselves in some way foreign to what they are. And this state cannot arise from arbitrary abolition of the State or of religion. For State and religion cannot be abolished; they will die out, their functions will wither away and hence will lose all reality at the conclusion of class struggles and of revolutionary transformations of society.

Thus interpreted, Marxism is the most critical, the most complex and the most difficult form of modern rationalism. At the same time, it is its most open form, for the paradox of Marxism lies in the fact that it can only continue to exist provided it never allows itself to become hidebound or to become a closed system, a state philosophy, on pain of death as a science and rebirth as religious dogma. It is on this condition that we can tie the process of knowledge in with the process of the revolutionary transformation of society.

YU. PETROVA-AVERKIEVA

Historicism in Soviet ethnographic science

In the USSR ethnography grew up as an historical discipline dealing with the peculiarities of the way of life and culture of ethnic communities at all stages of the development of human society. But while at earlier times ethnographers concentrated mainly on precapitalist societies, nowadays the majority of Soviet ethnographers study capitalist and post- capitalist socialist ethnic communities.

The leading principle of the ethnographic research in the USSR is historicism. By historicism is meant the study of every phenomenon of social life within a particular historical framework, in terms of the process of its origin and development, and its causal determination. The Marxist materialistic view of history underlies this approach. Soviet ethnographers have been working on the foundation of the Marxist theory of ethnographic science as a concrete social science based, first of all, on historical materialism and on Marxism in general. They substantiate this theory by the rich corpus of factual data accumulated by the ethnographic science, and take into account all the valuable findings of the pro-Marxist and non-Marxist theories.

Since one often comes across wrong interpretations of Marxist historicism in western ethnographic literature, I shall dwell upon some principal features of the approach in question, which guide Soviet scholars in their research work. Soviet ethnographers proceed, first of all, from the Marxist-Leninist teaching concerning social progress and the onward march of history.

Many western scholars have tried to refute Marxism by denying the very idea of progress in human history and stressing the absence of an objective criterion of progress. Indeed, the development of a society is highly contradictory and uneven in all spheres of social life. That is why Marxists pose the problem of social progress as related to concrete historical processes; they propose a concrete criterion of progress with regard to different spheres of social life – technological, socio-economic, and intellectual.

In the sphere of technology the objective criterion of progress is the level of the development of productive forces, the extent to which man has control over nature. As Lenin stressed, we find here the 'highest criterion of social progress.'[1]

But productive forces develop within particular socio-economic systems. A socio-economic formation is progressive when it provides the best possibilities for the development of human productive forces. Giving a generalised formulation of the objective criterion of social progress, the Soviet sociologist Semenov justly wrote:

> The better the possibilities which a society affords for the increase in the productivity of labour, for unlimited development and independent creation of history by working masses, for the satisfying of their growing material and cultural needs, for enriching one's personality – the more progressive that society is.[2]

At the same time, it is characteristic of the present historical epoch that for many economically underdeveloped countries there exists today the possibility of a revolutionary leap to socialism, bypassing the capitalist stage. They have much better opportunities for rapid progress in all spheres than developed capitalist countries. It is noteworthy that not only Soviet scholars point out this peculiarity. Service, for instance, notes it in his article on the evolutionary potential of 'backward civilisations.'[3]

Soviet ethnographers consider it their task to work out concrete criteria of progress with regard to the historical investigated epochs to determine the degree of progressiveness or of reactionary character of this or that social process or phenomenon, under the given conditions of time and place. This is the starting point in the study of the surviving traditions, or traditional social structures, such as, for instance, a village community.

Marx's formulation of fundamental principles of materialistic understanding of history is well-known:

> In the social production of their life men enter into definite relations that are indispensable and independent of their will, relations of production which correspond to a definite stage of development of their material productive forces. The sum-total of these relations of production constitutes the economic structure of society, the real foundation on which rises a legal and political superstructure and to which correspond definite forms of social consciousness. The mode of production of material life conditions the social, political and intellectual life processes in general. It is not the consciousness of men that determines their being, but on the contrary, their social being that determines their consciousness.[4]

About his own conclusions Marx wrote: 'The general result at which I arrived and which once won, served as a guiding thread for my studies.'[5] Evaluating Marx's findings, Engels said: 'For all historical sciences (and all sciences which are not natural sciences are historical) a revolutionary discovery was made with this proposition.'[6]

This discovery is gaining wide recognition nowadays even in non-Marxist and neo-Marxist literature, but at the same time it is this statement which often seems to be misinterpreted. It is often understood as 'economic materialism' or 'economic determinism,' and in this particular form it is popular with modern neo-evolutionists. Both Marx and Engels, and also Lenin, had warned against such interpretations. Engels in the letter to Bloch wrote:

> According to the materialistic concept of history, the ultimately determining element in history is the production and reproduction of real life. More than this neither Marx nor I have ever asserted. Hence if somebody twists this into saying that the economic element is the only determining one, he transforms that proposition into a meaningless, abstract, senseless phrase. The economic situation is the basis, but the various elements of the superstructure . . . also exercise their influence upon the course of the historical struggles and in many cases preponderate in determining their form.[7]

To Mikhailovsky's attempt to interpret Marxism along these lines, Lenin wrote:

> But where have you read in the works of Marx or Engels that they necessarily spoke of economic materialism? When they described their world outlook they called it simply materialism . . . The materialists (Marxists) were the first socialists to raise the issue of the need to analyse all aspects of social life, and not only the economic.[8]

The above quoted statement of Marx is often understood as a formulation of technological determination. The productive forces are reduced to technology and the development of technology is seen as the main driving force of history. One can even come across quite erroneous statements to the effect that in *Capital* Marx expounded the 'energy theory of evolution'.[9] Techno-environmental interpretations of Marxism have also spread recently.[10]

It is the central category of Marxist historicism – that of socio-economic formation – that is most misunderstood. Many western scholars recognise the importance of the concept of social formation, but they disagree on its meaning. As is known, the founders of Marxism, long before functionalism had appeared, emphasised the interdependence of all phenomena of social life and the dialectical character of this interdependence. Of all the various intra-social relations they singled out as primary the material and objective relations, namely the socio-economic relations, the study of which allowed them to establish several principal types of such relations. Lenin wrote: 'The analysis of material social relations at once made it possible to observe recurrences and regularity and to generalise the systems of the various countries under the single fundamental concept: social formation.'[11] Every formation is characterised by a particular mode of production of material life.

In the course of its development every formation passes through the stages of origin, climax and transition to a higher formation. Every formation, as Lenin says, 'is a specific social organism whose inception, functioning, and transition to a higher form are governed by specific laws.'[12]

In Soviet historiography these stages are usually called 'historical epochs.' It is in the character of historical epochs that the concrete historical process of existence of formation manifests itself.

The shift in socio-economic formations is a general law independent of chronological data. It is the logic of the historical process. As for historical epochs, they are associated with certain dates, events, and chronological periods. They represent the concrete march of history. The study of historical epochs introduces real historicism into the concept of social formation. Different kinds of processes may and do occur among different peoples and countries in one and the same historical epoch. It is necessary, as Lenin wrote, 'that account be taken of the specific features distinguishing this country from others in the same historical epoch.'[13]

Every epoch within a social formation is characterised by its own specific regularities, jointly with general laws of that social formation. Every social formation is a natural stage in the onward march of world history. The formation is both the embodiment of the discontinuity of historical process, and a link in the chain of progressive development of mankind. According to Marxist historicism, the sequence of successive formations expresses the objective logic of world history. But this order is not an objective necessity for every nation. We know of peoples who leapt from primative society directly to feudalism and even capitalism (American Indians) or even to socialism (minor peoples of the north of the USSR); there are peoples who passed from feudalism to socialism, with the help of socialist countries. No single socio-economic formation, except for the primitive one, dominated the whole world at a single period of time. Because of the unevenness and diversity of the historical process which followed the primitive formation, societies belonging to different formations co-exist in one and the same historical epoch. We ethnographers of the twentieth century are able to observe, for instance, societies which allow us to identify the basic general characteristic features of the primitive formation.

Soviet ethnographers, investigating primitive society from the point of view of historicism, set themselves the task of tracing, on the basis of ethnographic and archaeological data, the epochs of historical development of the primitive social formation. Most of our scholars adhere to the division of this formation into three major historical epochs: the primitive human herd, the matrilineal clan, and the transition to class society. We attempt to establish the specific features of every epoch, and their relation to the general regularities of this pre-class primitive-communist formation. Particular attention is given to the third of the above mentioned epochs of this formation; the task in this connection is to reveal the conditions and signs of the appearance in its innermost recesses of a new kind of relation characteristic of an emerging higher type of class formation. Apart from the great ideological and practical importance of such investigations, the material itself seems to be easily available, as most of the economically underdeveloped peoples of the world, available for direct observation by ethnographers recently, were living under conditions characteristic of this historical epoch.

In various works by our western colleagues one can come across a misunderstanding of the category of the mode of production of 'material goods' as a form or direction of economy; by production relations they understand a form of organisation of labour, or distribution of labour within this economy. A concrete society is then identified with a socio-economic formation. As a result, every tribe is considered to be a formation.[14] It is obvious that in this case the socio-economic formation is not viewed as a category of logic, as a type of society and a stage in the objective and logical world history process. Terray, for instance, identifies socio-economic formation with the mode of production, and the latter is defined as a '. . . three-part system: an economic base, a juridico-political superstructure, and an ideological superstructure. This economic base is, in its turn, a combination of a system of productive forces and a system of relations of production.'[15] Here the name of 'economic base' is given to the mode of production as a system of productive relations together with particular productive forces. As is well-known, Marx and Engels saw the 'economic basis', the system of productive relations, as a basis for all other kinds of social relations existing in a given society.

Such inaccuracies in the interpretation of the fundamentals of historical materialism are often explained as attempts to adapt them to the specific conditions of precapitalist societies, and in particular to primitive society.

Western ethnographic writings often contain statements about the inapplicability of Marxist historicism to the study of primitive society. We believe that Soviet ethnographers in their work have succeeded in refuting these misconceptions. In the study of the life of peoples at different stages of their history they always trace the operation of one fundamental historical law according to which 'the mode of production of material life conditions the social, political and intellectual life processes in general.' Primitive society was no exception and developed on the same basis. It was not stagnant, but the rate of its development was very slow.

Very important for our research is the following statement by Marx: 'Assume particular stages of development in production, commerce, and consumption, and you will have a corresponding social constitution, a corresponding organisation of the family or orders of classes, in a word, a corresponding civil society.'[16]

The classics of Marxism kept stressing that the materialist approach to history as a scientific theory of historical process should be seen as a general method of studying social phenomena, and not as a means of constructing abstract historical conceptions.

General sociological laws formulated by them do not exhaust all the diverse specific historical regularities. The founders of Marxism insisted on the necessity of concrete research into historical phenomena and events in order to reveal their objective interrelationship with other phenomena and facts, and to establish their essential traits. No general laws exist in their pure form. They operate under diverse conditions, embracing the unique traits of a given social and natural environment. They manifest themselves in various situations reflecting the dialects of the universality and diversity of historical processes. Comparative analysis reveals similarities of the objective tendencies in social development in spite of the diversity of natural environment, history and culture of ethnic and demographic structure of the given societies.

In the social life of an 'ethnos' ethnographers attempt to trace the interdependence and interweaving of economic, political, and ideological processes. They try to reveal the specific features of the relationship between basis and superstructure under the conditions of different historical epochs of different formations, and the long-term determinative role of the economic movement.

The diversity of the forms of social life of 'ethnoses' in one and the same historical epoch, demonstrated by ethnographic science, and the presence in the history of some of them of periods of stagnation and backward steps, do not contradict the Marxist understanding of history, nor do they refute the Marxist interpretation of history. According to Lenin's words, 'it is undialectical, unscientific and theoretically wrong to regard the course of world history as smooth and always progressive in direction, without occasional gigantic leaps back.'[17] Engels also has noted that, 'history often proceeds by leaps and zigzags.'[18] It is the recognition of revolutionary leaps, retreats and zigzags that distinguishes Marxist historicism from unilinear evolutionism, which emphasises the continuity of slow changes in history of human society. Marxism does not canonise one unilinear order of historical events as the only possible order; it denies the idea of predestined necessity. Such Marxist categories as possibility and reality refute the above interpretations of Marxism.

The method of historicism presupposes a thorough study of this or that process or phenomenon of social life in its historical perspective. Empirical knowledge and theoretical generalisations should be combined in such an inquiry. We do not accept the division of the science into two separate disciplines – ethnography as a 'fact-gathering' science and ethnology as a generalising one. However, Marxists do not deny the authority of fact. As Lenin stressed: 'Marxism does not base itself on anything other than the facts of history and reality.'[19] We only object to factual work being confined to merely discovering and describing facts, without interpreting them from the point of view of the historic regularities which are revealed by those facts. Every historic fact represents the unity of the general and the specific.

Accumulating facts is the first stage of a scientific investigation. Soviet ethnography, like any true science, comprises both a descriptive, empirical part and an 'explanatory,' theoretical part. Unimpeachable historical conceptions can and do grow only out of thorough factual studies. Materialistic understanding of history develops in correspondence with the concrete historical situation, as a result of the analysis of new facts and phenomena. This is the essence of Marxist historicism.

This approach is, however, often criticised as a method of 'preconceived schemes' and 'opinions.' Usually what is meant by these preconceived opinions and schemes are the sociological laws discovered by the founders of Marxism. This unfounded criticism on the part of the advocates of pure fact has often been denounced by many western scholars[20] who demonstrated by concrete evidence that the very choice of facts, their first rough classification, is based on certain philosophical promises and theoretical hypotheses of the researcher.

This unity of the concrete factual and general theoretical side of research is part of the Marxist teaching concerning the relationship between theory and practice, science and life. It also concerns science as a generalisation of experience. Another aspect of this teaching is the recognition of the fact that the knowledge of historical experience provides real possibilities of foreseeing the future and for planning it. In western literature this idea is often distorted and presented as 'politicisation' of social science, which threatens its 'honesty' and 'objectivity.' According to Harris, science should be above 'class interests.'[21] One might ask Harris to explain the 'class-independent' position from which he blackens Marxists, denounces Marx as a revolutionary, and refutes his teaching concerning proletarian revolutions? As the classics of Marxism established, the whole written history of mankind, except for the primitive epoch, is the history of class struggle. That is why Soviet ethnographers in their study of social phenomena of class societies, including early class societies, proceed from the assumption that the substance of a phenomenon or of an institution, or a custom under investigation, cannot be understood without the analysis of class relations in the given society. Lenin emphasises that no researcher describing social relations in a class society 'can help taking the side of one class or another.'[22] There is no such thing as objectivity independent of class – this has been stated in many western writings.[23]

The historical method of Soviet ethnography was especially productive when applied to the study of the genesis of ethnoses, the periods in the ethnic history of peoples, and their relation to the general history of mankind.[24] Soviet scholars single out three types of ethnic communities which succeeded one another in the process of history, they are tribes, nationalities, and nations. All these bore their specific features in different historical epochs of different socio-economic formations.

Much has been done by Soviet scholars to establish the regularities of the social development of mankind. In the ethnic and social features of a given ethnos, Soviet scholars see a display of the ethnically specific, and the specific is seen as the manifestation of the general laws of development of ethnic processes. The vast experience of nation building in such a multinational state as the USSR provided Soviet scholars with a mass of material and allowed them to work out a scientific typology of ethnic processes, to reveal the factors and rate of their development, and to specify stages of their history.

Comparative investigations of ethnic communities of various types have led these scholars to the conclusion that all the spheres of social life of the early ethnic communities – tribes – were permeated with specific ethnic features; that is why the tribal life as a whole has been the object of ethnographers' attention. At the subsequent stages ethnic peculiarities manifest themselves on a narrower scale. Nationalities still perpetuate them in their languages, traditional material and spiritual culture etc; but at the national level, ethnic character manifests itself most vividly in the consciousness of ethnic identity, which thus approaches the sphere of ethnic psychology. Having established that ethnic processes are slower than socio-economic ones, Soviet ethnographers, however, find it possible to reveal the ethnic specificity in other spheres of the social life of modern nations.

The priority of Soviet scholars in the investigation of ethnic problems has been recognised in the ethnographic literature of the West. I would mention here a recent statement of a noted Norwegian scholar, Gjessing, who wrote that 'ethnogenesis was never respected in western European anthropology, while in the USSR and Eastern European countries ethnohistory and ethnogenesis occupy a respectable place.'[25]

It is the Marxist historical approach to the social life of ethnoses that allows Soviet scholars to contribute markedly to the study of ethnic processes, including the problems of ethnogenesis.

In conclusion it should be noted that the work done by Soviet scholars in the field of ethnic history of peoples is not identical with what in the USA is called 'ethnohistory.' The latter, as far as I know, means the study of the past history of ethnoses on the basis of joint archaeological and ethnographic data and written sources. In the USSR this kind of investigation is called 'historical ethnography.' As for the subject-matter of ethnic history, it is the study of ethnic processes throughout the whole history of an ethnos.

NOTES

1 V.I. Lenin, *Collected Works*, vol. 13, Moscow, 1962, p. 243.

2 Yu.N. Semenov, *Social Progress and Modern Bourgeois Philosophy of Society*, Moscow, 1965, pp. 277–8 (in Russian).

3 E. Service, 'The law of evolutionary potential', in *Evolution and Culture*, 1960.

4 K. Marx and F. Engels, *Selected Works*, Moscow, 1970, p. 181.

5 Ibid.

6 K. Marx and F. Engels, *Selected Works*, vol. 1, Moscow, 1958.

7 K. Marx and F. Engels, *Selected Works*, vol. 2, Moscow, 1958.

8 V.I. Lenin, *Collected Works*, vol. 1, Moscow, 1960, pp. 151, 161-2.

9 M. Opler, 'Two converging lines of influence in cultural evolutionary theory', *American Anthropologist*, 1962, vol. 64, no. 3. G.S Berliner, 'The feet of the natives are large', *Current Anthropology*, 1969, vol. 3, no. 1, p. 60.

10 See, for example, M. Harris, *The Rise of Anthropological Theory*, New York, 1968.

11 Lenin, *Collected Works*, vol. 1, p. 140.

12 Ibid.

13 V.I. Lenin, *Collected Works*, vol. 20, Moscow, 1964, pp. 400-1.

14 C. Meillassoux, *L'Anthropologie Economique des Gouro de Côte d'Ivoire*, Paris, 1964. E. Terray, *Le Marxism devant les Sociétés 'Primitives'*, Paris, 1969. See also *Marxist Analysis and Social Anthropology*, London, 1975. For critical analysis of these conceptions see Yu.I. Semenov, 'Marxism and primitive society', *Sovietskaia Etnografia*, 1975, no. 4 (in Russian).

15 Terray, op. cit., pp. 97-8.

16 K. Marx and F. Engels, *Selected Works*, vol. 1, Moscow, 1969, p. 518.

17 V.I. Lenin, *Collected Works*, vol. 22, Moscow, 1964, p. 310.

18 K. Marx and F. Engels, *Selected Works*, vol. 1, Moscow, 1958, p. 373.

19 Lenin, *Collected Works*, vol. 1, p. 394.

20 See, for instance, 'Social responsibility symposium', *Current Anthropology*, 1968, vol. 9, no. 5. See also Harris, op. cit., pp. 2,290. G. Murdal, *Objectivity in Social Research*, New York, 1969. E. Gellner, *Cause and Meaning in the Social Sciences*, London, 1973.

21 Harris, op. cit., p. 221.

22 V.I. Lenin, *Collected Works*, vol. 2, Moscow, 1962, p. 531.

23 See, for example, *Anthropology and the Colonial Encounter*, London, 1973.

24 V.I. Kozlov, *Dynamics and Population Size of Peoples*, Moscow, 1969. Yu.V. Bromley, *Ethnos and Ethnography*, Moscow, 1973; *The Social and the National*, Moscow, 1974; *Ethnic Processes in the USSR*, Moscow, 1975 (all in Russian).

25 G. Gjessing, 'Socio-archaeology', *Current Anthropology*, 1975, vol. 16.

YU. I. SEMENOV

*The theory of socio-economic formations and world history**

I

The materialist conception of history is above all a way of seeing history as a natural-historical process, as the development and succession of socio-economic formations. Thus the concept of socio-economic formations naturally becomes the central and basic category of historical materialism. It is not possible to reach the heart of the materialist theory of the historical process without a deep understanding of this notion.

'Socio-economic formations' are defined as stages in the development of society, regularly succeeding each other in a strictly defined order. The definition may seem clear and simple; this simplicity is, however, deceptive, for it is not clear just how the word 'society' is being used. In philosophical and historical literature, the word has not one, but various meanings.

For one thing, it can be used to describe a concrete and distinct society. Such a society can be, in considerable measure, an independent unit in historical development. It is in this sense that the word is used when one speaks for instance, of Lagash, Athenian, Carthaginian, Venetian, French and Polish societies. In an earlier work I have suggested that, in this sense, we should use the expression 'social organism'.[1]

Secondly, the word 'society' is often used to indicate one or another concrete totality of social organisms. For instance, one speaks of the society of North American Indians, the society of Australian aborigines, or about western European or Near Eastern societies.

Thirdly, the term 'society' is used to designate all existing social organisms, past and present, i.e. to describe all human society as a whole. In this sense, one normally attaches the adjective 'human' to it.

Fourthly and finally, the word is also used to designate society as such, or this or that type of society.

It is only possible to make clear the proper meaning of the socio-

* Translated by Ernest Gellner. The translator has used the expressions 'global system' and 'world system' interchangeably (for stylistic reasons), whereas only one expression occurs in the original Russian.

economic formation, as a stage of historical development, by considering the genesis of this notion.

Human society has always represented the sum of a good number of
distinct concrete societies, i.e. social organisms. Correspondingly its
development, i.e. global history, is composed of a multiplicity of histories of these social organisms.

In the history of mankind, it is never possible to find wholly similar
social organisms. Every single society has its own particular traits,
which distinguish it from all others. Individuality and unreplicability
also distinguish the development of every social organism. Every distinct society has its own history, which is different from the history of all
other social organisms. The history of Athens differs from the history of
Rome, the history of England from that of France, the history of Russia
from that of China.

It was above all the uniqueness of the history of individual societies
which impressed historians prior to Marx. Hence global history appeared to them as the endless cumulation of events, devoid of any kind
of order. It was not possible to overcome the chaos and arbitrariness
governing visions of history without uncovering that which is common
to social organisms, and finding that which repeats itself in their development.

Pre-Marxist thinkers repeatedly made efforts in this direction.
Sociologists, for instance, endeavoured to find a concept which would
contain that which is common to all social organisms without exception,
and which would express the fundamental traits of any given concrete society. The concept which they obtained by means of abstracting
from the traits which distinguish one society from another, only resulted in empty abstractions, devoid of scientific value. Lenin provided
a profound and brilliant account of the indefensible nature of this kind
of idea.[2] There were also efforts to group social organisms together in
species and to define their types. But all these efforts proved abortive,
because sociologists and historians failed to separate the fundamental
aspects of social life from inessential and secondary ones. It is easy to
see that no classification of social organisms, which is based on secondary characteristics, can approach an understanding of the development
of society. As for the numerous attempts to show repetition in the evolution of single societies, they never reached further than one form or
another of 'cyclicalism'.

Social organisms do not merely exist and develop. They merge into
existence, and not infrequently they disintegrate, perish, disappear.
Literally before our very eyes there emerged from the ruins of Hitler's
'Third Reich' two new, previously non-existent social organisms – the
German Democratic Republic and the German Federal Republic.
Before our eyes Pakistan, as it had existed since its emergence in 1947,
disappeared, and in its place two new social organisms were formed,
one retaining the old name, the other adopting a new one: the Republic
of Bangladesh. If we turn to more distant periods, we find that the

emergence and disappearance of social organisms constitutes the most common of phenomena. The Hittite and Assyrian empires, the Athenian and Carthaginian republics, the Roman empire, etc. all emerged, grew, flourished, and then weakened and disappeared forever.

These and similar facts were at the root of the idea to which could make all social organisms (or their systems) pass through the same stages of development: they emerge, grow, reach maturity, age and, finally, perish. Global history then appears as the monotonous repetition of the very same processes, as the eternal movement of a wheel. In its time the emergence of this type of theory was in part connected with the effort to find at least some kind of order in history, and in this sense represented a definite contribution to the development of historical thought. This applies particularly to Vico and his *Scienzia Nuova* (1725). In our time, when the materialist conception of history has been in existence a long time, all kinds of 'cyclical' conceptions play a reactionary role. Their essence has now become the repudiation of the unity of the global historical process, and its fragmentation into basically disconnected histories of distinct social organisms or their groupings, which are then usually called civilisations.

But contrary to all theories of circularity, historical evidence bears such vivid testimony to the progress of mankind as a whole, as could hardly escape the attention of historians. Marx's predecessors notably perceived, in a highly defined form, the gradual development of human society. This insight found its expression in the delimitation of the basic epochs of global history. World-historical epochs such as the ancient, mediaeval and modern were already defined by the Italian humanist-historians of the fifteenth and sixteenth centuries (Bruni, Biondo, Machiavelli and others). Furthermore this three-term division came to be refined, and from the turn of the eighteenth and nineteenth centuries, historians came ever more frequently to treat the ancient east as a distinct period. This periodicisation of history had, for a considerable time, a merely empirical nature. A step forward towards endowing each of the three terms in the first-cited typology with theoretical import was taken by Saint-Simon, who related each of them to a definite social system: the ancient one was based on slavery, the mediaeval on feudalism, in which the labourer was tied to land and only indirectly belonged to the landowner, and the modern on the 'industrial' system, based on hired labour. Another significant effort was undertaken in this direction by Hegel in his *Philosophy of History* (1822-1831).

II

A revolution in conceptions of history arose when Marx and Engels succeeded in isolating, from all the other multiform social relations, just those which came into being independently of the will and knowledge of man and which determine their views, aims, strivings, their actions and comportment and thereby also all other social relations. These objective, material relations are the productive, socio-economic relations. In every concrete society, productive relations constitute a more or less integral whole, which is the base, the foundation of all other social relations, and thereby also of the entire social organism.

The separation of productive relations from all the others at the same time also amounted to the uncovering of the existence of some of their basic forms. It thus becomes clear that distinct social organisms could either have the same socio-economic structure. i.e. one constituted by relations of the same kind, or possess diverse structures, constituted by social relations of diverse types. In so far as productive relations are the fundamental, determinative ones, all individual societies, which have as their basis one and the same system of socio-economic relations, notwithstanding all their differences, in reality represent one and the same society, belong to one and the same type. On the other hand, social organisms with different socio-economic structures, whatever similarities they might display, are essentially distinct and relate to different types of society.

In this way, by means of the identification of productive relations as the basis of any given society and the discovery of several qualitatively different systems of such relations, the enormous number of social organisms was reduced to several basic types, to be called socio-economic formations. Lenin wrote: '. . . the analysis of material social relations provided the possibility of linking the repetitions and regularities, and of subsuming the social orders of various countries under the unitary conception of social formations.'[3]

The concept of socio-economic formations is not reducible simply to the idea of a social type. It is markedly more complex and many-sided. But one of its aspects is ever rooted in the fact that it is a concept of social species, which has as its base a definite type, a definite system of productive relations. This concept always brings home, on the one hand, the basic identity of all social organisms which have as their foundation one and the same system of productive relations, and on the other hand, the basic differences between concrete societies possessing diverse socio-economic structures.

The concept of socio-economic formations is altogether inseparable from the concept of concrete socio-economic formations. Without the concept of concrete types of society there neither is nor can be any concept of a type of society in general. It is evident that a socio-economic formation always exists as a concrete, definite socio-economic formation, which finds its existence only in definite societies, or social organisms. The relation of socio-economic formations to social organisms is essentially the relationship of the general to the specific. Lenin wrote: 'The general exists only in the specific and through it. Everything specific is (in one way or another) general. Anything general is (part, aspect or essence of) the specific.'[4]

A socio-economic formation has no independent being. A type of society can only exist in concrete societies of the given type. Any concrete socio-economic formation exists not alongside specific societies, but only in these very social organisms. It exists as their profound and shared basis, their internal essence, and thereby as their species. Lenin saw Marx's great achievement in that he 'did not confine himself to describing the existing system, to judging and condemning it; he gave a scientific explanation of it, reducing that existing system, which differs in diverse European and non-European countries, to a common basis – the capitalist social formation.'[5]

The common elements shared by social organisms, falling under the same socio-economic formation, naturally are not exhausted by their socio-economic structure. But what in the end unites all these social organisms, and above all determines their inclusion in one type, is the presence within them of one and the same system of productive relations. All else that binds them together derives from this fundamental shared trait. It was for this reason particularly that Lenin repeatedly defined the socio-economic formation as the sum of systems of definite productive relations.[6] At the same time, he never reduced the diverse socio-economic formations altogether to the system of their productive relations. According to him, each socio-economic formation was always the species of any society, when all its aspects were seen jointly. In the same work he characterises the system of productive relations as the 'skeleton' of socio-economic formations, which is always clothed in the 'flesh and blood' of other social relations.[7]

But this 'skeleton' always includes the essence of one or another socio-economic formation. Productive relations are objective and material. Accordingly, the system constituted by those relations is also material. And this means that this system operates and develops in accordance with its own laws, which are independent of the recognition and will of men who live within that system of relations. Given laws appear as laws of the functioning and development of socio-economic formations. The introduction of the notion of the socio-economic formation made it possible first of all to see the evolution of man as a natural-historical process, and made it possible to highlight not merely that which is common amongst social organisms, but also and at the same time that which is repetitive in their development.

All social organisms, which belong to one and the same formation, and have as their basis one and the same system of productive relations, are inevitably bound to develop in accordance with the same laws. However much contemporary England and Portugal, or contemporary Italy and Japan may differ from each other, they all represent bourgeois social organisms, and their development is defined by the same laws – the laws of capitalism.

The most serious task of science is the uncovering of the laws of the function and development of all socio-economic formations, i.e. the formulation of a theory of all formations. In relation to capitalism this task was carried out by Marx. The only path which can lead to the formulation of a theory of this or that formation is that which first uncovers those basic and general features which manifest themselves in the development of all organisms of that particular type. It is quite clear that one cannot uncover the shared features in phenomena unless one abstracts from the differences between them. It is only possible to lay bare the inner objective necessity of any given real process if one frees it from that concrete-historical form in which it manifests itself, and if one presents that process in its 'pure' form in its logical type, i.e. in a form in which it can only exist for theoretical comprehension.

Whereas concrete socio-economic formations exist in historical reality only when incarnated in social organisms, within theory the inner essence of single societies appears in a pure form, as something existing independently; as the ideal social organism of a given type. Marx's *Capital* may serve as an example. In that work, the function and development of capitalist society is considered, not as a definite society, e.g. the English, French or Italian, but as capitalist society in general. And the development of this ideal capitalism (the pure bourgeois socio-economic formation), represents nothing but the reproduction of the inner necessity, or objective regularity of the evolution of every particular capitalist society. Other social formations also appear in theory as ideal social organisms. It is for this reason in particular that Lenin, jointly with the characterisation of socio-economic formations as the general basis of individual societies, also called them: 'distinct social organisms, possessing distinct laws of their own emergence, functioning and transition to other forms, of transformation into other social organisms.'[8]

It is quite clear that a socio-economic formation in the pure sense, i.e. as a distinct social organism, can exist only in theory, but not in historical reality. In history, it exists in distinct societies as their inner essence, their objective basis. A failure to see this can lead to theoretical errors. Thus, for instance, certain Soviet historians, having failed to find in history pure, ideal socio-economic formations, reached the conclusion that formations do not exist in reality at all, that they represent only logical, theoretical constructions.[9] The endeavour to avoid such a conclusion led several other scholars to the direct, immediate identification of socio-economic formations with actually existing social organisms, with distinct concrete societies. The inevitable consequences were a schematisation, a simplification, and thereby a distortion of the historic process, the transformation of the theory of formations from a method of inquiry into a straitjacket into which historic facts had to be forced. Either of these approaches is equally misguided. Either can lead to a repudiation of the materialist conception of history.

III

So far we have spoken of socio-economic formations only as types of society, or social organisms. But they manifest themselves not merely as types of society. Every system of productive relations is connected with a definite level of the development of productive forces. Definite productive forces, together with a definite system of productive relations, constitute a unity – one or other of the modes of production. Hence it is possible to define a socio-economic formation as a type of society, which has as its foundation a definite mode of production. With the development of productive forces a system of productive relations is sooner or later replaced by another, more progressive one, which brings with itself the replacement of one type of society by another higher type.

What follows is that socio-economic formations are types of society which at the same time constitute definite stages in the gradual development of society. Correspondingly, the evolution of human society is nothing but the natural-historical process of the development and replacement of socio-economic formations.

The concept of socio-economic formations arose at the same time an idea of types of societies and of stages of social development. The foundation for the definition of socio-economic formations was laid by the delimitation, by pre-Marxist historians, of the basic epochs of global history: ancient oriental, ancient and mediaeval. Marx endowed this purely empirical classification with a theoretical basis.

The period of history in which the founders of Marxism lived was marked by the existence of social organisms based on the system of capitalist productive relations, the bourgeois mode of production. Capitalism celebrated its victory over feudalism before their very eyes. The capitalist social organisms, typical of modern Europe, were altogether absent from the middle ages. Specific to that period were feudal organisms with a feudal mode of production. In the earlier, or ancient period even feudal organisms were absent. It was the time of the existence of social organisms based on the slave-owning mode of production. The nature of productive relations which were at the root of ancient oriental social organism remained obscure in many ways during the 1850s. However, their shared idiosyncrasy and, at the same time, their qualitative differentiation, not merely from feudal and bourgeois, but also from ancient slave-owning societies, were not questioned at the time by Marx.

For this very reason he terminated his remarkable summary of the essence of the materialist conception of history in his Preface to the *Critique of Political Economy* with the words:

In general outline, the Asiatic, ancient, feudal, and contemporary, bourgeois modes of production can be designated as successive epochs of the economic social formation. Bourgeois productive relations appear as the last antagonistic form of the social process, antagonistic not in the sense of individual antagonism, but in the sense of an antagonist arising from the social conditions of the life of individuals; but the productive forces emerging in the bosom of bourgeois society will also create the conditions for the resolution of this antagonism. Hence with the bourgeois social formation the prehistory of human society comes to a close.[10]

Antagonistic social formations, in Marx's view, were preceded by pre-class, primitive society, and were destined to be succeeded by classless, communist society.

The scheme of the succession of socio-economic formations is accepted in its basic features by all Marxist scholars. The one contested element in it is the 'asiatic' mode of production and correspondingly the asiatic socio-economic formation. For a considerable time the asiatic formation was excluded from the schema, and ancient oriental social organisms were interpreted as slave-owning ones, i.e. as belonging to the same type as ancient societies. In recent years a vigorous discussion has taken place concerning the socio-economic structure of the ancient east. Many of the participants upheld the view that at the root of ancient oriental social organisms, there were distinctive antagonistic productive relations, distinguishable from both slave-owning and feudal ones, not to mention capitalist ones. Others did not accept this view. Even now a considerable proportion of Soviet scholars continues to view ancient oriental societies as slave-owning ones. Thus this issue remains open.

In this connection one must stress that neither solution of this problem is in conflict with the materialist concept of history, for in either case, the contention that human history is the natural-historical process of the evolution and succession of socio-economic formations, remains unshakeable. The question as to whether there were, in the ancient orient, socio-economic class formations distinct from slave-owning ones, is an issue of fact and not of principle.

IV

Another problem does however constitute an issue of principle. What did the socio-economic formations really represent, as stages of historical development, and in what manner did their succession occur in historical reality? At the level of theory, socio-economic formations appear as distinct social organisms, and their succession appears as the replacement of one such organism by another. Pure socio-economic formations appear in it as successive forms of existence of pure human society in general, constituting in itself one continuous social organism.

But in reality, socio-economic formations do not appear as distinct social organisms; nor does human society as a whole constitute a single social organism. It has always constituted a multiplicity of social organisms, which emerge, develop and disappear. Such a discrepancy between theory and reality is inescapable. We have already noted above, that at the level of theory, any given historical process appears in its pure, ideal aspect, in its logical form. As Engels showed, logic is 'nothing but the reflection of the historical process in an abstract and theoretically consistent form; a reflection which is corrected, but the correction corresponds to those laws which are given by historical process itself, so that every element is seen at the points of its development at which it reaches its full maturity and its classical form'.[11] So the theory of socio-economic formations is the reflection of the process of the development of human society in an abstract and theoretically consistent form.

The theory of every distinct social formation reflects the objective necessity of the development of all social organisms which have at their base the corresponding given system of productive relations. It is clear that the theory of socio-economic formations reproduces the objective necessity of the development of all social organisms in general, i.e. of all human society as a whole. But this contention requires refinement. One possibility is that, when we speak of all social organisms of a given type, we mean every one of them taken individually. But what have we in mind, when we speak of all social organisms on the second assumption: do we mean each social organism, taken in isolation, or do we mean all social organisms taken jointly? The interpretation of the theory of socio-economic formations hinges on the answer to this question. If we adopt the former alternative, the theory of socio-economic formations presents itself to us as the realisation of the inner necessity of the development of each social organism taken on its own. In the latter case, however, the evolution of a pure human society, the successive stages of which are pure socio-economic formations, is presented to us as the actualisation of the inner objective logic of the development of all social organisms taken jointly.

This question was not posed with clarity in Marxist philosophical and historical writings for a long time. But in practice an answer to it was always propounded. The overwhelming majority of scholars, often without clearly realising it themselves, in one way or another in the final analysis inclined towards the first solution. The treatment of the succession of social formations as successive changes of the type of individual social organism, corresponded all in all with the facts of European history, beginning with later feudalism. The replacement of feudalism by capitalism took place as a rule in the form of a qualitative transformation of existing social organisms. Qualitatively transformed from feudal into bourgeois, social organisms at the same time survived as such, as distinct units of historical development. France, for instance, transformed itself from a feudal into a bourgeois society, but at the same time preserved itself as France. Late-feudal and bourgeois France, notwithstanding all differences, do have something in common: they appear as successive stages of the evolution of French society. The transition from capitalism to socialism also generally has the form of the qualitative transformation of an existing social organism.

This made it possible to treat the theory of socio-economic formations as the actualisation of the development of each social organism taken on its own. The identification for practical purposes of the development of society as a whole, with the development of each society individually, was aided by the above-noted plurality of meanings of 'society'. The replacement of the notion of human society in general by that of social organism was virtually imperceptible. The consequence was the construction of the view of history of human society as the summation of the histories of a definite number of social organisms. Admittedly, the representatives of such a viewpoint spoke not of social organisms, but of 'nations' or 'countries'. This however does not affect the heart of the matter. The main point is that the succession of formations was presented as a process taking place exclusively within social organisms, and the formations themselves were conceived as the stages in the evolution of distinct concrete societies. Naturally, given such a view of socio-economic formations, based on their role as stages both of distinct societies and also of humanity of large, their inevitability can only appear as their applicability to all social organisms, as universality. The only basis for treating socio-economic formations as relevant for human society in general would then be the requirement that each individual society passes through them.

Of course, scholars who, consciously or unconsciously, adhered to such a view could not fail to see that there are facts incompatible with their conceptions. But amongst all such possible facts, they turned their attention to those which could be characterised as 'exceptions', as the omission by one nation or another of this or that socio-economic formation. Such an 'exception' they interpreted as an ever-possible or even inevitable deviation from the norm, brought about by the combination of some exceptional circumstances. But the matter is really much more complex.

Social organisms are known within which the feudal formation was replaced by capitalism, and the latter by socialism, but it is difficult to find any within which slave-owning was replaced by feudalism. The slave-owning social organisms of the ancient period did not transform themselves in the course of development into feudal ones, i.e. they did not 'pass over' into a higher stage, but disappeared, perished. It was not they, but new social organisms altogether, which emerged on their 'ruins', and which became feudal. Thus slave-owning society does not appear as a stage of the inner development of distinct societies, of social organisms. In so far as a considerable number of Soviet historians adhered to the conception of succession of stages outlined above, so the emergence of this fact appeared to them as equivalent to the demonstration of the proof that the slave-owning formation is not a regular stage of the evolution of human society. In the eyes of some of them ancient society emerged as a lateral, blind-alley branch of the mainstream of history.[12]

Moreover, antiquity is not exceptional. In general all global history, right up to late feudalism, presents itself to us not at all in the form of a process of transitions from stage to stage of a definite number of social organisms existing continuously, but as a process of the emergence, development and extinction of many social organisms. These co-exist not merely in space, alongside each other, but also in time, one after another. History knows no single social organism, which having once emerged, then 'passed through' *all* formations. Instead one knows an enormous number of social organisms, in the internal development of which a transition from one formation to another had no place whatever. In other words, in relation to these organisms, formations appear not as stages of their internal development, but only as their species. The majority of social organisms of the ancient world and of the early middle ages belong to this category.

This is particularly evident from the example of the ancient orient, all of whose history offers a process of the successive emergence and disappearance of social organisms and whole conglomerates of such organisms (the city-states of Sumer, Old Babylonia, New Babylonia, the Empires of the Medes, Urartu, Elam, Mittani and others). It is possible to disagree about the nature of the socio-economic structure of the ancient orient, but it seems unquestionable that the newly emergent social organisms belong to the same type as those which perished. Thus if we find, when we consider the history of Europe from the sixteenth to the twentieth centuries, a change in type of social organisms, while the organisms themselves preserve their identity as definite units of historical development, then the very opposite is characteristic of the ancient east: we see the emergence and disappearances of social organisms as units of historical development without any change of type, of allocation to species of formation.

These and similar facts prove indisputably not merely that there is no social organism that would have 'passed through' all formations, but also that there is no socio-economic formation, at any rate of a class type, through which all social organisms would have 'passed'. In essence this applies even to the primitive-communal formation, which is customarily seen as the one truly universal stage of development, which could in no case be missed out by any nation or country. However, one must not forget that the transition from a pre-class society to a class-endowed one never took place in the form of a qualitative transformation of any given, already existing social organism, as its metamorphosis from a pre-class into a class society. It was always a process of disruption of an old pre-class social organism and the emergence of new, previously non-existent class-endowed societies. Thus pre-class and the original class social formations never appeared as stages of the inner development of any given and defined social organism. This claim is not much affected by whether we speak in terms of 'nations' or 'countries'. For concrete nations and countries (unless the latter is used simply as a geographical expression) do not last for ever, but emerge and disappear. For instance, could one really say without qualification that the Russians, Germans, French and English 'passed through' the stage of primitive-communal structure, when it is well known that all these nations were formed long after the emergence of

class-endowed society, and in the course of its subsequent development. Furthermore, at the time of the disintegration of primitive
communal structure, there were as yet no Russians, Byelorussians or
Ukrainians, but Kriviachki, Biatichi, Polians, Dregovichi, Slovenes and
other East Slavonic ethnic groups. The existence of an overall continuity between the Novgorodian Slovenes, Kriviachki, and Biatichi on the
one hand, and the Great Russians on the other, must not obscure the
fact that we are here dealing not with one and the same ethnic community, but with different ones.

At present, the 'non-universality' of the slave-owning social formation is officially recognised by Soviet historians.[13] But, in the same
sense, the feudal and capitalist formations are not universal either. In
consequence, several Soviet historians reached the conclusion that not
only the slave-owning, but also all other formations, represent not
regular steps in the history of society, but only types of society.[14] This
was nothing less than a repudiation of the theory of socio-economic
formations.

v

The above-cited and similar facts are invoked by historians and sociologists representing non-Marxist positions to justify the rejection of the
theory of socio-economic formations. This theory appears to them
frequently as a purely conceptual schema, in conflict with historical reality. But in fact the contradiction with history does not apply at all to
the theory of socio-economic formations, but only to the interpretation
of it analysed above, which turns it into an account of the internal regularity of the development of every social organism treated as a distinct
unit.

At the base of such an interpretation there lies a view of the history of
human society as a simple summation of the histories of separate social
organisms, each of which develops independently. The unity of the
global historical process is thereby reduced almost exclusively to the
generality of the laws which operate in every social organism, and
thereby to the identity of their development. Correspondingly the
theory of social formations is understood as the reflection of the identity
of the development of all social organisms.

But in fact the history of human society, composed of the history of
distinct societies, does constitute a single whole, not reducible to the
sum of the developments of individual societies. And likewise the theory of
socio-economic formations expresses the unity of the global historic
process. It expresses the inner objective necessity of the development,
not of every social organism taken separately, but of all social organisms taken together, i.e. the evolution of the total human society seen as
a single whole.

It follows that socio-economic formations are above all stages of the
general development of human society. The history of every social
organism is but a small part of the history of the whole of human so-

ciety. Above all, that which applies to the whole need not apply to each
of the parts of which the whole is composed. The development of the
parts of social organisms, cannot but differ from the development of the
whole. All socio-economic formations can be 'passed through' only by
human society as a whole, and not by the distinct social organisms of
which it is composed. Some socio-economic formations may be represented in the history of specific organisms, and others in the history of
altogether different ones. And if some or other social organisms
perished and disappeared, this does not signify in the least that their
development did not embody one or other regular stage of the development of human society as a whole.

One has to remember that the very conception of socio-economic formations, as stages of development, arose not as a result of comparing
the histories of distinct social organisms and eliciting their stages,
which would then apply to all without exception, but by means of uncovering that which distinguishes one epoch of global history from
another. It is only by considering these epochs that one can understand
what socio-economic formations really mean as steps in the evolution of
society as a whole, and also understand how their succession and replacement take place.

Only in the primitive epoch did all social organisms belong to the
same type. From the moment of the emergence of the first class-
endowed societies, there have always simultaneously existed – as is the
case now – social organisms belonging not to one type, but to a diversity
of types. This being so, on what basis can one say that human society as
a whole finds itself in this or that stage of its development and what are
the objective criteria which enable one to judge in precisely which of
these stages it finds itself? The classification of a distinct social organism as belonging to one or another formation is decided by seeing what
system of productive relations is found at its base. But what can one say
of human society as a whole, if the social organisms which compose it
belong to diverse types?

If one adhered to the view of socio-economic formations above all as
similar stages of the development of distinct societies, then the criterion
could only be quantitative. One can assign society as a whole to that
stage of development which corresponds to the majority of social organisms existing at that moment, or which corresponds to the conditions
under which the majority of mankind lives at that time.

The concept of human society as a single whole also reveals the
possibility of quite another approach.

Social organisms of one kind or another as a rule do not exist in isolation. More often than not a definite number of social organisms of one
type form a more or less coherent whole. In this case the systems of productive relations, found at the base of each of them, appear as parts of a
more or less unified economic whole. And the social organisms are
united in such a case not only by the mere identity of economic structures, as is the case when they do not form a system, but also by the

presence of a unified economic base. Thus socio-economic formations exist not only in distinct societies but above all in systems of such societies. They are species not only of social organisms, but of whole systems.

Systems of social organisms of a given type can differ not only in scale, but also in the extent of their influence on neighbouring social organisms and systems. Social organisms of a single type did not constitute a single pan-global system even in the period of primitive society. It was characteristic of that type of society that a multiplicity of local systems of social organisms was in existence, no single one of which stood out from the rest. In consequence of the previously noted unequal development, not to mention other factors, a single pan-global system of social organisms of one type could not exist in the subsequent periods either, and this continues to be the case right up to our time.

But if it is not possible to speak of pan-global systems of social organisms of one type, then, after the transition to class society, it is possible to speak of global systems, i.e. those which were centres of the global-historic development, the existence of which is, even if not at once, at least in the final analysis, discernible in the total march of human history.

VI

The transition from pre-class to class society did not take place, as is well known, simultaneously throughout all the areas of human settlement. At first class-endowed society formed itself fully only in two delimited areas, the Nile valley and the area between the rivers Tigris and Euphrates. Thus there emerged the first regional centres of historical development surrounded by a historic periphery which remained backward in its development.

The subsequent development of mankind followed on the one hand the line of the emergence of new independent regional centres of historic development (the valleys of the Indus and the Hwang Ho) and on the other the line of formation of a broad system of class societies, embracing the entire Near East. The Near Eastern system of class societies, embracing Egypt and Mesopotamia, cannot be described as one of many regional centres of historical development. It constituted the centre of global-historical development and in that sense appeared not as a regional, but as a global system. With the formation of this system, class relations came to dominate the development of human society as a whole. One epoch of global history – the primitive – was finally and irreversibly replaced by a new one, the epoch of the ancient east. It is characterised by the fact that in it, the first class-endowed socio-economic formation assumes a leading role in the history of mankind. Following Marx, we shall call this the 'asiatic' formation.

The most striking peculiarity of the development of class society of the ancient east is the perpetual transformation of the political map, the

extinction of some and the emergence of other governmental formations. One of the main reasons for this is the alternation, characteristic
of all countries of the ancient east, of periods of the existence of strong
social organisms, and thereby also of strong centralised despotisms,
with periods of their disintegration into smaller social and hence also
governmental formations.[15]

In this connection one must stress that, whereas in modern history
the concepts 'country' and 'social organism' generally coincide in certain contexts, this is quite different in the ancient east. One and the
same country could at one period be one social organism, and in
another constitute a combination of semi-independent or even independent social organisms. Roughly the same can also be said of the
concepts 'social organism' and 'state'. If in later and modern history
every social organism as a rule also appears as a state, then in the
ancient east matters were more complex. The boundaries of a state
could coincide with those of a social organism, or fail to coincide with it.

As shown, it was a law of the development of the asiatic formation
that there was an alteration of periods of the existence of great social
organisms and of their disintegration into smaller ones. It is quite clear
that this could not be synchronised throughout all the countries of the
Near East. At that time, whilst one area experienced the formation and
existence of great social organisms, others could find themselves in a
state of decline. All this favoured the transformations of the political
map.

Great social organisms, at the height of their power and as a result of
a series of victorious wars of conquest, could subdue a considerable
number of other smaller, or weakened large social organisms. Hence
enormous empires arose, constituting complex conglomerates of social
organisms of diverse kinds. They could also embrace, jointly with class-
endowed social organisms, regions inhabited by peoples finding
themselves at the stage of the disintegration of clan or tribal society, i.e.
regions of the historic periphery. This situation speeded up the formation of class societies in those regions, and extended the area of the
centre of historical development at the expense of the periphery.

It is quite clear that the empires resulting from conquest could not be
stable and lasting. With the weakening of the social organism at the
core of such a political formation, the whole inevitably disintegrated.
Further weakening, or *a fortiori* the disintegration of the given organism,
led to a situation when it or the parts into which it disintegrated found
themselves under the power of a conqueror. Not infrequently these con-
querors were the peoples of the periphery, passing through the stage of
the formation of classes and of the state. They sometimes succeeded in
erecting great empires, covering considerable territories of the historic
centre. The consequence of all this was once again the extension of the
centre at the cost of the periphery. As is evident from what has been
stated, the disappearance and emergence of social organisms, the creation and disintegration of large political formations, the incursions of

peoples of the historic periphery into the region of the centre of historical development, can under no circumstances be interpreted as
deviations from normality, as anomalies. For the societies of the ancient
east all this appears as the norm or rule.

Whereas in the study of European history we encounter, beginning
with late feudalism, social organisms whose existence does not come to
an end even with such a radical transformation as is effected by a
change of socio-economic formation, in the study of the history of the
ancient east we do not find a single social organism which has continued in existence throughout the length of this epoch. All organisms
which emerged in the transition to class society disappeared long before
the termination of the ancient eastern epoch. Still less could ancient
oriental social organisms preserve themselves through the radical
changes involved in a replacement of social formation. Moreover, it is
possible to say *a priori* that the replacement of the asiatic formation by
another more progressive one, could not take place as the qualitative
transformation of continuous social organisms, which would have preserved themselves as such, as units of historical development. Nor did it
simply take the form of the destruction or ruin of asiatic social organisms and the emergence in their place of new, already slave-owning
ones. The real path of development was even more complex.

The point is that social organisms of a new type did not emerge at all
in that very same region in which asiatic society reached its greatest development, but at one of the edges of the world system of asiatic social
organisms, immediately adjoining the historic periphery of its time – in
the western part of Asia Minor and in the Balkan peninsula. This circumstance had in many ways obscured for the majority of historians
the fact of the existence of a continuous connection between the asiatic
and the ancient formations. Shtaerman maintains, for instance, that
'ancient society emerged on the basis of the disintegration of the primitive communal structure, and not as the result of the development of
earlier class endowed societies of the ancient oriental type, and cannot
in relation to them be considered a higher or any other stage of their development'.[16]

The contention that ancient society emerged directly from primitive-
communal society is passed on from one historical work to another.
Frequent repetition has made it seem axiomatic. But it is impossible to
agree with it without reservation. It seems unquestionable that ancient
societies were preceded on the same territory by class organisms, but of
another type. In so far as given data allow one to judge, Achaian king-
doms differed little in their socio-economic structure from the societies
of the ancient east. The view that Achaian Greece offers us the same
socio-economic formation as the ancient east is strikingly supported by
the particular features of the development of the older Greek class-
endowed societies. After their flowering there comes, as usual, a period
of decline, an irruption of tribes of the historic periphery, and the destruction of the older class social organisms.

At the moment of their invasion of the territory of Achaian Greece, the Dorian Greeks were at the stage of the formation of class society. The circumstance provided a basis for the claim that ancient society arose immediately from pre-class forms. There is an element of truth in this, but only an element, and not the whole. It is well known that a number of Greek regions, including Attica, were not conquered by the Dorians. The population of ancient Athens was composed of people whose more or less distant ancestors had lived in a society of the asiatic type. For this reason alone it would be incorrect to speak of Athenian slave-owning society as having replaced a primitive-communal one, even if one accepted the view that the degradation of the structure of Achaian Greece was complete enough to lead to the replacement of class relations by primitive-communal ones. In any case there are no data testifying to the existence of primitive-communal relations in the Attica at the turn of the second and first millennium B.C. Evidently, the regress went no further than the replacement of an early class society by a proto-class one.

But the issue hinges not merely on the existence of regions which escaped the Dorian invasions. The Dorians themselves could not escape the influence of the higher level of cultural development of the Achaians. It was all the easier for them to assimilate the achievements of Achaian culture, because on a technical level they were the equals of Achaia.

The replacement of the bronze age by the early iron age, which took place on the territory of Greece, made possible the transition to a new class-endowed socio-economic formation, and one more progressive than the asiatic one which emerged in the copper and bronze age. But this possibility would never have become a reality had Greece not represented an admittedly marginal, but nonetheless inseparable part of the old centre of the global historic development, and had it not been within the zone of the constant and many-sided influence of the lands of the old east.

Those historians who see the slave-owning not as an inevitable and regular stage in the evolution of human society, but as an exception, a deviation from the normal path of development, invoke as one piece of evidence the fact that nowhere on earth, except for Greece and Italy of the first millennium B.C., did the disintegration of the primitive-communal structure lead to slave-owning societies. This contention requires refinement. Nowhere on earth did the disintegration of primitive-communal structure on its own lead to the emergence of slave-owning social organisms, without the direct and immediate influence of previously formed class societies.

And this allows only one conclusion – slave-owning society does not appear to be the first class-endowed socio-economic formation. The only class formation which can arise exclusively on the basis of the disintegration of primitive society alone appears to be the asiatic one. In particular, because the transition from pre-class society to the asiatic socio-economic formation does not require or presuppose the agency of previously formed class-endowed socio-economic formations, asiatic societies can emerge as islands, to a considerable extent isolated from each other in a sea of peoples remaining in the pre-class stage, and constitute regional centres of historical development surrounded by the remaining periphery. All class societies, emerging in areas which at the time were outside the influence of previously formed centres of civilisation, inevitably had to be asiatic rather than slave-owning or feudal. The data available to science concerning the socio-economic structure or the proto-class and early-class societies of pre-Columban America, Oceania and sub-Saharan Africa fully confirm this claim.

Slave-owning society was not the first form of class society. Slave-owning society could not emerge as an island in the sea of primitive-communal structures. The conditions which are essential for the second class-endowed social formation can arise only as a result of a prolonged prior development of the first antagonistic formation. It is important to stress that these conditions could not be produced by the development of a relatively small system of asiatic social formations, constituting a local, regional centre of historical development. The first slave-owning social organisms could emerge only within the bounds of the global system of asiatic social organisms, such as was constituted by the Near Eastern one, and even that only after the completion of the transition to the iron age.

Thus the limitation in space and time of the emergence of slave-owning society is not in the least degree in conflict with the contention that the ancient formation was a regular stage in the development of human society. The emergence of the ancient formation was a law-bound and inevitable result of the development of the asiatic formation, notwithstanding the fact that slave-owning social organisms arose not throughout the territory of the old centre of global development, but only at one of its distant edges. The fact that the ancient formation could arise only as a result of prior millenial development of the asiatic society comes to be more and more recognised by historians. The well-known English archaeologist Woolley writes:

> We have outgrown the phase when all the arts were traced to Greece which was thought to have sprung, like Pallas, full grown from the brain of the Olympian Zeus; we have learnt how that flower of genius drew its sap from Lydians and Hittites, from Phoenica and Crete, from Babylon and Egypt. But the roots go farther back: behind all these lies Sumer.[17]

The emergence and consolidation in Ionia, Greece and later Italy of a system of social organisms of a new and much higher type, while the old socio-economic order survived in the Near East, meant nothing other than the transposition of the centre of global-historical development. The centre moved to the Mediterranean and the Near East became part of the historic periphery. Thus a new class-endowed periphery emerged alongside the old pre-class one. The emergence of the new world system marked the shift of the leading role in the history of mankind from the asiatic formation to the slave-owning one. One epoch of world history ended, namely the ancient oriental, and a new one, the ancient, commenced.

The ancient formation, like the 'asiatic', appeared as a stage in the development of human society, and not in the development of social organisms. Its replacement by a new and more progressive one, the feudal formation, took place in the form of the destruction of the old social organisms and the emergence of new ones, within which feudal relations developed and prevailed. As with the destruction of 'asiatic' social organisms, the destruction of slave-owning ones was connected with an invasion by peoples of the pre-class historic periphery.

The fact that the replacement of the ancient slave-owning formation by the feudal one took place not within distinct social organisms, but exclusively at the level of human society at large, obscured to a considerable extent the existence of a profound continuity between the ancient and feudal world systems. As I have already shown, it was this above all, along with some other factors considered above, which led various historians to the conclusion that ancient society does not in itself represent a regular stage in evolution, but rather a blind alley, branching off from the mainstream of human development. The total failure to see the continuous connection between systems of social organisms also lies at the base of a different kind of idea, which would fragment human history into the sum of histories of distinct, self-enclosed 'civilisations'.

In fact a deep continuity does obtain here as well. As the evolution of ancient society prepared the ground for the emergence of feudalism in conformity with social laws, in the final analysis it also did the same for capitalism. Engels pointed this out:

> Without slavery, no Greek state, no Greek art and science; without slavery, no Roman Empire. But without Hellenism and the Roman Empire as a basis, also no modern Europe. We should never forget that our whole economic, political and intellectual development has as its presupposition a state of things in which slavery was as necessary as it was universally recognised. In this sense we are entitled to say: without the slavery of antiquity, no modern socialism.[18]

All in all the continuity between ancient and feudal world systems is easier to see than that between the asiatic and the ancient, because feudal social organisms emerged not merely at the edges of the ancient centre of the global-historical development, but also on almost all of its territory. The fact that feudal social organisms also emerged on the territory of the pre-class historic periphery does not contradict this. The transition to feudalism was indeed accomplished, amongst all the peoples inhabiting this territory, only by those whose level of agricultural technology was no lower than that of the peoples of the ancient world, and who inhabited regions within the zone of influence first of the slave-owning, and later of the feudal world system of social organisms.

The most favourable conditions for the emergence of feudalism were found at the north-western edge of the ancient world system – on the territory of contemporary France. It was just there that feudalism emerged in its classical form, and it was just there that conditions arose for the formation of strong and lasting social organisms which, in their subsequent development, became capitalist. In this sense one can say that the transfer of the leading role in human history to feudalism, and the start of a new period in world history – the mediaeval – are connected with a new shift of the centre of global-historical development, this time to western Europe, where it remained even after the emergence of capitalism.

The fact that in the history of class-endowed society up to capitalism, every move to a new stage of development transpired not within the limits of distinct social organisms, but at the level of human society as a whole, was first recognised and at the same time obscured by Hegel. Behind the development and elevation of the 'Absolute Spirit', about which his *Philosophy of History* tells us, there are hidden the interconnected rise of new socio-economic formations and shifts of the centre of global-historic development.

The transition from the feudal socio-economic formation to the capitalist one took the form of the transformation of the social organisms, constituting the world feudal system, into bourgeois ones, which thereupon formed one world system. With the transfer of the leading role to the capitalist social formation, the middle ages were replaced by the modern period. This transformation initially involved only some of the social organisms. The others for some time maintained their old form. It is quite evident that the existence of a new capitalist world system could not fail to leave marks on the development of social organisms, which continued to be feudal, nor to give a considerably distinctive character to the process of their transformation into bourgeois ones. In contrast with all previous history, the replacement of feudalism by capitalism took place not only at the level of human society as a whole, but also inside every social organism. The world capitalist system was the first one which, for all practical purposes, drew every social organism on earth into its own sphere of influence. In this sense, global history in a literal sense only began with capitalism.

The great October revolution laid the foundation of a new world system – the socialist, which in the subsequent period emerges as the centre of the world historical developments, thereby opening up a further epoch of global history. The world socialist system appears as the only one which can be and necessarily will become global. And in the more distant future, with the transition to communism, human society will inevitably transform itself into a single social organism.

VII

In this way, though there had never been a pan-global system of asiatic social organisms, there did exist a global system of such societies. There had never been a pan-global slave-owning society, but a world system of slave-owning societies did exist. There was no pan-global system of feudalism, but there was a world system of feudal social organisms, a world feudal society.

In the course of world history, world systems of social organisms were replaced by others, which for a time took over the leading role in the history of mankind. Simultaneously, with the change of system, there was the replacement of one epoch by another. Between successive world systems there is a deep link of continuity. The development of each of them, with the exception of the communist one, prepares and makes possible the emergence of a new one, belonging to a higher type.

The successive replacement of world systems of social organisms appears in the form of the historic succession of socio-economic formations. If socio-economic formations as types of society exist incarnate in social organisms and diverse kinds of systems thereof, so the stages of development in which mankind as a whole finds itself have their existence only in world systems of social organisms of the appropriate type. The succession and replacement of world systems had already been noted by historians in some measure, which led to the delimitation of the epochs of world history. But its essence was revealed only by Marx and Engels, when they formulated the theory of socio-economic formations. The succession of socio-economic formations is the essence of the succession of global systems, and hence of historical epochs.

The old world system generally does not disappear at once with the emergence of a new one and its assumption of the leading role. The ancient system does seem to be an exception. When ceasing to be the centre of world historical development, a system may for some time preserve itself and, though no longer the leading one, may still remain a world system of a kind. Distinct social organisms, constituting this system, may preserve themselves for a long time even after the point when the system ceases to be global, and becomes a regional one (or several such), and even after the disintegration of such regional systems. As long as distinct social organisms exist, which have as their basis a given system of productive relations, the given socio-economic formation also survives, though no longer as a stage of human history as a whole, but only as a type of social organism and stage in which this or that individual society finds itself.

A world system which appears as the centre of the global-historical development shows its influence, not necessarily on all societies, as capitalism did at the time of its apogee, but at any rate on a large number of surrounding social organisms, which find themselves at a lower stage of development, or, particularly, at the primitive stage. Peoples which are retarded in their development and find themselves in the zone of influence of more progressive social organisms, are thereby given the option of acquiring their achievements in the spheres of material and intellectual culture, and of bypassing stages which mankind as a whole has already gone through.

The account of the results of the influence of advanced social organisms on backwards ones, which at the same time ignores their influence itself, is at the root of one of the variants of the idea of the multilineal of historic development. As the protagonists of this view say, history knows examples of the direct transition from the primitive structure not only to the asiatic, but also directly to the ancient, and, finally, directly to the feudal. From this they conclude that what we are dealing with here is nothing other than the existence of three equally valid, parallel lines of development.[19] But history is also familiar with cases of transition from the primitive formation directly to capitalism, or to socialism. However not one single representative of the viewpoint described has been able to bring himself to assert that we are here dealing with five parallel and equally valid lines of development. It is overwhelmingly clear that the transition from the primitive structure to capitalism or socialism is possible only through the direct agency of capitalist or socialist social organisms respectively. But really it is just the same in the case of the transition from the primitive-communal formation to the ancient or feudal. A basis for the emergence of ancient social organisms could only be provided by those disintegrating primitive ones which either found themselves in an area previously forming part of the world system of asiatic social organisms (the Dorians), or in the zone of the immediate influence of the world ancient system (the Romans). Similarly feudal social organisms could arise only on the basis of these disintegrating primitive organisms which found themselves either on the territory previously constituting the ancient world system (the Teutons), or in the zone of influence, first of the ancient and then of the feudal world system (the Slavs).

It appears as a characteristic trait of every world system which constitutes a centre of pan-global development, that it expands at the cost of retarded social organisms, which are drawn into the orbit of its influence. Not infrequently these societies provide the base for the emergence of social organisms of a new type, which then also enter the world system. The enlargement of the world system is accompanied by a further extension of the zone of its influence. More and more social organisms, belonging to lower types, are drawn into it.

In consequence history acquires an ever more marked pan-global character. Every time it takes a further step forward, the elevation of social organism which were retarded in their development to the level attained by humanity at large, becomes not merely possible, but also inevitable. This became manifest with particular clarity when mankind reached the capitalist stage of development, and the capitalist world system arose, which, step by step, drew the entire globe into its sphere of influence. Marx and Engels wrote:

The bourgeoisie, by the rapid improvement of all instruments of production, by the immensely facilitated means of communication, draws all, even the most barbarian, nations into civilisation. The cheap prices of its commodities are the heavy artillery with which it batters down all Chinese walls, with which it forces the barbarians' intensely obstinate hatred of foreigners to capitulate. It compels all nations, on pain of extinction, to adopt the bourgeois mode of production; it compels them to introduce what it calls civilisation into their midst, i.e. to become bourgeois themselves. In one word, it creates a world after its own image.[20]

The existence in Western Europe of the constituted world system of capitalist social organisms made the accelerated capitalist development of neighbouring lands both possible and necessary. Characterising the development of Russia, Marx stressed that she did not need 'like the West to pass through the long incubation period of developing machine production in order to obtain machines, steamboats, railways, etc'.[21] As he showed, Russian capitalists 'have managed to introduce in a flash the whole mechanism of exchange (banks, joint-stock companies, etc.) which took centuries to grow up in the West'.[22]

For a long time the process of 'catching up' by backward nations to the level attained by the leading ones took place spontaneously. The antagonistic character of the relationships of class society made its mark on the processes of incorporation of backward social organisms into the zone of influence of progressive societies. Not infrequently it took brutal and violent forms. All the colonial histories of capitalist countries can serve as an example. The following, for example, was written by Marx about British colonial domination in India:

England has to fulfil a double mission in India: one destructive, the other regenerating – the annihilation of the old Asiatic society, and the laying of the material foundation of Western society in Asia . . .

All the English bourgeoisie may be forced to do will neither emancipate nor materially mend the social condition of the mass of the people, which depends not only on the development of the productive powers, but on their appropriation by the people. But what they will not fail to do is to lay down the material premises for both. Has the bourgeoisie ever done more? Has it ever effected a progress without dragging individuals and peoples through blood and dirt, through misery and degradation?

The Indians will not reap the fruits of the new elements of society scattered among them by the British bourgeoisie, till in Great Britain itself the new ruling classes shall have been supplanted by the industrial proletariat, or till the Hindoos themselves shall have grown strong enough to throw off the English yoke altogether.[23]

The situation, was radically transformed by the appearance of the world's first socialist state and thereafter of a world socialist system. Already, in the early 1920s, Lenin gave the proletariat, which had taken power into its own hands, the task of providing pan-global help to nations retarded in their development, so as to ensure their transition directly to socialism, avoiding all other stages of development.[24] All the history of the USSR appears as the model example of the implementation of Lenin's great idea. Peoples, finding themselves at the moment of the October revolution at the stage of primitive structure (Nentsi, Nganasany, Oroki, Chikchi, Evenki and others), or of pre-capitalist class relations (Kazakhs, Turkmen, Uzbeks, Tadzhiks and others) live at present in a socialist society. Help from the workers of the USSR allowed the Mongol people to move on to socialism. The Soviet Union and other socialist states also provide an enormous amount of help for countries which have freed themselves from colonial dependency. In consequence many of them have adopted a socialist orientation and have entered on the path of non-capitalist development. The existence of a world socialist system provides the nations which are retarded in their development with a realistic possibility of a transition to socialism, which by-passes the long and tormented route by which mankind as a whole has passed.

VIII

Thus the transition from one socio-economic formation to another takes place in world history, with the exception only of the transition from primitive-communal formation to the asiatic, as the replacement of a world system of social organisms of one definite type by another, as the transfer of the leading role from one such system to another. But not even a single one of these systems ever embraced all the inhabited parts of the globe. Each of them always covered a more or less defined part of the oecumene. As the facts show, the centre of pan-global development more often did not remain static, but shifted, and in consequence the successive world systems generally occupied far from identical regions of the earth's surface.

All this makes it hardly probable that every sequence of social organisms existing in this or the other region of the oecumene – let alone any one distinct social organism taken on its own – could 'pass through' all socio-economic formations. That remains true even if we take as our unit entities such as continents. Only Europe, and even that only if taken as a whole, appears to be in some measure an exception to this.

Peoples existing in conditions of the primitive-communal structure were to be found on its territory. Quite clearly, this does not turn Europe into an exception. On the contrary, this links it with all other inhabited continents. Primitive-communal organisms existed throughout the oecumene, which led to the view of the primitive-communal formation as the universal one, as the one through which all nations without exception have 'passed'.

The world system of asiatic social organisms formed itself in Asia, where its centre was found, but it expanded and drew into itself a part of European territory (the southern part of the Balkan peninsula and Crete). Thus Europe also had its social organisms of the 'asian' type. On European territory, albeit in diverse regions of it, one would find the centres of the following world systems: ancient, feudal, capitalist. Finally, the world socialist system came to embrace a considerable part of Europe.

As we remarked above, the partisans of the theory of socio-economic formations, which was subjected to a critique in the preceding pages, did not altogether succeed in formulating their position with clarity. They did not take into account the multiplicity of senses of the word 'society' and they did not offer a theoretical clarification of the concept 'social organism'. Hence most of them saw the theory of socio-economic formations as requiring and presupposing that the historic development in all inhabited regions of the earth should be roughly the same. They would only permit, first, that development should proceed at diverse rates of speed, and secondly, that in one region or another, in virtue of exceptional circumstances, there should be the 'omission' of one stage or another.

This interpretation of the theory of socio-economic formations was presented as the only possible one and thus as identical with the theory itself. Hence the conspicuous fact, for example, that ancient social organisms existed only in a certain delimited area, basically in southern Europe, and a whole set of similar facts, were seen as grounds for the revision, not only of the given interpretation of the theory, but more generally of the basic contentions of the theory itself.

By way of example one may refer to the article by Danilova, 'Controversial problems in the theory of pre-capitalist societies'.[25] In this article the author adopts a position opposed to the so-called five-stage schema of formations (primitive, slave-owning, feudalism, capitalism, communism). But all her critique is equally effective against the six-stage schema (primitive, asiatic, ancient, feudal, capitalist and communist formations) and more generally against any given schema of the evolution of socio-economic formations.

In full accordance with Danilova's ideas, the five-stage schema appears to be the generalisation of the historical development of Europe alone, and not of human society as a whole. She writes: 'The successive replacement of the primitive and slave-owning structures by feudalism, and thereafter by capitalism in the other regions of the earth (and indeed also in Europe) which is so characteristic for the Mediterranean and the areas sharing its historic fate, is by no means to be found everywhere.' Showing that the criticised conception allows the omission of some formations but only as deviations or exceptions, Danilova stresses that 'there turned out to be more deviations and exceptions, than cases falling under the rule, and secondly – and this is the main point – the regularities operating here showed themselves to be so specific, that they could not be explained by the influence of historic environment alone.' All this led her to the conclusion that in human society there exist not one, but several diverse lines of development. In this way Danilova, without clearly realising it herself, arrives at the repudiation not merely of a five-stage, but more generally of any given scheme of the evolution of human society, i.e. to the rejection of the very core of the theory of socio-economic formations. Analogous conclusions were reached somewhat earlier by some other scholars.

The greatest paradox, if you like, lies in the fact that, at the root of this theory of history itself there lies the very same principle as is also found at the root of the interpretation of the theory of formations considered above, the untenability of which has led to this kind of conclusion. The followers of this interpretation of the succession of social formations and the partisans of the multilineal conception of history, both, and in equal measure, start from the rejection of the unity of the world historical process. Both groups alike see the history of mankind as a simple summation of parallel and predominantly independent processes in the development of distinct social organisms, countries, nations, areas, regions. There is only this difference between them, that according to the first, all these separate units develop basically in the same manner and along the same line, whereas according to the views of the latter group, they develop in an essentially diverse way, i.e. along different lines.

The issue of the unilineality or multilineality of historical development arises only if we are faced not by one, but by several independent objects. The question then is whether these objects developed in a basically similar or dissimilar way, according to the same or different laws. The conception of human history as a single process eliminates this question. The unity of an object already by itself presupposes the unity of its development, which not merely does not exclude, but on the contrary presupposes the idiosyncracy of the development of every part, of which the given whole is composed.

We have already shown above the total untenability of the conception of human history as a sum of histories of distinct units, bound only by the identity of the laws operating in them and their corresponding parallel development. But the idea of the multilineal development of mankind is just as untenable. In diverse regions, development took place in diverse fashions, but all these processes were in the end but parts of an unitary process of the evolution of human society, subject to one single set of regularities.

One of the factors conditioning the specificity of the development of diverse regions was the difference in the speed of their evolution.

At the time when the world capitalist system was emerging in Europe, Australian aborigines were still at the stage of primitive structure. This made the colonisation of Australia by Europeans inevitable. Capitalism was brought to Australia along with white settlers, and the aborigines were in part destroyed, in part pushed back into the least desirable locations. At present they face no prospects of development other than the organic information in the structure of Australian capitalist society.

Roughly the same took place on the territory of the present USA and Canada. The population of Mexico, central America and Peru already found itself, at the moment of European discovery, in the stage of the asiatic formation. Spain, whose dependency they became, was a feudal country. Initially, an idiosyncratic superimposition of the feudal mode of production on the asiatic took place in this area. Later, in proportion to its inclusion in the zone of influence of the world capitalist system, the capitalist mode of production emerged within it.

In sub-Saharan Africa, at the start of European colonisation, some peoples found themselves in the stage of primitive communal structure, and others at the stage of transition to the asiatic formation, and some of these had moved right up to the limit separating it from a genuine class society. Their inclusion in the zone of influence of the world capitalist system provided the condition for their development along the capitalist path. With the emergence of a world socialist system another possibility also arises for them – that of non-capitalist development.

The matter is more complex in the countries of Asia, especially those within which class society emerged sooner than in the majority of the regions of Europe (the Near East, India, China). All the efforts to discern in their development the same stages as those which apply to Europe, were hardly crowned with any great success. The social structure found there during the periods frequently called feudal by scholars, differed substantially from European feudalism, but it was very similar to that which was found there in an earlier period. Right up to their incorporation in the zone of influence of the world capitalist system, no trace of the bourgeois mode of production was to be found within them.

All this taken together would seem to give full support to the old idea of the existence in the East of its own line of development, qualitatively different from that followed by the West. Hence some Marxists, disenchanted with the above-described interpretation of the theory of socio-economic formations, came to be attracted by this view.[26]

However the solution to this problem was put forward by the authors of the theory of socio-economic formations, Marx and Engels. It consisted in proposing that from the birth of class society right up to the eighteenth and even nineteenth century, the asiatic mode of production continued to exist in certain countries of the East. In other words, these countries remained at the stage of the first class-endowed socio-economic formation, just as all the original population of Australia remained up to the same period at the stage of the primitive-communal structure. As is well known, Marx and Engels repeatedly wrote about the stagnant character of the evolution of the oriental countries.[28] The dragging of these countries into the zone of influence of the world capitalist system led to the overcoming of stagnation and the birth within them of the bourgeois mode of production. Marx upheld this viewpoint.[29] What we encounter here once again is a specific development, but not specific laws, nor an idiosyncratic line of development. To speak of a unique eastern line of development has hardly any better formulation than speaking of a unique Australian line.

Concerning the line of development which is frequently called western (European), it would seem that it is western in a purely geographical, but not in any historical sense. World systems of any given type, in which socio-economic formations were embodied, could not but be territorially bounded. Beginning with the ancient, they came to embrace Europe. From that time on, their successive replacement took place particularly on European territory. All this generates the illusion that we are dealing here with a regional, western, European line of development. In reality all these systems of social organisms, notwithstanding their territorial limitation were in their nature not regional, or European, but global ones, just as the pre-ancient Near-Eastern system of social organisms was global and not regional or asiatic.

The global significance of the formation of the capitalist system in Europe is indisputable. By the beginning of the twentieth century it drew into its sphere of operation not merely the whole world, but also through its operation provoked, in a large number of countries which were retarded in their development, the appearance of the bourgeois socio-economic mode. The matter is more complex with the asiatic, ancient and feudal systems. Not one of them extended its influence over the whole world. The degree of their influence on retarded society was correspondingly smaller. However, without the Near-Eastern asiatic system of social organisms there would have been no ancient one, without ancient society there would have been no feudal one, and without a feudal one, no capitalism. Only the successive development and replacement of these systems could prepare for the appearance of capitalism, and hence subsequently of socialism, thereby making not merely possible, but also necessary, the transition of all remaining peoples without exception directly to capitalism or socialism. In this way, in the final analysis, their existence and development was linked to the fate of all mankind.

The characteristic trait of a world system of social organisms of a given type appears to be the fact that their development inevitably prepares for the appearance of a new, more progressive world system, so that its existence appears to be a necessary link in the history of mankind. Thus not merely the capitalist and socialist, but even the old Near-Eastern asiatic, the ancient and feudal systems of social organisms were all stages of the development not of this or that region, but of humanity at large.

IX

In the light of everything said above it clearly transpires that one can in no way see the history of mankind as a simple sum of the histories of social organisms, and that one cannot see socio-economic formations as identical stages of the evolution of social organisms, obligatory for all of them. The history of human society is a single whole and socio-economic formations appear above all as stages of development of this single unity. Socio-economic formations may or may not appear as stages in the development of distinct social organisms, but this does not in the very least prevent them from being steps in the evolution of human society as a whole. The succession of socio-economic formations takes place above all at the level of all mankind, in the form of the replacement of world systems of social organisms of a given kind; and when mankind as a whole has reached this or that stage of its development, 'passed through' this or that formation, not merely does the need to pass through them disappear for retarded nations, but the very possibility disappears as well. Sooner or later it becomes not merely possible, but necessary for them to miss out all the intervening stages, and move onto the higher stage reached by mankind as a whole.

NOTES

1 Yu. I. Semenov, 'The category "social organism" and its significance for historical scholarship', *Voprosy Istorii*, 1966, no. 8 (in Russian).

2 V.I. Lenin, 'What the "friends of the people" are and how they fight the social-democrats', *Collected Works*, vol. 1, Moscow, 1972, pp. 136-45; 'The economic content of narodism and criticisms of it in Mr Struve's book', *Collected Works*, vol. 1, p. 411 (both in Russian).

3 Lenin, 'What the "friends of the people" are', *Collected Works*, vol. 1, p. 140.

4 V.I. Lenin, 'Philosophical notebooks', *Collected Works*, vol. 38, Moscow, 1972, p. 361.

5 Lenin, 'What the "friends of the people" are', *Collected Works*, vol. 1, pp. 157-8.

6 Lenin, *Collected Works*, vol. 1, pp. 142, 165.

7 Lenin, *Collected Works*, vol. 1, p. 141.

8 Lenin 'The economic content of narodism', *Collected Works*, vol. 1, p. 410.

9 See, for instance, A.Ya. Gurevich, 'To the discussion of precapitalist formations: formation and form', *Voprosy Filosofii*, 1968, no. 2, 118-19 (in Russian).

10 K. Marx, Preface to 'A contribution to the critique of political economy', in K. Marx and F. Engels, *Selected Works*, vol. 1, Moscow, 1973, p. 504.

11 Ibid.

12 See, for instance, E.M. Shtaerman, 'Ancient society: the modernisation of history and historical analogies', *Problems in the History of Pre-capitalist Societies*, vol. 1, Moscow, 1968, p. 647 (in Russian).

13 See E.M. Zhukov, 'Fifty years of Soviet historical science', *Voprosy Istorii*, 1968, no. 1, 25 (in Russian).

14 See G.A. Melikishvili, 'Concerning the question of ancient oriental class societies', *Voprosy Istorii*, 1966, no. 2, 73, (in Russian); and English translation in *Introduction to Soviet Ethnography* ed. S.P. Dunn and E. Dunn, vol. 2, Berkeley, 1974, pp. 560-1, 568-9.

15 See Yu.I. Semenov, 'The category "social organism"', *Voprosy Istorii*, 1966, no. 8 (in Russian).

16 See Shtaerman, in *Problems in the History of Pre-capitalist Societies*, vol. 1, p. 647 (in Russian).

17 C.L. Woolley, *The Sumerians*, Oxford, 1928, p. 193.

18 F. Engels, *Anti-Dühring*, Moscow-Leningrad, 1934, p. 206.

19 See L.S. Vasiliev and I.A. Stuchevskii, 'Three models of the emergence and evolution of pre-capitalist societies', *Voprosy Istorii*, 1965, no. 5 (in Russian). E.J. Hobsbawm, Introduction to K. Marx, *Pre-capitalist Social Formations*, London, 1964, pp. 36-8.

20 K. Marx and F. Engels, 'Manifesto of the Communist Party', *Selected Works*, vol. 1, p. 112.

21 K. Marx, 'First draft of the reply to V.I. Zasulich's letter', Marx and Engels, *Selected Works*, vol. 3, Moscow, 1973, p. 157.

22 Ibid.

23 K. Marx, 'The future results of the British rule in India', Marx and Engels, *Selected Works*, vol. 1, pp. 494, 497–8.

24 V.I. Lenin, 'Report of the Commission on the national and colonial questions, July', *Collected Works*, vol. 31, Moscow, 1974, p. 244; 'Tax in kind', *Collected Works*, vol. 32, Moscow, 1975, pp. 349-50.

25 L.V. Danilova, 'Controversial problems in the theory of precapitalist societies', *Soviet Anthropology and Archaeology*, 1971, vol. 9, 269–328 (a translation from the Russian). The Russian original appeared in *Problems in the History of Pre-capitalist Societies*, Moscow, vol 1, p. 27.

26 See. G. Lewin, 'The problem of social formations in Chinese history', *Marxism Today*, 1967, no. 1, 21-2.

27 Marx, 'The British rule in India', and 'The future results of the British rule in India', both in Marx and Engels, *Selected Works*, vol. 1, pp. 488–94; *Capital*, vol. 1, Moscow, 1965, pp. 357–9; 'The letter to Engels in Manchester, June 2nd 1853', K. Marx and F. Engels, *Selected Correspondence*, Moscow, 1975, pp. 75–6. F. Engels, 'The letter to Marx in London, June 6th, 1853', Marx and Engels, *Selected Correspondence*, pp. 75-7.

28 Marx, 'The British rule in India', and 'The future results of the British rule in India', both in Marx and Engels, *Selected Works*, vol. 1, pp. 490-6; *Capital*, vol. 1, p. 539; 'The letter to Engels in Manchester, June 14th, 1853', Marx and Engels, *Selected Correspondence*, pp. 79-80; Marx, *Capital*, vol. 3, Moscow, 1966, p. 796.

29 Marx, 'The future results of the British rule in India', Marx and Engels, *Selected Works*, vol. 1, pp. 494, 497-8.

E. GELLNER

A Russian Marxist philosophy of history

Yuri Semenov is a highly distinguished theoretician of Marxist and Soviet anthropology. His 'The theory of socio-economic formations and world history' is an elegant, coherent, beautifully argued and uncompromising defence of a unilineal interpretation of Marxism, and a defence of it as a valid account of human history.

This in itself is a matter of considerable interest. Unilinealism has of late had a bad press, both inside and outside the Soviet Union, among Marxists and non-Marxists alike. No consensus exists on this question inside Soviet scholarship, or outside of course, and the authors with whom Semenov polemicises include both scholars within his own country and westerners, Marxists and non-Marxists. Though Semenov does not raise this explicitly in the main part of his argument, the question is one of very great political interest, and is not at all a simple technical issue of concern to historians only. The question whether human history is One or Many is obviously fundamental for any philosophy of history. It is also central to most debates about Marxism, and to problems in Marxist political strategy.

One of the commonest criticisms of Marxism hinges on unilinealism, and runs as follows: Why did the socialist revolution occur in backward and peripheral Russia? Ought it not, according to the theory of universal obligatory successive stages of human society (i.e. unilinealism), to have occurred in the highly developed capitalist countries, in which the anticipated contradictions of the capitalist mode of production were becoming most acute? Or again, there is the well known dilemma facing Marxist revolutionaries in underdeveloped countries, endowed with peasantries and an emerging 'national bourgeoisie', but not yet with a numerous, powerful or effective proletariat. Ought such revolutionaries, in the light of unilinealism, to ally themselves with the national bourgeoisie and help further its ends in the patient expectation of a subsequent more favourable situation, or ought they to fight the ultimate enemy right now, and historic timetables be damned? (In Jewish theology, there is a special name for the sin of endeavouring to implement divine decrees prematurely, and the same might seem to apply within Marxism.)

It is an interesting consequence of Semenov's formulation of Marxist unilinealism, that if it is valid, these problems barely arise, or do not arise at all. If his position is correct, the questions themselves were profoundly misguided, and ought never to have been posed, at least in those terms.

The manner in which Semenov demonstrates his conclusion, as well as the conclusion itself, is of great interest. The argument is basically philosophical rather than specific and historical. Historical data, and those of a rather general kind, enter the argument only at relatively marginal and tangential points. The burden of the proof hinges on rather abstract and philosophical issues, and on two in particular – the unity of human history, and the question of nominalism versus realism (in the platonic sense). These two issues turn out, once again, to be related.

Consider the second of these, the problem of the relationship of abstract concepts to reality. It may be as well to invoke a contemporary authority, the American logician Quine, for a restatement of the available alternatives:

> The three main mediaeval points of view regarding universals are designated by historians as *realism, conceptualism,* and *nominalism.* Essentially these same three doctrines appear in twentieth-century surveys . . . under the new names of *logicism, intuitionism* and *formalism.*
>
>   *Realism* . . . is the Platonic doctrine that universals or abstract entities have being independently of mind; . . . *Conceptualism* holds that they are universal but that they are mind-made. . . . the *nominalists* of old, object(ed) to admitting abstract entities at all . . . [Willard van Orman Quine, *From a Logical Point of View,* Cambridge, Mass. 1953, pp. 14,15]

This was and evidently continues to be a central issue in philosophical thought, and in its time it could send those who were in error to their death:

> Then the Cardinal of Cambrai . . . questioned Master Jan Hus if he regarded universals as real apart from the thing itself. And he responded that he did, since both St Anselm and others had so regarded them. Thereupon the cardinal argued . . . that . . . it follows that with the cessation of the particular there also ceased the universal substance of itself. Jan Hus replied that it ceased to exist in the substance of that particular bread . . . but despite that, in other particulars it remains the same. [Report of the trial of Jan Hus in 1415 by Petr z Mladoňovic, quoted in *Unity, Heresy and Reform, 1378-1460,* ed. C.M.D. Crowder, London, 1977, pp. 88-9]

Within a month Jan Hus paid for his realist views at the stake. But the issue of realism/nominalism underlies not only the problem of transubstantiation, of the relationship of bread-in-general to the specific bread used in the Eucharist, but equally the relationship of socio-economic formations in general to specific, concrete societies.

Semenov clearly seems also to be a realist, and moreover he holds realism to be an essential prerequisite for the correct interpretation of Marxism. What is at issue now is the correct assessment of the ontological status, so to speak, of 'socio-economic formations'. Is there nothing in the world over and above concretely existing societies with which socio-economic formations must then be identified if the term is to refer to anything at all, or, on the other hand, are they merely logical arte-facts of the mind, conceptual conveniences? These would seem to be the nominalist and conceptualist options, and they seem to be repudiated:

> . . . a socio-economic formation in the pure sense . . . can only exist in theory, but not in historical reality. In history, it exists in distinct societies as their inner essence, their objective basis. A failure to see this can lead to theoretical errors. Thus, for instance, certain Soviet historians, having failed to locate within history pure, ideal socio-economic formations, reached the conclusion that formations do not exist in reality at all, that they represent only logical, theoretical con-structions. The endeavour to avoid such a conclusion led several other scholars to the direct, immediate identification of socio-economic formations with actually existing social organisms, with distinct concrete societies . . . Either of these approaches is equally misguided. Either can lead to a repudiation of the materialist con-ception of history. [Yu.I. Semenov, 'The theory of socio-economic formations and world history', translated by E. Gellner. All subse-quent quotations, not otherwise identified, are from this work]

Though socio-economic formations cannot exist independently of concrete individual societies, nevertheless they are not mere ab-stractions or conceptual conveniences. They exist as the inner essences of concrete societies, and determine their development. That inner essence is described, in so many words, as existing independently of the consciousness and will of men. Though this last remark seemed to be intended to apply above all to the minds and wills of participants in the historic process, it must presumably apply with even greater force to the historical observer. His mental acts do not make these systems of productive relations; they make him.

The question of the reality of abstractions may seem scholastic. Its relevance may however emerge more clearly if one looks at Semenov's other main consideration, namely the unity of human history and its implications for unilinealism and rival theories. What is unilinealism? It is the doctrine that, for the understanding of human history, we need to consider one and only one list of historic stages through which human society has passed (or is passing and will pass). Semenov quite cogently notes that the issue of unilinealism as such is quite independent of the subsidiary (though also important) question concerning just how many stages there are, or just what they are. (E.g., are there just five of them, or is the 'asiatic mode of production' a distinct stage, to be inserted between primitive communism and slave-owning society?)

Semenov's argument from the unity of human history runs as follows. To what could the *n* stages of human history (whatever the correct number may be) be meant to apply? There would seem to be two possibilities: First that they are meant to apply to the development of each and every society, taken individually. Secondly that they are meant to apply to the history of mankind at large (in some sense which is yet to emerge).

It is extremely interesting that Semenov concedes that the theory of socio-economic formations has generally been interpreted in the first sense. It wasn't even that the first interpretation was consciously preferred: it was unreflectively taken for granted:

> The overwhelming majority of scholars, often without clearly realising it themselves, in one way or another in the final analysis inclined towards the first solution. The treatment of the succession of social formations as successive changes of the type of individual social organism, corresponded all in all with the facts of European history, beginning with later feudalism . . . This made it possible to treat the theory of socio-economic formations as the actualisation of the development of each social organism taken on its own. The identification for practical purposes of the development of society as a whole, with the development of each society individually, was aided by the above-noted plurality of meanings of 'society'.

The last sentence of the quotation refers to the ambiguity of 'society': it can mean a concrete society, with co-ordinates in time and space, a local habitation and a name, but it can also mean the generic thing, which is, for Semenov, both abstract and yet inherent, essential, explicative. The passage quoted highlights, amongst other things, the inter-dependence of the platonic-realist and the historical-unity arguments. The unity applies to the generic essence, not to the individual society. But what is perhaps most interesting about it is the admission that the majority of scholars have in the past interpreted Marxism as requiring the unilineal succession to apply to individual societies – and this majority of course includes Marxists at least as much as the critics of Marxism. Hence Semenov's reformulation is a very significant advance within Marxism or, at the very least, the recovery and the making explicit of something which had long been lost and which, if originally present at all, had never been articulated with sufficient clarity or emphasis to make subsequent generations of scholars aware of the fact that they were contradicting it. Those who sinned against it generally did so, as Semenov stressed, without being aware of making any contentious assumption at all. 'This interpretation of the theory of socio-economic formations was presented as the only possible one and thus as identical with the theory itself.' If it was possible to do this, the correct interpretation could not have been very easily available, at least in explicit form.

Leaving aside the question of the originality of his formulation – is it valid? I find this central point in Semenov's argument entirely convincing. The idea that unilinealism requires every individual society to pass through every stage, (a view which, like the rest of Semenov's silent majority, I had always taken for granted, without even being aware of it), only needs to be stated clearly to be seen to be absurd. Every society could only pass through every stage if societies were generally immortal, like Jonathan Swift's Struldbrugs, or alternatively if societies lived out their lives in isolation. But each of these assumptions is blatantly absurd. No contemporary northern European society has a history going back beyond (at best) the middle ages. Through religion, modern Greece and Israel may perhaps claim some kind of rather dubious identity with ancient Byzantium and Israel respectively, though this identity immediately lapses if we insist on continuity of territorial occupation or of organisation or of political sovereignty or anything of the kind.

It seems to follow that if, for instance, both slave-owning society and feudalism are such 'stages', then it is somewhat implausible to suppose that the same continuous society had at one period been slave-owning and at another, feudal. There was presumably never a time when slave-owners were required to hand in their deeds of ownership of slaves, and have them replaced by land-deeds to appropriate territory, carrying with them a given number of serfs, and corresponding military obligations to overlords, and so forth. It is a nice idea – one likes to think of queues of disgruntled slave-owners, waiting at the municipium, complaining to each other about the bad rate of exchange – 'ten erstwhile slaves for one acre with two serfs, now is that fair I ask you, the government is clearly making a packet out of this transition to feudalism, it's just one further hidden form of taxation' – and perhaps denouncing those who cheat – 'now Lucanius over there, he hands in sick old slaves whom he had quickly bought up cheap when the change from slave-owning to feudalism was announced, but then he manages to collar the very best land with the youngest serfs! And I tell you another thing, this *ius primae noctis* which we are promised in the decree promulgating feudalism, it really isn't a patch on the fun we used to have with the Nubian slave-girls. If you ask me, it's a very retrogressive step, and it's always the middle classes who pay for it in the end . . .'

It is an attractive picture, but to the detriment of the continuity of history, it never happened that way. Semenov is so clearly right on this point that one is a bit puzzled that it had not been made with emphasis earlier. It is not plausible to expect every, or even any, concrete continuous society to pass through all stages. This being so, why had critics of Marxism and revisionists made so much fuss about the absence of some stages in some societies in particular? We shall have to return to this question.

If the succession of stages cannot plausibly be credited to single, continuous societies, which seems to be the case, a number of other questions arise which include: What is a single society? And in what sense can the series of stages be credited to human history or society as a whole? The former question is not answered in Semenov's article, but it is clearly highlighted by his whole approach. The second and crucial question is answered quite explicitly and very clearly. It is here that we shift from his negative position (stages may not be credited to the life stories of individual societies) to his positive doctrine (they must be credited to something else). But just what?

Though the history of mankind may be unitary, yet mankind, except perhaps in the very last stages of its history, does not form some kind of organic unity, recognising itself as such and acting as one. For most of history so far, it is split into large number of units, often quite unaware of each other. In what sense then can such an history have 'stages'? Semenov quite explicitly, and plausibly, rejects any statistical answer to this. It would be quite pointless, for instance, to say that mankind at large is in the feudal stage at a time when the majority of societies is feudal. For one thing, how do you count feudal 'societies' – is there one per king, baron or knight? Nor would it make sense to select a time when the majority of mankind lived under feudal regimes (if such a time existed, which is doubtful). What then?

Semenov's answer is profoundly Hegelian, and he does indeed invoke Hegel in his argument. The answer can best be summed up as the torch relay theory of history. The torch of leadership is passed on in the course of human history from one area to another and from one social system to another. Mankind as a whole is at a given stage, when the most advanced, and at the same time most influential area happens to be at the stage in question. The criterion for being the most influential seems to be in part that it exercises a great deal of influence on surrounding backward, peripheral areas; another criterion seems to be that it is also preparing the ground for the next stage. It would seem to follow that one can only identify the torch-carrying region with confidence after the event, when the next stage has arrived (provided it in turn can be identified), unless one can, which seems unlikely, do it with the help of a kind of sociological-genetic X-ray, identifying the seeds of the future before they have borne fruit. (But the owl of Minerva only flies at dusk.)

It also follows that parallel replication of the same stages in diverse societies is not merely no longer required by the theory, but becomes positively implausible, and would perhaps even contradict the theory. The powerful *rayonnement* of the torch-carrying zone, at any stage, changes the rules of the game so much that societies lagging behind will no longer pass through the same stages as the pioneers. This principle is in fact applied in another interesting work, L.E. Kubbel's *Songhaiskaia Derzhava* (Moscow, Nauka, 1974). The author appears to share this view of Semenov's, and invokes it to explain why West African sahelian societies did not move from the primitive-communal stage to a slave society, but to an early form of feudalism.

A number of things have happened in this reformulation. History acquires a strongly purposive, moralistic tinge. Though Semenov insists on the independence, from human consciousness and will, of the basic productive relations which determine all else, nevertheless the pattern which they generate can only be characterised in highly evaluative terms, and the story told seems dominated by a purpose which is both inexorable and which means well by mankind, in the end. But over and above this, it is diffusion which is heavily stressed, and which plays an absolutely indispensable part in this interpretation, in this reunification of human history, so to speak. Diffusion is indeed a very important process. In the nineteenth century, when anthropology was born, Europeans had the fact of diffusion under their very noses; they could see it happening all the time. The rival idea of evolution took a little more thought; one had to put together what the biologists were saying, with the history of one's own society, and then surmise that other societies moved along similar lines (only more slowly), and that the whole thing was similar to the biological story. The third idea, functionalism, starts from the observation that some societies do not change much, and the inference that this requires mechanisms for keeping them stable, and that it may be a bad thing to disturb those mechanisms. (This idea had long been available in conservative thought, it suited some styles of colonial policy, and, contrary to the belief of some anthropologists, it was not invented within anthropology.) The question is, which of these three ideas (if any) provides the clue to understanding human society and history.

Marxism as conventionally interpreted (and in harmony, I think, with the intentions of its founders) is basically evolutionist. I apologise for the term, especially to Russian Marxists, for whom I think this immediately conjures up the association of doctrines about evolutionary rather than revolutionary development. The question about smooth continuity versus occasional dramatic jumps is quite a separate one, not connected with the present argument. The term 'evolutionism' is here used in a generic manner, covering both these alternatives, and designating a stress on endogenous development as the main and crucial process in human history. The conventional interpretation repudiates the functionalist stress on stability and functionality as spurious, as a case of taking the façade for the reality: within the social sciences in the West, Marxists tend to consider functionalists to be the main opposing trend. In Semenov's reformulation, we shall see that the matter is more complex.

Now obviously Marxism never denied the fact of diffusion. It is clearly implied in any unilineal version of Marxist philosophy of history at two points at least: in as far as primitive-communal societies are small, whereas asiatic or slave-owning ones are large or at any rate larger, obviously the relationship between the displacing and displaced social forms must be of a few-many kind, if not actually of a one-many kind. Such absorption by few or one of many is the extreme form of diffusion, of course. Then again, with the coming of capitalism, its absorption of the rest of the world is not merely implied, but explicitly commented on, by Marx and Engels. In between these two transitions, the matter is not clear. The progression asiatic – slave-owning – feudal is not necessarily, or at all, a progression in size, and thus does not require absorption of new territory and/or population at each stage.

However, though Marxism, as conventionally interpreted, clearly allows and requires diffusion at two points at least, and does not exclude it elsewhere; nevertheless it stresses it much less than is the case in Semenov's version, where diffusion features very conspicuously. Thus Semenov stresses the impact of the torch-carrying centre on peripheral regions, and on the continuous expansion of both centre and affected periphery (as opposed to the backwoods which remain isolated). There is a further extremely important point: on occasion, not only is the centre an essential precondition of the attainment of the next stage, but so is the periphery. The periphery becomes, at least on occasion, quite indispensable.

This seems particularly true, according to Semenov, at the point of transition from Near-Eastern asiatic society (ancient-oriental) to Mediterranean slave-owning society.

> . . . it is possible to say *a priori* that the replacement of the asiatic formation by another, more progressive one could not take place as the qualitative transformation of existing social organisms, which would have preserved themselves as such . . . Nor did it take place simply in the form of the destruction or ruin of asiatic social organisms and the emergence in their place of new, already slave-owning ones.
>
> The point is that social organisms of a new type did not emerge at all in that very same region . . . but at one of the edges of the world system of asiatic social organisms . . .
>
> The replacement of the bronze age by the early iron age, which took place on the territory of Greece, made possible the transition to a new class-endowed socio-economic formation, and one more progressive than the asiatic one which emerged in the copper and bronze age. But this possibility would never have become a reality had Greece not represented an admittedly marginal, but nonetheless inseparable part of the old centre . . .

The influence of the old 'asiatic' society was an essential precondition of this miracle. (There can be no doubt about Semenov's sympathy with it. One is reminded of what Hegel had said – in the ancient orient, only *one* was free, but here *some* were free.) Moreover, the miracle apparently occurréd once only – which, I suppose, justifies one in calling it a miracle (my term, not Semenov's).

> . . . Slave-owning social organisms arose not throughout the territory of the old centre of global development but only at *one* of its distant limits. [My italics.]

But this single *Wirtchaftswunder* is the precondition of all the others in the western historical sequence. The authority of Engels' *Anti-Dühring* is invoked for this: 'Without slavery, no Greek state, no Greek art and science; without slavery, no Roman Empire. But without Hellenism and the Roman Empire. . . no modern Europe.'

Earlier, we are given an account of the ancient Near East which does indeed make it seem unlikely that the transition to a higher stage could have occurred internally, rather than at its limits:

> . . . the ancient orient, all of whose history offers a process of the successive emergence and disappearance of social organisms or conglomerates of such organisms . . . It is possible to disagree about the nature of the socio-economic structure of the ancient orient, but it seems unquestionable that the newly emerging social organisms belonged to the same type as those which perished.

Change of personnel, but not of structure. Ibn Khaldun would endorse such a view. Semenov also puts forward an oscillation theory for this region and period of human history:

> The most striking peculiarity of the development of class society of the ancient east is the perpetual transformation of the political map, the extinction of some and the emergence of other governmental formations. One of the main reasons for this is the alteration, characteristic of all countries of the ancient east, of periods of the existence of strong social organisms, and thereby also of strong centralised despotisms, with periods of their disintegration . . .
>
> It is quite clear that the empires resulting from conquest could not be stable or lasting. With the weakening . . . at the core . . . the whole inevitably disintegrated . . . the parts into which it disintegrated found themselves under the power of a conqueror. Not infrequently these conquerors were the peoples of the periphery . . . the incursions of the peoples of the historic periphery into the region of the centre of historical development can under no circumstances be interpreted as deviations from normality. For the societies of the ancient east all this appears to be the norm or rule.

It is difficult to see how this could have normally led to any progress. If so many perished without ever producing the next stage, why should one of them some day creatively produce something new? This seed showed no sign of sprouting. But once only, in the far west of the ancient eastern world, one of those incursions did eventually lead to an higher stage.

The unprogressive, stagnant nature of the asiatic socio-economic formation, its low potential for self-propulsion to the next higher stage, is further visible from that second great incarnation of it, in the East proper (as opposed to the ancient Near East). In those regions, '... class society emerged sooner than in most of the regions of Europe ...' but did not proceed to develop. Semenov does not altogether exclude the possibility that they might properly be characterised as feudal:

> The social structure found there during the periods which are frequently called feudal by scholars, differed substantially from European feudalism ...

But this hardly matters; feudal or asiatic, either way it was static: '... but [it] was very similar to that which was found there in antiquity.' Whatever it was, it was stagnant. The authority of Marx and Engels is invoked for this theory of asiatic stagnation:

> ... the solution ... was proposed by the very authors of the theory of socio-economic formations, Marx and Engels. It consisted of proposing that from the birth of class-endowed society right up to the eighteenth and even nineteenth centuries, the asiatic mode of production continued to exist in certain countries of the East. In other words, these countries remained in the stage of the first class-endowed socio-economic formation, just as all the original population of Australia remained up to the same period at the stage of primitive-communal structure. As is well known, Marx and Engels repeatedly wrote about the stagnant character of the evolution of the oriental countries.

As we have seen, Semenov overcomes the misguided interpretation of unilinealism by means of a judicious blend of diffusionism and what I have called the torch relay view of history, and what may also be called the displacement effect, or the doctrine of the essential periphery. The historic periphery, one might say, is a subject not object of history in Semenov's view: during various crucial transitions, i.e. the asiatic/slave and the slave/feudal, it played a crucial role in the attainment of the next historic step (Though Semenov does not really spell this out, the same would now seem to be true for the capitalism/socialism transition.) The fact that historic leadership is displaced, that the torch is passed sideways, that its new erstwhile retarded recipients are also essential for further progress, dispenses both them and their predecessors from that irksome theoretical obligation to 'pass through all stages'. If the sideways displacement effect is essential not accidental, if the active participation and contribution of the periphery is a necessary precondition of further progress, it follows not merely that societies need not, but actually *cannot*, parallel each other's 'stages'. At the very least, the periphery (according to the hypothesis previously backward by 'stage' criteria) must leapfrog forward when it takes over leadership. If the participation of the periphery was essential for the attainment of the next stage, then parts of the old centre not affected by the agency of the newly active periphery are *ipso facto* debarred from being the originators of the next round, the next step up. Some transitions positively require a radical change of world leadership, it would appear.

As stated, this theoretical adjustment or reinterpretation of the theory contains a great amount of implicit diffusionism, of the invocation of the important process by which societies affect each other sideways, and have impact on each other, to the point of transforming each other. (This is in contrast with the 'evolutionist' model of an 'internal' or endogenous development.) This diffusionism is rather specific in the importance it attributes to what might otherwise be considered the passive, 'backward' or influence-receiving regions.

But functionalism is also present in this theory (and it has perhaps always been one of the constituents of Marxism). Evolutionists start from the fact of endogenous development (and the development of mankind as a whole must be endogenous, as Semenov might insist, if we exclude extra-terrestrial intrusions); diffusionists start from the equally conspicuous fact of lateral influence; and functionalists start from the sometimes most conspicuous fact of stability or stagnation. We have seen how much Semenov stresses the stagnation of the orientals and the native Australians.

> The dragging of these countries into the zone of influence of the world capitalist system led to the overcoming of stagnation . . . Marx took this view.

From all this it would seem to follow that functionalism – the doctrine that the main trait of societies is stability, self-perpetuation, and that consequently the job of the social analyst is to locate the mechanisms, the functions, which contribute to this end result – would seem a pretty good approximation to the truth, at any rate for the majority of societies, though not for all. Admittedly, this self-preserving equilibrium or stagnation of oriental societies (though not of Australian aboriginal ones), is one of class-endowed and hence antagonistic structures, so that the stability is conflict-ridden rather than peaceful. Such a view however would in no way differentiate Semenov from many 'western' functionalists, who often delight in finding conflict functional and seeing functions in conflict. The only difference would be that they would extend such a conflict-stressing account to primitive-communal societies as well, whether or not they possess 'classes'.

We now possess, I think, the outline skeleton of Semenov's position, sketched out as accurately and fairly as I am capable, though not at all times in his own words. Consider now the problems faced by this position.

First of all it is worth repeating that its central contention seems to me correct. If one considers the importance of diffusion in human history, and the ephemeral nature, on a historic time scale, of concrete societies, and the fact that 'stages' are inspired by historic epochs not by individual national histories, it does indeed follow that what Semenov rightly calls the customary interpretation of unilinealism is so implausible that it should never have been adopted, and that only certain idiosyncrasies of European history led to its implausibility remaining hidden. By abandoning that interpretation, socio-economic formations or stages are freed from the need to 'apply' to each and every society. *Ipso facto*, the critic of that theory finds himself deprived of a large part of his armoury, if not all of it. So is all well? Can the matter rest there?

There is in the West a well-known and influential theory of science, formulated by Sir Karl Popper, which runs roughly as follows: the merit of scientific theories lies in their exposure to risk. The more possible facts they deny, the more they are at risk, the greater their content and merit. So the misguided interpretation of unilinealism was clearly full of content, in so far as it denied all the facts assiduously assembled by its critics, concerning the failure of this or that society to pass through appropriate stages. Semenov's version is not vulnerable to these facts (or at any rate, not vulnerable to an important proportion of those facts). Does that mean that it is virtually without content, or at any rate that the substance of Marxism has been drastically impoverished?

Semenov's adjustment would seem to be *ad hoc* in the sense that it clearly appears to be provoked by those criticisms, and to be designed to render them harmless. But his reasoning is not merely in this sense *ad hoc*, it is also entirely cogent. The trouble with any uncritical or unselective repudiation of *ad hoc* adjustments is that arguments may be both *ad hoc* and good. Popperians may be in danger of forgetting that such theories, like all others, must benefit from the principle that the origin of a theory is unconnected with its merit. Being *ad hoc* is a kind of origin. Such bastardy should not disqualify a candidate of merit.

The truth of the matter would seem to be that although Semenov's reformulation withdraws unilinealism from the reach of some objections, it does not withdraw it from the reach of all of them. Moreover, not only does it not lose all the empirical content and testability-exposure of the old formulation, it actually highlights some new and interesting problems, which, by the criteria of the philosophy of science mentioned above, is a hallmark of a good and fertile theory. Both the retained-old and the newly-acquired problems deserve discussion.

First of all, whilst the reformulation frees societies from the obligation to pass through all stages, it surely cannot give them *carte blanche* to do entirely as they please. They were exempted from the old obligation in virtue of the importance of diffusion, of the lateral influence of world-leaders, in the sociological sense. Hence they can only claim their exemption from the old obligatory stages when such lateral influence does operate. It can only permit them to evade the proper sequence under the influence of a world centre which drags them into another 'stage'. But if insulated (and does insulation never occur?) they must either follow the proper order of stages, or perhaps be stagnant. Otherwise, they continue to pose a problem for unilinealism, Semenov's reformulation notwithstanding.

Take a concrete example. In the West, scholars concerned with the phenomenon of slavery disagree about the exact number of societies actually based on the institution of slavery, but they seem to be agreed that the Caribbean and the southern states of the USA, in the appropriate parts of the eighteenth and nineteenth centuries, fall into this category. This retrogression, from late feudalism or early capitalism, without the benefit of the influence of any global centre of slave owning, (which in any case would not be a torch-carrying world leader but itself a case of retrogression), must continue to pose a problem for unilinealism.

Or take the problem of stagnation – in other words, the fact that 'static' functionalism does seem true for such a large proportion of human societies. Although Semenov's reformulation rightly allows the phenomenon of primitive-communal societies being dragged from their periphery into 'higher' world systems, it must presumably still be true that had this not occurred, those laggards would eventually propel themselves upwards by their own inner resources. I suppose we can now never know whether indeed they would have done so. For my own part, I would quite gladly accept a modified quasi-evolutionist version of the transition from primitive-communal to asiatic, which might be called the frequency or statistical theory, and which would run as follows: not every primitive-communal society contains adequate or sufficient seeds of change. The conditions of upward development are more complex, and require additional propitious circumstances (say, an alluvial river valley suitable for intensive irrigation agriculture – a theory which admittedly looks plausible only for the 'old world', but I am using it only for the sake of argument). The theory would only require that this combination of circumstances is sufficiently probable to ensure that it should occur sooner or later. Once it occurred, the processes or torch-of-leadership assumption and of diffusion, so much stressed (in other terms) by Semenov, would ensure the perpetuation of the new stage. It would constitute no objection to such a theory that the initial endogenous transformation would only occur in a minority of primitive-communal societies.

Semenov does not actually elaborate such a theory, but it seems to me consistent with his position, and in its spirit, and moreover to be intrinsically plausible and attractive. What the theory really requires is that the spontaneous, endogenous primitive/asiatic transition should have occured at least often enough for us to be able, so to speak, to rely on it. This seems to be the case, and Semenov also holds it to be so:

> A first class-endowed society formed itself fully only in two delimited areas, the Nile valley and the area between the rivers Tigris and Euphrates . . . The subsequent development of mankind followed, on the one hand, the line of the emergence of new independent regional centres of historic development (the valleys of the Indus and the Hwang Ho) . . .

> The only class formation which can arise exclusively on the basis of the disintegration of primitive society alone appears to be the asiatic one . . . asiatic societies can emerge as islands, to a considerable extent isolated from each other in a sea of peoples remaining in the pre-class stage . . . All class societies, emerging in areas which at the time were outside the influence of previously formed centres of civilisation, inevitably had to be asiatic rather than slave-owning or feudal. The data available . . . [from] pre-Columban America, Oceania and sub-Saharan Africa fully confirm this . . .

Given the multiplicity of these independent, isolated 'asiatic islands', in four or five continents, we seem to be safe. If by some accident of geography, the Nile flowed into the Indian ocean and the Sahara stretched to Suez, there would have been no pharaonic Egypt, but the transition from primitive to asiatic would have been safe. The Chinese or the Hawaians, the Aztecs and the Incas would still have been there. History might have been delayed a bit, but its basic laws would have remained unaltered. Only the timetable would have been amended.

But what does make one feel rather nervous is when one sees the torch of progress in one pair of hands only. If those feet had stumbled, if that leader had faltered, if those hands had failed . . . what then? It makes one scared to think of it.

For just this seems to have been the situation, on at least one crucial occasion:

> . . . the limitation in space and time of the emergence of slave-owning society . . . slave-owning social organisms arose not throughout the territory of the old centre . . . but only at one of its distant edges . . .

Semenov does not discuss the question of the existence of other slave-owning societies, but as far as the successors to the old Near-Eastern world system are concerned, the ancient Mediterranean seems to have been an unique case. This is curious, in as far as the three pre-conditions he specifies – iron, pre-existing asiatic society, and early-class invaders – must often have come together. For one thing, why did the new formation not spread with Alexander? And after Alexander, there have been many invaders of asiatic societies, endowed both with an early class structure presumably comparable to that of the Dorians, and with iron, and yet asiatic society remained stubbornly stagnant, and it took the brutal prince of capitalism to rouse that sleeping beauty from her slumber.

Here we come to a profound methodological problem which faces Semenov's reinterpretation. The endogenous, acorn-to-oaktree vision of human history seems essential to Marxism and to evolutionist theories generally; in fact, it defines evolutionism. But how do we know that acorns generate oak trees? The answer is that we have numerous examples of this particular development. No oak tree is known to have sprung from something other than an acorn. But the matter becomes more difficult if we only possess one instance only of a particular transition. Too many factors are present for us to be able to single out the crucial ones. It may be different in modern genetics. It may be that microscopic investigation of the genetic equipment enables the geneticist to identify its growth potential *a priori*. But in history and the social sciences, we simply cannot read the genetic code – whether because our theories are not good and precise enough, or because social structures are not as tightly organised and uniquely determined in their effects as biological ones, or both. If there is only one specimen of slave-owning society, at any rate within the mainstream of history, and that one is in turn the precondition of all subsequent progress, then we are methodologically in a very difficult situation. One of Semenov's opponents on this issue within the Soviet Union, whom he very fairly quotes, does indeed single out this problem as absolutely central:

> . . . there turned out to be more deviations and exceptions than cases falling under the rule [of unilinealism], and secondly – and this is the main point – the regularities operating here showed themselves to be so specific, that they could not be explained simply by the influence of historic environment alone. [L.V. Danilova, 'Controversial problems in the theory of pre-capitalist societies', also quoted in Semenov's article. An English version is available in *Soviet Anthropology and Archaeology*, 1968, vol. 9, pp. 269–328]

This may indeed be the main point. If one specific conjuncture of circumstances produced an unique event – the emergence of slave-owning society – which however also turns out to be an essential link in the chain leading to the present, what happens to the necessity of historical development? Semenov does not abjure historical necessity. He asserts it in the abstract:

> The theory of every distinct social formation reflects the objective necessity of the development of *all* social organisms, which have at their base the corresponding system of productive relations.
>
> The characteristic trait of a world system of social organisms of a given type appears to be the fact that their development *inevitably* prepares the appearance of a new, more progressive world system, so

that its existence appears to be a *necessary* link in the history of mankind. [My italics]

He is also willing to implement this abstract historical determinism by specific historically guaranteed predictions:

> The world socialist system appears as the only one which can be and necessarily will become global. And in the more distant future, with the transition to communism, human society will inevitably transform itself into a single social organism.

This final prediction is interesting. By what criterion will the global communist society be one organism? Presumably not by political criteria, in as far as there can be no room for state authorities in a classless society. The other plausible criterion would be a shared culture, which is indeed in our age the most important criterion of 'nationality'. But why should we expect mankind in the communist stage to become culturally homogeneous? Many people would find such a prospect depressing. But what is interesting about the prediction is the implied suggestion – it is no more – that lateral boundaries (between 'social organisms', or 'nations') also express antagonisms. What else, other than the absence of antagonisms, would account for the inevitable erosion of lateral boundaries? If this is so, one could indeed expect lateral boundaries to go by the board, if one anticipates a stage of human history which will be free of social antagonisms. The idea that lateral inter-organism relations, or at least some of them, are also antagonistic is indeed implied in Semenov's scheme. It would seem to follow from the importance given within it to the relation between the periphery and the centre. Certain crucial transitions can only take place through the interaction between centre and periphery. The relationship between the two is not immediately a relation between classes, but it is a relationship between organisms at different stages, and hence containing diverse classes at their helm. In this sense, it is also a kind of class antagonism. The stress on centre-periphery relations and the attempt to extend the notion of class relation to it is of course shared by Soviet and western Marxists, and is prominant in the recent work of influential western Marxists such as Wallerstein (I. Wallerstein, *The Modern World System*, New York, 1974). The whole notion of 'periphery', as recently used, is I suppose an attempt to turn 'under-development' into a timeless and generic notion, available for use retrospectively on the historic past.

However these are tangential issues. The one central methodological issue facing the Semenov reinterpretation arises from the essential and yet more or less unique character of at least one stage, namely Mediterranean slave-owning society. The obverse of this uniqueness (which Semenov does not assert in so many words) is the fact that we cannot rely on this formation to arise on the foundation of its predecessor, asiatic society, in the orient. (This failure Semenov stresses explicitly.) Slave-owning society, if not unique, at least is not a reliable consequence of its historic antecedents, unlike asiatic society itself, which appears to be a hardy plant flowering irrepressibly in many parts of the globe.

The most influential single sociologist in the West is I suppose Max Weber. It would be bizarre to reduce his disagreement with Marx to the issue of idealism/materialism. The real difference is something else: it is the issue between the acorn/oaktree model and the gatekeeper models of human progress. In the Hegelian/Marxist tradition, the seeds of progress are there and will come to fruition one way or another. On the gatekeeper model, the way forward is barred, but one gate happened, fortuitously, to be open. The former model naturally leads to a sense of the unity of mankind and its history (a sense which Semenov shares so strongly), because it is as it were guaranteed by the potency of those shared seeds, whereas the latter vision implies the opposite. Weber was indeed obsessed by the distinctiveness of western history, its non-universality. It is significant that the real international popularity of Weber's thought came at a period obsessed with the failure of non-western acorns to grow easily and quickly into western oak trees, i.e. at the time of preoccupation with the difficulties of 'economic development' (and/or of its desired political accompaniments.) This is the heart of the matter. The one crucial opening in the gate was for him a consequence of an accidental combination of circumstances. (Like Semenov, he thought he could nevertheless give a causal account of it, despite its uniqueness.) He was only an idealist in the thin sense that one element in the set of circumstances was an ideological one. The other elements were not, and for most societies and situations, he was as materialist as they come.

Semenov's nearly-unique gate or opening is located much further back than Weber's. It is, as we saw, located at the emergence of slave-owning in the Balkans and Italy, over 2000 years prior to the passage of Weber's special gateway. But this does not affect the logical aspect of the problem. What happens to historical inevitability, to the generation of one stage by another, if one of the stages is quasi-unique or in any case simply cannot be relied upon to emerge from its predecessor? This is one of the problems Semenov's reformulation will have to face.

Whilst Semenov successfully demonstrates that individual societies do not need to pass through each and every stage, and that they may skip stages when they come under the influence of more advanced, torch-carrying centres, nevertheless certain possibilities presumably must still remain excluded; there is still a certain overlap in requirements between Semenov's unitary-history unilinealism, and the old parallel-unilinealism. Societies must not jump stages when not impelled to do so by any outside advanced centre, for instance. Semenov does not discuss the case of Japan, the one society which, though asiatic in a geographic sense, is widely held to have had a genuine feudalism. If

slave society was absent in the East, but is held to be a precondition of
the emergence of feudalism, how was this possible? Societies must not
go into reverse gear and regress into 'earlier' stages, with or without the
impulsion of some more powerful centre. Can there be centres of retar-
dation too which also exercise an influence? In brief, the unity of world
history, the stress on diffusion of more advanced modes of production
from centres of excellence, does not remove all the problems facing unilinealism. The reinterpretation does not give unilinealism a completely
clean bill of health, it merely removes some of its difficulties.

But let us leave these problems, and consider some of the new tasks
which the interpretation suggests. Semenov's insistence on the importance of the periphery and of the sideways passing of the torch is
reminiscent of a certain familiar philosophy of history, which has often
been formulated: civilisations or nations or societies must, like three-
quarters in rugby football, pass the ball sideways if they are to advance.
There is a poetic formulation of this idea by the Austrian poet and
playwright Grillparzer, for instance:

> Denn alle Völker dieser weiten Erde,
> Sie treten auf den Schauplatz nach und nach,
> Die an dem Po und bei den Alpen wohnen,
> Dann zu den Pyranäen kehrt die Macht.
> Die aus der Seine trinken und der Rhone,
> Schauspieler stets, sie spielen drauf den Herrn.
> Der Brite spannt das Netz von seiner Insel,
> Und treibt die Fische in sein goldnes Garn.
> Ja, selbst die Menschen jenseits eurer Berge,
> Das blaugeaugte Volk voll roher Kraft,
> Das nur im Fortschritt kaum bewahrt die Stärke
> Blind, wenn es handelt, thatlos, wenn es denkt,
> Auch sie bestrahlt der Weltensonne Schimmer,
> Und Erbe aller Frühern glänzt ihr Stern.
> Dann kommt's auf euch, an euch und eure Brüder,
> Der letzte Aufschwung ist's der matten Welt.
> Die lang gedient, sie werden endlich herrschen,
> Zwar breit und weit, allein nicht hoch, noch tief;
> Die Kraft, entfernt von ihrem ersten Ursprung,
> Wird schwächer, ist nur noch erborgte Kraft.
> Doch werdet herrschen ihr und euren Namen
> Als Siegel drücken auf der kunftgen Zeit.
>
> (Grillparzer, *Libussa*, Act V).

Thus spoke Libuše, while presiding over the transition from
matriarchy to early state formation and urbanisation among the western
Slavs; the occasion of the prophecy was the foundation of the city of
Prague. My translation follows:

Thus all the peoples on the expanse of earth
The worldly stage ascend, each turn by turn,
Those living by the Po and in the Alps,
Then to the Pyrenees the power shifts.
Those who drink from the Seine and from the Rhone,
Were actors ever, then they played the lords.
The Briton spreads a net from his fair isle,
And drives the fish into his golden snare.
Yea, even the men who live beyond your hills,
The blue-eyed nation full of uncouth strength,
A folk which barely holds its place in progress,
Blind when it acts, and deedless when it thinks;
They too will feel the rays of the world's sun,
Their star will shine, succeeding all the rest.
Your turn will come, for you and for your brethren,
The final upsurge of a weary earth.
Those who have served so long will rule at last,
Though far and wide, yet without height or depth;
The strength, so far now from its primal spring,
Grows weaker, being now but borrowed force.
Yet you will rule, and press your name as seal
On time to come, time which is yet to be.

But there is a certain asymmetry in Semenov's version. The torch needs to be advanced sideways on numerous occasions, but not always. In the first transition (primitive/asiatic), the question of it being passed from a more advanced centre to a retarded periphery simply did not arise, as there weren't any advanced centres. If you break up 'primitive society' into a number of sub-stages, as is done by the Soviet scholar Maretin, this point then applies once again to the first of these sub-stages. (See Yu. V. Maretin, *Community and its Types in Indonesia*, separately published offprint, Proceedings of the VII World Congress of Anthropology, Nauka, Moscow, 1964.) Thus, in the first transition, everyone is equally retarded, or if you like, no one is retarded, and without any centre, there can be no periphery. At the next transition (asiatic/slave) the side-step was essential: the asiatic heartlands do not seem to have the potential for endogenous growth, but sink into canonically documented stagnation. The same is repeated next time: the slave/feudal transition once again takes place at the edge of the old centre. But the feudal/capitalist transition is exceptional: it is, so to speak, a centre-preserving transition, and this is quite idiosyncratic, if one spells out Semenov's schema in detail. Is this connected with the fact that it is the one transition to which western historical sociology is really sensitive? If there is at present any kind of philosophy of history at all in the West, it is an unsystematised one, which concentrates on the big social transformation wrought by industrialisation. It perceives two historical transformations – the neolithic and the industrial revolutions. In be-tween, there are conquests rather than inwardly-destined and deep metamorphoses. No one has yet articulated this vision with philosophic depth. The philosophy of 'industrial society' has not yet found its Hegel. But if the feudal/capitalist tradition is so unusual, how is it to be explained? Why is one particular transition centre-preserving, whereas all others (except the first, which had no choice) are centre-shifting? The last transition, which is yet to come, will also be unique, in that it will be neither centre-preserving nor centre-displacing, but centre-dissolving.

Strictly speaking, not one but two contrasts are involved here. Some transitions preserve leadership, and some can only be accomplished by means of the displacement of the advanced centre. But further-more there is also the contrast between society-preserving and so-ciety-destroying transitions (irrespective of the question of national leadership). The two distinctions are not identical and cut across each other. As far as the very first epochal transition is concerned, the issue of society-preservation does already arise (whereas the issue of the preservation of leadership could not yet arise, there not having been any prior leaders). Semenov explicitly says that the first class-endowed societies emerge not through a metamorphosis of primitive ones, but through their destruction, and on their ruins. Both questions arise in the second and third transitions, which are both 'displacement of leadership' and 'discontinuity of societies' transitions. The next transition is doubly contrasted with them: leader-ship stays put, and societies preserve themselves. But the transition from capitalism to socialism is the most interesting one, from this viewpoint: leadership does shift sideways, but at the same time societies are preserved. The last transition, Semenov predicts, will dis-solve the previously existing distinct societies, and we can on general Marxist grounds assume that leadership will move only in the sense of dissolving altogether. It will move, but not to anyone. It will just move away.

This second contrast between society-preserving transitions and others, obviously crucial and central for any further development of this philosophy of history, in effect brings to the fore the whole question of why there are, and also why sometimes there are not, continuous soci-eties, nations, cultures or whatever. Traditional Marxism can be accused, at best, of not highlighting the question, and at worst of treating it as something epiphenomenal and of no great interest. A dis-missive attitude to this question simply is not possible within Semenov's schema. The diversity and plurality of nations and cultures is not a contingent accident, a by-product of the isolation and hence of the linguistic and other idiosyncrasies of primitive communities, but an essential fact, without which the whole process of world history could not work. This seems to follow, if from nothing else, from the crucial role played by peripheral nations on those three supremely important occasions in world history. If a backward and distinct periphery is essential for some steps forward, there could be no progress in a world with one nation only.

The schema highlights a point which others have reached by different paths: that ethnicity seems to have a different role in the later stages of history, and in the course of the later transitions, from the one it had during earlier epochs. In connection, for instance, with the asiatic mode of production and its epoch, Semenov notes the non-congruence between political organisation and 'social organism'. Though he does not say so, the same is also conspicuously true of slave-owning society, whose political units varied from small city states to the ecumenical Roman empire, without apparently any corresponding radical change in the underlying relations of production. (The same appears to be true in Mongolia and central Asia, according to the material of a Soviet scholar, S.I. Vainstein. In her introduction to his study of the Tuvinians, *Nomads of South Siberia*, Cambridge, 1979, Caroline Humphrey writes, 'Vainstein's material adds up to the following conclusion: there are no transformations in the technology of herding, nor of agriculture, nor of craft or commodity production, which "account for" the rise and fall of the steppe empires.') Non-congruence between ethnicity and polity also seems hardly disputable for the feudal age, with its shadowy larger units and its fragmented political micro-units. It is during the subsequent two stages that two of the things occur which may well be connected: societies acquire a kind of persistence, become continuous and 'pass through' the transitions, and ethnicity becomes an important (though not the exclusive) principle of political-unit delimitation. One can add to this the idiosyncratic fact that no sideways passing of the torch occurs during the first of the two great modern transitions, which at the same time looks like being the big and crucial transition for bourgeois sociologists: the emergence of 'rational' production.

One can of course think of good *ad hoc* reasons why the transition from feudalism to capitalism had to be endogenous and society-preserving. It was a transition in which commercial and production-oriented strata took over from a predatory or display-oriented military nobility – a contrast which of course greatly struck the early European sociologists. This being so, it could hardly be a transition in which the historical midwife would be a war of conquest and domination. It was the un-martial ones – at least in their outward aspect – who were the victors then. It was the warriors who were the vanquished. They could hardly be defeated at their own game and in their own field by newcomers ill-suited for it. The victory had to be effected by internal mechanisms inside a society. If it was decided by war at all, it was civil war, which preserved the continuity of state and society even if it changed the identity of rulers within it. One can also put the case negatively: is it conceivable that the emergence of bourgeois society out of a feudal one would have been the work of peripheral – bluntly: barbarian – invaders? There is something bizarre about the idea of such tribal invaders demolishing the baron's castle and then settling down in its ruins as burghers, traders, financiers and entrepreneurs.

No, this transition for once had to be endogenous, and hence both society- and national-leadership-preserving. But I must confess that I find the *ad hoc* reasons which I have sketched out above, in order to explain the idiosyncrasy, rather inelegant precisely because of their *ad hoc* quality. They are plausible as far as they go, but if history is such a unity – if transitions generally involve a side-step, but not on this one occasion – I'd like to see some good general reason for this asymmetry. What I have described as the implicit, unformulated western philosophy of history, does seem to have the advantage here: by treating the transition to industrialism as in any case quite unique, it is not embarrassed by then finding further unique traits in it. Semenov's version of the Hegelo-Marxist vision transforms it from an essentially Eurocentric self-congratulatory one – which it had been normally – into an encouraging pat on the back for late developers. But in doing this, it finds one particular transition, the feudalism/capitalism one, embarrassingly idiosyncratic.

Let us return however to the overall conceptual strategy of Semenov's work and its place in the intellectual world of Soviet scholarship. He has saved unilinealism from at any rate some of the historical objections to it by means of his strong stress on the unity of history, on the inequality between centre and periphery which nevertheless are parts of one single process, on the diffusion from centre to periphery, which is however accompanied by an essential role of periphery in the course of crucial transitions; in brief he adopts what may be called the relay torch pattern of historical leadership, which stresses the importance of leadership and emulation. The last shall be first. This was always a Marxist view, but Semenov's schema gives it an ethnic twist in addition to its old class meaning. The consequence of all this has been a schema which highlights not only the highly problematical nature of the historical continuity of societies or nations, but also certain specific and intriguing oddities in this field – that the patterns of social continuity and of global leadership by societies are rather different at different stages and in the course of diverse traditions. Once noted and stressed, these questions can hardly be ignored.

But the suggestiveness of Semenov's ideas in this direction is not, so to speak, simply an irrelevant price or by-product of the main objective, namely the defence of unilinealism. Though the relevance is not spelt out, let alone underscored by him, it is there: the most conspicuous research innovation within Soviet anthropology recently has been a concern with ethnicity, with the ethnos, and moreover a concern with it in the modern, non-archaic period, which is marked by the idiosyncratic persistence of ethnoses. In other words, there is a sense in which the world-historical theoretical formulation proposed by Semenov, and the concrete research into ethnicity led by Bromley, dovetail very neatly.

The argument would not merely explain why the existence of

distinctive ethnic groups is essential to world history, it would also, and in intimate connection with the previous point, help explain the persistence and historic importance of real war, as opposed to the metaphorical class war. In a remarkable book (*Philosophers of Peace and War*, Cambridge, 1978) W.B. Gallie argues (p. 99):

> This problem arises . . . from the fact that the existence of war . . . cannot be considered or dealt with or controlled, simply as one facet or by-product of mankind's great constructive task of achieving a just and satisfying economic order. Or to speak more simply, from its first beginnings Marxist overall social theory was defective, through its failure to place and explain the different possible roles of war in human history.

Whatever other functions warfare may have – and Semenov no doubt would not disagree with Marx's account of its essential role in ancient slave-owning society – during the crucial side-stepping movements it would be an inevitable agent of the diffusion or even the very establishment of the new social order. Gallie quotes that devastatingly accurate prediction by Engels of the nature of the First World War, published as early as 1888; but goes on to add that Engels misunderstood the practical implications of his theoretical insight, whilst Lenin understood the practical implications without necessarily appreciating the theoretical point. War was essential to the emergence of a new order on the periphery. As Gallie puts it (p. 98):

> For, contrary to Marx and Engels, who had maintained that Tsarism would fall only to a revolution from within, Lenin was persuaded that it would fall only as the result of an utterly disastrous war – and that meant as long a war, and as generalised a global war, as possible . . . In sum, Lenin's stance in 1914 was not simply good Marxism, a faithful adherence to its classic doctrines . . . it was also a necessity of his particular task as leader of the Russian Marxist Socialists . . . Lenin was committed, in fact if not in word, to international socialism *for the sake of one country*, from 1911 onwards, if not from the outset of his revolutionary career.

Semenov's schema is also suggestive or expressive in other intriguing ways. These additional ideas or suggestions are implicit in the arrangement of the material and not articulated by Semenov himself, who consequently cannot in fairness be held in any way responsible for them, one way or the other. They are in the eye of this beholder or interpreter, who must consequently assume complete responsibility for them.

A striking trait of the schema is its strong sense, not of world-historical individuals (none are mentioned, and there is conspicuous absence of any cult of personality in this philosophy of history), but of, so to speak, *welt-historische Voelker*. (Bryce Gallie for instance said about Lenin that 'he was to become the one unquestionably "world-historical individual" of our century'. But no world-historical individuals appear on Semenov's tableau. His heroes are nations or collectivities.) They are the nations who assume leadership, and the criteria of leadership are ultimately moral – a contribution towards the fulfilment of the ultimate destiny of mankind as a whole, a destiny whose culmination, both in a chronological and an evaluative sense, is known. The West has lost all such confidence, and despises its Victorian predecessors for having had it. A western anthropologist who dared speak, without irony, of the *mission civilisatrice* or of the 'white man's burden', would be more or less ostracised by his professional community. Semenov has no hesitation in using the notion of differences of level of development and referring to the obligations of global leadership which this carries with it.

The major mechanism of progress in the past has been the leadership and influence exercised by an advanced centre over the retarded periphery. This influence defined leadership and the location of leadership in turn defined the world-historical epoch. Secondly, Semenov tells us that the most advanced world-system in existence now is the socialist one. The joint implication of these two assertions is not spelt out, but it is obvious. The moral obligations of leadership which this imposes on that system and on its centre are clear. If such leadership is exercised in the course of aiding nations which had been for too long committed to stagnation, it may well fail to be properly appreciated. It may be no accident that it is precisely the previously most stagnant society which is also now the most recalcitrant in accepting guidance from the leading centre.

But that is not all. Russia was once expected to be the third Rome. This did not come to be – at least not literally. However, three times in our single and united pan-human history did mankind advance only by taking a step sideways; thrice was the torch of progress handed over to a nation on the periphery, advance being blocked by the centre. Once it was passed to the Dorians when they established a slave-owning society at the far West of the ancient orient; once it was handed to the Franks when they built the centre of feudalism in the outlying marchlands of declining slave society. More recently the banner of leadership was transmitted for the third time.

PART II

The distinctiveness of the primitive

A. I. PERSHITS

Ethnographic reconstruction of the history of primitive society

The history of primitive society looms large in the Marxist under-standing of history. This is because it helps to solve a number of prob-lems. Above all there is the great significance of the general concept of primitive society for the Marxist theory of the historical process. It asserts that primitive society – or the primitive communal system – was the first socio-economic formation in the history of mankind, and was the only one which knew neither private property, nor antagonistic classes, nor state power. The concept of pristine collectivism enables the founders of scientific communism to demonstrate not the primor-dial, but, on the contrary, the historically conditioned and, therefore, transient character of all these basic institutions of class society. It will be recalled that in their concept of the history of primitive society, Marx and Engels drew on the research carried out in the nineteenth century, especially on the works by Morgan. A large amount of new material has been accumulated since then and some of the old conclusions could not but become outdated as science developed. This confronted scientists with the alternative of deciding which conclusions need to be refined or revised – the more specific and secondary, or those which are of prin-cipal, methodological significance? It is the second solution which is prevalent in western anthropology. Some scientists have continued to try to prove the pristine character of the rudimentary forms of private ownership, state power, etc.[1] It is noteworthy that even those scholars who, like Gellner, give in principle a positive assessment of the theory of socio-economic formations, are rather sceptical about the first such system – the primitive one.[2] Hence the great importance attached by Marxist science to the reconstruction of primitive society and its history on the basis of all the facts available today.

Another important goal of this kind of reconstruction is to provide science with more knowledge. Here we proceed from the conviction that any cultural phenomenon can be understood only if it is studied in the historico-genetic context, and not only from the structural-cum-functional viewpoint. Many elements of culture are rooted in the primeval past and later manifest themselves in a modified form.

Lastly, there is still another purpose of studying the history of primitive society, which is of practical significance. Today there are quite a few backward peoples who have retained various pre-class forms, often those which were fused with the latest class relation. The ethnographic assessment of phenomena like the remnants of the clan and communal traditions, the activity of secret societies, tribalism, etc. may help these peoples in their social, economic, political and cultural advancement.

Another reason why special importance is attached to the history of primitive society, apart from the goals concerning world outlook, knowledge and practical tasks, is the distinctiveness of its methodology and sources. While other sections of historical science are based mainly on written monuments, the history of primitive society, at least prior to the emergence of the first class societies, wholly pertains to the preliterate stage in the development of humanity and is reconstructed on the basis of other sources. Hence the tendency, which is traced back to Radcliffe Brown and Lowie and is characteristic of the western conception of scholarship, to draw a distinction between scholarship proper, which studies only the civilised peoples with a written language, and prehistory or prehistoric (sometimes also protohistoric) archaeology, studying primitive society before it reached that level of civilisation.[3] A kind of a compromise and, at the same time, marked headway was made in the 1950s when 'ethnohistory,' a new subdivision within American socio-cultural anthropology, emerged in order to undertake, as it is often conceived, a reconstruction of the history of preliterate peoples by combining the written sources of neighbouring civilised societies with ethnographic and other data.[4] In methodological terms, this idea resembles another one, formulated in West European science somewhat earlier, of singling out 'parahistory', commencing in preliterate societies with the emergence of written sources in other parts of the globe, which provided certain possibilities for 'historising' the peoples before they reached the civilisation level.[5]

It is obvious that here the formal historiographical approach replaces the substantial approach to classification. In reality, however, all peoples, whatever the sources used to reconstruct their history, are the subjects of one single historical process. Hence, the development of all peoples is studied by one historical science, although, naturally, one or another aspect of this science (and of the adjacent sciences) comes to the foreground for the study of diverse stages of history. This is precisely why we look to the history of primitive society, although it is based almost wholly, not on written information, but rather on archaeological, paleoanthropological, ethnographic and other data, as an organic element of one historical science. At present this approach to the question, which Marx and Engels stressed (in 'German ideology' that history should not be contrasted with prehistory) often attracts western researchers as well.[6] Most recently, it has become relevant for the contrast of history and 'ethnohistory.' Thus, C. Hudson notes with good reason that 'by consigning preliterate peoples to ethnohistory, however, we remove them from the category of humanity to which we ourselves belong.'[7]

I believe that the singling out of proto- or para- or ethno-history should be transferred into another level. Being part and parcel of total historical science, the history of primitive society is subdivided into history dealing with the period ending with the emergence of most ancient civilisations, and the history of a society coexisting with the class society and developing at the outskirts of civilisation. These subdivisions of the history of primitive society, like the societies themselves, may be defined as preclass and epiclass (here the prefix 'epi' means existing at the same time). Belonging to similar types of primitive societies, the preclass and epiclass societies differ in the degree of the spontaneity of their development, which I am going to dwell upon somewhat later. This differentiation allows us to avoid a possible ambiguity of the word 'primitive' and is clearer (as regards notions and terminology) than the differentiation between the historically primitive societies and those lagging behind in their development. So far, this is merely a recommendation, and in this paper I am using the traditional term 'primitive' in the sense of preclass, and 'lagging behind in its (their) development' in the sense of epiclass.

So what are the possibilities today of reconstructing the history of primitive society? How much pertinent information is there in the different sources, and what part of it is properly ethnographic? These questions can be answered differently with respect to diverse periods in the development of primitive society.

As for the most ancient epoch of the early paleolithic era, the data provided by paleoanthropology, primatology to some extent, and especially archaeology, are of primary, if not exclusive, significance. The evidence supplied by paleoanthropology, such as skulls, endocrans, signs of injuries on bone remnants, burial places, etc. offers material by which we can judge about the psychology, demographic structure and even the social life of the collectivities of archanthrops and paleoanthrops. Their significance, however, is not to be overestimated: they are not very large and, at least as far as sociological conclusions are concerned, do not always make it possible to decide what is the rule and what is the exception. The area in which one can use primatological results, however one assesses the legitimacy of this method, is restricted to the earliest stage of sociogenesis. In this context, the fast growing data of archaeology are becoming increasingly important, though here too, when applied to a given delimited epoch and a well-defined sphere, the truth is evidently somewhere halfway between the cautious optimism of Childe and the moderate pessimism of de Laet.[8] It is no accident that in archaeology, as well as in paleoanthropology, the same data lead various scholars to diametrically opposed conclusions. Take, for instance, the recent excavations of the early paleolithic settlements in Soviet territory (Kudaro, Tsona, Azykh, and others), in which some archaeologists see evidence of a universal existence of communes, i.e. collectivities that were well knit together socially, and others see in them only distinct harbingers of subsequent communal organisation in a so-called primitive human herd.[9] Generally speaking, the lack of sufficient ethnographic parallels for that epoch makes it an area of most vigorous debates which, in theoretical terms, concern the question of the legitimacy of placing the material within the framework of the primitive social formation.[10]

True, the adherents of the so-called 'new archaeology' trend that took shape in the USA in the 1960s believe that the methods of historical reconstruction can be based on systems analysis of any one of the interrelated elements making up archaeological complexes. The reconstruction of the absent elements is done in this case by a comparison of some subsystems with others, aided by an analysis of a mass of facts by statistical and computer methods. However, even the most outstanding representatives of this trend do not deny the significance of ethnographic data as a means of modelling reconstructed social relationships and checking purely archaeological hypotheses.[11] I shall not analyse here the archaeological methods proper, but confine myself to noting their relatively great significance for the study of the socio-cultural complexes of those early epochs for which we have no ethnographic parallels.

As primitive man exceeded the bounds of the early paleolithic, we came to possess, apart from the facts of archaeology, the data of ethnography on the peoples of the world which lag behind in their development. Perhaps it is not worth giving much thought to finding a comparative evaluation of archaeological and ethnographic sources for the reconstruction of the history of primitive society as from that landmark. The former attract us by their unquestioned simultaneity with the epoch which is being reconstructed; and the latter by their all-embracing and solid character. A comprehensive application of both is necessary (and written sources should also be used whenever possible) and it is this approach that is getting most widespread. But, as it was aptly observed by a Soviet ethnographer, while archaeology is offering us merely a skeleton, ethnography enables us to judge the texture and the functioning of a living organism.[12] This raises a cardinal question for the evaluation of the history of primitive society: just how representative are ethnographic data for the understanding of the history of the primitive community?

There are two methods of using ethnographic data for the reconstruction of primitive history: the historical comparative method and the method of survivals. The former is the basic one, according to which the primeval past of mankind is reconstructed by comparing its stages with the corresponding nations which are at present lagging behind in their development. The historical comparative method appeals to the unity of the world historical process, and for anyone who recognises this unity the validity of this method is beyond doubt. Nevertheless, its concrete application comes up against definite difficulties, arising from the question of the comparability or congruence of the compared entities.

In contrast with such classics of evolutionism as Bastian and Taylor, we know full well that the unity of the world historical process is determined not merely by the nature of sociological laws but also by contacts between various groups of mankind which steadily increase in the course of historical development.[13] These contacts took place in the primeval epoch of mankind as well, but they acquired a special importance with the emergence and expansion of the area of civilisations whose influence, in one way or another, was felt by their close and distant primitive periphery. Even the isolation of Australian aborigines in the precolonial period was not absolute, and the influence of more advanced societies on the less developed ones increased many times over since the time of great geographic discoveries. This influence should not be exaggerated either: on more than one occasion, attention was drawn to the fact that external influences are effective above all when the ground has been prepared by internal development of the recipient societies. Likewise, it cannot be underrated. I cannot but agree with those researchers who consider that a large number of underdeveloped societies which have been studied by ethnographers in modern times, had been subjected to outside influence in previous epochs, and that their representativeness is correspondingly limited for the history of primitive society.[14]

There is another factor to be reckoned with. The very fact that certain tribes have lagged behind in their development poses the question whether they may be identified with the primitive tribes of the 'old world' which advanced at a far higher rate and, therefore, whether the geographic and historical factors which, among other things, caused stagnation did not play a significant role. This is especially true about the less developed tribes of hunters and gatherers aptly described by M. Sahlins as 'displaced persons.'[15] Such societies probably degenerated in part and may be regarded as deformed.

It is not without reason that in recent times many western scholars, while recognising the validity of archaeological-ethnographic comparisons, confine their possibility merely to the regions where the continuity of cultural development can be traced archaeologically.[16] This view, however, in which the method of 'controlled comparison' proposed by Eggan in 1954 is used as a starting point, seems to be too extreme. Elaborated in Soviet ethnography, the theory of economic-cultural types opens up possibilities for comparing societies of a similar type, regardless of the area of their location and cultural continuity.[17] A similar stand is taken by such prominent foreign archaeologists as Clark. In his view, uninterrupted development adds to the authenticity of comparisons but the latter, however, are admissible whenever it concerns the societies with similar levels in their manner of securing of means of subsistence and ecology.[18]

All this goes to show that modern societies (in the broad sense of the word) which lag behind in their development are not the equivalents, but merely the analogues of primitive societies, and that in using the historical comparative method one should be guided by the general principles of drawing conclusions by analogy, with due respect for the usual conditions of enhancing the probability of such conclusions. As is known, an analogy should be based on as many relevant traits as possible. Considering our goals, this means that to reach conclusions about a primitive-historical model A, we should ascertain its similarity with ethnographic model A^1, with which it is being compared in a considerable number of important features revealed archaeologically in the former case, and ethnographically in the latter. The larger this number, the more probable the analogy, and vice versa. If some of the significant features of the models obviously do not coincide, an analogy is rendered invalid. It is important to bear in mind another requirement of increasing the probability of conclusions made by analogy: the feature to be revealed should be linked with other features as closely as possible, and be as closely determined as possible.

So what are the limits, in terms of stages and subjects, of applying the historical comparative method which may also be called 'the method of ethnographic analogues'?

As far as archaeological eras are concerned, this method is now often applied to the late paleolithic, because the material culture of the aborigines of Tasmania and, to some extent, of Australia bears a resemblance to the late paleolithic culture. But for all that, this parallel is disputable since the differences are not less significant. Here we deal with different forms of hunting activity and different levels of settled life, which, even when other essential elements are almost similar, could not but influence the social organisation in the whole. It is no accident that other scholars are trying to reconstruct the social organisation of classical settled hunters and gatherers, who lived in the late paleolithic, by analogy with the communities of settled horticulturists, which, by the way, is also contestable. Perhaps we have no reliable ethnographic analogues of late paleolithic communities at all. But, beginning with the next archaeological epoch, at least when it concerns many regions of the globe, the availability of ethnographic analogues is certain: tools and implements of production, direction and level of economic development, the character of settlements and living quarters, and some other characteristics are identical at the stage of classic mesolithic, on the one hand, and among the wandering tribes of hunters and gatherers of the modern times on the other.

Now, as far as subject matter is concerned, this method is far more effective when applied to socio-economic, rather than to socio-ideological, structures. This is only natural, since the former are more rigidly determined by material elements of production. Thus, the social organisation of wandering hunters and gatherers is, as a rule, of the same type and consists of local groups composed of nuclear families, and kinship links among them may be either matrilineal or patrilineal. Furthermore, the lack of a rigid determination of causal connection in many cultural spheres, revealing merely statistical rather than dynamic regularities, leaves open vast opportunities for the further use of ethnographic analogues. Interesting in this respect are attempts of Soviet and western scientists to outline certain complexes of interrelated socio-cultural structures. Thus Butinov singles out a complex traced in the material on Papuans and characteristic for the neolithic era. In that complex the previously productive economy is combined with the clan form of community and the nuclear form of the family, clan form of kinship and inheritance.[19] Trigger and other 'new archaeology' adherents are evolving the notion of a component (or subsystem) of an interrelated combination of cultural features, which develops in certain ecological conditions.[20] Opportunities, which are evidently fairly large, are offered in this field by mathematical methods of systems analysis.

Since the ethnographic method is restricted by limits of time and of subject matter, the method of survivals is an important supplement to it. It may be extended to all the stages of the history of primitive mankind and is used for the study of super-structural phenomena (i.e. institutions and ideas) to the same extent as for basis phenomena (those pertaining to the economic sphere). This is explained by the fact that super-structural forms have a relative autonomy and the further away these forms appear to be from their socio-economic foundation, the greater the autonomy. True, the method of survivals, like the very notion of survival, has come up against strong criticism in the West, especially from functionalist-ethnographers, and also from some researchers in the Soviet Union.[21] The objections concern, above all, Taylor's comparison of a survival with rudiments in a living organism, the singling out of a survival's discrepancy from a given state of culture as the main trait of that survival; its inexplicability in terms of a given culture. This interpretation of a survival is doubtful indeed: hardly anyone will find such survivals of the past which would not undergo a change through conditions of a later period, and which would not acquire a new content or become the functional elements of the system which has absorbed them. If this is so, the very method of survivals would lose its foundation.

However, another view of the survival is possible: a survival of the past which has retained its old form but acquired a new content. In this case the analysis of the outward specifics alone offers certain opportunities for the ethnographic reconstruction of phenomena belonging to the previous historical epochs. There is the classical example of the custom of avoidance among affines. Radcliffe-Brown seems to be right in saying that, functionally, they prevented quarrels. But this function obviously does not correspond to the very strict form of interdictions which, as was convincingly proved by Taylor, could arise only with a change of customs, in this case the locality of marriage.

The method of survivals is not an easy one, of course, and may open up a possibility of different, and sometimes arbitrary, interpretations. Thus, various researchers associate the customs according to which children are brought up in other families (fosterage), with the echoes of group marriage, or with avunculate, or with the same processes arising during the epoch of class-formation, or with relationships between vassal and suzerain in early feudal society.[22] Of these interpretations, the last two find confirmation in historical-ethnographic material indicating a gradual transformation of given custom in the process of the disintegration of the tribal system and the formation of society. On the other hand, the first two interpretations present a purely logical construction and can hardly be substantiated, since the fosterage custom has not been noted in any of the pristine tribes. Thus, a proper application of the method of survivals for retrospective reconstruction requires a necessary analysis of their firm roots in another stage.

The evaluation of sources, which is the foundation of the history of society, is considerably enlarged by complementing the method of ethnographic analogues with the method of survivals. Thus, although there are no reliable ethnographic analogues for the late paleolithic, a researcher can 'plunge' into that epoch by studying the survivals preserved in the analogues of the subsequent archaeological epochs. An example of this is furnished by the interesting attempts of Yu. I. Semenov to reconstruct the early forms of relations of production, the original localised clan, and the non-local group marriage on the basis of survivals.[23]

There are other, narrower, methods by which ethnographic analogues enter the historical past. Among them is the study of oral traditions, in particular, views of the historical past of the given peoples, i.e. the oral historiography of the aborigines. Soviet and foreign ethnographers alike have devoted special works to the method employed in this kind of research.[24]

I would like to stress here the increasing role played by the elaboration of the ethnographic methods used in the reconstruction of the history of primitive society. As distinct from paleoanthropology and archaeology, with their virtually inexhaustible possibilities of obtaining new factual data by way of excavations, ethnography has, on the whole, exhausted its field resources. The few tribes that have not been studied and now live, according to some sources, in the backwood regions of Australia, New Guinea and Amazonia, are unlikely to add much to the total volume of the information accumulated by ethnography. This also applies to the official and narrative sources containing ethnographic information. In these conditions a primary significance is attached to the further improvement, in keeping with up-to-date demands, of the methods used in the theoretical interpretation of the data which our science possesses today.

It would be a mistake, however, to overestimate the potential of the methods described here for a reliable ethnographic reconstruction of all concrete institutions and forms of the primitive social formation. More often than not, we are compelled to make up for the lack of factual data by hypotheses, and are able to produce judgments with certainty only about the outlines of social development. But hypotheses, and not merely empirical observations, are necessary for the development of theoretical generalisations, and their role in the history of primitive society is no smaller than it is in any other science. As new facts are being accumulated, some hypotheses are inevitably scrapped, as were some of the suppositions by Morgan concerning the early forms of marriage, while others are refined and find a new confirmation, as was the case with his thesis about the emergence of a 'political' society on the basis of the establishment of private ownership, which was specified and developed by the Marxist science. Such a logical process of perfecting scientific knowledge does not detract from the important role of theory and of broad theoretical inquiry. These constitute the only way of getting one's bearings in the vast, and at times controversial, amount of factual data provided by the study of the history of primitive society.

NOTES

1 W. Nippold, *Die Anfange des Eigentums bei den Naturvolkern und die Entstehung des Privateigentums*, The Hague, 1954; 'Uber die Anfange des Staatslebens bei den Naturvolkern', *Zeitschr. f. Ethnologie*, 1956, vol. 18. The latest bulletin on modern Anglo-American and French literature: N.M. Keizerov and G.V. Maltsev, 'Contemporary bourgeois theories of the origin of political power', *Sovietskaia Etnografia*, 1974, no. 6 (in Russian).

2 E. Gellner, 'The Soviet and the savage', *Current Anthropology*, 1975, vol. 16, no. 4, 599.

3 See E.A. Hoebel, *Anthropology: the Study of Man*, New York, 1966. D.S. Marshall, 'General anthropology: strategy of human science', *Current Anthropology*, 1967, vol. 8.

4 N. Oestreich Lurie, 'Ethnohistory: an "ethnological" point of view', *Ethnohistory*, 1966, vol. 13, 1–2. C. Hudson, 'Folk history and ethnohistory', *Ethnohistory*, 1966, vol. 13.

5 K.J. Narr, 'Vorderasien, Nordafrika und Europa', *Abriss der Vorgeschichte*, Munich, S. 5, 1957.

6 See Yu. P. Averkieva, 'Ethnology and cultural (social) anthropology in the West', *Sovietskaia Etnografia*, 1971, no. 5, 15 (in Russian).

7 C. Hudson, 'The historical approach to anthropology', *Handbook of Social and Cultural Anthropology*, Chicago, 1973, p. 112.

8 V.G. Childe, *Social Evolution*, London, 1951. S.J. de Laet, *L'Archaeologie et ses Problèmes*, Berchen-Bruxelles, 1954, p. 138.

9 V.P. Luibin, *The Stone Age in the Territory of the USSR*, Moscow, 1970, p. 40 (in Russian). P.I. Borisovskii, 'The problems of the formation of human society and the archaeological discoveries of the last ten years', in *Lenin's Ideas in the Study of the History of Primitive Society, Slave-Owning Society and Feudalism*, Moscow, 1970, p. 74 (in Russian).

10 Yu.V. Bromley and A.I. Pershits, 'F. Engels and the problems of primitive history', in *The Problems of Ethnography and Anthropology in the Light of the Scholarly Inheritance of F. Engels*, Moscow, 1974, p. 34 (in Russian).

11 L. Binford, 'Methodological considerations of the archaeological use of ethnographic data', in *Man the Hunter*, ed. R.B. Lee and V. DeVore, Chicago, 1968, p. 270.

12 V.R. Kabo, 'The history of primitive society and ethnography: to the problem of the reconstruction of the past on the basis of ethnographic data', in *Hunters, Gatherers, Fishermen*, Leningrad, 1972, p. 61 (in Russian).

13 S.N. Artanovskii, *The Historical Uniqueness of Mankind and the Mutual Influence of Cultures*, Leningrad, 1967, p. 5 (in Russian).

14 A.M. Khazanov, 'The primitive periphery of pre-capitalist societies', in *Primitive Society: Basic Problems of Development*, Moscow, 1975, p. 194 (in Russian).

15 M. Sahlins, *Stone Age Economics*, Chicago-New York, 1972, p. 8.

16 K.C. Chang, 'Major aspects of the interrelationship of archaeology and ethnology: some thoughts on comparative method in cultural anthropology', in *Methodology in Social Research*, New York, 1968, p. 240.

17 M.G. Levin and N.N. Cheboksarov, 'Economic-cultural types and historico-ethnographic regions: towards the formulation of the problem', *Sovietskaia Etnografia*, 1968, no. 2. N.N. Cheboksarov and I.A. Cheboksarova, *Nations, Races, Cultures*, Moscow, 1971, pp. 169ff (both in Russian).

18 J.G. Clark, 'Archaeological theories and interpretation: old world', *Anthropology Today*, Chicago, 1957, p. 335.

19 N.A. Butinov, 'Primitive-communal structure: basic stages and local variations', *Problems in the History of Pre-Capitalist Societies*, vol. 1, Moscow, 1968, p. 155 (in Russian).

20 B. Trigger, *Beyond History: the Methods of Prehistory*, New York, 1968.

21 V.R. Kabo, 'The problem of survivals in ethnography', *Documents of the Eastern Commission of the Geographical Society of the USSR*, Publ. 1(2), Leningrad, 1965; 'The history of primitive society and ethnography', *Hunters, Gatherers, Fishermen*, pp. 56ff (both in Russian).

22 M.M. Kovalevskii, *Law and Custom in the Caucasus*, vol. 1, Moscow, 1890, pp. 14ff. M.O. Kosven, *Ethnography and History of the Caucasus*, 1961, pp. 111ff. A.Ya. Gurevich, *Problems of the Origin of Feudalism in Western Europe*, Moscow, 1970, pp. 79ff. V.K. Gardanov, *Fosterage*, Moscow, 1973 (all in Russian).

23 Yu.I. Semenov, *The Origins of Humanity*, Moscow, 1966; *The Origins of Family and Marriage*, Moscow, 1964 (both in Russian).

24 J. Vansina, *Oral Tradition: a Study of Historical Methodology*, Chicago, 1965. C. Hudson, in *Ethnohistory*, vol. 13. S.M. Abramzon and L.P. Potapov, 'Folk ethnology as one of the sources for the study of ethnic and social history: on the basis of data drawn from Turkic-speaking nomads', *Sovietskaia Etnografia*, 1975, no. 6 (in Russian).

JAMES WOODBURN

Hunters and gatherers today and reconstruction of the past

In the past few years a substantial amount of important new detailed field research has been carried out among contemporary hunting and gathering societies.[1] This is an appropriate time to take stock and to think carefully about what these societies have in common and how they may differ, if at all, from the hunters and gatherers of the past. What inferences, however tentative, can we make about hunters and gatherers of the late pre-neolithic period, the few thousand years before the development of agriculture and pastoralism? Projection backwards seems to me as a social anthropologist to be an enormously difficult task and likely to yield no more than, at best, plausible hypotheses. But it is a pleasure to be asked to make the attempt at a conference with Soviet anthropologists who are, by long tradition, so much more accustomed to think in historical terms than we are.

The major issue I shall discuss is what, if anything, is really distinctive about the economy and social organisation of contemporary hunters and gatherers when compared with other non-literate, non-centralised, non-industrial peoples. In other words, do those societies which by definition share the characteristic that their members obtain their food and other requirements directly from wild, natural sources, also *in consequence* share a particular type of economy? Does direct extraction of material requirements from nature constrain the way in which people work and the way in which the yield of their work is distributed? And does obtaining requirements in this particular manner determine or limit the type of social relationships and social groupings that are established in these societies?

Of course, even if we are able to establish distinctive characteristics of contemporary hunters and gatherers, it does not automatically follow that these are a product of hunting and gathering *per se*, or that they would apply to ancient hunters and gatherers. We would have to pose the following additional supplementary questions:

1. Is what is distinctive a product of the particular environments

(often tropical forest, arid and infertile semi-desert, or arctic wasteland – areas commonly both isolated and relatively unsuitable for agriculture or pastoralism) in which contemporary hunters and gatherers live as compared with the very much wider range of environments used by hunters and gatherers in the pre-neolithic period?

2. Is what is distinctive a product of the contact situation, of the political and economic relationships which exist, and have long existed, between many hunting groups and their non-hunting neighbours?

3. Is what is distinctive a product of a long period of cumulative evolution (or of degeneration or breakdown) *since* the so-called neolithic revolution?

The two most obvious ways of proceeding would be either to aim to select out particular hunting and gathering societies which are claimed to be in some way virgin, uncontaminated by the events of the past ten thousand years, and suitable representative models for true pre-neolithic man; or, alternatively, to try from the start to generalise from a reasonably wide range of studies of contemporary hunters and gatherers without prejudgments about their virginity. I favour this alternative procedure. I do not believe that a hunting and gathering way of life can be instantly created by any set of individuals who choose to start to live by hunting and gathering. The development of the complex knowledge, skills and social relationships necessary to exploit any habitat efficiently by hunting and gathering, while maintaining adequate nutrition and relative stability of population numbers and density, can only be achieved over a time-span of many generations. But it is of no concern to me here to establish whether the ancestors of members of those societies which I shall be discussing have always been hunters and gatherers: provided that they are efficient hunters and gatherers today, whether their ancestors may at some time or other have lived by farming seems to me to be irrelevant. My concern is not with hunters and gatherers as fossils, as survivors miraculously preserving palaeolithic or mesolithic traits into the present, but as the living and efficient practitioners of a mode of subsistence which, if understood, may allow us to make some limited generalisations about others with similar modes of subsistence both in the present and the past.

Until quite recently conventional views of the nature of hunting and gathering societies were based to a remarkable extent on evidence from the Australian Aborigines. Especially in matters relating to kinship and religious organisation, the Australians were usually given pride of place. In the work of Morgan, Durkheim and more recent writers, the kinship and marriage practices of Australian Aborigines were, directly or indirectly, taken to represent archetypal early or elementary forms of social organisation. It became customary until only about ten years ago to think of hunters and gatherers as typically living in exogamous, patrilineal (or, at least, patrilocal) hordes or bands, each of which jointly and exclusively held a clearly defined territory for its members. Recent data have altered the stereotype in two different respects. Hiatt[2] and others have denied the general existence of hordes in Australia and have argued that the socio-economic units of Australian Aborigines were far more flexible in membership and were not restricted to the use of a particular territory.

But a far more fundamental challenge both to the patrilocal band stereotype and to other conventional ideas about hunters and gatherers has come from new data on societies which differ radically from the Australians. These societies are ones in which organisation – not just local organisation – is very flexible and in which individuals are relatively free to select or reject those with whom they are to associate socially – in residence, in the food quest, in trade and exchange, in ritual contexts. In these societies kinship and contract link individuals but constrain them far less than they do in most other societies. People are not heavily dependent on specific other people for access to their basic requirements. In general, food, water, raw materials and other necessities are obtained relatively easily without elaborate and sustained cooperation and with little, if any, competition or conflict over access to resources. Territories, if they are defined at all, do not substantially constrain individual choice of residence or use of resources. Nomadic residential groupings change constantly in size and composition. If lineage, clan or any other type of kinship group is recognised, it may give the individual a sense of identity but provides him with no substantial rights, and burdens him with no substantial duties. The limited material assets which are held are mostly self-acquired and both inheritance and succession are unimportant. But I should say at once that although these societies lack many of the institutions familiar to anthropologists, it would be entirely misleading to see them as being in some way deficient or defective; their social organisation is certainly not anarchic, disordered or lacking in system.

To understand the new data, I think we must make a distinction between two types of economic system – those in which the return for labour (the yield for labour) is delayed and those in which it is, in general, immediate.[3] In the vast majority of human societies, the return on the labour of most people, most of the time, is delayed. Among farmers – ranging from nomadic pastoralists and swidden farmers with a relatively simple technology to the most technologically sophisticated farmers of today – the system of production involves *intrinsic* delay. There is always a period of weeks, months, or even years, between planting and harvesting, or between rearing and milking or killing a domestic animal, in which people apply their labour before a yield becomes available as a reward for their labour. This yield, or some part of it, is then allocated in some way or other to provide for the requirements of the participant or participants. While recognising the immense variety of systems of production and of allocation, it is important not to disregard certain fundamental similarities: the existence of delay imposes basic organisational requirements for a set of ordered, differentiated, jurally defined relationships through which crucial goods and services will be transmitted in a specified and regulated manner.

In which societies is there immediate return on labour? I want to talk here mainly about those hunting and gathering societies in which individuals and groups go out for part of most days to obtain their food and other requirements which are then consumed for the most part on that particular day or casually over the days that follow. Members of such societies avoid long-term commitments in using their labour and they are not concerned to develop stores of food or other possessions; even their tools and weapons and other technical items used in obtaining food and other requirements are, in general, of types which do not involve substantial investment of time. What I want to stress is that both economic systems based on delayed return and systems based on immediate return are common among hunting and gathering societies,[4] but only delayed-return systems occur among farmers.[5] To classify hunting and gathering societies into those with economy and social organisation based on immediate return, and those with economy and social organisation based on delayed return, is surprisingly easy. The polarity is nearly always marked. In each type there are a whole range of phenomena which appear to be closely dependent on each other.[6]

Hunters and gatherers with delayed-return systems

In this category I would include, provisionally, the following:

1. *Part-time hunters*, who also, for at least part of the year, cultivate their own crops or herd their own stock (such as the Sirionó, the Nambikwara, the Lele, the Bisa, the Nyamwezi, the Lapps, the Barasana). Even in those cases in which agriculture occupies a rather small proportion of their time and energy, if it is to be efficiently practised with systematic labour input at appropriate times, then the social organisation will be of the delayed-return type.

2. *Sedentary or semi-sedentary hunters and gatherers* (such as the Haida, the Kwakiutl and the Ainu). A sedentary way of life seems always to involve a measure of property accumulation and storage and some division of fixed resources among the members of the community.

3. *Fishermen who invest*: hunters and gatherers who depend heavily on fishing with boats, or man-made dams, weirs and large-scale fish traps (such as some, at least, of the Eskimo).

4. *Trappers who invest*: hunters and gatherers who make extensive use of pit traps, dead-fall traps, stockades or other traps involving a substantial input of labour. (Contemporary peoples in this category are usually part-time hunters – but many prehistoric hunters and gatherers, some sedentary and some not, fall into this category.)

5. *Beekeepers who invest*: hunters and gatherers who make extensive use of man-made beehives. (Again usually these are part-time hunters. But groups such as the Mountain Dorobo[7] can be included.)

6. *Mounted hunters*: hunters who invest in horses (such as the Plains Indians).

7. *The Australian Aborigines*. In this case alone, I specify only the people without at this stage mentioning any aspect of their mode of subsistence. I will, of course, return to this subject.

The argument is that hunters and gatherers falling into the first six of these roughly defined groupings, are, in terms of both their economy and their social organisation, more like farmers (though useful distinctions can be made between them and farmers) than they are like those hunters and gatherers with systems based on immediate return.

Immediate-return systems

Among hunters and gatherers with economic systems and social organisation based on immediate return I would include, provisionally, the following peoples: the !Kung Bushmen of Botswana and Namibia[8], the Mbuti of Zaire[9], the Hadza of Tanzania[10], the Malapantaram (Hill Pandaram) of South India[11], the Paliyan of South India[12] and probably the Batek Negritos of Malaysia[13]. All these societies are nomadic and positively value movement. They do not accumulate property but consume it, give it away, gamble it away or throw it away. Most of them have knowledge of techniques for storing food but use them only occasionally to prevent food from going rotten rather than to save it for some future occasion. They tend to use portable, utilitarian, easily acquired, replaceable artefacts – made with real skill but without hours of labour – and avoid those which are fixed in one place, heavy, elaborately decorated, require prolonged manufacture, regular maintenance, joint work by several people or any combination of these.[14] The system is one in which people travel light, unencumbered, as they see it, by possessions and by commitments.

Perhaps to illustrate what I mean by immediate return I should quote a trivial but graphic instance described by a colonial administrator travelling among the Hadza in Tanganyika more than fifty years ago. He wrote:

At the end of one of my visits to them I found myself with a live ox, originally intended as bait for a troublesome lion, on my hands. The beast was certain to die, having been for days among the tsetse fly, and as we had meat in abundance I presented it to the Kangeju [Hadza], who had never tasted beef. Although I was leaving them with more game meat than they could possibly consume, including the carcasses of two rhinoceros, they scouted my suggestion that they should keep the ox alive until they actually needed it, and as I started I saw them shooting it with arrows.[15]

The behaviour which surprised the administrator need not surprise us. It is neither aberrant nor irrational but is wholly consistent with Hadza values and Hadza organisation. Encumbrances are unacceptable and people simply do not take on even short-term commitments which might provide a few additional days of desirable food. There is no basis for anyone to take on the work and the responsibility of looking after the animal, the meat of which would by custom be shared by all. Equally, whatever opposition individuals might conceivably have to the policy of immediate slaughter, they would have no basis for intervention to dissuade those who wished to kill the animal at once. I am confident that if a similar incident had occurred during my own field research, the outcome would have been much the same.

The available data on these societies demonstrate quite clearly that we cannot attribute the distinction I am making to simple environmental factors. It is easy to assume from our own sedentary ethnocentric standpoint that people who have the means to be sedentary, will be sedentary, who have the means to store food, will store food, and who have the knowledge and skills to make and accumulate property (for themselves or their group), will do so. None of these groups live in a harsh environment in which, given the knowledge and skills available to them, they have to live in the way they do. None are excluded by the difficulties of their environment or by the limitations of their technology from having a system with the stress on delayed return. (As the argument in the later part of this paper will show, I am not arguing environmental factors are *totally* irrelevant).

Land use by hunters and gatherers is not as different from land use by farmers as might at first appear[16]. Both hunting and gathering and agriculture involve modification of the environment, partly deliberate, partly inadvertent. Nomadic hunters and gatherers always live at very low population densities (usually far less than one person per square mile) and their effect on the environment is accordingly less obvious. It is also less obvious because increase in some wild species of plant or animal and decrease in others is far less visible (and far less readily ascertainable) than the replacement of wild species of plant or animal by domesticated species. Yet the ecological effects of, for example, those hunters and gatherers who systematically use fire to burn the vegetation from very large areas in order to drive game or in order to induce fresh growth of young grass that will attract the game, are very substantial – far more substantial sometimes than the clearance and cultivation of some few acres by the farmer.[17]

All contemporary hunters and gatherers are highly skilled and selective users of their environment: choices are constantly being made about which animals to hunt and which vegetables to gather. These choices have an effect on the future avilability of the resources. It is quite misleading to argue, as some writers do, that the so-called neolithic revolution gave increased control over the environment. What it did was to provide control of a new and different type which permitted a much greater population density. Hunters and gatherers may control their future food supplies by culling game animals selectively, by operating restrictions on hunting which have the effect of providing a close season, by using vegetable sources with discretion and replanting portions of root so that the plants regenerate, by extracting only part of the honey from wild bees' nests so that the sites are not deserted and by many other similar techniques of conservation which suggest that the distinction between hunting and gathering as a system of unplanned extraction, and cultivation as a system of planned production is not valid. Some hunting and gathering techniques – the making of stockades, pit traps, weirs, dams etc. – may even involve more substantial planned capital investment than is usual in simple systems of agriculture not involving irrigation.

The distinction which should be made is between narrowly extractive hunting and gathering – which in its extreme form may involve what amounts to a repudiation of all measures of conservation, of all investment in fixed assets, and of all attempts at planned development of resources – and hunting and gathering with an emphasis on, at least, short-term conservation and resource development which is analogous in many respects to farming.[18] I use the term *repudiation* deliberately. The extractive approach to hunting and gathering is a strategy developed over time usually as an alternative to a conservation approach, and not in ignorance of the possibility of conservation; although I can imagine ecological and other factors which might favour one approach rather than the other, I cannot imagine any environment in which either of the two strategies is impracticable.

A preliminary review of some of the literature suggests the obvious: those who consume most of their food on the day they obtain it and who are unconcerned about storage, also appear to be relatively unconcerned about conservation and about the planned development of their resources. The point can be most conveniently illustrated from my own field research. The Hadza do not replant any part of the roots they dig up; they select the biggest and best game animals to kill – usually the mature males – not because they are males and can be culled without reducing the breeding potential of the herd, but simply because they offer the best immediate return; in harvesting berries, entire branches are often cut from the trees to ease the present problems of picking without regard to future loss of yield; all honey and grubs in wild bees' nests are extracted and more often than not consumed at once,[19] without leaving any of the contents of the nest to encourage the bees to stay.[20] The Hadza constantly set fire to grass and dry scrub in their area. Usually this happens by accident or as a consequence of some children's game. I do not recall anyone expressing anxiety about the effects of bush fires except on rare occasions when they threaten a site where people are camping.[21] Most camp sites are located in rocky areas away from vulnerable areas of dry vegetation.

In societies with systems based on delayed return, for any individual to secure the yield, or some part of the yield, from his labour he depends on others. Usually this dependence (or interdependence) will be manifest in the work process itself where the farmer, for example, will almost invariably pool his labour with others – at least with his wife, and usually during the labour peaks of the agricultural cycle with several others – but, equally important, he depends on cooperation with others for the protection of the growing crops, of his use-rights to the land on which they are growing and of the yield when he obtains and stores it. Societies with systems based on immediate return are potentially free from this dependency. Individuals have much more direct access to their basic subsistence requirements – food, water, raw materials for their tools etc. – without entering into necessary commitments to and dependencies on others. The adult individual is *potentially* autonomous, and it is not, in practice, rare in some of these societies to find individuals living entirely on their own as hermits for long periods. (According to Marshall[22] this does not, however, apply to the !Kung.)

Let me illustrate the access to subsistence requirements enjoyed by the Hadza. Among the Hadza, groups of women go out almost every day with some of the children to gather wild roots and berries. There are no boundaries and they can go wherever they choose. Decisions about where to go and what food to seek are made casually, on an *ad hoc* basis, without systematic planning. Each adult woman collects for herself. Usually, though, especially when roots are being gathered, one or more fires are lit where the work is going on and the women congregate and eat together much of the food they have obtained. This is done in a free and easy way with the various women providing food and each woman not necessarily eating the same food, or even the same amount as she has provided. Children also work, if they choose, and contribute if they choose. Each woman carries her residual food back to camp, though she may well give some away either where the food is obtained or on arrival in camp or, more particularly, when she has cooked the food in camp. But she is under no obligation to provide vegetable food for anyone apart from her small children: even her husband has no clear right to food gathered by his wife. However, anyone who is present when food is being eaten, whether or not it is cooked food, cannot, in practice, be refused.

Men obtain most of their food through their own efforts. Unlike the women, they usually go off into the bush individually. While walking around looking for game animals to hunt or a wild bees' nest to raid, they pick enough berries to satisfy their hunger. If they succeed in obtaining some honey or killing a small animal, it will usually be prepared, cooked and eaten on the spot. Only when the hunter has satisfied his own hunger will he bring the surplus back into camp. My impression is that on the majority of occasions when a man returns to camp, he is empty-handed but his hunger is satisfied. Only when a large animal is killed are there important obligatory sharing rules and what happens then will be discussed later. A crucially important point is that the obligatory sharing rules relate not to basic subsistence but to an eagerly desired increment above basic subsistence. Individuals can and do meet their nutritional requirements easily without entering into dependency on others.

The hunting and gathering techniques of some of the other peoples included in my list as having systems based on immediate return involve less individual activity and more cooperation than in the case of the Hadza. The Mbuti Pygmies apparently gather wild fruits and roots in a manner not very different from the Hadza.[23] But hunting is a cooperative venture: women and children drive game animals, large and small, into a semi-circle of nets set up by the men. The yield is shared out among the various participants as soon as they return to camp.[24] The point that I want to stress here is that this is cooperation of a very specific sort. Within the rather broad limits set by the optimal numbers for an efficient hunt,[25] anyone who is present may participate and is entitled to a proportion of the yield. There is no commitment to participate and no basis for exclusion from participation. Each hunt is complete in itself and participation today apparently carries no obligation to participate tomorrow.

The !Kung Bushmen hunt large game animals in groups usually composed of from two to four or five men. Marshall[26] tells us:

> The composition of the hunting party is not a matter of strict convention or of anxious concern. Whoever the hunters are, the meat is shared and everyone profits. The men are free to organise their hunting parties as they like. No categories of consanguineous kin or affines are prohibited from hunting together, whether or not they have the joking relationship or practice the sitting and speaking avoidances. Men from different bands may hunt together.

Both Mbuti and !Kung cooperation in the hunt is fundamentally different from cooperation in agricultural systems where at least the core members of the productive group are not an *ad hoc* aggregation but are a set of people bound by more enduring ties of kinship or of contract.

In hunting and gathering societies, rules governing the distribution of large game animals commonly differ from rules governing the distribution of other food. Even if the animal has been killed by a single individual hunting entirely on his own and using a personally-owned bow and arrow or other weapon, he will be obliged to share the meat and cannot hoard it for his own use or the use of his own domestic group. Whatever the mode of hunting – whether hunters go out as indi-

viduals or as part of a team – the system of distribution seems uniformly
to require extensive, obligatory sharing. But the type of sharing varies.

Among the Hadza part of the meat is reserved for the initiated men
who eat it in secret. Elaborate sanctions protect their rights. Part of the
remainder is given to the hunter's wife's parents, if they are present,
and the rest is distributed widely among all in the camp. Indeed the
number of people in a camp is affected by this system of distribution:
people – especially good hunters – will not remain for long in a camp
where the number of people is too great for an adequate amount of meat
from each kill to be obtained.[27] I should perhaps stress again that the
camp is an extremely unstable unit: people are constantly moving in
and moving out but all who are present receive meat irrespective of their
relationship to others who are present. The system of distribution
marks out and reinforces the mutual interests firstly of initiated men as
a category and secondly of the members of a camp at any particular
time. It does not mark out and reinforce specific kinship ties (apart from
the tie with parents-in-law which I shall discuss later) or any type of
contractual tie between, say, hunting partners. The individual hunter
surrenders his yield to an *ad hoc* ephemeral group of initiated men and
an equally ephemeral community. His subsequent rights to meat from
other kills are no greater and no less than those of other men, whether
they be hunters or those who choose not to hunt. What I am concerned
to show here is that the system of distribution does not provide for
delayed return. Individual hunters are not able to invest the yield of
their labour in specific social relationships (apart from the relationship
with parents-in-law) in order to establish future claims on those who have
received meat from them.[28] From the limited evidence available, I have not
so far established to my satisfaction the extent to which the same principle
applies in other hunting and gathering societies but, since this is
intended as a paper to provoke discussion rather than as a definitive
statement, I am willing to hazard the guess that in those societies in
which immediate return is stressed, roughly similar arrangements will
apply,[29] while in those societies with delayed return individual hunters
will, in general, surrender their rights to a substantial part of the meat
of animals they have killed to specific individuals on whom they will in
future be able to make enforceable claims which are greater than the
claims they enjoy simply as male members of the same residential
community. Of course, if they are expected to give meat to a particular kinsman, the claims established are likely to be expressed in terms
of the unspecific and long-term moral obligations of kinship. If, on
the other hand, they are expected to give to a contractual partner of
some sort, the claim established is likely to be more specific, more
carefully calculated and probably relatively short-term.

In these societies with systems based on immediate return, the emphasis on generalised mutuality rather than on specific individual
commitments applies not only in meat-sharing contexts but more
generally. Individuals are not bound to others by what can, for con-

venience, be described as load-bearing relationships;[30] relationships do not carry a heavy burden of goods and services transmitted between the participants in recognition of claims or obligations. To avoid misunderstanding I should stress that I am certainly not suggesting that kinship is unimportant in immediate-return systems – only that its significance is different. It is quite usual in immediate-return systems for kinship terms to be very widely used to address and to refer to other members of the community: indeed many of these systems are universal kinship systems in which everyone – or at least everyone within the political community – is able to define a kinship or quasi-kinship tie to everyone else. The kinship metaphor (which, of course, intrinsically suggests connectedness) is an appropriate way of marking out categories of people with whom one has something in common, with whom social relationships are, in principle, amicable, and mutual sharing can occur. However whether or not they are universal in the sense described above, kinship systems in societies with an organisation of immediate-return type are usually, in contrast to delayed-return systems, not elaborately differentiated. The total number of distinct categories of kinsmen (and of affines) is usually very small and often many of the category terms are used self-reciprocally in address. The absence among adult members of the same sex of differential access to resources, to wealth and to knowledge together with the absence of differentiated binding claims and obligations (and of the relations of authority and dependence that are implicit in those particular claims and obligations which are both important and significantly asymmetrical) leaves for kinship in immediate-return systems the role of defining a limited range of variations on the theme of expected mutuality. (I leave aside for the present the variable ways in which marriageable categories are defined in immediate-return systems.) The distinction between these different types of mutuality is often not much stressed and individuals may be able to reclassify their relationships with others casually and opportunistically without evoking disapproval. In some instances classification by kinship is merged with classification by age (as in the Mbuti instance) and by personal name (as in the !Kung instance) which makes application of terms to a wide range of people simpler than it would otherwise be and increases the possibilities for opportunistic classification in terms of whatever type of mutuality seems appropriate at a particular time.

All Hadza treat each other as kin and apply kinship terms to each other; kin expect mutuality from each other and should not be antagonistic but there is no expectation, even in the closest kinship ties, of strong moral commitment. Hadza abandon the seriously ill whether they are their close kin or not. They recognise the obligation to leave the sick person his or her personal possessions and a small supply of food and water but they do not usually accept the commitment to carry the sick and to care for them until they recover.[31] The evidence suggests to me that the strong morally-binding commitment to kin that we find so commonly in societies with delayed return is created by the constant transmission of important goods and services. As between different immediate-return systems, there does seem to be a gradient in the extent to which active mutuality is fostered. Among the !Kung the importance of mutuality is greatly emphasised both in ritual contexts and in ordinary secular life in which the constant and widespread transmission of small gifts and services seems to contribute substantially to amicable social relationships. Marshall brings out well the texture of these relationships. The gifts are simple tokens of generosity and friendly intent. The trivial 'debts' incurred are quite unlike the binding jural obligations of delayed-return systems. And as Marshall says 'no one was dependent upon acquiring objects by gift-giving'.[32]

Systems of immediate return offer to the individual, so long as he retains his health and strength, a rather special type of personal autonomy and security. His lack of dependence on others for access to crucial assets and the ease with which he can segregate himself from all with whom he is in dispute without sacrificing any important interests, greatly reduce the scope for conflict. In contrast, systems based on delayed return offer greater security in sickness and frail old age but involve serious risks of competition and conflict over access to crucial assets and much less personal autonomy.

I have stressed the lack of both individual and joint investment in material assets in societies with immediate-return systems. But what about investment in 'social capital', in culture, in knowledge and skills? How is this acquired, replenished and transmitted from one generation to the next? If inheritance is negligible, if children are not dependent materially on their parents or on other members of the parental generation for long, if parents have little authority and there is little formal instruction by parents in knowledge and skills, how then is cultural continuity maintained? All I can do here in relation to these important issues is to make a few brief comments.

Immediate-return systems are strongly oriented to the present. The almost total absence of strong commitments to specific other people deriving from the past (and similarly of obligations incurred in the present which would require careful planning for future reciprocation) is linked, as I have suggested in an earlier publication, with a lack of concern about the past or the future.[33]

It is also the case that in immediate-return systems people often do not, at least explicitly, seem to value their own culture and institutions very highly and may, indeed, not be accustomed to formulating what their custom is or what it ought to be. Dispute procedures which in other societies often provide an important public platform for the assertion of cultural norms and values, do not usually provide such a platform in these societies.

We have here an apparently unpropitious combination: custom which is not clearly formulated, apparently not very highly valued and where the mechanisms for transmitting it from one generation to the next might seem to be deficient. Yet cultural continuity seems to me to be maintained in these societies without special problems. Claims old and new that these societies may be culturally impoverished and have 'regressed' are often based on curious and misleading conceptions of progress and, even when more satisfactorily formulated, have not so far been supported by convincing evidence and have not taken adequate account of the cultural complexity that has been described by recent fieldworkers. In societies with immediate-return systems, transmission of knowledge and skills within the peer group is often particularly important. Among the Hadza, for example, boys learn their bow-and-arrow hunting knowledge and techniques and their tracking skills mainly informally from other boys only a little older than themselves and this mode of transmission operates effectively in passing on what is certainly complicated and difficult material – more complicated and difficult, I would guess, than the knowledge and skills required by members of many farming societies. If anthropologists still believe that the transmission of knowledge and skills in small-scale societies from one generation to the next depends on the authority of the senior generation over the junior, on the at least partial acceptance by the junior generation of that authority and on ties of binding kinship linking the two generations, then, I think, the evidence from immediate-return systems shows that this view should now be discarded. The authority and the binding kinship which are so characteristic of delayed-return systems are associated with the transmission of exclusively-held rights to important property but are not necessary for the inter-generational transmission of knowledge and skills available either to all members of the community or at least to all members of the same sex or age group.

The point in the discussion has now been reached at which I must come back to the Australian Aborigines and the issue of whether they do, or do not, have a system of delayed return.

Let us start by looking very briefly at some aspects of their culture and social organisation which differ radically from those of immediate-return hunter-gatherers. They have a variety of bounded kinship and other groups, membership of which involves specific, ascriptive entitlements and duties. Interpersonal kinship relationships are very obviously load-bearing: kinsmen recognise a wide variety of specific differentiated rights and obligations to each other and to their various affines. The moral commitment of kin to each other appears, even in ecologically difficult areas, to rule out the abandonment of the sick and the aged. Some kinsmen are dependent on others for access to 'assets' which they need to achieve fully-fledged adult status and those who are dependent are subject to the authority of those on whom they depend. There are conflicts of interest between individuals and between groups over assets and these lead to fighting and accusations of witchcraft and sorcery. The Australians have an elaborate religious life which is controlled by the older men who partially exclude women and younger men from access to secret religious knowledge. Men give and receive women in marriage.

In spite of much local variation in culture and social organisation, these characteristics I have outlined – in general so unlike those of immediate-return systems – appear to be common to all Australian Aborigines. It would be hard to argue that these characteristics, or some of them, are derived in some way from the ecology since Aborigines live, or until recently lived, in a strikingly wide range of different habitats from very fertile areas rich in wild food to some of the most arid and least fertile areas inhabited by human beings anywhere in the world. Are there, then, consistencies in the tools, equipment, techniques and work practices used to obtain food and other necessities, and in the social relations utilised in the food quest, which transcend the variation in habitat? Interestingly enough, there are indeed some consistencies both in the technology and the social relations of production but what is striking is that what is general is relatively simple tools and techniques involving relatively little investment of time and effort (and not *in this respect* dissimilar from the technology of immediate-return hunters and gatherers) together with a rather limited degree of coordination and co-operation in the work of producing the equipment and in the food quest itself (the extent of cooperation appears in general to be no greater than we find among those with an immediate-return system). Moreover the food obtained in hunting and gathering is, in general, obtained and consumed on the same day. So, in what can be generalised about the means of subsistence and the most obvious relationships used in obtaining subsistence, we find little that is coordinate with the elaboration of, and the strength of, Australian interpersonal and group relations. However, there are some rather rare but very interesting local exceptions to the general situation I have described in which there is substantial investment in hunting and gathering technology and delayed return on labour deployed. I shall discuss some of these rather exceptional cases later.

In order to understand Australian systems in general we must broaden the notion of production. In Australia, as in many farming systems, the notions of production and reproduction are linked. All over Australia, irrespective of the local ecology, men consider themselves to be concerned in a long-term productive enterprise in which they assert control over and bring up their daughters (or their sisters, their sisters' daughters or other junior female relatives), negotiate over their marriages and eventually decide when they will marry and who the husbands will be. Men combine with other men in asserting control over the women and in asserting the right to determine their destination in marriage. Men are dependent on their fathers or on their mother's brothers or other senior relatives for help in obtaining wives and await the right in their turn to acquire control over the disposition of their own junior female relatives. I don't think it would be too misleading an analogy, crude though it may appear at first sight, to describe Australians as farmers in disguise who are concerned with farming (and farming out) their women. Of course, in any more detailed discussion it would be essential to discuss the part played by the women themselves. Obviously much the greater part of the work of looking after and bringing up daughters falls on their mothers rather than on their fathers. In some Australian societies women have much influence on the destination of their daughters in marriage. And the brides themselves are not to be treated as no more than mere objects to be manipulated in a game played by their senior male (and female) relatives.

Control over women is also used to convert what would otherwise be only immediate short-term rights in self-acquired and group-acquired foodstuffs and other materials into specific long-term claims. In Australia, it seems to be generally the case that a wife is obliged to go out and gather food for her husband and that a man is obliged to hunt for his father-in-law or for other senior male kin of his wife. My argument, then, is that the Australian system is clearly based on a system of long-term return on labour.

I am not, of course, suggesting that the Australians are in any way unusual except in comparison with other hunters and gatherers who obtain food in a similar way. Many primitive and peasant farmers (who, of course, also have delayed-return systems) can also be said, in a sense, to 'produce' or to 'farm' women.

But my argument does not depend on the analogy I am making and I do not insist on it. The important point, on which I do insist, is that, whether or not Australian men (or men of other societies) can be said in any sense to 'produce' or 'farm' women, they do maintain and transmit long-term rights over their female kin, and traditional Australian social organisation in all its variety is to be seen as centrally and essentially connected with the maintenance, manipulation and transmission of these long-term rights.

Let me now return to two rather interesting local exceptions in which there is evidence of a substantial element of delayed return in the system of food production:

> Contrary to the general idea the main food supply among aborigines, except at certain restricted seasons of the year, is not animal, but vegetable, and in Arnhem Land upwards of sixty food plants are known. Some of these are local and are obtained more or less casually and in small quantity. But a comparatively small number, which constitute staple foods, are gathered in great bulk, which can be measured in tons, and these plants provide as regular a harvest of food as cultivated gardens. In Eastern Arnhem Land the most important of the staple foods are ŋätu, the fruit of a Cycad, ...
>
> The fruit of the Cycad, ŋätu, which was mentioned above, must be soaked for a period of from three to five days to leach out soluble poison which it contains. After this it is ground, moulded into a cake which may weigh several pounds, wrapped in a neat parcel in paperbark, and cooked in hot ashes, when it bears a resemblance

to a very heavy, coarse, unleavened bread. Vast quantities of *ŋätu* are gathered in the course of the year. It has the merit that, unlike most other foods of the aborigines which must be eaten immediately after preparation, it can be kept for some days or weeks. The fact that it is very abundant gives *ŋätu* a special value in native economy, for it enables the women to maintain an adequate food supply on ceremonial occasions when hundreds of people are gathered in one camp for weeks or months at a time, who could not otherwise be supported for such periods on local resources.[34]

This is a particularly interesting instance and one that would be surprising in a system based on immediate return. Thomson mentions the storing of two uncooked plant foods, *Buchanania Muelleri* and *Parinarium Nonda*,[35] but nonetheless it is clear that most sources of food are not stored here or, apparently, elsewhere in Australia.

From a very different part of Australia, South Western Victoria, there is a recently published report of elaborately constructed eel traps:

At the confluence of this creek with the marsh observed an immense piece of ground – trenches and banks resembling the work of civilised man but which on inspection were found to be the work of the aboriginal natives – purpose consisted for catching eels – a specimen of art of the same extent I had not before seen . . . these trenches are hundreds of yards in length – I measured in one place in one continuous triple line for the distance of 500 yards. The triple water course led to other ramified and extensive trenches of a more tortuous form – an area of at least 15 acres was thus traced out. . . . These works must have been executed at great cost of labour. . . . There must have been some thousands of yards of this trenching and banking. The whole of the water from the mountain rivulets is made to pass through this trenching ere it reaches the marsh. . . .[36]

There are other occasional instances in the literature of direct delayed return in the system of food-production and Professor D.J. Mulvaney tells me that there is some additional archaeological evidence. But what is surprising, when the social organisation of Australian Aborigines is compared with that of hunter-gatherers elsewhere, is not that these instances of direct delayed return in food production occur, but that they are so rare. Australian organisation would seem to be particularly well-adapted for the direct use of delayed return in food production.

What can be said with confidence is that the delayed return which operates so generally in the assertion of rights over women in Australia is not to be treated as a product of the relatively rare delayed return operating in the technology and of the social relations of their food and other material production. The developmental scenario which the Australian data suggest is that delayed return operating in the 'production' of women provides, as I have described above, for the conversion of what would otherwise be only immediate short-term rights in self-acquired and group-acquired food into specific long-term claims. And, at the same time, delayed return operating in the 'production' of women facilitates (but, surprisingly, only in a few special cases) the development of food-production systems with a substantial and direct delayed-return ingredient as in the Arnhem Land and S.W. Victoria instances I have described.

Looking again at some immediate-return systems – the Hadza and the !Kung for example – in the light of the Australian data, it becomes clear that, although in both societies (as generally in immediate-return systems) women give themselves in marriage (or at least have a clear and unambiguous right of refusal of any husband chosen for them), nevertheless the bridegroom does take on various long-term economic obligations to his affines.[37] In both societies the relationship to affines can be said to involve a delayed-return element though one that is apparently far less clear and less burdensome for the bridegroom than is usual in Australia. The routes in the difficult transition from immediate to delayed return are likely to be many and varied but one broad highway among them lies, I think, in the intensification of control by men of rights over women who are to be given in marriage.

I should stress that I am not seeking to reduce social organisation in general in hunting and gathering societies to no more than a mere epiphenomenon of technology and the organisation of the work process. What I am saying is simply this: there does appear to be a direct connection between one particular aspect of the work process – its application through time in a systematic way to produce a delayed yield in the form of some recognised asset[38] – and certain specific aspects of social organisation. The connection is this: if there are delayed yields, then there must be organisation having the general characteristics I have outlined to control and apportion these delayed yields. The particular form the organisation will take cannot, however, be predicted nor can one say that the organisation exists in order to control and apportion these assets because, once in existence, the organisation will be used in a variety of ways, which will include the control and apportionment of assets, but which are not otherwise determined by this function. In societies without delayed yields and assets, we do not find delayed-return social organisation.[39]

One task remains to be carried out in this paper: I must attempt to put the material in the paper into a historical framework and, in the process, to answer the questions posed at the beginning of this paper. The bulk of the paper provides the answer to the major issue raised on p. 95. What I see as distinctive about the economy and social organisation of hunters and gatherers should by now be clear.

The first question on pp. 95–6 has been answered in part. Systems of immediate return and systems of delayed return can both occur in any environment. I do not believe that abundance and scarcity of food and other resources are, in themselves, likely to be crucial variables. The

Australian delayed-return system operates in both harsh and fertile areas. However, areas where food storage is easy and obviously desirable – such as the arctic – are likely to favour the development of delayed-return systems; it is, perhaps, also relevant that in the arctic coordinated investment of time and effort in making dwellings and clothing is much more likely since in this climate elaborate and effective dwellings and clothing are so much more necessary. The availability of some prolific valued food or other major resource located at some particular site is likely to favour long-term settlement, together with the development by those who exploit the asset of conservation measures and/or organisational measures to protect the asset from outsiders. The salmon rivers of the north-west coast of North America may fall into this category. Delayed return is probable here. Finally the specialised exploitation of some single resource, and a concentration on this resource to the exclusion of almost all other sources of food, may, even when the resource is not localised, tend to favour delayed-return systems. Specialised reindeer hunters may be an example. The use of a wide range of different resources and the dispersal of those resources so that they cannot readily be controlled or developed exclusively by any individual or group is likely, not to favour immediate return, but to be neutral in relation to the two alternatives.

The answer to the second question on p. 96 is that the contact situation and the political and economic relationships with non-hunting outsiders are relevant. Turnbull[40] and Gardner[41] both discuss societies with systems of immediate return, and attribute the systems directly to the relationships with outsiders. Turnbull, in his discussion of the Mbuti Pygmies, argues that their mobility and flexibility are a means by which they seek to avoid political domination by their agricultural neighbours. Gardner sees the situation more starkly and argues that the immediate-return system of the Paliyan groups which he studied is pathological and the result of breakdown caused by the dominance and exploitation of their predatory peasant neighbours. Both authors are, I think, wrong in treating immediate return as an unusual system which requires special explanation. As the examples I have listed earlier in this paper illustrate, the system is widespread and not all the societies in question suffer from exploitation by neighbours. At the same time I think the idea should be treated seriously and we should consider whether pressure from outsiders is one of the factors which tends, in combination with other factors, to push societies towards immediate-return systems. I think it is plausible to suggest that it is and that in a world consisting exclusively of hunters and gatherers, a higher proportion might have had delayed-return systems. I would add that systems of immediate return seem to be particularly well adapted to change – in habitat, in the food base, in technology and in personnel.

In the final question, I raised the issue of whether what is distinctive about hunters and gatherers is a product of evolution (or degeneration) since the so-called neolithic revolution. In ten or twelve thousand years much can happen, and I feel distinctly uneasy about speculating about such a vast period. What I would say is that the archaeological evidence suggests that most of the basic technical equipment available to modern hunters was already available in the pre-neolithic period. I doubt whether the availability of metal for spear- and arrow-heads has greatly altered hunting techniques or much increased productivity. The use of the horse by the Plains Indians and others was a far more profound change and had a dramatic effect on hunting success and consequently on game populations. The development of arrow and spear poison may have some significance. The earliest record of arrow poison, as far as I am aware from my own limited knowledge, is from a Southern African hunting site of the mid-third millenium B.C.[42] Whenever it was first developed – and it may well long pre-date this finding – I suppose that it would tend to increase yield and to inhibit group hunting and accordingly perhaps lead to various consequential changes in economy and social organisation.[43]

In principle, I can see no reason why modern hunters should be substantially unrepresentative of those in the past. The major difficulty is, I suppose, that our modern sample is small and, given the much greater abundance of hunting societies at that time, I would expect greater diversity in economy and in social organisation than occurs in modern representatives of this way of life.

I should stress, though, that I am not saying that individual groups of hunters are likely to have remained unchanged. It seems plausible to suggest that some modern hunters will have cultivated at some period in their history. Indeed we know this to be the case with some of the Plains Indians. I think it highly probable there will have been occasional changes from delayed-return hunting and gathering to systems of immediate-return hunting and gathering, and vice versa.

The clear archaeological evidence for large trap sites and substantial sedentary communities in the pre-neolithic period is, I think, an unmistakable indication that systems of delayed return existed at that time. Immediate return is a simpler system and one which is more adaptable to climatic and other change: it is likely, in certain circumstances, to have provided advantages then as now, and I would expect that some pre-neolithic societies will have had systems of this sort. Sadly, unlike some cases of delayed return, it probably leaves no distinctive archaeological evidence. Highly mobile groups with simple equipment are as likely to have had systems based on delayed return as on immediate return. Systems of delayed return can hardly have sprung fully fledged into existence and are likely at some stage to have been based on immediate return. There must presumably have been a time when all societies had systems based on immediate return.

I will end with a comment on polarity. Most anthropologists reading this paper will be familiar with Edmund Leach's discussion of hierarchical *gumsa* and egalitarian *gumlao* political systems in Highland Burma. These systems are seen as intrinsically unstable and the societies discussed by Leach oscillate between the two.[44] The modalities that I am describing here are obviously far more stable and contain no obvious internal contradictions to cause a shift in polarity.[45] My suggestion that shifts in polarity can and do occur in both directions is speculative. But whether shifts do or do not occur, the polarity itself is, on the available evidence, a fact. Hunting and gathering societies are not arranged on a continuum but tend to cluster at one or other pole. Within each modality a whole range of aspects of the economy and the social organisation are congruent: I hope to explore further implications of the polarity and the congruence within each polarity in future papers.

Finally let me stress that in making the distinction that I do, the aim is of course not just to construct yet another simple dichotomous classification. Unless the distinction I make allows us not merely to describe *some* of the variability between different hunting and gathering societies, but also to begin to explain it, my approach should not be accepted.

*

I would like to acknowledge very helpful comments on material in this paper from the participants at Burg Wartenstein Seminar No. 70, from members of the Department of Anthropology at Cambridge and from my colleagues and students at the Department of Anthropology, London School of Economics. The material on the Hadza included in this paper was collected during seven periods of field research between 1958 and 1969 and generously funded by the following bodies: The Royal Society; the World Health Organisation; the Wenner-Gren Foundation for Anthropological Research; the East African Institute of Social Research; the Goldsmiths' Company; the Smuts Memorial Fund; the Sir Bartle Frere Fund; the Mary Euphrasia Mosley Fund.

NOTES

1 See, for example: R.B. Lee and I. DeVore (eds), *Man the Hunter*, Chicago, 1968. M.G. Bicchieri (ed.), *Hunters and Gatherers Today*, New York, 1972. A.M. Reshetov (ed.), *Hunters, Gatherers, Fishermen*, Leningrad, 1972 (in Russian).

2 L.R. Hiatt, 'Local organisation among the Australian Aborigines', *Oceania*, 1962, 32.

3 This same distinction is further explored in others of my recent papers including 'Minimal politics: the political organisation of the Hadza of North Tanzania' in *Politics in Leadership: A Comparative Perspective* (ed. P. Cohen and W. Shack), Oxford, 1979, and a paper on Hadza sex roles read initially at a conference of the Association of Social Anthropologists in Swansea in 1977 and presented in revised form at a conference on *Hunting and Gathering Societies* in Paris in 1978. There is some overlap between these papers in the descriptive formulation of the distinction.

4 In an important paper ('On the mode of production of the hunting band', in *French Perspectives in African Studies* (ed. P. Alexandre), London, 1973), Claude Meillassoux has independently developed a similar distinction though he uses it to draw out a contrast between hunters and gatherers and agriculturalists and does not acknowledge that many hunter-gatherers have delayed-return economies. As will be clear from my analy-

sis I do not accept Meillassoux's major claim that 'the mode of exploitation of the land is determinant of the social, political and ideological processes of the hunting band' (ibid., p. 187).

5 Immediate-return systems are found in a few highly restricted and specialised contexts in industrial societies, discussion of which is outside the scope of this paper.

6 Perhaps though I should register a note of caution: this paper is not intended as a definitive statement. It is a preliminary formulation intended to elicit discussion.

7 R. Blackburn, 'A preliminary report of research on the Ogiek tribe of Kenya', *Discussion Paper* no. 1, *Institute for Development Studies, University College, Nairobi,* 1970. R. Blackburn, 'Honey in Okiek personality, culture and society', unpublished PhD thesis, Michigan State University, 1971.

8 R.B. Lee, '!Kung Bushman subsistence: an input-output analysis', in *Environment and Cultural Behavior* (ed. A.P. Vayda), New York, 1969. R.B. Lee, 'The !Kung Bushmen of Botswana', in Bicchieri (ed.), op. cit. R.B. Lee, 'Work effort, group structure and land-use in contemporary hunter-gatherers', in *Man, Settlement and Urbanism* (ed. P.J. Ucko *et al.*), London, 1972. R.B. Lee, 'Male-female residence arrangements and political power in human hunter-gatherers', *Archives of Sexual Behavior,* 1974, 3, 2. R.B. Lee and I. DeVore (eds), *Kalahari Hunter-Gatherers: Studies of the !Kung San and their Neighbors,* Cambridge, Mass., 1976. L. Marshall, 'Marriage among !Kung Bushmen', *Africa,* 1959, XXIX, 4. L. Marshall, !Kung Bushman bands, *Africa,* 1960, XXX, 4. L. Marshall, 'The !Kung Bushmen of the Kalahari Desert', in *Peoples of Africa* (ed. J.L. Gibbs), London, 1965. L. Marshall, 'Sharing, talking and giving: relief of social tensions among !Kung Bushmen', in Lee and DeVore (eds), 1976, op. cit.

9 C.M. Turnbull, 'The Mbuti Pygmies: an ethnographic survey', *Anthropological Papers of the American Museum of Natural History,* 1965, 50, 3. C.M. Turnbull, *Wayward Servants,* London, 1966.

10 J.C. Woodburn, 'An introduction to Hadza ecology', in Lee and DeVore (eds), 1968, op. cit. J.C. Woodburn, 'Stability and flexibility in Hadza residential groupings', in Lee and DeVore (eds), 1968, op. cit. J.C. Woodburn, 'Ecology, nomadic movement and the composition of the local group among hunters and gatherers: an East African example and its implications', in Ucko *et al.* (eds), op. cit.

11 B. Morris, 'An analysis of the economy and social organisation of the Malapantaram, a South Indian hunting and gathering people', unpublished PhD thesis, University of London, 1975. B. Morris, 'Tappers, trappers and the Hill Pandaram (South India)', *Anthropos,* 1977, 72.

12 P.M. Gardner, 'Symmetric respect and memorate knowledge: the structure and ecology of individualistic culture', *Southwestern Journal of Anthropology,* 1966, 22. P.M. Gardner, 'Paliyan social structure', in *Contributions to Anthropology: Band Societies* (ed. D. Damas), *National Museums of Canada Bulletin,* 1969, no. 228, *Anthropological Series* no. 84. P.M. Gardner, 'The Paliyans', in Bicchieri (ed.), op. cit.

13 K.M. Endicott, 'Batek Negrito religion', unpublished PhD thesis, University of Oxford, 1976.

14 Production of artefacts may, however, involve some planning and some assembling of materials which cannot be done on the spur of the moment. For example, a Hadza poisoned arrow is made from a particular kind of wood which grows mainly in one area, a set of vulture wing-feathers, glue made from a bulb to stick down the feathers, a thread made from impala ligament to hold them in place, a metal arrow-head beaten cold from traded iron and arrow-poison made either from the seeds of *Strophanthus eminii* or the sap of *Adenium sp.* None of these raw materials is very difficult to obtain, but obviously to assemble them does require some forethought. See J.C. Woodburn, *Hunters and Gatherers: The Material Culture of the Nomadic Hadza,* London, 1970, pp. 28-31.

15 F.J. Bagshawe, 'The peoples of the Happy Valley (East Africa). The aboriginal races of Kondoa Irangi, part II: the Kangeju', *Journal of the African Society,* 1924-5, XXIV, XCIV, p. 122.

16 Meillassoux's (op. cit., p. 192) interesting application of the distinction between

land as an *instrument of labour* for farmers and a *subject of labour* for hunter-gatherers cannot, I think, be sustained if the cross-cultural evidence for hunter-gatherer land-use is taken into account.

17 As Desmond Clark points out, the recently developed hypothesis that man may have been responsible for the extinction of a number of the earlier Pleistocene faunal species is easier to accept if this was accomplished through the destruction of their habitat and food supply by the continued and uncontrolled use of fire, than if it had been achieved by killing them off by the more conventional use of hand weapons. (J. Desmond Clark, *The Prehistory of Africa*, London, 1970, p. 101.)

18 Conservation is, of course, usually practised in a rather limited way even in most delayed-return economies. While protection of domesticated animals, growing crops and use rights to land are pursued and maintained vigorously and relatively effectively, the long-term conservation of the land over periods of many years to avoid damaging erosion and to maintain fertility is far more rarely a matter of real and active concern even where the necessary knowledge, skills and technology are available. Long-term planned conservation is only likely in conditions of unusual political and economic stability.

19 Sometimes the honey, but not the grubs, is kept for use in trade.

20 Most wild bees' nests are in hollow trees. Access is obtained by cutting a hole large enough to insert one's hand and arm. If, after extracting the contents, a stone or piece of wood is jammed into the hole to block access by creatures larger than bees, in time the bees are likely to return. Hadza will occasionally take the trouble to pick up a stone or piece of wood and to use it for this purpose if one happens to be immediately to hand.

21 In our film about Hadza hunting and gathering, at one point two men, out seeking honey, walk away from a fire they have lit without extinguishing it. I have seen this done so many times by the Hadza that, in making and editing the film, my colleague and I were entirely unaware that their behaviour might strike audiences as unusual. Yet almost every time the film is shown, someone asks why the fire was not extinguished. (J.C. Woodburn and S. Hudson, *The Hadza: The Food Quest of an East African Hunting and Gathering Tribe*, London, 1966 (16mm film).)

22 Marshall, 1976, op. cit., p. 350.

23 Turnbull, 1966, op. cit., pp. 166-8.

24 Ibid., pp. 157-8.

25 Ibid., p. 154.

26 Marshall, 1976, op. cit., p. 357.

27 Woodburn, 1972, op. cit., p. 199.

28 Of course successful hunters who provide meat regularly earn widespread goodwill – one might say they acquire prestige but I think this is perhaps misleading as they enjoy no special standing in the community. The general goodwill they earn, although it, too, can be in a sense 'drawn on', is to be clearly distinguished from the claims established by investing in specific social relationships.

29 In the light of material given by Marshall (1976, op. cit., pp. 357-63) the distinction I am making should be drawn less starkly.

30 I use the term 'load-bearing relationships' for the close kinship and contractual relationships of non-industrial, delayed-return societies to convey in simple terms the point that these relationships, unlike those in immediate-return systems, carry a heavy and specifiable burden of goods and services transmitted between the participants in recognition of claims and obligations and that this set of commitments constitutes an essential, basic, supportive component in the operation of the wider system of social relations and social groups in such societies.

31 I discuss this practice, and the insufficiency of ecological explanations, in J.C. Woodburn, Discussions part IIc in Lee and DeVore (eds) 1968, op. cit., p. 91.

32 Marshall, 1976, op. cit., p. 367.

33 Woodburn, Discussions part IIc in Lee and DeVore (eds) 1968, op. cit., p. 91.

34 D.F. Thomson, *Economic Structure and the Ceremonial Exchange Cycle in Arnhem Land*,

Melbourne, 1949, pp. 21-3.

35 Ibid., pp. 23-4.

36 Material dated July 7th 1841 in G.A. Robinson, Manuscripts and Papers, Port Phillip Protectorate, 1839-49, Mitchell Library, Sydney. Cited in H. Lourandos, 'Aboriginal settlement and land-use in South Western Victoria: a report on current fieldwork', *The Artefact*, 1976, 1 (4), pp. 182-3.

37 Among the Hadza, the main obligation is to the mother-in-law. The father-in-law will only be provided with meat or any other food if he happens to be living in the same camp. Even then the son-in-law makes his own decision about whether or not to go hunting. It is common for fathers-in-law to be given nothing.

38 Work does not produce assets in a mechanical way. To be assets they must be recognised as scarce, as valuable, as controllable and as available for allocation to some people and not to others, or on some occasions and not others. For example, however much work may be put into the rearing of daughters, rights over the sexuality of daughters only become an asset to be allocated by their fathers or other senior male relatives if these men have enough control over their daughters to be able to determine their destination in marriage, or at the very least, to be able to break a marriage if a daughter's husband fails to provide recompense to his wife's senior male relatives for the asset he has received.

39 I would be particularly grateful if any reader of this paper could draw my attention to ethnographic instances which appear to be exceptions to this assertion.

40 Turnbull, 1966, op. cit.

41 Gardner, 1966, 1969 and 1972, op. cit.

42 Clark, op. cit., p. 157.

43 For nearly 20 years I have been trying to interest archaeologists in a systematic search for evidence of use of arrow poison or spear poison in the mesolithic and upper palaeolithic of Europe and in comparable material from elsewhere. For reasons that are not entirely clear to me, not much work seems to have been done so far on this topic. Any references to such work would be much appreciated by the author.

44 E.R. Leach, *Political Systems of Highland Burma*, London, 1954.

45 I take up, and modify, this point in a paper on Hadza sex roles read initially at a conference of the Association of Social Anthropologists in Swansea in 1977 and presented in revised form at a conference on *Hunting and Gathering Societies* in Paris in 1978.

J. GOODY

Thought and writing

In his book *Thought and Language*[1] Vygotsky discussed the two distinct functions of language: external communication with other human beings and secondly, and equally important, the internal manipulation of inner thoughts. I don't wish to enter into any controversy about the relationship between thinking and language, partly because the definitional problems are more to the fore than the evidential ones, and partly because it is enough for my purpose to make the self-evident assumption stressed by Vygotsky that 'speech plays an essential role in the organization of higher psychological functions'.[2] By this assertion he meant that while practical intelligence was clearly to be found in non-linguistic animals and in the pre-speech child, the interweaving of the symbolic (linguistic) and practical (e.g. tool-using) activities of the child were the very essence of complex human behaviour. The most significant moment in the course of a child's intellectual development is when speech and 'activities' converge. From there on speech not only accompanies much of the child's practical activity, but it plays a specific role in carrying it out. Social speech as well as egocentric speech, for example, enables him to plan more effectively. At a later stage the capacity to use language for problem-solving is turned inward, taking on an intrapersonal function in addition to the inter-personal one: 'The history of the process of the internalization of social speech is also the history of the socialization of children's practical intellect'.

So while language is clearly both the result and prerequisite of communication between human beings, it is also critical for human cognitive processes in a more general sense, that is to say, for the internal as well as for the external manipulation of human thoughts. And while particular languages and dialects differ in the kinds of manipulation they encourage and permit, they clearly have an enormous amount in common in promoting classification, storage, organisation, retrieval and planning, not in a Whorfian (cultural) sense, but in a more general (structural and functional) sense.[3] In saying this I would wish to sidestep the Whorf-Chomsky debate concerning the particular or universal character of the relationship between language and ways of thinking, since there are viable alternatives to cultural particularism and genetic universality, and it is to those that Vygotsky points when he insists on the importance of the changes in the mode of communication and of the historical dimension in a more general sense.

If we presume some functional relation between language-using and the higher psychological functions, there is an *a priori* case for assuming that further changes in the mode of communication might affect internal cognitive processes. In terms of the development of human society, and hence of human potentialities as well as achievements, the most important subsequent change is from oral to written language, a shift which of course adds to rather than replaces the cultural equipment available to a society. Moreover, it is an addition in terms of individual as well as historical development; men first learn to hear, then to speak, later to read, finally to write (though in the historical sequence, the hearing and speaking, like the reading and writing, are synchronic). The order is intrinsic in two ways. First, because the perpetuation of a complex human culture depends at every level upon the individual being a receiver before becoming a transmitter, a copyist before being a creator. Once again, we do not need to enter the empiricist-rationalist debate, since an internal structure is obviously required before any message can be received at all, though the important question is the relation of that structure to earlier simpler grammars the child has to operate, and the relation of these to earlier messages. Secondly, because even with the advent of writing it is still in many ways an oral language that one is engaged in writing (though the relationship varies from near identity to extreme diglossia).

Reacting against their nineteenth century predecessors, most linguists in this century have given their exclusive attention to oral language and have tended to treat written language as a purely derivative phenomenon.[4] They have allowed little or no autonomy to the written channel (or register) and hence have tended to discount the possibility of its effect on cognitive processes. Anthropological theory, too, has often accepted the equation 'man = language', but avoided that which runs 'civilisation = writing'; a pervasive relativism blinded many to the possibility that changes in the means of communication subsequent to the adoption of speech may have important implications for the structure of ideas, as well as for the structure of society. Consequently their analyses tend to limit the implications to the most obvious material changes alone – changes that centre around inscribing clay, stone or paper with verbal signs, and their use as a bureaucratic device. Precisely the same tendency results from genetic and other universalisms; the search for a universal grammar, while taking forms that are peculiarly literate, tends to neglect the field of investigation into the differences between the syntactical structures of the written and the oral registers. The assumption of a common deep structure plays down the significance of differences that lie at the level of use rather than usage, of manipulation rather than structure. It is strange that a group of human beings, who probably spend more time reading and writing than they do speaking and listening, have been so oblivious to the social and psychological implications of their craft. Has the inclination towards a mainly 'mentalist' social science, which an attachment to 'individualism' often encourages (so too can an overdose of culturalism), led to a disregard of the 'historical' and 'material' factors that Vygotsky's environment encouraged him to explore? In making this point we should of course acknowledge the work done by the Toronto School, and by those they have influenced in various ways, e.g. Innis, Havelock, Carpenter, McLuhan, Goody, Goody and Watt, Olsen.[5] On the linguistic side, we should also recognise the insistence on writing as a separate channel, a distinct register, another style, in the work of Vachek and of Smith.[6] However, these linguists are mainly interested in problems in the learning of an orthography (in this case, English) or in the teaching of reading. And while they both recognise the independence of the written register (which is not seen simply as a matter of coding and encoding sound), Smith emphasises the lack of difference between the visual and the spoken modes, both referring back to a common deep structure.

The position suggested here is different. However we may visualise the deep structure (and it has been variously and confusingly formulated) we assume that, while the mind is in no sense a *tabula rasa*, its basic processes can and must be influenced by changes in the means of communication. Neither the spoken nor the written language are simply manifestations of some abstract linguistic ability that lies for ever hidden in the depths, unchanging, sempiternal. We accept a 'functional' view of cognitive processes. Changes in the means of communication, changes that are external to the actor at least in the Durkheimian sense, alter the range of possibilities, internal as well as external.

The point can be illustrated by means of what may seem a trivial example. In the train journey from the outskirts to the centre of many capital cities, a considerable number of individuals spend the first half hour of each day engaged in attempting to solve the crossword puzzles that appear in their favourite newspapers. A special kind of ability and motivation is required for such activity, the kind of ability that is summarised in the phrase a 'crossword puzzle mind'. From the standpoint of an immediate calculation of means-ends relationships, such activity is pointless, invented for its own sake, a 'game'. But pointless as it is in the short term, it leads to a heightened consciousness of linguistic usage as well, perhaps, as stimulating an interest in other types of problem-solving. Yet such an activity is entirely dependent upon the existence of writing and indeed appears early on in the history of written cultures. The first crossword has been recorded by Zandee[7] in ancient Egypt, but acrostics, the visual manipulation of linguistic signs, were a common feature of Egyptian texts and form an important element in the Old Testament.[8]

The example of the crossword puzzle is less trivial than it might appear, since the kind of problem-solving it involves comes close to the definition of the cognitive process itself: 'going beyond the information given'[9], 'information, extraction and organisation'.[10] Yet this particular activity might perhaps be regarded as a special cognitive style which, while not absent from oral cultures, is encouraged by literacy in a whole variety of ways. For reading and writing, which are frequently solitary pursuits, seem to stimulate self-reflection, which in turn stimulates certain forms of problem-posing and problem-solving. These forms of activity have an obvious relationship to certain dominant elements in the thought processes of our own society. However, in other situations and in many simpler cultures, problem-solving was perhaps of less importance than problem-avoidance.

The crossword is based on a matrix of columns and rows, the elements of which (letters) add up in various directions. The numerical counterpart is the magic square, which substitutes numbers for letters in a manner common to many cabalastic, astrological and magical works that emanated from the Middle East after the development of writing and which still command a large and enthusiastic following. Substitute words for letters as the elements of the matrix and we get a table, that God-sent instrument of much early written activity, bureaucratic and intellectual, an instrument that is still used by anthropologists, psychologists and seekers after knowledge of all kinds, to organise and formalise their information into classificatory frameworks, systems of verbatim recall and plans for future action. While all writing adds a visuo-spatial dimension to language (which hitherto had only an audio-temporal one), such formalised graphic arrangements provide precise spatial locations for (principally) nouns and numbers. At the same time they not only extract, codify and summarise a great deal of information otherwise embedded in the flux of experience, but they also make it possible to manipulate, re-organise and reformulate this information in a manner that is virtually inconceivable in the purely oral context. It is on this latter point that I want to place the major stress.

The results of this 'external' activity (the making and manipulation of tabulated information) are frequently internalised by being placed in the long term memory, from whence they are retrieved as oral products. Oral arithmetic is of this kind, based as it is upon the multiplication tables universally found on the backs of copy books or exercise books. The table itself as well as its contents are both products of the visual rather than the aural mode, for as an activity multiplication (as distinct from successive addition) seems dependent upon the existence of graphic system, at least beyond the elementary stage. Just as the electronic calculator has made oral multiplication partially obsolete, so the arithmetic table improved upon earlier processes of calculation. In oral society multiplication is virtually non-existent. While addition itself is based upon counting a set of objects themselves or, more abstractly, by direct visual representation (as with the abacus), counting individual items could be replaced by the cognitive process that has been called subitising, a kind of visual estimating of items of six and below, limits that seem to be set by structural features of the human brain.[11]

What is significant about the dominant use of language in early writing systems is that so much of the product displays a very different syntactical structure from speech. Indeed the written register is also, but less radically, to be distinguished from the oral on the level of semantics, stylistics and pragmatics. On the syntactical level, much linguistic usage does not possess a sentence structure, much less the continuous pattern of give-and-take that marks most oral discourse. In some cases the flow of speech may be arrested by the 'reduction to writing'. But in much earlier verse what is reduced is not speech, though it is clearly language. These early written products often consist not of sentences but of separated words, arranged in some kind of list. In Mesopotamia, most of these lists are of a bureaucratic kind, involved in some aspects of the economy or the polity. The same is true of other Mediterranean societies. Remember the excitement provoked by the decipherment of Linear B? But disappointingly to many, the secrets revealed were not earlier versions of Homeric or Hesiodic myth. The secrets unlocked were rather of the order

rams	2
ewes	4
goats	7

Apart from these bureaucratic lists we find a large number of lexical lists of trees, roles, classes of various kinds etc. which possess several characteristics that make them differ from the categories that usually emerge in oral communication: First, they consist of isolated lexemes abstracted from the flow of speech, and indeed from almost any 'context of action' except that of writing itself. Secondly, the lists are formalised versions of classificatory systems that are to some extent implicit in language use, but they go beyond those classificatory systems in important ways that I have tried to indicate elsewhere.[12]

Let us now consider the relation of this argument concerning the role of writing in the development of 'thought' to the evidence from recent linguistic and psycholinguistic work. We shall be concentrating here, not so much on the issues of how far the content and indeed the strategy of communication differs, which we have touched upon in other discussions, but on three central issues that have been of more immediate concern to contributors to these fields: first, the differences between languages that have been written and those that have not, secondly, between the written and oral registers of the same language, and thirdly between the performance of individuals in the written and in the oral registers. The available material on these differences is very limited, mainly because (as I have suggested) the real significance of the problem has not been recognised. Systematic treatment of the difference between those languages that have been written and those that have not is virtually non-existent, although the number of hints, guesses and as-sumptions are legion. The second aspect, the difference between the written and oral registers of the same language, has been the subject of some discussion. One recent contribution by Huddleston [13] compares a rather limited range of material, namely the use of relative clauses, in scientific texts and in the oral discourse of university-educated individuals (see also Quirk; Crystal and Davy[14]). Internal and non-restricted clauses, which represent elaborate interruptions of the flow of speech, are more common in the written texts. So too is the avoidance of the relative pronoun at the end of the sentence, a point which leads Huddleston to comment that 'the influence of the prescriptive gramma-rian is clearly greater in the more carefully constructed written language'.[15] The comment is illuminating for it indicates the connection between the construction of 'grammars' and the existence of the written register, as well as suggesting the feedback of those formalised state-ments of 'rules' on the written, and to a lesser extent, the spoken language (see Bourdieu[16] for his criticism of the notion of 'rule').

Little systematic work has been done on the general problem but it is possible to indicate some of the likely differences between the written and spoken registers, anyway as far as English is concerned. These turn upon:

1. The length of sentences (increasing in writing)
2. Differences in construction, with dependent clauses becoming more frequent than conjunctions
3. Increased nominalisation as against a preference for verbalisation in speech, a process that is connected with abstraction[17]
4 The completion of sentences is more imperative: sentences are rarely left hanging in the air but the written language systematically extracts lexemes (especially nouns) from the context of the sentence, as in a dictionary.
5. Rules are more clearly restraining, e.g. in the matter of split infini-tives in English
6. There is a tendency to use longer words
7. There is greater variety in e.g. the selection of adjectives
8. The order becomes more complex, partly because of the ability to scan backwards as well as forwards (e.g. in written German). As Levin-son points out, sentence complexity is difficult to define and hence there is some inconsistency between this observation and that of Portnoy (below). Both, however, seem to me reconcilable. It is a question of a more adequate definition of the variables.
9. Greater lexical stability

On the third question, concerning the differences in the linguistic behaviour of the same set of individuals, depending upon which register, oral or written, they are using, psycholinguistic studies appear to shed some light on the influence of modes of communication. A recent paper by Portnoy[18] summarises previous investigations as well as analysing the author's own empirical results.

Before discussing these results it is in order to make some general points. First, the samples in these various studies were relatively homogeneous and consisted mainly of well-educated individuals, that is, those possessing great familiarity with the written mode. The exception to both the rule of homogeneity and of advanced education (though see also the study of Bushnell[19]) is the comparative work by Simmons on deaf and hearing children aged eight to fifteen. In other words these investigations did not attempt to assess the influence of differences in literate attainment on oral behaviour. Nevertheless some interesting points emerge on which there is a considerable degree of agreement and which are confirmed by the tests carried out by Portnoy. She found that oral and written samples varied systematically with respect to word diversity and word redundancy; the written samples showed more diversity and the oral more redundancy. Indeed increased word diversity in written samples had earlier been reported by a series of investigators working with college students. As far as the general characteristics of words are concerned, shorter words are generally found in oral discourse, longer ones in written language (Kaump, Green, Devito,[20] but Bushnell[21] found no difference). Sentence characteristics tend to reverse the trend in that the oral sentences were longer, in a sense more complex, and they contained more imperative, interrogative and exclamatory sentences but less declarative ones.

Portnoy also tested for the comprehensibility of the oral and written utterance of a set of individuals. This was done by means of the 'cloze' procedure, which involves the elimination of every fifth word from a passage composed either orally or in writing (other 'cloze' procedures use existing texts). After a certain delay the passages are fed back to the respondents who have provided them, as well as to others. The degree of fit between the later response and the earlier text, assessed both grammatically and semantically, provides a measure of comprehensibility. It turned out that, taking the two samples as a whole, there was no significant difference. However, taking each pair of responses for every respondent, significant differences in comprehensibility were found between the productions of individuals in these two registers and they were therefore grouped into Speakers and Writers. It is the latter who, both in speaking and writing, tend to use longer words; the use of shorter words by the Speakers corresponds to the general tendency of oral communication, where comprehensibility is often a matter of repetition and simplicity.

These consclusions reinforce everyday observation. Writers are not necessarily Speakers, nor Speakers Writers. Indeed, one is struck by the fact that some students who seem inarticulate in seminars may write excellent answers to examinations. Had one been judging from speech alone, the linguistic performance of such students would have been a prime example of Bernstein's 'restricted code', demonstrating their urban working-class origin. But this particular use of language is not simply a matter of a restricted pattern of communication brought about by the intimidating context of the seminar; the same restricted vocabulary, the repetitive use of words and simplified grammar can be observed in relaxed as well as in formal situations. Yet some of these individuals, who displayed a restricted code in speech, employ a very elaborate one in writing.

What does this say about the relationship of speech to writing and of both to language? What does it say about the relationship of class to codes? To take the last point first, while urban working-class speech may be more restricted (on a series of simple criteria such as word diversity) than that of the middle class, this restriction may be connected to two rather contradictory factors. In the first place, it may result from a deliberate restriction on verbal interaction in a group situation where the use of word diversity is held to be fancy, intellectual, unmanly. Communication in an army barracks, for example, may involve the deliberate suppression of diversity, in word, dress and action, and the use of all-purpose adjectives such as 'bloody' which convey little except emphasis; the schoolchild's superlatives do the same job, and one might adapt the phrases of Bernstein and Malinowski to speak of 'a restricted code of emphatic communion'. In the second place, while the content of utterance may restrict the exploitation of linguistic resources, it seems likely, given the evidence quoted earlier, that writing encourages elaboration. Landsberger's comment upon the divergence of written from oral forms in ancient Mesopotamia makes this point quite clearly; the written register systematically prevents 'archaic' forms from sliding into oblivion.

Thus on the one hand we can see Bernstein's restricted code[22] as being a deliberate limitation on the total range of linguistic expression in some contexts (e.g. group conversation) as distinct from its more comprehensive exploitation in others (e.g. the address to the union meeting). The implication is that such a 'code' is not limited to one class nor does it represent the total linguistic behaviour of those who adopt such restrictions. On the other hand, education in literate forms is clearly related to the system of stratification (though by providing a channel of mobility as well as confirming higher status). It could be said that literacy institutionalises a criterion of achievement which appears to (and to some extent does) replace ascription. But in fact, family circumstance plays a notable part in such achievement and hence disguises a certain perpetuation of the *status quo*. The greater elaboration of the written register is likely to affect the oral style of those who spend a high proportion of their time in reading and writing, not only on oratorical occasions but in ordinary discourse as well. On the other hand, performance in these different registers may differ substantially between individuals so that we have to be careful about allocating them to one particular category; it is another matter with their performance in a particular register (or in a particular context). There is one other factor to be taken into account: working-class speech may be restricted by the urban environment and industrial conditions. On the other hand, the limited access to literacy that urban life offers provides an opportunity for the autodidact and the scholarship boy.

This discussion raises a general point about the nature of 'restrictive codes' or non-standard speech. Before typing individuals according to these terms and relating such typing to class, one should bear in mind that individuals are not limited to operating in one such code, and that an individual's performance in the written register may be at odds with his performance in the spoken one. Since in most literate cultures upper speech is closer to the written register, it is plainly more difficult for those accustomed to so-called non-standard English to learn how to read and write. For, contrary to the views of Chomsky and other linguists, the problem of teaching reading is not simply one of 'bringing into consciousness a system that plays a basic role in the spoken language itself';[23] it is a question of learning a variety of language that may be considerably different in significant features from, say, Lowlands Scots or Birmingham English. Such a task is perfectly possible; everyone succeeds at it to some extent. But it has to be recognised that for some groups the process may be quite different from learning to read one's maternal tongue and closer to the task of schoolchildren in West Africa who have to do their lessons in Arabic or English, that is, in non-maternal languages. The reasons why children whose maternal tongue is of limited circulation work in these other languages are similar to those that force English children to learn to read a special type of language, and they are reasons which, given the nature of literate culture, are not easy to set aside.

Bernstein's distinction between 'restricted' and 'elaborated' codes,[24] characterising working-class and middle-class children respectively, is seen by Kay as a matter of the increasing autonomy of the linguistic channel; the 'richer speech style' or code is 'precise and logically explicit'.[25] It is associated with the difference between local and world languages and the mechanisms appear to be increasing specialisation (which involves lexical specialisation) and the introduction of writing. The lexical elaboration of world languages is paralleled by the lexical usage of the middle classes who employ those languages, and has to be contrasted with the languages of local cultures or subordinate classes. Lexical elaboration entails (according to recent theory) grammatical structure, for 'lexical items are inextricably intermeshed in the semantic and transformational structure of language'.[26]

Lexical elaboration is not simply a matter of using more words, but of the nature of the lexical increase was well as the different use of the same words. If lexical elaboration is associated with the increasing autonomy of the linguistic channel, then one of the prime movers in this trend is the use of writing. For written language is partly cut off from the context that face-to-face communication gives to speech, a context that uses multiple channels, not only the purely linguistic one, and which therefore does not have to be so decontextualised, so abstract, so formal, either in content or in form.

But is the difference between lower and upper speech only a matter of the latter having adopted the more autonomous mode? Surely there is also a 'hierarchical backlash' which means that, for example, the adopted or transformed speech of an immigrant community might be less elaborate than their African language, and hence one might possibly talk of actual impoverishment, of underdevelopment (while recognising the problems of measurement and the errors of those who have failed to treat 'dialect' differences in their own right) in a sense more concrete than the notion of relative deprivation would alone suggest. Relative deprivation may actually restrict speech forms.

In discussing the relationship between oral and written behaviour in the same and different individuals belonging to a single 'speech community', it hardly needs saying that oral behaviour is learned earlier and informally, in a family setting, whereas writing is learned later, and usually in the more formal setting of the school; though this is not theoretically necessary, the teaching of reading and writing often involves a more authoritarian situation and set of procedures than the transmission of spoken language. Moreover, while the latter is critical to the human condition, the former is in a sense optional.

I remarked earlier that little systematic work had been done on the first problem area, namely the relationship between oral and written languages (e.g. Hopi and English), as distinct from the difference between written and oral registers of the same language[27] and individual performances in these registers.[28]

A tentative link between the two themes is provided by the work of some writers concerned with problems of orthography, and specifically with the teaching of English both as a foreign language (e.g. Pulgram, Vachek[29]) and to native speakers themselves. The general situation, both empirically and theoretically, has recently been reviewed by Smith[30] who has summarised research and tried to integrate relevant findings with the work of Chomsky and Halle.[31] He starts from an assumption we have been concerned to stress, that writing is not simply a matter of recording sound, that is, speech. In English, he argues, there is a lack of correspondence at the level of spelling; the correspondence is at a 'deeper', 'underlying' level, for 'English orthography is more closely related to underlying aspects of language involving meaning than to the sound pattern of any one dialect'.[32] Looking at evidence from linguists and psychologists (Wardhaugh, Joos, Miller[33]) he sees no evidence of differences in the grammatical structure or lexicon of written and oral registers, only of different proportions of occurrence and degrees of complexity,[34] leading him to conclude that 'Speech and writing are variants or alternative forms of the same language', while rejecting 'the more superficial proposition that writing is speech written down'.

Smith is led by the argument of Chomsky and Halle to state that since English orthography is related to 'an underlying abstract level of language and not to sound', 'differences in spoken dialect should not be relevant to reading'.[35] English orthography is the optimal system for all dialects and it is an 'egregious error to assume that written language is somehow a closer representation of a particular . . . standard dialect than of any other'. In apparent modification of this assertion he notes that if anything, written language should be regarded as 'a dialect in its own right'. If this is so, then surely one dialect can resemble a second more closely than a third, and the dialect of written English is likely to resemble the speech of clerical rather than manual workers, not necessarily because of closeness of representation (it has been argued that classical Chinese never was a spoken language) but because of feedback, syntactical, lexical and stylistic, of the written on the oral register. While Smith recognises the 'independence' of text from utterance, his particular use of the model of deep and surface structure treats the former as a constant (among variable dialects) and as dominating, in a vectorial sense, the surface. This rationalist position, which fails to take account of the historical situation, turns language into an entity of dubious status and fails to allow for any feedback from external changes either over the short or the long term.

The position is not altogether dissimilar from that adopted by liberal-minded psychologists who regard capacities as constant and achievement as the variable. In a general sense this is obviously true. But at another level it distracts from interesting possibilities relating to research and policy. Glick[36] suggests that cognitive processes can be thought of as:

1. the extraction and organisation of empirical information by means of concept behaviour, systems of classification, which are partly dependent upon specific languages, and partly on the world out there (Rosch[37]),
2. the formation of plans for behaviour (Miller, Gallanter and Pibram[38]),
3. the elaboration of more general theories about the world (Werner and Kaplan[39]).

I would suggest that in each of these areas there is substantial if unsystematic evidence to suggest that cognitive processes are affected in important ways by writing, as we have seen in the reference to administrative lists, conceptual listing, the whole development of more regular and systematic observations of the world around us and the incorporation of religious ideas in holy books. For an exception to the general neglect of this topic, see Greenfield.[40]

These brief comments suggest how the material we have examined on the difference between written and oral languages or registers, limited as it is, displays some striking similarities to another difference, which has been talked about in vague cultural terms. This is the difference between what Lévi-Strauss refers to as the domesticated and the savage, what others refer to as primitive and advanced, or simple and complex. Some major differences touched upon in this discussion can reasonably be attributed to the advent of writing and its subsequent developments – the formalisation of discourse, the extension of abstraction, of logic (e.g. the syllogism) and of rationality, not in the sense that philosophers usually mean, but in a more restricted fashion that refers to the analysis of formal propositions in ways that seem to depend upon visual inspection and material manipulation.

The different implications of oral and written communication for cognitive development may also have important physiological correlates, arising out of the hemispheric differences in the brain which influence the processing of sensory material. Laterality studies have shown that the left hemisphere is superior in the recognition of oral materials, while the right is specialised for the recognition of non-verbal shapes, patterns and nonsense figures.[41] The hemispheric preferences for nominal as against physical analysis emerge in a preference for serial as against parallel processing of linguistic stimuli that can be performed either verbally or visuo-spatially.[42] 'The perceptual specialization of the left hemisphere extends to . . . virtually any type of acoustic material with a linguistic referent.'[43] Interestingly the effect increases the more language-like the material. Zurif and Sait[44] 'presented dichotically lists of syllables read as a list and read as a sentence, with proper intonation, and found greater laterality with sentence-like material'.[45] We may note in passing that lateralisation appears to be a specifically human trait (animals are randomly left or right-handed) and probably connected with the development of language; moreover the only demonstrable sex differences in cognitive processes among humans have to do with differences in lateralisation that affect visuo-spatial ordering and verbal ability. The profound social, psychological, and possibly physiological effects of language on cognitive processes need little stressing; that other changes in the system of interpersonal communication may have parallel effects should occasion no surprise.

I want to conclude with a remark on reading rather than writing, for it is of more general relevance, particularly in an era when the printed word supplements the written. Travelling in a commuter train I have had the experience of observing over three-quarters of the individuals present engaged in the same pattern of 'linguistic' communication, with the same set of absent actors, ignoring all those who were physically present. They were reading the one available evening newspaper. This kind of activity involves the shift from the largely interactional, contextual use of language (often with an emphasis on strategies that minimise linguistic elaboration and have immediate reference) to a use that is silent, impersonal and decontextualised (often with an emphasis on maximal elaboration, encouraging self-reflection upon a text rather than participation in an utterance). The full implications of such a shift for cognitive processes have hardly begun to be assessed. Some of the implications are emerging from cross-cultural research in the sphere of education. In the review of psychological work on cognitive development to which I have already referred, Glick acknowledges the need to break down the global variables of schooling. When we do so we find that a good candidate for the effective factor is 'training and reading',[46] where the work of Gibson *et al.*[47] has shown how achievement in this area alters the way in which 'form discriminations' are made, and may increase the relevance of 'form' when there are alternative systems of classification. Another important finding is that of Greenfield *et al.*[48] where the authors argue for the importance of training in the written language to increase the use of the hierarchical devices that a language contains. For writing must take language out of the 'immediate referential context'. Concepts are then more easily manipulated, more easily turned upside down. The individual 'is freed from the immediate contexts of the things thought about.'[49] Here once again, external factors play an important role in internal processes. For example, the particular activity in which my commuters were engaged clearly depended not merely upon writing, but upon the presence of the printing press. In this way the example serves as an illustration of how developments in the technology of the intellect (and specifically in graphic systems) affect cognitive processes. Which is not, of course, to deny that other factors such as class, ideology or position in the sibling group do not also have a part to play in these processes, and it is the attempt to uncover these different influences in social situations that is the task of the social sciences. The decontextualisation, impersonalisation and complexity are to be linked not only with literacy in itself, but with communication in class or caste societies, where the experiential context of speakers and listeners cannot be assumed to be similar, making it necessary for linguistic acts to be made more explicit. Both writing and class are linked to historically specific situations, and seem to have some similar influences upon processes of communication.

*

I am most grateful for the thoughtful comments of Ernest Gellner, Mike Smith and Steve Levinson, as well as for discussions with Penny Brown on the differences in registers. The use of the pair, 'utterance' and 'text', I have borrowed from David Olsen.

My paper is perhaps a curious example of 'western' anthropology, both in its concerns and in its method. I can only say that it emerges from a conception of the interaction of intensive and extensive methods which implies not only the mating of theoretical and empirical enquiry, but also the use of an historical frame of reference as well as a systemic one.

NOTES

1 L.S. Vygotsky, *Thought and Language*, Cambridge, Mass., 1962 (English translation).

2 L.S. Vygotsky, *Mind and Society: The Development of Higher Psychological Processes*, Cambridge, Mass., 1978 (English translation).

3 F.H. Lenneberg, 'Cognition in ethnolinguistics', *Language*, 1953, 29, 463–71, reprinted P.Adams (ed.) *Language in Thinking* (Penguin Modern Psychology Readings), London, 1972.

4 L. Bloomfield, *Language*, New York, 1933.

5 H. Innes, *Empire and Communication*, Oxford, 1950, and *The Bias of Communication*, Toronto, 1951. E.A. Havelock, *Preface to Plato*, Cambridge, Mass., 1963, *Prologue to Greek Literacy*, Cincinnati, 1973, and 'The origins of western literacy', in *Monograph Series*, 1976, no. 14, The Ontario Institute for Studies in Education. E. Carpenter, *Oh, What a Blow that Phantom Gave Me!*, New York, 1973. M. McLuhan, *The Gutenberg Galaxy*, Toronto, 1951. E.A. Havelock, *Preface to Plato*, Cambridge, Mass., 1963, *Prologue to Greek* and I.P. Watt, 'The consequences of literacy', *Comparative Studies in History and Society*, 1977, 5, 304–45. D.R. Olsen, 'From utterance to text', in H. Fisher and R. Diez-Guerrero (eds) *Language and Logic in Personality and Society*, New York, 1976.

6 J. Vachek, *Written Language: General Problems and Problems of English* (Janua Linguarum, Series Critica, 14), The Hague, 1973. F. Smith, 'The relations between the spoken and the written language', in E. and L. Lenneberg, *Foundations of Language*, vol. 2, London, 1975.

7 J. Zandee, 'An Egyptian crossword puzzle', *Ex Oriente Lux*, Leiden, 1966.

8 J.J. Clère, 'Acrostiches et mots croisés des anciens Egyptiens', *Chronique d'Egypte*, 1938, 25, 35–58. A. Demsky, 'A proto-Canaanite abecedary dating from the period of the Judges', 1977 (unpublished).

9 J.S. Bruner, *Beyond the Information Given*, London, 1974.

10 J. Glick, 'Cognitive development in cross-cultural perspective', in F.D. Horowitz (ed.) *Review of Child Development Research*, Chicago, 1975, 4.

11 E.L. Kaufman *et al.* 'The discrimination of visual number', *Am. J. Psych.*, 1949, 62, 498-525. G.A. Miller, 'The magical number seven, plus or minus', *Psychol. Rev.*, 1956, 63, 81-97.

12 J. Goody, *The Domestication of the Savage Mind*, Cambridge, 1977.

13 R.D. Huddleston, *The Sentence in Written English*, Cambridge, 1971.

14 R. Quirk, 'Relative clauses in educated spoken English', in *Essays on the English Language*, London, 1968. D. Crystal and D. Davy, *Investigating English Style*, London, 1969.

15 Huddleston, op. cit., p. 262.

16 P. Bourdieu, *Outline of a Theory of Practice* (translated R. Nice), Cambridge, 1977.

17 G. Fielding and E. Coope, 'Medium of communication, orientation to interaction, and conversational style', paper presented at the Social Psychology Section Conference of the British Psychological Society, 1976. P. Brown and C. Fraser, 'Nominal and verbal language styles' (forthcoming).

18 S. Portnoy, 'A comparison of oral and written behavior', in K. Salzinger and R.S. Feldman (eds) *Studies in Verbal Behaviour*, New York, 1973.

19 P.P. Bushnell, *An Analytic Contrast of Oral with Written English*, Bureau of Publications, Teachers' College, Columbia University, 1930.

20 E.A. Kaump, 'An analysis of the structural differences between oral and written language of 100 secondary school students', unpublished PhD dissertation, University of Wisconsin, 1940. J.R. Green, 'A comparison of oral and written language: a quantitative analysis of the structure and vocabulary of a group of college students', unpublished PhD dissertation, New York University, 1958. J.A. Devito, 'Comprehension factors in oral and written discourse of skilled communicators', *Speech Monographs*, 1965, 32, 124-8.

21 Bushnell, op. cit.

22 B. Bernstein, 'Elaborated and restricted codes: their social origins and some consequences', in J. Gumpertz and D. Hymes (eds), *The Ethnography of Communication, American Anthropologist*, 1964, 66, 6, pt 2.

23 N. Chomsky, 'Phonology and reading', in H. Levin and J.P. Williams (eds), *Basic Studies in Reading*, New York, 1970.

24 Bernstein, op. cit.

25 P. Kay, 'Language evolution and speech style', 1971 (unpublished).

26 Ibid.

27 Huddleston, op. cit.

28 Portnoy, op. cit.

29 E. Pulgram, 'Phoneme and grapheme: a parallel', *Word*, 1951, 7, 15–20, and 'Graphic and phonic systems: figures and signs', *Word*, 1965, 21, 208–24. Vachek, op. cit.

30 Smith, op. cit.

31 N. Chomsky and M. Halle, *The Sound Pattern of English*, New York, 1968.

32 Smith, op. cit., p. 347.

33 R. Wardhaugh, *Reading: A Linguistic Perspective*, New York, 1969. M. Joos, 'The five clocks', *Int. J. Am. Linguistics*, 1962, monograph 28. G.A. Miller, *Language and Communication*, New York, 1951.

34 Smith, op. cit., p. 348.

35 Ibid., p. 352.

36 Glick, op. cit.

37 E. Rosch, 'Human categorisation', in N. Warren (ed.) *Advances in Cross-Cultural Psychology*, vol. 1, London, 1976.

38 G.A. Miller, E. Gallanter, and K. Pibram, *Plans and the Structure of Behavior*, New York, 1960.

39 H. Werner and B. Kaplan, *Symbol Formation*, New York, 1963.

40 P.M. Greenfield, 'Oral or written language: the consequences for cognitive development in Africa, the U. S. and England', *Language and Speech*, 1972, 169–78.

41 M.J. White, 'Laterality differences in perception: a review', *Psychological Bulletin*, 1969, 72, 387–405. G. Cohen, 'Hemispheric differences in serial versus parallel processing', *J. Exp. Psychol.*, 1973, 97, 349–56.

42 Cohen, op. cit., p. 355.

43 M.P. Bryden and F. Allard, 'Dichotic listening and the development of linguistic processes', in M. Kinsbourne (ed.) *Hemispheric Asymmetry of Function*, London, 1974.

44 E.B. Zurif and P.E. Sait, 'The role of syntax in dichotic listening', *Newspsychologia*, 1970, 8, 839-44.

45 Bryden and Allard, op. cit., p. 15.

46 Glick, op.cit., p. 627.

47 E.J. Gibson *et al.* 'A developmental study of the discrimination of letter-like forms', *J. Comp. and Phys. Psych.*, 1962, 55, 897–906.

48 P.M. Greenfield *et al.* 'On culture and equivalence II', in J.S. Bruner *et al.* (eds) *Studies in Cognitive Growth*, New York, 1966.

49 Glick, op. cit., p.634.

LAWRENCE KRADER

The origins of the state among the nomads of Asia

Theory of the state in general

The state is the product of that society which is divided into two classes of people, a class composed of those directly engaged in social production, and a class of those who are not so directly engaged. The social product is conformably divided into two parts, a part which is applied to the reproduction of the direct producers as a social class, and a surplus which is appropriated to the maintenance of the class of those whose relation to production in the society is indirect. The direct producers in the society labour, work and toil both for themselves and for these others, whose relation to social production is either indirect or nonexistent; it is these others that the social surplus supports. The state is the organisation of society for the regulation of the relations both within and between the social classes. Yet the relations of the two social classes to the state differ; it is in the interest of that class in the society which appropriates the social surplus produced that the agencies of the state are active. The class-divided society is composed of the rulers, who have appropriated the social surplus, and the ruled, who are the direct producers in the society. The nature of the class interest and the class oppositions is a matter that must be explored in another context. The relation of the individuals of the ruling class to the interest of this social class and to the state will be considered in the following pages.

The social class of the direct producers has no immediate interest in the formation of the state. On the contrary, as we shall see, this social class maintained a number of archaic collective institutions, which had been evolved long before the formation of the state; these institutions, as gentes, sibs, clans, kin village communities, continued in being among them long after the state was formed as the over-arching power in the society. These institutions of the collectivity had long maintained the functions of keeping the peace, resolving conflicts both within and between the clans and villages, attacking and defending in war, and continued to do so after the formation of the state. The agencies of the state, when established, took over these same functions of the administration of justice, conduct of war and diplomacy; at this point the interests of the social classes were divided. The archaic collective institutions had formerly resolved conflicts or maintained the peace internally in the interest of the social whole, in this case the whole community, clan or tribe. The agencies of the state now defended, warred, both in the interest of the state and that of the social whole. It is a double interest, conflicting internally within itself; on the one side it is the interest of the state as the representative of the social class for whom it is organised, on the other the interest of the social whole.

The state is formed by and out of the relations of these classes in society to one another and to the social whole, it is formed as the society is divided and internally opposed. It is not formed by the ruling class, for that class has to be established in the first place by the process of social division in order to fulfill its ruling function. It would be an error to take the interest of the ruling class to be the process of formation of the state itself, for that class did not form the state in its own interest. On the contrary, the interest of the ruling class emerged out of the formation of the ruling class. The two are mutually supportive, and reinforce each other, they are not identical. To hold that the ruling class formed the state in its own interest would be a teleological interpretation of history.

It is sometimes held that the state is identical with the society in which it is found; that the state is composed directly of people. This usage merely multiplies terms without necessity. The state is neither identical with human society in general nor with class-divided society, nor with any particular society. The state is the organisation of a particular kind of society, which is class-divided society; the state is in its abstract meaning the principle of that society, though concretely it is the organisation itself. We will consider its further concretion below.

Human societies have been classified according to habitat, whether tropical, desert, temperate or polar; they have been classified according to their mythologies, whether solar or lunar; they have been classified as matriarchal or patriarchal. Here one principle will be applied: human societies are of two types, on the one hand they are non-divided, forming an undifferentiated whole; on the other they are divided into classes according to the relations of the members of the society to social production, to the surounding nature and to the technology of the society. The non-divided, undifferentiated society is the primitive society; the divided society is civilised society, or civil society, it is the society with the state, or political society. The primitive society is founded on the primitive economy, primitive relation to nature and technology, whose principle is that the unit of production coincides with the unit of consumption; the relations of production are such that each works for the other, and this work relation is reciprocated by the other. The civil society is founded on the division and opposition between the social classes, whereby one of these classes labours and works in the society

and on the natural surroundings both for its own maintenance and reproduction as a class; at the same time it labours and works for another
social class, which labour and work is not returned. The latter is the
principle of non-reciprocity; it is the principle of the political as
opposed to primitive economy; it is that on which the state is founded,
and is presupposed by the latter.

The society with the state is a small part of the number of societies of
the human kind, and covers an extremely small time period of the entire
history of humanity. It is a recent phenomenon, perhaps no more than
five thousand years old, but has engulfed virtually all humanity during
the few millennia since its inception. It has come to dominate the history of mankind because no power on earth is comparable to it. There
are those such as David Easton and Radcliffe-Brown who would suppress the idea of the state by the elimination of the term. Their main
reason appears to be that the term has proved too complex. This is the
opposite of the multiplication of terms without necessity: it is its dim-
inution or reduction, likewise without necessity. The fact that a term
has been misused, or that its object is too complex is no reason in itself
to discard it. There have also been those in the past, such as Meyer or
Koppers, and the present, such as Hoebel, who would make the state
identical with human society as a whole. Not only is this the multiplication of terms without necessity, as in the preceding case; it further
confuses the issue of government versus the state. The element of
self-government may be found in any human society, however informal
that government may be. The mode of government of the Eskimos,
Pygmies, Andaman Islanders and Tierra del Fuegians, is informal, dis-
continuous, detectable with difficulty, and scarcely vested, but it is
government, and as such is concerned with the resolution of conflict,
maintenance of internal and external peace of the society and the conduct of war. Government is a function of the state which, however, is
conducted outside the limits of the state. In the matter of justice there is,
moreover, a contradiction between government and the state, for while
justice is concretely the concern of government, it is not concretely the
concern of the state. On the contrary, the state is in the abstract concerned with justice as abstractum.

In the society with the state the distinction between authority and
power is made. Power lies with the organisation of society that has centralised its internal means of regulation and control; authority lies with
the people as a whole. (This distinction was affirmed by Cicero, in
ancient Rome.) The centralisation of the power in turn is negated in
civil society. On the one hand, it is there negated by the division and
opposition between the social classes that make it up; an external
negation. On the other hand, it is internally negated by the opposing interests of the individuals within the ruling class. These latter individuals have in common their private interests as a class, which is their
class interest. These class interests come into conflict with each other.
The means of social regulation by the state are directed to the overcom-

ing of the oppositions between the social classes as they are to the overcoming of the oppositions between the individual interests within the
ruling class. The social organisation is thus made into the political
regulation and control of the society in this case; it is, above all, regulation and control through the political economy. The opposing
interests between and within the classes that make up the society of the
political economy are the subject of the political regulation and control.

The state is the formal organisation of the society of political economy; the informal elements of the organisation of the human being and
human society fall outside its purview. The human individual exists
only as a formal being in relation to the state; the human individual
extrudes the formal being, as the legal person, civil person, *persona civilis*
or *moralis, Rechtsperson*, etc. to meet the relation required of and to the
state. The human society extrudes the formal side of its organisation as
the state to define and relate to the legal or civil personality of the individual human being.

The state is the formal organisation of class-composed and class-
opposed human society. On the one hand, we have seen that it is the
abstract principle of this formal organisation, whether it be the society of
the asiatic, slave or servile modes of production, or that of the modern
society of production of capital. On the other hand, the state is concre-
tised in particular states, ancient and modern.

The state in nomadic society

The nomadic societies of central and middle Asia developed the state,
both in its abstract and concrete forms, in the course of their history
over the past three millennia. The states of these nomads first appeared
during the first millennium prior to the modern era on the margins of
the history and territory of the argricultural peoples of China, India,
Persia. It is sometimes maintained that the Turks, Mongols and other
nomads of inland Asia had not developed the state. That they had developed the state a thousand or more years after the agricultural peoples
had done so is clear; that they had developed the state in relation to,
and in opposition to the state formation of the agricultural peoples no
less so. But this is not to say that the nomads developed no state at all.
On the contrary, they developed the state, at first as a marginal and
emergent historical phenomenon in Eurasia and Africa, later as a fully-
fledged element of the history of these regions of the world.

In order to comprehend the place of the nomads in world history, it is
first necessary to grasp the division of labour in society between nomads
and agricultural peoples, which will be here set forth in the light of the
history of East and Central Asia. The nomads of Central Asia make their
historical appearance in the confederation of the Hsien Pi during the
latter part of the first millennium before the modern era, in conflicts
with the Chinese of the early Ch'in dynasty. The records from the

annals of this early Chinese dynasty mention briefly their relations with the nomads. At a later time, during the course of the first millennium of the present era, the relations were made firm, were deepened and extended between the Chinese on the one side, the Turks, Mongols, and Manchus on the other. With the subsequent development of writing among the latter, we have come to have not only the viewpoint of the ruling class of the Chinese but also that of the nomads. The Tatars are social groups which comprise the Altaic language community. Among them are the Uygurs, Kök Turks (Blue Turks), Orkhon and Yenisey Turks, T'o Pa, T'u-chüeh, Yüeh-chih, Kyrgyz, Jou-Jan (Juan-Juan?), Mongols proper, Naiman, Kereit, Kara Kitan, Pohai, Chin, Liao, Manchus. They were commonly termed Tatars singly or collectively. The Hsien Pi were perhaps a confederation of the ancestors of some of these, together with non-Altaic speakers whose descendants live in Siberia, or lived there.

The inhabitants of the Mongol steppes during the past two millennia have been sometimes Turks, sometimes Mongols. Their main economic basis has been pastoral nomadism. It is sometimes claimed that they also practiced agriculture. It is difficult to deny this, but that is not the point. The inhabitants of Mongolia, such as have been already mentioned, were mainly pastoralists, supplementing their subsistence by a minor amount of agriculture, and by exchanging their pastoral (also hunting and gathering) products with the products of their agricultural neighbours. The forces that held the Tatars to their major economic concern, pastoralism, were both internal and external. The internal force was the weight of tradition, or customary practice; the external was the weight of the production by the agricultural neighbours and the exchanges with them. The transcontinental network of exchanges held both sets of practices in place.

Behind and underlying this exchange network lies a vast system of the division of labour in society in Asia, such as is comprehended with difficulty within European history, extending quantitatively and qualitatively beyond European historical experience and categories of history. The nomads of Asia lived and still live in tents, being without fixed abode, breeding domesticated livestock in herds, primarily sheep, goats, cattle, horses and camels, and moving from one pasture to the next, according to the season, with them. They exchanged the surplus products of their nomadic life with those of the agricultural peoples: livestock on the hoof and its products – wool, peltries, leather, felt – for agricultural products. The Chinese exchanged their products, such as rice, tea and cotton, to meet the wants of the nomads. The nomads met the wants of the Chinese, providing sheep flesh for their diet, cavalry for the armies, post horses, ceremonial steeds and transport camels.

In other parts of Eurasia there is a division of labour within the village, or within the producing unit, whether the country, province, or the nation as a whole, whereby the exchange of pastoral for cultural products is carried out. In North China and neighbouring Central Asia, however, there has been a great specialisation of social production on either side of the Great Wall of China, whereby the nomadic Turks and Mongols have had a major concern with stockbreeding, and but a minor concern with agriculture, and the Chinese, predominantly agricultural, devoted only a small part of their social labour and land to cattle, camel, sheep or horse raising. Each side was dependent to this degree on the exchange of products.

The agricultural production is intensive, the pastoral extensive. The herds of the nomads extend over vast areas, the agricultural production by comparison is concentrated. In consequence, the same number of people live by the pastoral production in a territory which is one hundred times greater in extent than that of the agriculturalists. The nomadic peoples of Turkestan, in Middle and West Asia, have a pattern that is neither as extremely specialised as the pastoralism of Mongolia nor as diversified as the European. The traditonal European rural economy was maintained by agricultural and animal husbandry practices generally within the village, from the Iberian peninsula to the Alps and Russia. The Kazakhs and Uzbeks of Middle Asia, traditionally pastoralists, undertook an appreciable if limited amount of agriculture in their winter camps and pastures. These peoples, together with the neighbouring Kirgiz, and Turkmen, were engaged historically in exchanges of their pastoral product with their agricultural neighbours, just as were the Mongols. The social division of labour in traditional European practice fell thus within the ethnic groups. In West Asia the social division of labour was maintained between the ethnic groups; in East Asia there was developed to a greater extreme the division of labour between these ethnic groups and peoples than in West Asia.

This vast, continent-wide exchange system in Asia was frequently interrupted; it was defective. The institutions which were engaged in the exchanges were not well or efficiently developed, in contrast with the world-wide oil, coal, steel, cotton, rice, meat and wool markets of the modern period of capital production. The interruptions of the great exchanges produced raids and wars, indeed they led to conquest of either side by the other, thence to conquest dynasties which appear from time to time in Chinese history: the T'o-pa Wei, Chin, Liao, Yuan (Mongol) and Ch'ing (Manchu). Attention has frequently been drawn to the wars of conquest between nomadic Tatars and Chinese. This is the abnormal condition. Customarily the Chinese and the nomadic Tatars exchanged surplus products with one another – they did so over a period of thousands of years.

The Turks and Mongols had a class-divided society during the period of our concern. The social class of direct production, the herdsmen and their families, were engaged in part in the production of their own maintenance, and in part in the production of a surplus. A part of this surplus was set aside for the purpose of exchange. These immediate producers (*arat* in Mongol) at the same time produced a surplus which was applied in part to the maintenance, in traditional times, of their ruling class, the Khans, and the military leaders, ministers, courtiers and retinue of the Khans. The ancient and modern Tatars were alike divided into two social classes, the class of herdsmen, who were direct producers in the society, and the class of aristocracy or nobility, for whom a social surplus was produced. We have seen that the social surplus was circulated in two directions: to the neighbouring agricultural peoples and to the ruling class of the Tatars. The product of the exchange from the agricultural side was in turn divided between the common people and the ruling class: silks, jewels and other sumptuary wares were for the use of the ruling class, while the tea, rice, etc. were consumed by both classes in society. Slaves are also found in the the old, or traditional Tatar polity, but their economic importance was minor.

The ancient Hsien Pi had a ruling stratum of princes, or aristocracy. Whether they actually formed a social class or not is difficult to perceive from the written record, which has come to us only from the Chinese side. The chiefs of the Hsien Pi may have been the leaders of a confederation of tribes, or alternatively they may have been an actual ruling class. If the former, then we have a case of an emerging state; if the latter, then the state was already in being. Without stirring up this problem of the early form of the Tatar polity, we note that the state amongst these peoples has undergone its historical development. It is of interest to observe that the state amongst them can be traced from its early beginnings, in the period of its coming into being, through its full historical florescence during the past two thousand years among the Turks, Mongols and Manchus (who were originally nomads of a different type from the others).

The historical records of Blue (Kök) Turks, the Orkhon and Yenisey Turks, the Mongols and the Manchus provide good accounts of the formation of particular states among the nomadic peoples. The best-known of these, in the European accounts, is that of the Mongol empire of the twelfth to fourteenth centuries. The Mongol society at the beginning of this period, in the twelfth century, was already a society divided into hereditary classes. The father of Chingis Khan, Yesügei Bagatur, belonged to the lower stratum of the nobility. Mongol society was divided into social classes of rich and poor, Chingis Khan himself in the course of his life passed from the extreme of poverty to that of wealth. During this period, the classes in Mongol society were stabilised and the oppositions between them were carried forward principally in the same form, with certain modifications to be mentioned below, down to the beginning of the twentieth century.

The Mongol empire in that period was founded on the conquests effected over neighbouring parts of East, South and West Asia and Eastern Europe by the Mongol State. That state was the product of a class-divided society, the classes of the society having mutually-opposed relations to the means of production. On the one side, there were the direct producers in the society: the herding people and their families who had been organised from time immemorial into kin-villages, lineages and clans. The 'Secret History' of the Mongols, a document compiled in the thirteenth century, traces the genealogy of the emperor, Chingis Khan, over twenty-four generations; the Secret History covers the transition from myth to history, and the transition of the Mongols before the formation of the state. The twenty-four generations of the genealogy are not to be taken in the literal sense, in which five centuries of human history are covered, but indicate that the transition had been made by them from a primitive forest people to the pastoral society of the steppes, with a political economy and the state. At the same time, the social organisation of kin-village communities, clans and clan confederations which was maintained by them from the pre-historical period through the empire of Chingis Khan, is recorded in the Secret History; this organisation survived even into the twentieth century, although it has been much disrupted latterly. The folk-historical element of the Secret History is relevant to both the ancient past and to the recent history of the Mongols.

The social class of the Mongol herding families maintained its traditional communal and consanguineal organisation down to the period of state formation among them, and indeed long after the first introduction of the state, after the stabilisation of the relations between the social classes, and indeed even into the period of its disruption of the traditional economy and society in the early twentieth century. The institutions of collective life survived among the clans of herdsmen, the institution of individualism was developed but in a very minor degree among this class.

The ruling class of traditional Mongol society on the contrary was early on formed along the lines of individualism; central to this formation was the figure of the Khan, who personified the state. Chingis Khan gathered about himself in the last decades of the twelfth and the beginning of the thirteenth centuries warriors who had given up their occupation as herdsmen, had been torn forth from their kin-villages. They swore their allegiance to the Khan, served him as soldiers, advisers, ministers, and bore a personal relation to him, which was formalised as the relation of *nöxüt*, 'friends'. Much has been written about the *nöxüt*, retainers of the emperor. It has even been thought that they were feudal lords. That of course they were not. They took their oath as the followers of the Khan, and stood in a relation that was bound to his person. They maintained a private relation as the intimates of the emperor, each side knew the strengths and weaknesses of the other. This is the subjective aspect of their relation. Objectively, their relation was a formal one; it is a relation to the state personified in the Khan, the oath of allegiance was to the personification of the state. The state is the sum of the formal relations of the individual human being, just as it is the sum of the formal relations of the society. For their service to the state, the retinue received great rewards and punishments as great for their disservice, for negligence, misfeasance, malfeasance or non-feasance in office. It is for this public career that they had formally broken with their birthright. They were the broken men on the one side, the men torn forth from the villages on the other.

These retainers were individuals, their individuality was expressed within the framework of the thirteenth-century Mongol society and state. The brief statements of the Secret History recount their names, their characteristic traits, whether bravery or cunning, and the particularities of their relations to the Khan, whether of jealousy, generosity, zealous service, fear or pride. The Secret History is an account in the service of the state, and the individualism is that of the ruling class in that service and selfservice. This contradiction was no more overcome in the history of the particular form of the state among the Mongols than it was in the history of the particular form of the state in nineteenth-century European capitalism. At that later time the ideology of individualism achieved one of its high points of expression in philosophy, romance, poetry and song, again centred on the figure of the emperor (Napoleon and Napoleonism). Yet one of the functions of the state is to contain the extreme forms of individual interests as they conflict with each other within the ruling class.

The formation of the state is therefore asymmetrical in the history of the Mongols, as it is in the history of the state in Europe, Africa, and elsewhere in Asia. On the one hand, the tradition of the collectivity is carried forward in the communal organisation of the villages and clans of the Mongols; this is the characteristic of the herdsmen, labouring among the herds. On the other hand, the individuality is developed among the warriors, the great men, ministers in the service of the prince, as it is among the nobility and the princes themselves.

We have said that a modification was introduced into the Mongol class structure. Following the conversion to Buddhism in the late sixteenth century, many herdsmen entered into the service of the Buddhist lamaseries, serving there not as monks or disciples, but as herdsmen. These families of herders no longer served the traditional princes and clan chiefs, but laboured in the monasteries, tending, herding, milking, shearing wool, making butter, or kumys, etc. Their relations were new, and at the same time traditional. The lamaseries profited from the surplus produced, exchanged and sold by the herdsmen; the herdsmen paid a form of tithe or tribute to the lamaseries, but were freed from imposts to the secular authorities by this means. They were bound to the service of the lamaseries, just as the traditional herding families were bound to the service of the princes, *noyot*. Both forms of labour in the Mongol society were unfree.

The theory has been circulated about that the Mongol *arat* were feudal serfs. This may be true, but if so, then feudalism is given a different interpretation and meaning thereby. The feudalism of the European model, in the middle ages, had a number of characteristic features in common with the Mongol. Each society was divided into classes, each had formed a state. The state sovereignty in each was acknowledged, personified in a ruler, or overlord. Social labour in both cases was unfree. The labouring class in each society produced a surplus that was appropriated by the ruling class, the surplus being in the form of surplus labour or a surplus product which was extracted in kind; money played virtually no role whatsoever in either case. The ruling class in Mongolia as in European feudalism was an aristocracy, the overlord was a prince, king or emperor, frequently elected by his retainers, the broken men in both societies. The overlord had a personal relation to his vassals in the European society, to his retinue in both. They stood, in one sense, in relation to him as clients to patron.

The difference between traditional Mongol and European feudal society and the state is no less profound. All Mongols, commoners and nobility, had a common descent. This was not so in European feudalism, where it was a grave insult to impute common blood to a noble family. The opposition between town and countryside, as between the product of town industry and the product of the land, which was present in European feudalism, was absent in the traditional Mongol economy. In both the traditional Mongol economy and in that of European feudalism a surplus was extracted from the direct producers, as we have seen. That surplus was appropriated, whether in labour or in kind, by the representatives of the ruling class acting at once as landowners and as landlords in feudal Europe. As landowners they extracted the surplus, whether in labour or in kind, as groundrent, in their private capacity; as landlords they extracted the surplus labour or surplus product as tax in their public capacity. Rent and tax coincided in feudal Europe during the middle ages, the relation of landowner and landlord coincided, the public sphere was not distinguished from the private sphere. In traditional Mongolia, the private and public spheres were not at first differentiated, rent and tax coincided, landowner and landlord were one and the same person. But during the nineteenth and twentieth centuries, an important distinction is to be noticed in the traditional herding economy of the Mongols. The secular princes had private herds as opposed to the herds of the state treasure; the relation of the herding families of the commons to the one differed from their relation to the other. Social labour of the Mongol herdsmen in the private capacity, *xamjilga,* in the service of the prince, was distinct from the social labour of the *arat,* which was neither distinctively public nor private. It was, in either case, bound labour, unfree labour.

That which is shared between the Mongol society in its traditional form and European feudal society is not in any way specific to the two of them, but is shared with society in ancient Rome, and with traditional civil society and state in Africa. This has to be resolved if feudalism is to be imputed to the mediaeval Mongol society.

The traditional Mongol nomadic society was a society with a form of political economy, civil society and the state. The economy underwent an inner evolution, particularly with regard to the appropriation and distribution of the surplus produced in the society. That surplus, at first indistinguishably private and public, later came to be differentiated as private on the one hand, public on the other, in one sector of the economy, while at the same time, the identity of the two sides was maintained in another sector of the Mongol economy. It has been sometimes held that the surplus produced in the political economy and society is not different from that produced in the primitive economy and society. Thus, in the latter 'something extra, for a guest, or for a feast' is offered in proof that the surplus is found in both primitive and political economies. That is not relevant to our matter, for in the primitive economy no differentiation is made between production in the family and production in society, just as no differentiation is there made between the division of labour in the family and the division of labour in society. In the political economy, on the contrary, a family may produce and set aside for a guest or a feast, but this surplus is distinct from the production in society of surplus value as surplus labour or product. The distinction between the two forms of surplus was mantained in the traditional Mongol society, just as the division of labour in the family was distinct from the division of labour in society, in the form of the division of labour between the agricultural and pastoral societies. These differentiations were maintained in the traditional Mongol political economy and society, where they continued to exist side by side from the era of the Mongol empire down to the beginning of the twentieth century.

The state among the nomads underwent its inner evolution. Consider the beginnings of the state in the first millennium before the present era among the nomads of Asia: it is barely evolved. The records pertaining to its existence are few, the nomads themselves had no writing, their state was ephemeral, and soon disappeared from view. The state among the later nomads was more stable, and from the beginning of the first millenium of the present period was almost continuously in existence. The history of the state among the nomads is epitomised by the history of their indigenous written records and of their script. (The relation between the formation of the state and the development of the script is not a chance correlation, but a coordination with interacting consequence in the service of the former.) The script and records of the ancient Uygurs, the 'runic' inscriptions of the Orkhon and Yenisey Turks, the writings of the Mongols in the scripts which are derived from the Indo-Tibetan (Phagspa, Indic Devanagari) and from the Uyguric, and the Manchu records in a script derived from the latter, together make up a thesaurus of the activities of the nomadic state in the first and second millennia of the present era. The nomads evolved the state in relation to the more stable, more continuous, more advanced, more ancient and more 'civilised' state of their agricultural neighbours. The two sides together formed a great, barely integrated, defective economic and social unity in the past, which was composed of an interconnected network of economic, political and bellicose relations, between the specialised agricultural and herding peoples. This network spread over the larger parts of East, Central, West and South Asia, determining the formation on the state as abstractum in its several parts, and as concretum in the history of the particular peoples, agricultural on the one side, nomadic on the other. The network was, to begin with, an exchange system of the specialised farming and herding production unities. The social division of labour between them was integrated in a great market and tribute system that spread over the entire continent. The evolution of the market system over the world to the point attained in the present capital market can be traced. The religious, political, etc. systems over Asia reinforced this defective unity of exchange.

Historically, the state was not discovered by the nomads of Central and Middle Asia, nor was it invented by them; the state is no one's discovery or invention. The state is the product of particular social conditions, whereby society, divided into opposed social classes, produces a central organism of political authority within its midst, the entity in its abstract form which arches over the entire society. Concretely and historically, the state controls and regulates the relations between and within the social classes by means of particular agencies. The state is not there for control and regulation; that is a false teleology. The state is the abstract expression of this centralised control and regulation. The means for that control and regulation are the concrete social agencies of extraction of surplus labour and surplus product from the immediate producers in society, the distribution thereof, the collection of rent and tax, juridical administration, military and police actions, the maintenance of records and archives, post and communication at home and abroad. The state in concrete-historical form was developed among agricultural people in the 'old world' and the new, and among nomadic peoples of Eurasia and Africa. The state is older, more stable, associated with more complex development and undertakings among certain agricultural peoples in ancient Egypt, China, or Persia than among nomadic peoples. Yet it is false to consider the latter as the reflex of the former, or as merely occupying the interstices between the agricultural spaces. On the contrary, the state, in its inner nature, form, content and function is the same abstract entity throughout its various concrete-historical changes in external form.

Comment on theory and method

The history of nomadism and of the state among the nomadic societies of Asia is complex, for, just as there are many nomadic societies, so there are many histories, which interact with each other and with the neighbouring agricultural and hunting societies. In order to elucidate the historical process of state origin and formation, one may take as the point of departure those societies wherein the state has not been formed historically by inner moments, or insufficiently formed, e.g. among the

Tuvinians; or one may take as the point of departure those societies in which the state has been formed by inner moments of their history, e.g. the Kök Turks, the Mongols, the Orkhon and Yenisey Turks. It is from the latter history that the analysis made here has taken its point of departure. The formation of the state has been followed from its foundation in history, the formation of the opposed social classes in the nomadic societies. Plainly, one does not start with the history of those nomadic societies in which the state has not been developed, if one proposes to write the history of the formation of the state; on the contrary, classless societies are introduced into the analysis in order to demonstrate the presence or absence of the historical conditions necessary for the phenomenon under investigation.

Next, the hypothesis is sometimes advanced that the state, if formed among nomadic societies, is formed only in conjunction with the formation of the state among the agricultural societies. Such an hypothesis is founded on the theory of diffusionism, which has little to offer to the present stage of the discussion of the theory and history of the state. The state was first formed in Asia, in all probability, among the agricultural peoples. The nomadic societies stand in both direct and indirect relation to this early state formation. However, to limit the discussion to these historical phenomena is to focus the attention only on the surface, the superstructure, and to withdraw it from its proper object, the foundation. The presence of class-divided societies among nomadic Turks and Mongols in ancient and mediaeval times is historically attested; these societies have formed the state among themselves. The historical moments of state formation among them, issuing from the formation and opposition of the social classes there, as between the common herding families on the one hand, and the nobility on the other, are different from the historical moments of state formation among the agricultural Chinese, Persians, or peoples of India. The first thing to be said therefore is that the state in the nomadic societies had a different historical origin and course than that among the agricultural peoples. The second is that all these historical phenomena are variants of a single institution, the state, whose variant forms are in interaction with each other and with the whole.

The theory of the origin and nature of the state in general has been well developed in the nineteenth and twentieth centuries. The historical process of the state formation among the nomads of Middle, Central (Inner) Asia in particular has been brought out by the orientalists, historians and ethnologists in the same time period. Here the general theory and the particular historical process are brought together.

PART III

The distinctiveness of the contemporary world

YU. BROMLEY

The object and the subject-matter of ethnography

As is generally known, two opposed but dialectically related tendencies mark the rapid development of contemporary science. On the one hand there is an increasing specialisation of scientific disciplines in an attempt to deepen the analysis of the area studied; on the other the emergence of new 'border' disciplines, dictated by the need for a comprehensive study of objective reality. The contemporary advance of science as a whole is achieved by the fusion of these contrary trends.

This pattern should be taken into account when outlining the profile of any science, and in particular when considering the question of the profile of contemporary ethnographic investigations. It applies, first of all, to their specialisation, which requires a more specific delimitation of ethnography from contiguous disciplines.

A pre-condition for attaining this end is to delimit the specific object of investigation, and then its subject-matter. It is true that the concepts 'the object' and 'the subject-matter' in scientific knowledge are still defined in diverse ways, and sometimes the two are not differentiated at all. However, these concepts do not coincide, and their confusion makes it rather difficult to delimit those sciences which study one and the same object.

As far as the concept of 'the object' of cognition is concerned, it is best to use it, in our view, to denote that part of objective reality which is the area investigated. When speaking of 'the subject-matter' of knowledge we mean that which constitutes for every given science the aggregate of specific properties and regularities which govern the development of objective reality and which are investigated by that science alone. The singling out of these properties of the investigated area already constitutes a result of the study of it.

Thus the object of investigation in different sciences may be the same, while the subject-matter of investigation is different. For example, in the broad sense of the word, the object of investigation in physics and chemistry is nature as a whole, but the subject-matter of the first science is its physical properties (the physical form of the motion of matter), whereas the subject-matter of the second is its chemical properties (the chemical form of the motion of matter).

At the same time the above-mentioned identification of the object and the subject-matter of investigations can be explained, in our opinion, by the fact that in some cases their delimitation is either very difficult or simply impossible. This applies above all to those sciences which express the existence of different scientific methods of discovering objective reality (for example philosophy, logic, mathematics, statistics, etc.).

The hierarchical structure of objects of investigation should also be taken into account, as it allows us to identify not only the total object of the given science taken as a whole, but also the immediate objects of separate investigations carried out within its framework. Thus if the object of investigation in genetics is the whole organic world, the immediate objects of particular genetic studies may be flies, mice or human beings. The subject-matter in most sciences is stratified, and the presence of different investigation zones in them is so manifest that it does not require any special illustration.

From the moment that ethnography (ethnology) emerged, the most diverse viewpoints concerning the object of its inquiry were aired. Some scientists considered this object to be man, some culture, and others society. But according to the most widespread opinion, it is peoples which form the main object of ethnography.

In our opinion, there ought to be no direct contradiction between the name of a scientific discipline and the name of its object (or subject-matter) of investigation (for example, it is hardly suitable to apply the term zoology to the science studying plants), otherwise serious difficulties will arise in achieving the necessary consensus and the term will not be able to convey meaning and scientific sense. In other words, there should be a certain conformity between the name of a scientific discipline and the objective reality studied by it (identity is, however, not obligatory or even desirable, as for instance in the case of the word 'history').

In our particular case we find that the name of our science – ethnography (or ethnology) – points directly to a definite category of objective reality, the 'ethnos'. As for the second part of the term, even if derived from the ancient Greek 'grapho', it does not necessarily mean that the science in question is merely descriptive. In this connection geography is a good illustration, since it studies also the regularities of certain spheres of nature. The same applies to ethnography which in the USSR combines both descriptive and theoretical levels of investigation. That is why in the USSR ethnography and ethnology are practically synonyms, though traditionally the first is used more often. Hence our understanding of ethnography largely depends on the kind of social community we define by the term 'ethnos'. In ancient Greek this word had approximately ten meanings, including such variations as a people, a tribe, a crowd, a group of people, aliens, a herd, etc. The term 'ethnos' in modern science is not polysemantic to the same extent, but so far there is no consensus on the interpretation both of the term itself and of its main derivatives: 'ethnic communities' and 'ethnic'. All existing interpretations can generally be divided into two main groups. On the one hand, there is the notion that 'ethnos' is 'a comparatively small community with a predominantly archaic character'.[1] On the other hand, this term can be regarded as an equivalent for the word 'people', including not only small communities but also those with millions of members and embracing not only backward peoples but also those in highly developed states.[2]

In Russian ethnography the term 'ethnos' was used from the very beginning to denote 'a people'.[3] This interpretation of the term survives in Soviet ethnography and its use has become particularly widespread in recent decades.[4]

To define the object of ethnographic-ethnological studies by using the term 'ethnos' as meaning 'a people' in a general sense is, in our opinon, perfectly justified. It would hardly be correct to limit the scope of this object to small and backward communities. It is not only comparatively small communities, such as the Hopis, Botocudos, and Aleuts, but also such large 'ethnoses-peoples', as the Russians, the English, the Japanese, the French, etc., which are composed of many millions.

In an effort to determine these common characteristic features of ethnoses-peoples which distinguish them from other human communities we must bear in mind that ethnoses belong to that variety of communities which emerge as a result of the natural-historical process and not as a result of the given people's will. At the same time we must remember that ethnoses are complex formations; each possesses not only a certain internal unity but also specific features which distinguish it from all other formations of the same type. A particular role is played by the ethnic consciousness of the members of an ethnos both through mutual identification and by differentiation as a whole from other similar communities with a 'we-they' antithesis. And when we speak, for example, about the French ethnos-people, it always implies that it has definite features distinguishing it from all other peoples and that this difference is consolidated through everyday ethnic consciousness.

At the same time it would be an oversimplification to confine the essence of ethnos to the ethnic consciousness of its members, which delimits a given ethnos from all other similar communities; underlying this ethnic consciousness are the distinctive features of each ethnos which exist independently and which express its inner integrity. Evidently it is the stable properties of the ethnos that should be considered, since ethnoses-peoples as a rule continue to exist over many, many centuries. But what are the spheres of the objective existence of these properties?

At first sight it may seem that these are predominantly the external distinctive peculiarities of physical types of people, i.e., racial features.

However, in reality racial features do not as a rule play any essential ethnic-differentiating role. This is due not only to the fact that 'pure', racially unmixed, peoples do not exist, but also to the fact that there are no clear-cut anthropological boundaries between contiguous ethnoses-peoples belonging to one of the great races. That is why the attempts to determine a people's ethnic identity on the basis of external physical-anthropological features are usually of a very indefinite character. This also explains the fact that cases where racial features act as the main ethnic indicators are rather exceptional. Such cases generally occur when the neighbours of an ethnos belong to other great or small races.

Among all human characteristics the group-specific features of culture, using this word in its broadest sense, are of more significance for ethnic delimitation than physical appearance. By the group-specific features of culture we mean an aggregate of specifically human activity and its results. It is in the very sphere of culture thus interpreted that all the principal distinguishing features of ethnoses-peoples are usually concentrated. It is not by chance that we notice in everyday life such stable components of culture as language, religion, folk art, folklore, customs, rites, norms of behaviour, habits, etc. It is true that for some time now attention has been drawn to the fact that no single cultural component may be regarded as an indispensable ethnic-differentiating indicator. However, it would be incorrect to deny on these grounds that culture has its ethnic functions. It shows merely that no one single specific individual cultural component, but the whole complex of inherent, specific cultural features characterise an ethnos. And if, say, language and ethnos, linguistic and ethnic division, always coincided, then the differentiation of these concepts would be devoid of sense.

Ethnoses differ from each other also in some various psychological particulars, mainly in the nuances and style of expressing psychological traits common to all mankind. These particular features in the aggregate may be designated as the ethnic (national) character.

Ethnic consciousness, i.e. the realisation by members of an ethnos that they belong to it, is an indispensable ethnic feature. It is connected with the ability to separate themselves from other ethnoses and manifests itself first of all in the use of a common name which the ethnos gives to itself (ethnonym).

An important component of ethnic consciousness is the belief in a common origin. Its reality is derived from common historical destinies of ethnos members throughout the whole period of its existence.

Common characteristics of culture and psychology, ethnic consciousness and an ethnonym may be regarded in our opinion as ethnic features proper. To a greater or lesser extent the members of every ethnos necessarily possess such features, irrespective of whether they live within a compact area or are dispersed (for example, the Armenians of the USSR, Syria and the USA.).

Accordingly, an ethnic community proper or ethnos in the general sense of the word may be defined as an historically formed aggregate of people who share relatively stable specific features of culture (including language) and psychology, an awareness of their unity and their difference from other similar groups, and an ethnonym which they have given themselves. We propose to use the term 'ethnicos' to denote the ethnos in this general sense. But ethnicos is not an isolated phenomenon. In reality it has no existence apart from social institutions proper at various levels (from family to state). It is necessary to note the conventional delimitation of ethnic phenomena proper and social phenomena proper; by the latter we understand essentially class and professional relations and corresponding institutions. The 'social' in the richer sense of the word, of course, includes the 'ethnic' and, consequently, ethnoses themselves are social phenomena. Often the main part of a given ethnicos is contained within the boundaries of a single state (a social organism). In such cases we deal with special formations which we propose to call 'ethnosocial organisms', (abbreviated *ESO*). Such formations, together with ethnic (cultural) unity usually possess territorial, economic, social and political unity (that is, so to say, the maximal variant).

But the main components of the ethnosocial organism are undoubtedly on the one hand ethnic, and on the other socio-economic factors.[5] Socio-economic factors which form the basis of all social phenomena, including ethnic phenomena, are more flexible than the latter. It is this relative conservatism and a certain independence of strictly ethnic features that make it possible for one and the same ethnicos (in reference to its ethnic parameters) to continue its existence during several socio-economic formations. For example the Ukrainian ethnicos has existed under feudalism, capitalism and socialism.

But an ethnosocial organism is another matter. It belongs to a definite socio-economic formation which unavoidably gives it a specific character. It is this fact that essentially underlies the way ethnic communities can be distinguished by type according to the stages of the historical evolution of society. Examples of this are the tribe, the nationality (*narodnost*), the bourgeois and the socialist nation, which are terms used in Soviet social scientific literature. The first of such types of community is regarded as the main type at the stage of primitive society; the second is typical for the slave-owning and feudal periods; the term 'nation' is used to denote only the *ESO* of capitalist and socialist societies. In contrast to the *ESO*, the nation, the remaining ethnicoses of capitalist and socialist societies (and sometimes even of pre-capitalist societies) are generally called 'nationalities' (*natsionalnost*).

Such a concept of ethnoses as the main objects of study by ethnography (ethnology) does not, however, rule out disagreement on the definition of its subject-matter. This manifested itself vividly in the oped, whether small or large, which existed in the past and which still exist are encompassed by the scope of the ethnographer's scientific interests.

The idea that all ethnoses-peoples form the main object of ethnography (ethnology) does not, however, rule out disagreement on the definition of its subject-matter. This manifested itself vividly in the formative period of Soviet ethnographical science. At that time there was a tendency, on the one hand, to confine ethnography to studying only archaic 'survival' phenomena and, on the other hand, to consider ethnography, or rather ethnology, as a super-discipline claiming to study practically all the components of social life. Such disagreement in determining the subject-matter of ethnography still to some extent persists. It is evident, however, that the first of the above-mentioned tendencies implies the notion that the subject-matter of ethnography (ethnology) is a kind of *peau de chagrin* since archaic phenomena are increasingly disappearing from the life of peoples. Despite its apparent breadth, the second tendency affords no better prospect for the science of ethnoses. It creates insuperable difficulties in delimiting the spheres of inquiries of ethnography and those of numerous other scientific disciplines which study different aspects of peoples' lives. Such difficulties have become especially evident in connection with the rapid development of concrete sociological investigations, since these themselves claim to embrace practically all aspects of the everyday life of society.

All these circumstances urgently raise the question of criteria for determining the sphere of the subject-matter of ethnographic (ethnological) science (as well as of socio-cultural anthropology), and delimiting it from contiguous disciplines.

One of the traditional answers to this question in our literature is that ethnography studies 'folk' culture. However, this cannot be regarded as sufficient, and not only because the adjective 'folk' is polysemantic. The main problem is that reference to 'folk' culture inevitably raises a new question; in what way does ethnography differ from such disciplines as the history of folk architecture, the history of folk music, folklore studies, etc.

Sometimes the main specificity of the ethnographic study of culture, as well as that of peoples as a whole, is seen in its method of direct observation. However, it is difficult to accept this viewpoint, too. First, this method is widely used in other disciplines (in folklore art studies, for example). Secondly, ethnography does not confine itself to this method in studying contemporary peoples.

The opinion has been recently expressed that the specific viewpoint of ethnography (ethnology) concerning its subject is determined by its problems.[6] But then the question arises: what are the criteria for singling out these problems? The absence of an answer to this question leaves open the possibility of making arbitrary choices in such problems.

It is generally known that the subject-matter of science cannot be determined arbitrarily and depends, above all, on singling out from the sum total those properties inherent in its object which form the object of investigation by the science in question. Hence the viewpoint is determined not by an arbitrary choice of problems but by the presence in the object of certain specific properties. In our case such an object is the ethnos-people. It is evident therefore that it is among its typological characteristic features that we should look for criteria for determining the subject-matter of ethnography (ethnology).

What features can be considered as such? Doubtless those which can be called ethnic and through which the ethnos may be distinguished from other human communities. On the one hand, these are the features which bring together all the members of the ethnos (intra-ethnic integration), and on the other hand, the features which separate it from other similar communities (inter-ethnic differentiation). As mentioned above, such functions are carried out, together with language, mainly by the components of traditional everyday culture (customs, rituals, folk art, folklore, etc). The specific peculiarities of these components distinguish one ethnos from another.

Accordingly, the criterion for singling out the subject-matter of ethnography (ethnology) should, in our opinion, be an examination of ethnos components through the prism of the ethnic functions carried out by these components. Owing to the greater obviousness of their ethnic-differentiating properties (ethnic specificity), it is precisely these features which serve as a starting-point for singling out the scope of the subject-matter of ethnographic investigations.

But ethnography (ethnology) is called upon to reveal a picture of an ethnos as a whole – not only its ethnic-differentiating features but also those which it shares with other ethnoses. The identification of the specific and the shared is always an indivisible process. That is why a comparative study of ethnos components as the main method of determining its specific features inevitably presupposes also locating those features which it shares with other ethnoses. Some features may turn out to be characteristic of all ethnoses past and present, i.e., to be common to all mankind; other features may turn out to be specific to only some groups of ethnoses and thus these will be specific in their own way.

The main zone of ethnographic (ethnological) investigation is determined through the study of the ethnos and its components which reveals their ethnic-differentiating features. It seems self-evident that given such an approach to the problem the nucleus of ethnography (ethnology) will be the study of that layer of culture, in its broadest meaning, which fulfils ethnic functions, and above all, of traditional, everyday culture.

However, the role of traditional, everyday culture is far from identical at different stages of social development. Moreover, the temporal parameters of traditions are different: in some cases old archaic traditions prevail, and in others new ones are formed.

In pre-class and early class societies culture is co-extensive with its everyday traditional-archaic layer. It is owing to this long-recognised fact that when dealing with backward peoples who have no written language ethnography (ethnology) studies their culture as a whole; ranging from their methods of economic activity to their religious beliefs and language. Moreover, owing to the syncretism of social life, in this case the whole social sphere of their life, a 'socionormative' culture enters the framework of ethnographic studies. The effective monopoly of ethnography in the study of archaic features of economically backward peoples has led to its active participation in the working out of the problems of the primitive society.

However, in our own time scientific and technological revolution and social progress are accompanied by the rapid disappearance of archaic phenomena. Hence one of the most important tasks of ethnographers today and in the near future is to record such archaic phenomena as still exist. The character of these records and their significance largely depend on whether the ethnographer deals with archaic phenomena of backward peoples or with the survivals which still exist in highly industrialised societies. In the first case, data on the archaic components of the life of peoples in some measure throw additional light on the problems of the history of early class and sometimes of pre-class societies. In the case of archaic forms surviving in the everyday life of peoples of highly industrialised countries, the study of these forms frequently makes it possible to get an idea of the everyday life led by such peoples at least a century or more ago. It should be borne in mind, however, that in such cases the survivals of archaic phenomena are being rapidly replaced by professional, urbanised culture. Therefore the problem of recording them acquires great urgency. It is not by chance that ethnographers who study the peoples of highly industrialised countries pay special attention to this aspect. The widespread publication in recent years, in most European countries, of historico-ethnographic atlases, an important way of recording traditional culture, constitutes striking evidence of this.

Though the uncovering of archaic phenomena is very important for ethnography it would be a mistake to devote this discipline wholly to the study of surviving social antiquities.

This concerns especially the ethnoses of highly developed class societies. True, in studying them the aim of investigation remains in the final analysis the same as in studying ethnoses of pre-class and early-class societies, i.e. to shed light on the whole complex of characteristic features of ethnic communities. But such unity of final aim cannot, nevertheless, serve as sufficient grounds for transferring mechanically to the studies of the peoples of developed countries those ideas about the profile of ethnographic science which had been formed in studying peoples without written languages and whose whole life, as mentioned before, is full of archaisms.

It is necessary to take into account the fact that in class socio-economic formations the content of the object of ethnographic investigations changes substantially. It becomes exceedingly complex and many-sided. Certain spheres of social life become greatly insulated as a result of the development of the productive forces. Economic specialisation and differentiation of the spheres of production and consumption occur and this process becomes especially intensive with the rise of capitalism. The social structure becomes more complex. The former syncretism in culture disappears, its components become differentiated. Profound differences appear in the mode of life of classes and social groups, rural and urban inhabitants, between folk and professional culture.

The scientific and technological revolution influences ethnic communities greatly. True, this influence is dual in character; on the one hand, it promotes an equalisation of the cultural levels of ethnic communities, the interpenetration of cultures, their standardisation and unification; on the other, mass media may strengthen ethnic consciousness among the broad masses of the population. And this, in turn, has a reverse influence on intellectual culture, imparting ethnic significance to those of its components which formerly were of little importance in this respect, or even fulfilled no ethnic functions at all. On the whole, as standardised forms of culture spread more widely, the ethnic specificity of contemporary peoples is gradually, as it were, shifting from the sphere of material culture into the sphere of intellectual culture.

The emergence of new traditions, including those in the sphere of everyday culture, should be borne in mind. At the same time, professional activity in the sphere of intellectual culture is playing an ever greater ethnic role in highly developed countries, especially in those cases when its achievements penetrate into the everyday life of people. As a result, ethnic functions are carried out by new, comparatively stable components of intellectual culture rather than by archaic survivals. These new components frequently include elements of old traditions though in modified forms.

All this raises a set of problems for modern ethnography (ethnology) connected with the study of contemporary peoples (including those of industrially developed countries) as a living reality. Naturally, in this case most attention should still be paid to those spheres of a people's life in which its characteristic features manifest themselves most vividly. And this, as already mentioned, mainly concerns the intellectual culture of peoples, their social psychology.

In providing a concrete outline for ethnographic investigations and its prospects, we must not forget that ethnoses are not merely a sum of separate components but constitute integral systems. The necessity for a comprehensive study of these systems has led to the emergence of a series of borderline disciplines linking ethnography with related sciences; ethnic geography, ethnic anthropology, ethno-demography, ethno-linguistics, ethno-sociology, etc. Some of these border disciplines have already existed for some time and have succeeded in more or less proving their significance; others, though they are only now making their first steps, undoubtedly have good prospects.

Ethnoses are dynamic systems. Hence one of the most important tasks of ethnography is to study the changes which take place in them, i.e., the ethnic processes. Though in the past these processes were rather slow, in the end they led to the disappearance of some ethnic units and the emergence of others. It is for this reason in particular that Soviet ethnographers pay considerable attention to the question of the origin of peoples (ethnogenesis) which they study jointly with archaeologists, anthropologists, linguists, etc.

The ethnographic study of modern ethnic processes is of quite a different character. In the course of these processes intensive changes take place in the various components of ethnic communities. Consequently, the scientist studying modern ethnic communities should focus his attention on the changes which occur in their demographic, social, cultural, linguistic and other parameters. The increasing intensification of ethnic processes in the modern world gives special significance to these studies and predetermines their further prospects.

Thus, the concept of ethnography (ethnology) as the science of ethnoses does not encourage pessimism about the progressive disappearance of its own subject-matter. So long as peoples exist, ethnography (ethnology) preserves its object of investigation, and not only as the historic past but also as current reality. But the relative significance of diverse zones in the subject-matter of ethnographic investigations is changing with changes in ethnic specificity. Moreover, in the course of social progress the subject-matter of ethnography is becoming increasingly complex, setting itself ever new areas of inquiry.

NOTES

1 R. Naroll, 'On ethnic unit classification', *Current Anthropology*, 1964, vol. 5, no. 4.

2 F. Barth, *Ethnic Groups and Boundaries*, Bergen, 1970.

3 N. Mogilyansky, 'Ethnography and its tasks', *Russian Anthropological Society Journal*, St. Petersburg, 1909, vol. 3 (in Russian).

4 P. Kushner, 'National consciousness as an ethnic indicator', *Brief Reports of the Institute of Ethnography*, Moscow, 1949, no. 8; 'Ethnic territories and boundaries', *TIE AN SSSR*, Moscow, 1951, vol. 15. S. Tokarev, 'The problem of types of ethnic communities', *Problemy Filosofii*, Moscow, 1964, no. 11. V. Kozlov, *The Dynamics of the Numerical Strength of Peoples*, Moscow, 1969. Yu. Bromley, 'Concerning the characteristics of the concept ethnos', *Races and Peoples*, Moscow, 1971, issue 1. K. Chistov, 'The ethnic community, ethnic consciousness and some problems of intellectual culture', *Sovietskaia Etnografia*, 1972, no. 3 (all in Russian).

5 Yu. Bromley, 'The term ethnos and its definition', *Soviet Ethnology and Anthropology Today*, The Hague-Paris, 1974.

6 S. Tokarev, 'The tasks of ethnographical studies of peoples of industrial countries', *Sovietskaia Etnografia*, 1967, no. 5.

T. DRAGADZE

The place of 'ethnos' theory in Soviet anthropology

An endeavour to place anthropology amongst the sciences can imply establishing boundaries for the discipline. It seems to me that this is the way mainstream Soviet scholars in recent years have expressed their understanding of what anthropology is about, by enunciating in advance the scope of the field and, through a process of elimination, arriving at an unequivocal definition of the subject. In the West we have also been struggling over the nature of the discipline, one form of the debate being the discussion on 'new anthropology' as well as 'old'.[1] I know that several colleagues share my embarassment whenever students ask me to define anthropology even in academic terms. It was therefore with great pleasure that I embarked on an attempt to learn a little about the Soviet understanding of the discipline. There has been a new appraisal of its place in the social sciences, although Soviet scholars, when assessing the development of their subject, have generally preferred to stress continuity rather than new departures.

I think that Soviet social scientists, and anthropologists in particular, can be said to operate in a closed conceptual system in that it is spelled out *a priori*; the 'rules of the game' are known by the participants and they are the terms in which ventures into analysis are assessed. However, within this system, discussion is intense and lively. Indeed, the present debate on 'ethnos' is such that nearly every statement I shall record here has been challenged, so this can merely be a summary of some of the main contentions, each of which has by no means received full acceptance. In this system, however, the unchanging emphasis which Gellner sensed so well is on the close connection between history and anthropology.[2] The historical principle is the main analytical tool and historicism the main explanatory device to have been used throughout the Soviet period. The historical dimension included in every study – seeing social phenomena as being in a state of flux, containing elements of the past and moving towards some new form – nevertheless antedates the adoption there of Marxist theory. This way of thought stems from an uninterrupted, deep-rooted intellectual

tradition which was universal until it was rejected by the struc-
tural-functionalists in the West.[3] It is useful to add that human history
had been seen by Soviet scholars as following a universal 'stages of history' development, the implications of which are usually studied by the
philosophers and adopted subsequently by the anthropologists for their
own use.[4]

It is imperative to state here that in the West we also operate within
closed frameworks, although less obviously so, and the Soviet approach
is salutary since it enhances our awareness of our inherent limitations.
Above all, we find with our Soviet colleagues the freshness of a theoretical framework which is relatively straightforward and uncluttered.

You need only refer to Professor Bromley's definitive work *Ethnos and
Ethnography*[5] to realise that an understanding of the term 'ethnos' is central to any appreciation of recent views on the nature of anthropology
which Soviet scholars offer. In no uncertain terms Bromley states that
the object of anthropological enquiry is the ethnos as a social unit. Man
as a social being can be examined in a great number of ways, as can the
collectivities in which he participates. Unlike other researchers, however, anthropologists should specialise in studying man in his capacity
as member of an 'ethnos', the nature of these 'ethnoses' and their history.
For example, ethnic consciousness is the anthropologist's special field,
whereas 'collective consciousness' *tout court* is not. Through this division
of labour among the human sciences anthropology acquires an autonomy which sets it apart from history and sociology, the latter being a
discipline which has been gaining momentum in the USSR since the
late 1960s.

The concept 'ethnos' has undergone a long process of refinement and
redefinition since it was first elaborated by Shirokogoroff.[6] But I shall
take my cue from the most recent publication I have received from
Moscow, *Contemporary Ethnic Processes in the USSR*.[7] Giving an overall,
working definition, Bromley and Kozlov write:

> Ethnos (in the narrow sense of the term) can be defined as a firm
> aggregate of people, historically established on a given territory,
> possessing in common relatively stable particularities of language
> and culture, and also recognizing their unity and difference from
> other similar formations (self awareness) and expressing this in a
> self-appointed name (ethnonym).[8]

Why such a group is called an 'ethnos' and not by some other name can
be partly accounted for by pointing out that in Soviet terms the word
'society' is the Marxian term for a particular socio-economic formation: feudal society, capitalist society. Similar difficulties arise with the
use of terms such as 'community', 'group', 'nationality', 'nation' and
'people' – *narod* in Russian – which for some time have had definite, acknowledged meanings which are best not tampered with. They too are
all associated with and confined to particular stages of history. I would

venture the remark that anyway Marxists cherish their use of terminology more than most non-Marxists, regardless of which translation. Soviet scholars have maintained that some British anthropologists will talk of the Nuer 'people', the Bantu-speaking 'peoples' or the Chinese 'people' without a particularly precise sociological definition of the group in question. But more fundamental is the argument that the term 'ethnos' is seen to be the embodiment of an assumption which reflects the special type of corporateness felt by those who belong to it. An ethnos is only an ethnos if its members perceive it as such. This cannot be said so blithely of such western conventions as the use of the term 'tribe', the very notion of which is sometimes confusing to those to whom it is supposed to apply.[9]

An ethnos is an unit, at least for the most committed Soviet contenders, which is not bound to any particular historical stage of societal development. Its character is dependant, but not its very existence. To draw a simple analogy: the existence of a language is not bound to any particular stage of history although it undergoes modifications in any particular circumstances. An overflogged remark, but one which highlights the analogy, is that the basic grammar of any given language changes little over time, although its vocabulary is transformed considerably. For ethnographers caught in the trap of the system of historical stages, an ethnos is a useful analytical device, being an unit which can be traced vertically through history. A nation or a society cannot be treated in the same way. They dissolve at certain stages and form again. This means that for 'societies' one has a conceptual vision of horizontal strata. An ethnos is an entity that can be analysed vertically up through these strata, a very handy model for an historically minded Soviet anthropologist. Indeed, these ethnoses change their character as they pass through the strata, but they do not lose their identity as ethnoses and their boundaries as units. 'The Ukrainian ethnos', for instance, 'existed under feudalism and capitalism and continues to exist under socialism' writes Bromley.[10]

This assertion has by no means found acceptance among all the participants in the current ethnos debates, which have been sparked off by Tokarev's attempt to formalise the links between historical stages and types of ethnos.[11] Some have maintained that ethnoses can only exist within the conditions of pre-capitalist formations. Others, such as Gumilev, although using questionable and unpopular arguments, steadfastedly proclaim the ubiquity of ethnos in the contemporary world scene. He writes: 'There is not a single person in the earth who is not in an ethnos. Every person when asked, "Who are you?" will answer, "Russian, French, Persian or Masai", without thinking.'[12] But he perturbed his readers by suggesting that since this phenomenon is omnipresent, it expresses such a deep psychological element in humans which causes them to ascribe themselves to an ethnos, that it can almost be said to be biological. All Soviet ethnographers are anxious to disavow any 'biological' element in the study of ethnos especially if it could denote some sort of racist overtone. (Gumilev would share this concern and so it was unfortunate that he should have misused his vocabulary.) For instance, when studying the relationship between intra-ethnic endogamy and the survival of an ethnos, Bromley stresses that it is the capacity for the reproduction of culture alone which is affected by intermarriage.[13] An ethnos is never equated with a particular physical type, although the two occasionally coincide at a given stage of history.

For Shirokogoroff 'ethnos regulation' was dependant on the interplay between three factors: the ecological conditions to which the ethnos had to adapt, its relations with other ethnoses and the size of its population. He then set these factors out in equations to qualify the potentialities of each element. For example, the higher the 'level of culture' of the ethnos, the less intensive the variations in population.[14] This tended to evoke a picture of the ethnos in its state as a primitive horde, which for some scholars is all an ethnos ever is, anyway. For those who see its continuity into complex society, a 'stages of history' framework has to be elaborated more thoroughly.

Specifically, during my research in Moscow, I was told that the great difference between the Soviet understanding of 'ethnos' and the American school of Mead and Benedict (cf. *Patterns of Culture*) is that the Soviet notion of 'ethnic specificity' cannot be seen, to use sociological jargon, as an independent variable. If a static model for society were to be used, if the 'ethnographic present' were to be an accepted convention, it would be different. But if, like all social phenomena, ethnos categories must be observed throughout their path of historical evolution, then these will appear more fluid, more versatile, and thereby more enduring.

Inevitably, the current Soviet axiom is that an ethnos is always a system whose binding characteristics are dependent on the economy, history and politics of the day. I will not try to paraphrase the accounts of a favourite theme offered by Soviet authors elsewhere, in English.[15] The implications are obvious enough: in its path the ethnos unit will be moulded into very different shapes according to the type of society in which it exists. Predictably, Bromley and Kozlov distinguish three types of community in which an ethnos might find expression: the tribe for 'primitive' society, where its members stress the closeness of kinship ties and common descent from a usually mythical ancestor; the nation for capitalist and socialist society; whereas characteristic for slave-owning and feudal society is the *narodnost*, a 'people' somewhere between a tribe and nation for which there is no adequate English translation.[16] Sometimes it will be the common language which appears as the salient binding characteristic, at other times the religious belief system, or the shared economy (e.g. pastoralism) or the war machine in times of political expansion. You name it and you might find it. An analogous approach is used in the West when we teach the history of the family, but in the Soviet case opportunist choices do not stem from an argument in functionalist terms.

Ultimately, an ethnos might be said to be a group in the Durkheim-ian sense insofar as its members share a collective representation: they believe that they are a group of people apart because they share some unique features in common. The components – the 'meaning' – of this particular collective representation will vary through time, as it is transmitted from generation to generation. But what is the 'constant'? I would suggest that this is seen to be the actual label. Ethnos is not a 'geist'. It is a group of people giving themselves a common label – the ethnonym. This label, which expresses their distinctiveness from other similar groups, is the basis of their self-definition (and therefore the basis of the ethnos's existence). This point was made succinctly, I think, by Kriukov in a seminar paper last year in Moscow, 'The evolution of ethnic self-awareness and the problem of ethnogenesis', which he illustrated with reference to the ancient Greeks and the ancient Chinese. I do not know whether this interesting paper has been published yet.[17]

The boundaries of the ethnos might or might not coincide with those of a group participating in any given social organisation. It is important to remember this when Soviet authors follow an ethnos across the great divide between the antagonistic and the non-antagonistic forms of society. It seems to me that an ethnos is seen to be moving along a sort of continuum from social organisation in its early stages to cognitive field in its later (socialist) stage. (By the same token can I submit that one is moving towards what can be called a 'cultural' model?)[18]

There has recently been increasing interest in ethnicity among western social scientists. For instance, Glazer and Moynihan published a large collection of articles in 1975,[19] and an ASA Monograph was brought out in 1974 on urban ethnicity.[20] Ethnicity is studied within the context of conflict theory with inequality as its theme. Ethnic groups are culturally bounded but politically and economically maintained. David Parkin, following Abner Cohen, writes:

> I would put my view [on a definition of ethnicity] in the form of a simple equation: ethnicity = a) the articulation of cultural distinctiveness in b) situations of political conflict or competition.[21]

According to this school, ethnic self awareness arises as a reaction to the social forces of actual or potential deprivation.

In these terms a dialogue with Soviet scholars would be problematic. This is not because, when they write about ethnoses in the USSR today, they never depict them as suffering in competition one with the other. It would not be enough merely to question whether Soviet society is non-antagonistic and classless. You could use your own convictions and rewrite some ethnographies[22] but you would not have grappled with the essence of Soviet ethnos theory.

To my knowledge there has not been any recent Soviet literature devoted specifically to the relationship between class and ethnos. My motive for mentioning it here is merely because western colleagues continually question me about it, although I would have preferred to leave this discussion to the Soviet scholars at the conference. As far as I can tell, they maintain that ethnoses can be cut across internally by class divisions but ethnos and class are not seen as alternate but as complementary analytic categories. For class concepts belong to the horizontal strata of social analysis, ethnos concepts to vertical analysis. They would maintain that the history of class struggles and the history of ethnoses can be analysed concurrently, thus adding a further dimension to a Marxian study of social change. Members of the same class from different ethnoses – each with their unique ethnic character – can come together for purposes of class solidarity, and ethnic self awareness is not seen as a 'false consciousness'.

According to most Soviet scholars, self ascription to an ethnos is not a form of spontaneous response. In particular it is not merely a response to the agonies of capitalism. It arises from the inner experience of countless generations who simply perceive that, for example, as Turks they are different to the French. Over a long period, surviving the convulsions of social change, Turkishness *per se* is continuous and stable although it will assume very different forms. The interplay between the ethnoses is such that Turks and French might combine to fight common oppressive forces, they might share the same level of technology, they might even share a common government, but they will fight in the Turkish style and the French style, will speak Turkish and French, will have a Turkish and a French symbolic order. It is the paradigmatic nature of Turkishness and Frenchness – which, for example, Ardener in an early formulation would perhaps have called a 'template'[23] – which should form the object of our enquiries as anthropologists. Thus it is the residue category one can turn to when, having exhausted the possibilities of analysis according to the canons of socio-economic history, one seeks to perceive what remains as a recurring theme within the boundaries of Turkishness and Frenchness. The study of ethnic specificity will entail comparative analysis throughout. A strand of thought arising from this position is that ethnic specificity can be seen as the objective justification for a subjective awareness of affiliation to a given ethnos. It is in these terms that Bromley elaborated his typology of ethnos hierarchies to account for the phenomenon of people seeing themselves as, for example, Slav, Russian and Don Cossak simultaneously.[24]

More important in understanding Soviet 'ethnos' theory is to note the approach used to diagnose the oncoming death of an ethnos. Again, this point has been dealt with admirably in English translation and I shall not repeat arguments expressed so much better by the Soviet authors themselves.[25] In brief, intermarriage with other ethnoses's members, conquest by and intense contact with other ethnoses, removal from a common territory and other similar conditions can erode the salience of ethnic self-labelling. But the study of ethnic specificity through time is nevertheless deemed to be the main task of Soviet anthropologists, because it is believed that the specifics of a dominant, host ethnos will always be modified by the ethnoses they absorb (or the 'ethnicoses' they absorb – the term Bromley has used to denote ethnic groups not living on their own territory). The extreme position, admittedly one which I have not encountered in the literature yet, which follows, would be to maintain that ethnic specific qualities will all die totally only if all members of the given ethnos who possess them were to be physically exterminated, in isolation. In the case of the USSR, Bromley and Kozlov declare that, should it become a melting pot of ethnoses, the new macro-ethnos would contain ethnic specifics of every ethnos present today.[26]

Chlenov, a young Soviet scholar – again his views would be challenged by several of his colleagues – has tentatively put forward a practical proposal to help the acceptance of the importance of ethnic specificity as the object of our studies. Thus, although it is not entirely representative of the main opinions, I have found guidance to clues for understanding how anthropology[27] can be comprehended as a discipline in Chlenov's article: 'On the internal articulation of ethnographic science'[28] where he suggests alternative ways of classifying information in libraries. He gives a humourous account of current library catalogue titles devised for this purpose. He maintains that *etnografia* is not the social history of primitive society as has been traditionally thought in the USSR, but rather is the study of ethnos in all its manifestations, where social history is only relevant when it deals with ethnic specificity. He suggests that material should be classified according to new indices:

The specificity of *etnografia* compared with other social sciences, (sociology, history, law, economics and so on) is to be found in its 'conjunctive character'. An ethnos contains many of the same traits as human society as a whole. It is well known that it is difficult to trace the boundaries between an ethnos and a social group of another character. And the various aspects of human society's existence (social organisation, production, law, etc.) are studied by different sciences. Accordingly, *etnografia* is made up of a conglomeration of scientific disciplines, each of which is tightly linked to a 'corresponding' social or natural science and can only be distinguished from it by the specifics of its subject matter. Before characterising the actual system of internal articulation, a few remarks on the terminology used here: it seems to me that in Russia the use of the term *etnografia* has become traditional and habitual and there is absolutely no need to substitute it with any other term, for example with '*narodovedenie*' [*volkskunde?*] or 'ethnology' or others. As for the internal subdivisions of *etnografia*, there is no [established] tradition yet and so I propose to use the right combination of the element 'ethno-' with other words to depict the separate components of *etnografia*:

1. Ethnology. Subject matter: ethnos as a system in synchrony and diachrony. The more general questions concerning the existence of an ethnos, ethnos philosophy, the relationship between ethnos and culture, ethnos theory, ethnos typologies, ethnos origins, the character of ethnic contacts, ethnogenesis, ethnic history. Corresponding sciences: history and philosophy.

2. Ethnosociology. Subject matter: social organisation of the ethnos. Social organisation, social control, interrelations of people within an ethnos, traditional social structures, legal ethnology, political ethnology and so on. Corresponding sciences: sociology, law, political science and history.

3. Ethnoeconomics. Subject matter: the organisation and culture of production and its uses within an ethnos. General questions of economic ethnology, economy (*khozaistvo*), material culture. Corresponding science: economics.

4. Ethnofolkloristics. Subject matter: ethnic expressions of 'spiritual culture'. Way of life [*byt*], oral folklore, decorative art and music folklore, ideas about the world, rudiments of scientific knowledge. Corresponding sciences: folkloristics, art and music studies.

5. Ethnolinguistics. Subject matter: language as a means of communication within and between ethnoses. Language and ethnic thought, ethnosemantics, genetic ethnolinguistics, bilingualism, language contacts, politics of language, ethno-onomastics. Corresponding science: linguistics.

6. Ethnogeography. Subject matter: the relationship between ethnos and geographical environment. Ethnos ecology, ethnodemography, ethnocartography, ethnobotany, ethnozoology. Corresponding sciences: geography, demography, ecology and cartography.

7. Ethnopsychology. Subject matter: stable psychic characteristics of the ethnos. General questions of ethnopsychology, culture and personality, axiology, the ethnography of teaching and education, ethnosexology, the position of *unsocial* groups within the ethnos (youth and the aged), relations between the sexes, attitudes to women, etc. Corresponding science: psychology and social psychology. [Italics mine. T.D.]

8. Ethnoreligious studies. Subject matter: ethnic particularities of religion. Comparative studies of religious systems, the relationship of religion with other characteristics of the ethnos, popular beliefs, superstitions, mythology. Corresponding science: religious studies.

9. Ethnobiology. Subject matter: biological characteristics of the ethnos. Physical anthropology of the ethnos, medical anthropology, the relationship between an ethnos and race, social and cultural aspects of inter-racial relations. Corresponding sciences: physical anthropology, medicine and sociology.

10. Subsidiary disciplines in *etnografia*; the history of *etnografia*,

teaching methods for *etnografia*, museum work, archive work and source studies.

It is easy to take issue with Chlenov over several components of his scheme, in particular numbers seven, eight, and nine, except that he is attempting to catalogue material already written as well as that which he anticipates in the future. Above all he tends to assume that the material to be classified concerns ethnoses in what he would see as their pre-scientific stage. It is true that Soviet anthropologists do accept an unquestionable distinction between pre-scientific and scientific 'modes of thought', and the bulk of excellent Soviet ethnographic field work has traditionally been concentrated on issues untypical of modern life. Nevertheless, I still am under the impression that the theory of ethnos is seen as a means by which Soviet anthropology can successfully claim a unique stake in the study of contemporary society.

As for the particular study of ethnos, ethnicity and ethnic specificity, ultimately the difference between the western and Soviet approach is perhaps merely a question of emphasis. When trying to untangle the frequent confusion of ethnic character and ethnic group, of culture and structure, western scholars see ethnic self-awareness as implying a cohesive social organisation, whereas on this point the Soviet emphasis is often minimal.

I am intrigued, however, as to whether in simple terms one must assume that an ethnos is merely some sort of epi-phenomenon where, from a particular socio-economic formation, the arrows of causality point in one direction only, or whether – more interestingly – there is a sense in which an ethnos, or at least some elements of ethnic specificity, have a general, 'paradigmatic' autonomy.

In conclusion, I must confess that I have overstated the argument in order to be polemical. But this is because I looked forward so greatly to an opportunity at the forthcoming conference to learn more from our Soviet colleagues who have so much to contribute to enrich our discipline.

NOTES

1 I have in mind such statements as those of R. Needham, 'The future of social anthropology; disintegration or metamorphosis', *Anniversary Contributions to Anthropology: Twelve Essays,* Leiden, 1971. Banaji, 'Crisis in British anthropology', *New Left Review,* 1970, no. 64. Previously published in the *Journal of the Anthropological Society of Oxford.* E. Ardener, 'The new anthropology and its critics', *MAN,* 1971, n.s., vol. 6, no. 3; also discussions at the decennial meeting of the Association of Social Anthropologists, 1973, entitled 'New departures in anthropology'.
2 E. Gellner, 'The Soviet and the savage', *Current Anthropology,* 1975, vol. 16, no. 4.
3 See my comments on E. Gellner in *Current Anthropology,* 1975, vol. 16, no. 4.
4 For a fine example of recent philosophy, see Y. Boroday, V.J. Kelle and E. G. Plimak, *The Principle of Historicism in the Cognition of Social Phenomena,* Moscow, 1972 (in Russian).

5 Yu. V. Bromley, *Ethnos and Ethnography*, Moscow, 1973, (in Russian).

6 I am indebted to E. Leach for information. S.M. Shirokogoroff (1887-1939) lectured in Vladivostok in 1921 and 1922 before leaving the Soviet Union for good, so his influence there has been indirect. He published *Ethnos*, Shanghai, 1923, a book based on these lectures. An English version, *Ethnical Unit and Milieu*, was published in Shanghai, 1924.

7 Yu. V. Bromley *et al.* (eds), *Contemporary Ethnic Processes in the USSR*, Moscow, 1975 (in Russian).

8 Ibid. p. 11.

9 E.W. Ardener, 'Language, ethnicity and population' in 'The population factor in African studies', paper presented to the African Studies Association, 1972, published in *Studies in Social Anthropology* (ed. J. Beattie and Y. Lienhardt), Oxford, 1975, pp. 343-53.

10 Yu. V. Bromley, 'Ethnos and the ethnosocial organism', *Ethnologia Slavica*, vol. 3, Bratislava, 1971 (in Russian).

11 S.A. Tokarev, 'The problems of types of ethnic community: notes towards ethnographic methodology', *Voprosi Filosophii*, Moscow, 1964, (in Russian). He revived the interest in 'ethnos' which was touched on by P.I. Kushner as early as 1949, and in the early 1950s.

12 L.N. Gumilev, 'On the term "ethnos"', *Papers of the Geographical Society*, Leningrad, 1966 (in Russian).

13 Y.V. Bromley, 'Ethnos and endogamy', *Sovietskaia Etnografia*, 1969, no. 9; and the discussion on this paper in *Sovietskaia Etnografia*, 1970 (in Russian).

14 Shirokogoroff, *Ethnical Unit and Milieu* (in Russian).

15 Y.V. Bromley (ed.), *Soviet Ethnology and Anthropology Today*, The Hague, 1974.

16 Bromley *et al.* (eds), op. cit., p. 12.

17 M. Kriukov, Institute of Ethnography, Academy of Sciences, Moscow.

18 I know 'culture' is a term needing a re-think. See Z. Bauman, *Culture as Praxis*, London, 1972.

19 N. Glazer and D. Moynihan (eds), *Ethnicity: Theory and Experience*, Harvard University Press, 1975.

20 A. Cohen (ed.), *Urban Ethnicity*, ASA Monograph 12, London, 1974.

21 D. Parkin 'Congregational and interpersonal ideologies in political ethnicity', in Cohen (ed.), *Urban Ethnicity*.

22 See the position of D. Lane, 'Ethnic and class stratification in Soviet Kazakhstan, 1917-1939', *Comparative Studies in History and Society*, vol. 17, Cambridge, 1975.

23 E.W. Ardener in M. Douglas (ed.), *Witchcraft: Confessions and Accusations*, ASA Monograph 9, 1970, p. 156.

24 Yu.V. Bromley in *Papers Presented to the 8th World Congress of Sociology*, Toronto, 1974.

25 See in particular *Papers Presented to the 8th World Congress of Sociology*, Toronto, 1974. Bromley (ed.), *Soviet Ethnology and Anthropology Today*. Also, forthcoming, T. Dragadze (ed.), *Readings in Contemporary Soviet Anthropology*, Oxford University Press.

26 Yu.V. Bromley and V.I. Kozlov, 'Leninism and ethnic processes in the USSR', *Sovietskaia Etnografia*, 1970, no. 1 (in Russian).

27 *Etnografia* in Russian, not simple to translate. Except in the extract from Chlenov I have rendered it throughout as 'anthropology' or 'ethnology', as appropriate in English usage. Etnologia is rendered only as 'ethnology'.

28 M.A. Chlenov, 'On the internal articulation of ethnographic science', *Paper to the Moscow branch of the Geographical Society*, 1973 (in Russian).

L. DROBIZHEVA

Ethnic sociology of present-day life

In the Soviet Union ethnography does not confine itself to archaic societies, but also undertakes the study of well-developed urbanised nations, of their past and present. When modern urbanised nations become the object of research, ethnography, while maintaining a fairly broad range, nevertheless restricts its scope, since ethnographers can use data concerning the life of these nations drawn from other sciences. So they do not need to investigate all the aspects of the life of a nation, as specialists in historical ethno-sociology are obliged to do when studying archaic nations, or as social anthropologists do in their work.

But since the ethnical development of a nation is influenced by factors other than ethnical (social and economic above all), in its study of modern nations ethnography co-operates with other sciences, and especially with sociology. This interaction has led to co-operation with the two sciences and given rise to such new scientific mixtures as ethno-sociology. (In the USSR modern ethno-sociology researches into present-day life, as distinct from historical ethno-sociology which studies the past.)

When the object of study is a community possessing not merely shared cultural elements, but also socio-economic ones, which makes it an ethno-social entity, then ethnographers and sociologists enter a common area of research. So ethno-sociology studies the interaction and the mechanism of this interrelation of ethnic, social and socio-psychological phenomena.

Socio-economic changes determine not only internal ethnic development, but also influence the ethnic processes stimulated by inter-ethnic contacts. The direction of ethnic influence depends largely on the political position, educational level and social structure of the interacting nations. Ethno-social processes and their mutual influence are the object of ethno-sociological study.

Ethno-sociology undertakes research into the social structure of nations, the impact of social factors on the preservation of cultural traditions, the spread of innovations, and inter-ethnic relations. It particularly stresses social variety and the socio-economic conditions of the functioning of culture.

Of the two trends that have emerged in ethno-sociological studies, one deals with social processes and characteristics in the ethnic environments, and the other with ethnic processes in social groups. Therefore, while ethnography most frequently undertakes research into the separate subsystems of the ethnic organism, such as, for instance, rites, interiors and exteriors of houses, food, ethnic features of a family, etc., ethno-sociological study is focused on ethno-social processes. It is difficult, consequently, to share the view that all studies of ethnic phenomena in present-day life should be regarded as ethno-sociological.[1]

Some scholars maintain that ethnology and sociology differ in their methods.[2] But it is common knowledge that the same methods may be applied in different sciences. Therefore it would be wrong to describe research as sociological or ethnological processing solely from the method used.

The problems studied by Soviet ethno-sociologists are close to those examined by social anthropologists and western sociologists dealing with 'ethnic groups'. A classical example of this kind of sociological research written from the viewpoint of an 'ethnic group' is the well-known study by Thomas and Znanecki, *The Polish Peasant in Europe and America* (1918). In such cases researchers concentrate on an ethnic group which is normally an explicit minority in one or another state.[3] However, in contrast with this, ethno-sociology in the Soviet Union gives priority to studying large peoples of the Union and Autonomous Soviet Republics.

In western sociology there are other trends as well. They focus attention not on an individual ethnic group but on relations between two or more groups. This area of research is often referred to as the sociology of racial and ethnic relations. The terms they use are: competition, conflict, accommodation, assimilation and the like.

In the postwar period western sociologists have turned more to problems of discrimination and prejudice. In *Racial Cultural Minorities: Analysis of Prejudice and Discrimination* by Sympson and Inger (3rd ed., 1965), a very well-known work of this kind, the two approaches, one from the viewpoint of social interaction, and the other dealing with social problems and with prejudice, are combined. In such studies,[4] the investigation of the social structure of the contacting groups, of cultural and historical factors, is pursued with a view to the analysis of inter-ethnic relations and intercourse.

In Soviet ethno-sociology the study of the social structure of peoples and their cultural development has a special significance. A change in the social and cultural characteristics is examined in order to trace the development of the peoples and the directions of socio-ethnic processes. The study of relations between groups, of the real inter-ethnic intercourse and contacts – attitudes, say, at home, at a factory, an office, and in other spheres – is one of the trends of ethno-sociological research in the Soviet Union. This trend also borders on psychology. The scholars working in this sphere concentrate on bringing out conditions promoting the development of friendly relations among nations. This is closely linked to the study of the interaction of cultures, since social interests and orientations obviously canalise this process.

The shift of specifically ethnic elements in modern society to the sphere of its cultural life accounts for the greater attention paid by Soviet scientists to such socio-psychological phenomena and processes as ethnic attitudes, orientations, interests and values. This tends to broaden the range of questions to be studied by ethno-sociology, which brings it nearer to psychology. Recent years have seen an increase of interest in such socio-psychological themes as the link of social stratification with the ethnic awareness of peoples, and the cross-fertilisation of cultures, etc. It is only natural that, being located at the crossroads of ethnography, sociology and psychology, these aspects are viewed as intermediate.

Although its boundaries are quite relative, the 'research area' substantially determines its special methodology. The difference between ethnographic and sociological research lies in the fact that the ethnographic approach rests above all on the examination of a single aspect, aiming to reveal what is ethnically specific, while the sociological approach to the object of research requires that general similarities be studied in the first place. The monographic studies of rural areas by ethnographers and sociologists are a case in point. The ethnographers were interested in the ethnic features of a specific village, while the sociologists seek in it a reflection of general phenomena, of something that is generally characteristic for members of a socialist farm cooperative.[5]

Ethno-sociology develops on the borderline of the two sciences, and hence must evolve an approach which will ensure the study of that which is ethnically specific in close connection with that which is general. Ethno-cultural phenomena are viewed by ethno-sociology in connection with economic, socio-political and psychological phenomena of the life of a society. This goes to show that a comprehensive, aggregate approach is indispensable for ethno-sociological research.

True, ethnographers also have in mind the influence of a social system as a whole when they describe marriages, birth and burial rituals, the habits of people living in cities and in the countryside. The tendency toward a comprehensive approach in studying ethnic processes and phenomena does not imply a sharp distinction between ethnographic and ethno-sociological research. This approach is sought by all specialists, but it is not always possible to achieve it (for instance, because of the lack of the required sources, or of their comparability). For this reason one will often find an all-round approach in ethnography within its own bounds.

When studying culture, this approach requires, for instance, that all its aspects be covered by a given piece of research, while the study of those economic and political phenomena which determine cultural development but are outside the cultural sphere is not necessary. For this reason, in the course of ethnographic research into the life of modern urbanised peoples, changes in the socio-political system, social structure and economic progress are viewed as fundamental elements, but are not studied by the ethnographers directly. Ethnographers use knowledge accumulated by other special sciences. Herein lies one of the differences between ethnographic and ethno-sociological research, for the latter takes the economic, social, psychological and, of course, ethnic phenomena in the life of nations as the direct objects of study. Each of these phenomena is examined in close relationship with all the others, and the very mechanism of this relationship is studied. This is achieved through a comprehensive approach involving several sciences.

Ethnic sociology requires that ethnic, social, economic and psychological phenomena should be recorded in a way which would allow scientists to regard them in close correlation and within the limits of a clearly defined object.

Such a comprehensive approach in ethno-sociological research is already adopted at the stage when a research programme is being drawn up, when questionnaires, interviews and plans for observation are being prepared, and statistical and other clerical documents are being selected to ensure the objectivity of information. For instance, during the ethno-sociological investigation conducted in the rural areas of the Tatar Autonomous Republic, Moldavia, Georgia, Estonia, Uzbekistan and the Russian Federation, so-called 'passports' were made for the countryside in the regions where field interviews were taken. This was done so as to combine the socio-psychological information concerning people's opinion and behaviour with information concerning the field of their activity. Recorded in those 'passports' were data on the economic situation on collective farms, on material and cultural conditions of life and other factors of the environment which, when processed in a computer, were tied in with the data registered in the questionnaires.[6] In other cases the necessary objective data on the environment were recorded in the questionnaires so that they could be compared directly with the views and estimates given by the subjects.

In ethnography it is permissible to establish the composition of a population on the basis of the statistical data and through information provided by questionnaires, while the rites, customs, folk poetry and other aspects are studied on the basis of the information obtained from the people interviewed. In ethno-sociology, on the other hand, mass processes are analysed. In this case research is focused on the participation of specific groups of the population in folk arts and crafts, in ritual behaviour, etc. Participation in feasts and one or another traditional manner of behaviour is examined in combination with the socio-cultural characteristics of groups of people and the specifics of their social environment.

Ethno-sociological researchers take into consideration both the general social conditions of a macro-environment and the specific conditions of a micro-environment. For this reason some or other ethno-social interactions are analysed in cities and villages with different levels of urbanisation, in a concrete social environment and in various types of situations (for instance, a situation of social changes or stability, of long-established or recent inter-ethnic contacts, their character, etc.). This methodological approach leads to a situation in which the conclusions and hypotheses in ethno-sociological research are often formulated in a manner consonant with probability theory. For instance, direct contacts promote ethnic relations between persons, provided there is mutual interest, and provided interaction among ethnic groups is durable enough.[7]

Both the ethnographer and sociologist always bear in mind that the common elements to be examined undergo change with time. Therefore an historical approach is applied in studying them. Besides, in ethno-sociology the changes are always registered in a quantitatively definite form, making it possible to forecast processes.

The forecasting of phenomena and processes is also facilitated by the study of an ethnic attitude in different age-groups, the approach to various ethnic distinctive traits in material and intellectual culture, and to diverse norms of behaviour. For example, a questionnaire asks in what manner a person's wedding party was held and what kind of wedding he would like his children to have; or whether a person wears national costume and wants to see it available at large. Although it is known that in various situations men's actions often diverge from their expressed views, they none-the-less reflect possible changes.

The developmental trends are further identified by studying qualitative changes in growing social groups. Here is a simple example of this: a growth of the urban population in an ethnic environment will obviously bring about a unification in the material culture of a nation.

In ethno-sociological studies, analysis is conducted on the basis of various sources: statistical data, documents provided by government offices and public organisations, observation, etc., with public opinion polls normally being the main source. More often than not the polls are carried out in accordance with a standard programme, and more rarely they are based on open-ended interviews. During the polls the individual is a source of information. In archaic societies one or another person or a small group of persons could have a fairly true picture of what was common among them all, whereas this is not the case with advanced and socially differentiated peoples. The individual is not only a representative of an ethnic community, but also of a social group. In modern society, which is socially differentiated, age difference, too, is of great significance. Hence opinion polls are held on a mass scale and thus become representative.

In this way ethnic sociology, like sociology in general, is concerned with the individual qualities of a person (such as his capability for comprehension, communication and other similar qualities that may interest a psychologist), but in their typical aspects: social, professional and demographic traits, including those which are characteristic of a person as a member of an ethnic group. Hence in studying an individual there also arises a special aspect, namely, that of the individual in interaction with other members of the ethnic community.

The methodological premise of research into intra-ethnic and inter-ethnic orientations and into the behaviour of the individual is the notion that the individual is in interaction with his environment in which some cultural values or other are predominant, and that they are influenced by a specific situation.

Thus the changing attitude to the elements of material and intellectual culture reflects their transformation in the life of society.

Since it is the mass processes which are studied by ethno-sociology, they are analysed through statistical regularities. Recently ethnographers have been making use of statistical descriptions and questionnaires which were sometimes processed by computers. So the use of quantitative methods does not necessarily mean that a given research should be regarded as ethno-sociological. Likewise the use of some or other methods of research, such as, for instance, an opinion poll or observation, still allow one to class a study as either ethno-sociology or ethnography. Only the subject as a whole, the methodological approach, and the methods of research in combination with the technique ensuring the required professional level of a research, can enable one to determine whether a research is ethnographic or ethno-sociological. But we do not at all insist on such a strict delimitation. All that is professionally necessary, and is most important in a research, is an adequate reflection of real life.

In the past decade representative ethno-sociological investigation has been carried out in the USSR among such large peoples as Georgians, Uzbeks, Moldavians, Estonians and Tatars, and also among the Russians living in some areas of the Russian Federation and in the republics of the peoples listed above. This investigation was conducted in accordance with the programme called 'Optimisation of socio-cultural conditions for development and for bringing the Soviet peoples closer together' (research was headed by Yu.V. Arutyunyan); furthermore, a research that was close to ethno-sociology was carried out among Udmurts and Mordovians (supervised by V.V. Pimenov).[8]

The first results of ethno-sociological studies were published in the book, *The Social and the National* (Moscow, 1973, in Russian), and a number of articles. The research conducted in the Tatar Republic, representative for the Tatar and Russian population, was in its way experimental. Later its programme was extended[9] and researches were carried out in the various Union Republics.

As has been stated, ethno-sociological research was conducted in two inter-related directions. In one of them comparative analysis made it possible to determine the influence of ethnic distinctive traits on social processes and phenomena; the other determined the dependence of ethnic changes on social factors.

These ethno-sociological studies have considerably extended our knowledge of modern nations, including their culture, social pattern and way of life. Previously the proportion of workers, farmers and intellectuals in a nation could be established on the basis of sociological data. Now there is a possibility of showing their internal composition, the professional and educational level of different strata of the population, and of their social and cultural needs and interests.

The research has also made it possible to bring out the significance of various strata-forming factors for socialist nations today. Thus the theoretical elaboration and practical investigation of such factors as the nature of work, and the role of the individual in the organisation of labour, have revealed their most essential significance for the distinctions between industrial workers and intellectuals and, inside these categories, between various groups according to their professional level and function.

The study of this problem also had its ethnic aspect. The internal proportions of the socio-ethnic groups of the Soviet Union have a steady tendency to approach the same level, which reflects the process in which the levels of their economic and cultural development are drawing closer to one another. However, because of the specialisation and co-operation of the national economies of the constituent republics, and also because of historical traditions, the proportion of the rural population, and in particular of collective farmers, will also continue to be of considerable size in the future. Therefore the increasing similarity between the socio-class groups, caused by the growth of skilled and educated strata, is of great significance for overcoming the existing differences in the social pattern of diverse peoples. The ethno-sociological investigations have shown that the professional and educational level tends to rise among the rural population, among collective farmers, and especially among young people. This points to an important direction in the convergence in the socio-class pattern of nations. Not only are the proportions of the socio-class groups becoming more similar in the Soviet Union, but also, as was confirmed by concrete studies, the differences between them are disappearing as their professional and educational levels even out.

The research undertaken in Moldavia has shown, for instance, that Moldavian and Russian young people within the age-group twenty to twenty-four have the same professional level, while among those who are in their forties the level is twice as high for Russians.[10]

Ethno-sociological studies have shown the significance of the factors determining social mobility among Soviet nations, education being the most effective channel of social advancement. The Soviet state has provided conditions for eliminating the social and cultural backwardness of nations. Ethnic sociologists have recorded instances of accelerated social mobility, such as the mobility of Tatars, Moldavians and Uzbeks in comparison with Russians. Under present-day conditions, however, nationality has no substantial influence on the socio-professional position of a person.

High social mobility affects ethnic changes. Research in the republics mentioned above has shown that in the growing groups of the population, where the professional level keeps rising, forms of culture appear to be the most integrated; their interest in the literature and art of other nations is greater. But it would be an oversimplification to believe that ethnic distinctiveness is on the wane.

The mobile strata, above all the recent village dwellers who arrived in cities, have not only adapted themselves to the new environment but have also carried folk traditions along with them, adding a new ethnic dimension to the urban environment. Thus, the study of the cultural characteristics of social groups often helps one to look into the nature of ethnic changes.

In the cultural sphere, ethno-sociological studies have made it possible to discern the changes in the orientations toward professional and folk cultures, toward the ethnically original and integrated forms, or the forms existing in other nationalities. The functioning of culture was studied in various socio-professional groups. This has enabled scholars to show interaction between cultures.

Among Tatars, Moldavians, Georgians, Estonians and Russians living together in the national republics, one generalisation is valid today: there is more in common in the culture of the people who are of different nationalities but are in one social group, than among different social groups of one nationality. Cultural similarity is more obvious on the educational level, in the extent to which various ethnic groups are informed in scientific and socio-political spheres. The distinctive elements are retained more in the perception of emotionally-coloured cultural information, and in the norms and manners of social intercourse.

It has been proved by using mass data that the cross-fertilisation of cultures is most vigorous in professional spheres. The more advanced a professional culture is, the more it is capable of mutual penetration. The folk arts and folklore are less susceptible to mutual borrowings.

The folk traditional forms, including customs and rites, are retained in the versions which are in keeping with present-day norms of the life of society. For instance among Georgians, Moldavians and Uzbeks, the love of folk songs and dances happily co-exists with their interest in music hall songs, or symphony music and ballet. (Sixty to eighty per cent of those polled in the three republics have said they are keen on folk dances and music.)

At the same time the customs that used strictly to regulate men's behaviour are dying out. This process is more active in the groups whose professional and educational level is the highest. The disappearance of the traditional norms of behaviour associated with religion is proceeding especially fast with the rise in the professional skills.

Ethno-sociological studies in general have shown on a broader scale the norms, values and orientations in life among the nationalities of the Soviet Union. This area of research which borders on psychology is now attracting great interest.

The family is known to play a considerable role in the transmission of cultural traditions to the next generation. Ethno-sociological studies have notably extended the range of questions about the family previously investigated by ethnographers. Further aspects are considered today when studying the social and cultural characteristics of the family and the social status, educational level and cultural interests of the family members; also the influence of these characteristics on the relationships in the family, the number of children born to it, and the change of traditions in the bringing up of children. The social advancement of the husband and wife and their children's careers are analysed, and the psychological climate of the family is examined.

Special attention is given to mixed families, to their growing number in view of the theoretical probability of mixed marriages in an ethnic community and the self-identification, in ethnic terms, of the juveniles of these families.[11] The study of inter-ethnic relations as relations between ethnic groups is one of the aspects of ethno-sociological research, as we have mentioned above. These relations are studied through the analysis of the concrete actions of men and through their attitudes and orientations.

Here, as the empirical investigations have shown, the socio-political conditions of contacts are of decisive significance. The socio-cultural, historical, individual and situational factors determining inter-ethnic relations are studied in concrete terms. The research has shown with quantitative precision that the favourable, friendly type of inter-ethnic relations is predominant.

The attitude to various types of contacts – business, neighbourly, family and friendly – is, according to ethno-sociological research, influenced amongst different peoples of the USSR both by general and specific factors. Thus, the attitude to mixed (inter-ethnic) marriages is precisely determined by cultural factors, while the attitude to production and business contacts is determined by social and professional interests and situational factors. There is a certain connection between the attitudes toward various forms of social intercourse. But it is not so rigid as to ensure that the attitude to the closer kinds of contacts (as those in a family) automatically entails a similar attitude to any other contacts. (The so-called Bogardus gradation of social distance is based on the assumption that such a direct dependence does exist.)

This is probably explained by the fact that friendly and favourable attitudes are most widespread in the inter-ethnic relationships in the USSR (for instance, such attitudes were observed among eighty to ninety per cent of the largest groups of Moldavians, Tatars and Russians living in Tataria and Moldavia).[12] A considerable part of the population is neutral to contacts with other nationalities. Therefore, a negative attitude of some people to one or another type of contact is very rare and does not conform to the favourable attitudes to other types of contact.

Ethno-sociological studies have also shown that attitudes to inter-ethnic intercourse and to national culture are influenced by diverse factors.

NOTES

1 See 'Session on the outcome of field research in 1973', *Sovietskaia Etnografia*, 1974, no. 65 (in Russian).

2 R. Cresswell, 'Ethnologie et sociologie: problème de collaboration', *L'Homme*, 1967, no. 1, 84.

3 See J. Harding *et al.*, 'Prejudice and ethnic relations', *The Handbook of Social Psychology*, vol. 15, 2nd ed., 1969.

4 See D. Sympson and D.M. Inger, 'Sociology of racial and ethnic relations', *Sociology Today: Problems and Prospects*, New York, 1972. T.F. Pettigrew, 'Race relations in the USA', *American Sociology*, New York–London, 1968.

5 Yu. V. Bromley, *Ethnos and Ethnography*, Moscow, 1973, p. 249 (in Russian).

6 See Yu. V. Arutyunyan, *Social Structure of Rural Population of the USSR*, Moscow, 1971, p. 351; 'Socio-cultural aspects of development and drawing nations together in the USSR', *Sovietskaia Etnografia*, 1972, no. 3 (both in Russian).

7 See Yu. V. Arutyunyan (ed.), *The Social and the National*, Moscow, 1973, pp. 282-3 (in Russian).

8 See Arutyunyan, in *Sovietskaia Etnografia*, 1972, no. 3.

9 See E.K. Vasilyeva *et al.*, 'Contemporary ethno-cultural processes in Udmurtya', *Sovietskaia Etnografia*, 1970, no. 2 (in Russian).

10 *Soviet People: New Historic Entity*, Moscow, 1975, p. 315 (in Russian).

11 See L.N. Terentyeva, 'The determination of the national identity by teenagers in nationally-mixed families', *Sovietskaia Etnografia*, 1969, no. 3 (in Russian).

12 See Arutyunyan (ed.), *The Social and the National*. L.M. Drobizheva, 'The strengthening of similarity in the cultural development of nations', in *Istoria SSSR*, 1972, no. 4 (in Russian).

T. SHANIN

The conceptual reappearance of peasantry in Anglo-Saxon social science

One of the most interesting manifestations of human thought is the way concepts and problems appear and disappear in the public eye and in the scholar's mind. That seems particularly true within the social sciences. The unfolding reality and its contradictions – the stuff human biographies and social history are made of – doubtless provide a determinant of it. Yet that is not all, for human consciousness and thought are not simply reflections of 'the objective', but display complex and partly-autonomous characteristics of their own. Those include the rich texture of 'meanings and designs and communications . . . symbols . . . manipulative interpretations . . . (which) stand . . . between consciousness and existence'.[1] Furthermore, specific items of thought are embedded in general *Weltanschauung*, categories and theoretical stands, conscious and unconscious as they may be and linked in turn in mutual interdependence with the collective experience.

The study of peasant societies within 'western' scholarship is a case in point. As in conjuror's tricks or hairdressing fashions, tendencies have appeared, disappeared and reappeared again. The underlying reasons for this chequered intellectual history is neither frivolous nor accidental. To understand it is to learn something about the history and political economy of the world at large as well as about the way ideologies work and change.

Now you see it, now you don't

The crucial historical experience which has influenced collective consciousness the world over has been that of the industrial revolution and the establishment of a world-wide system of capitalist political economy. Whatever its origins and causes, still under debate, the results envelop us all, colouring perception, determining plausible taxonomies, weighing heavily on knowledge. It was linked directly with a general outlook which assumed and preached the unilinear, necessary, never ending and positive 'progress' of humanity from barbarism to true civilisation – which was more or less synonymous with advanced science and technology. Large-scale, mechanised mass-production was taken as necessarily advantageous and so was accumulation of capital, urban life and formal education. In our field of interest, the results of all this differed in different regions. A three-fold division can be clearly spotted between countries at the core of industrialisation/capitalism processes, their class periphery to the East, and the colonial or semi-colonial countries.[2]

During the five decades divided by the beginning of the twentieth century the mainstream of thought within the capitalist 'core' equated peasant economy and society with 'our' past and with backwardness of less developed and less fortunate 'others', to be eradicated as soon as possible. Specificity of peasant social structure, economy, behaviour was discarded altogether or else defined as cultural inertia and/or prejudice. Rural sociology first flourished in the USA. It was first taught at Chicago University in 1892. In 1917 a section of rural sociology was established within the American Sociological Association. It aimed at the maximisation of the profits of a capitalist farmer/entrepreneur and at the ironing out of patches of 'backwardness' still evident in the countryside. So did its counterpart within agrarian economics. Conceptually, both in scholarly and popular images, peasant communities came to play the implicit role of the opposing pole, counterpart and at times 'bogeyman' to those communities which were modern, advanced and successful within dualistic societal taxonomies. Even the word 'peasant' was disappearing from usage or else was used as an abuse signifying crassness, illiteracy and stupidity.

The sidelines of this prevailing view came to reflect the beginnings of disenchantment with the 'new world'. On the one hand, a variety of reactionary ideologies came to exult in the virtues of peasantry, from poetic expressions of belief in joys of natural living to fears of the German and French general staff of losing a pool of healthy and stupid army recruits. More seriously, the social critics of capitalism from de Tocqueville onwards have generated some light from peasant/non-peasant comparison, pin-pointing some lost qualities within modern life, or else, like Durkheim, have considered the possibilities of recapturing some of these qualities for contemporary use within a process of 'social engineering'.

The centre of systematic studies of peasantry was during this period firmly placed in Central and Eastern Europe. In those countries a highly sophisticated intelligentsia politically committed to nationalism and/or liberalism and/or populism and/or socialism was faced with a massive peasantry – the poorest and most oppressed segment of its nations. The ideologies and politics of the struggle for modernisation and/or democracy and/or justice necessarily related to the peasant majorities in those societies, both the major object and the possible carrier of change or else the main bottle-neck of any advance. On the eve of the

First World War the intellectual and political attempts to look at and activate peasantries were often matched by the peasants' own efforts to establish viable political movements in defence of their own political interests, e.g. in Poland, Rumania, Bulgaria, Denmark, etc. All this resulted in a flourishing of studies of peasantry on both the empirical and theoretical levels. Works like those by Kautsky or David in Germany, Boyer in Austria, Chuprov, Lenin and Chernenkov in Russia, and Znaniecki in Poland, or, on the more empirical level, Russian budget studies of peasant households or Polish studies of peasant correspondence, are still relevant and often in many respects unsurpassed. A variety of disciplines shared in this: sociology, ethnography, economics, history, etc. Nor was it merely an extension of prevailing disciplinary models, theories and methods, for much of it assumed, delineated and analysed the peasantry as a social entity and attempted to build the theoretical tools necessary for this task.

Within 'the third region' of colonial and semi-colonial countries 'western' domination was reflected in the growth of anthropology as a discipline specifically devoted to the primitive, small scale and exotic, if not bizarre. A basic conceptual dualism between West and East, with an underlying connotation of advanced as opposed to backward or even good or 'as-it-should-be' versus bad and 'to-be-overcome', led to concentration on the 'primitives', i.e. the temporarily or eternally backward. The ideological support of colonial rule implicit in it or even explicitly offered, was answered especially in the twentieth century by 'native' literature of protest often concerned with peasant life and conditions.[3] The work of a few liberal scholars within the colonial establishment has aimed at similar issues.[4] While often very illuminating, it suffered badly from the limited, unstructured and particular character of the relevant sources, part and parcel of the way the educational and research world-system was organised, centred and controlled.

It is the character of the increasingly global scholarly establishment which determined the place of peasant research within its central Anglo-Saxon component. On the one hand, the disregard of specific studies of peasantry in the West was partly mitigated by the cross-fertilisation of Central and East European perspectives with the works of Thomas and Znaniecki, Lenin, and Sorokin acting as bridges, and as accepted classics of sociological and economic thought (Chayanov and Prokopovich's work caused a similar effect in Germany).[5] On the other hand, such organisation of study accepted a hierarchy of importance and assumed necessary direction of development by which, in Plekhanov's remarkable phrase, 'peasantry did not exist, historically speaking'. To be forward-looking and progressive was to assign concern with peasants to the past, the transient, and the irrelevant. The alternative was to denounce them as cruel barbarians who block the advance of well-being and humanism; this gave a strong emotional charge to the issue.

This was behind the nearly total silence concerning peasants which commenced at the end of the 1920s and continued for about three decades. The West entered an economic crisis and then a world war. As usual, crisis bred self-centredness which makes 'fringes' disappear. In Germany and in Eastern Europe, the rapid spread of nationalist ideologies and dictatorships led to the oppression both of peasant political movements and of radical social sciences mainly concerned with social underdogs. Pro-peasant reactionary rhetoric was increasingly used instead of studies of peasantry, as well as all sorts of social critiques. In the USSR collectivisation has both abolished the very subject matter of small-holder economy and destroyed or restricted the most brilliant of its students, Marxist and non-Marxist alike. As usual, studies in colonies and semi-colonies faithfully reflected metropolitan social sciences or else were closely controlled and repressed. With few exceptions[6] the scholarly field of peasant studies passed rapidly into oblivion.

Looking back it seems clear that by the 1950s the main factors which eventually led to a major upswing of peasant studies were already present or surfacing. Yet the awareness of them was lagging. The analysts of industrial societies were happily experimenting with development theories of planning, econometrics, functions of further advance and new technologies of computing. The non-industrial societies were optimistically tackling the task of joining the 'industrial' club. The Anglo-Saxon modernisation theories repeated on a somewhat more sophisticated level the basic beliefs of its evolutionist predecessors of half a century ago: the necessity for everybody was rapid unilinear and positive advance from barbarism to civilisation – envisaged as industrial capitalist society – with the possible addition of the components of a welfare state. In this context, peasantry has indeed not existed or else has existed as a marginal nuisance, spontaneously disappearing or to be finally removed from the scene by state institutions, education, etc. The few critics of 'modernisation theory' were usually disregarded as eccentrics as were the still very few academics who began the initial slow rehabilitation of specific concepts and terminologies concerning peasant studies.[7]

Back into the scholar's eye

The Anglo-Saxon academic literature of the 1960s has experienced a virtual explosion of studies devoted to peasantry. Both the term and its scholarly content were suddenly revitalised. A virtual flood of articles and books was supplemented by a mounting 'consumer pressure' of scholars and students which brought dozens of seminars and conferences into being. The actual interests and potential results are probably even greater than the remarkable list of new publications indicates, for figures of publications and numbers of new students coming into the field are still on the increase. Even the politicians seemed to join the stampede, led by Ministers of State urgently gathering in Rome in 1975 to discuss 'world hunger' while the chief of The International Bank was defining the problem of 'world poverty' as revolving primarily around the economics of 'the millions of small subsistence farms' which meant the need 'to redefine the objective and measurement of development'.[8] This all raises the questions of 'why?', 'what?' and 'so what?' concerning this shift of scholars' attention.

Before turning to the content and significance of this particular renaissance of concern with peasantry, let us say something about the roots of its re-appearance. These seem to reflect the collapse of 'modernisation' both as a policy and a theory explaining the contemporary world, along with a number of other developments both of a political and conceptual nature.

'Not so long ago the earth numbered 2,000,000,000 inhabitants: 500,000,000 men and 1,500,000,000 natives. The former had the Word, the others had the use of it.'[9] Sartre's pronouncement took its dramatic force from the real enough drama of colonialism and its rapid disintegration. It was closely followed by a not less shattering discovery that, in some essentials, colonialism is very much still with us, part of a world suddenly enlarged by increasingly global politics, economics and communications. All this provides the setting for the conceptual re-appearance of peasantry in our times.

By 1960 it became painfully clear that developing societies do not 'catch up' with industrial ones – the gap was widening. Nor were these societies simply proceeding along the path of those who did it already. Franks' phrase 'the development of underdevelopment' grasped it neatly – it was not simply backwardness and slowness in 'take off' but something different in character, unexpected and disagreeable, shattering political structures and optimistic modernisation theories alike. Not only in a relative but in an absolute sense, poverty has been spreading in sections of the world population depicted by scholars as mainly rural, small-holding, village-bound, family-farming: in a word, peasant. New awareness of numbers and trends began to come to the surface. For example, the share of peasants within the Mexican population was decreasing but their actual numbers are today larger than at the beginning of the century and continue to rise. Indeed, Brazil[10] has been undergoing virtual 'repeasantation' in some of its regions as part of the rapid capitalist advance of the society as a whole. The collapse of simple technological solutions based on 'more and more', the fact that the green revolution could simultaneously increase production of food-stuffs and lead to increasing hunger of the peasant majority, placed the stress again on social and political structures rather than technologies.[11] Nor did the political or military strategists fare much better than the sociologists and economists of the modernisation school. Chinese peasants were manifestly producing something socially different from rapid industrialisation and urbanisation, without a drop in standards of living and with marked political devotion. The Vietnamese peasants proved 'historically existent' to the point of making history – the first power to achieve the impossible by defeating the USA militarily and politically. Peasants stubbornly refused to fit concepts and predictions.

A variety of 'dependency theories' has recently entered the breach left by the collapse of 'modernisation' perspectives as a new accepted vogue, to claim that exploitation on a world scale is at the root of the 'underdevelopment'.[12] They claim multi-directionality of development determined by inequalities within the world society. Capitalism did not simply turn everything it touched into its own image, but rather stabilised, reproduced or even produced anew non-capitalist social structures. Nor was simple parallel development enough of an explanation – the global interdependence came into focus. Industrialisation in the core countries could, at least in principle, stabilise some basic peasant characteristics of a majority of mankind. The exceptional significance of studies of peasantry, not only past but present, was theoretically clinched by Barrington Moore's claim that the way the peasantry disappears makes a decisive impact on a society's subsequent development.[13] The character of peasantry and its social setting seems crucial even to the future of post-peasant societies.

Concepts and blinds

The conceptual content of the re-appearance of peasants as an issue of primary and long-term importance within the social sciences reflects three basic sub-problems: the definition and the delineation of the phenomenon, the claim to its specificity and its disciplinary setting.

There are two major ways to make peasantry disappear, by definition or, more exactly, by the lack of one. Firstly, it may result from adopting a taxonomy of societies which make peasants fall into a mixed bag or into a residual category, together with pastoral nomads, traditional merchants, non-Christian priests and oriental gentry, undivided and conceptually indivisible. The second is to focus attention on heterogeneity or changeability of the peasant societies, concluding thereby that any generalisation about them is spurious or misleading.

The developments in the theoretical stand of a large majority of American anthropologists can be used here as a relevant example. On the one hand the empiricist tendency has been rife, focussing specifically on a single village or tribe 'of one's own'. Endless specifications of detail were often misconstrued as proof of the necessity of methodological nominalism. Simultaneously, basic taxonomy of 'modern versus primitive' was often adopted with a clear undertone of 'us versus them' and with the disciplinary assignment of 'them' to anthropology. A small tribe or a tribal village was then accepted explicitly, or implicitly, as the basic archetype of what is to be studied. Peasants have subsequently disappeared as an analytically definable entity into the general category of 'backward' or else into the residue of those who do not quite fit either of the polarities assumed.

The ability of a conceptual framework to focus as well as to disperse attention can be amply demonstrated here. A conceptual re-tooling was directly related and mutually determined with the current regeneration of the interest in peasants. These conceptual changes took shape in a two-pronged way, closely related to the works of Redfield and Wolf respectively. Redfield has found both the accepted taxonomic dualism and the consequent definition of anthropologists' tasks as relating exclusively to 'folk-communities' increasingly restrictive and disorientating in relation to peasants. His solution was to try and develop an earlier cryptic remark by Krober, who defined peasantry as 'part societies with part culture'. The restrictive dualistic taxonomy was thereby opened up into a tripartite or a three-stage conceptualisation within which every society progressed from a 'folk-community' (autonomous, self-centred and of 'mechanical solidarity' to use the Durkheimian notion) to a modern society (necessarily inter-dependent and of 'organic solidarity'), via a third type, or stage, defined by the necessary relation between rural segments and an urban centre, the second 'societal half' focussing political power and formal (written) culture.[14] Peasantry as a social entity was structurally defined by the character of its relation to the urbanites and delineated thereby from other inhabitants of the pre-industrial and pre-capitalist societies. The historicity and heterogeneity of peasant societies were partly provided for in Redfield's discussion of 'peasants on the make' and peasants' 'conceptual edge'.[15]

On the other hand, Wolf has dropped altogether the formal dualism of cultures as the starting point of the definition of peasants and turned to the content of peasant economy and societal life.[16] Specific agricultural production, and the way of living attached to it, was used as the basic way to delineate the entity under investigation. Its diversity and basic dynamics were consequently conceptualised by the analysis of agricultural eco-types as well as the content of its societal setting and participation in market economy.[17]

Turning from the example to the general characteristics of the conceptual field, there seemed to be four major, partly over-lapping, traditions in operation. First, peasants were approached as the productive and oppressed majority at the historical stage directly preceding capitalism (feudal?) or its remnants in the contemporary world. Secondly, peasants were defined in terms of a cultural lag, i.e. as representatives of patterns of consciousness typical of earlier national traditions. Thirdly, peasants were defined in terms of a specific economy rooted in either particular agriculture or in the way the family-farm unit of production operates, or both. Fourthly, Redfield's and some other definitions placed peasants in relation to the basic societal dualism suggested by Durkheim, Tönnies and Maine, etc. Each of these approaches focusses on specific aspects of peasant social life, and, whilst illuminating them, obscures other aspects. The growing awareness of the limitation inherent in each single approach explains the growth of attempts to combine these various viewpoints. These integrations of diverse theoretical tendencies are sometimes consistent and sometimes merely eclectic.[18]

The issue of specificity and academic disciplines

Whichever definition is adopted, the conceptual significance of peasantry as a problematic is rooted in the approach adopted to the underlying issue of the specificity of peasant economy and society. It goes without saying that peasants differ in different societies, regions, villages and households and that such an assumption does not challenge, as such, the possibility or need for relevant generalisations. Also, typical characteristics of peasantry change in time. (So does the character of other social entities – characterisation and typification are not evidence of stagnation but tools of analysis and yardsticks of processes.) If peasant social structures do not consistently differ from others or cannot be meaningfully delineated as such, two things would follow.

First, all one can hope to achieve is to collect and classify additional data reflecting various areas, periods and samples. No significant theoretical advance is possible or necessary here, for theoretical tools developed elsewhere can be put to use more or less directly, e.g. neo-classical economics or sociological studies of mobility within urban society.

Secondly, the wave of peasant studies and publications is to be treated partly as an answer to pragmatic needs of governments, otherwise as an intellectual fashion due to subside, but not as a conquest of new conceptual fields.

On the other hand, should the conceptual specificity of peasants be accepted, the importance of the recent advance increases. This has been indeed the approach of the most significant recent writings, which describe 'vertical segmentation' as a specific characteristic of political action, and strategies of the use of family labour defying narrowly economic rationales, etc. provide examples of application of such a general attitude. The first publications in English of two earlier classics were particularly significant here: Marx's *Grundrisse* and Chayanov's *The Theory of Peasant Economy*.[19] It is in the attempts to develop, often to integrate and to relate these theoretical approaches to more recent empirical findings, that recent studies of peasantry have made their most significant theoretical advance.

Closely related to the discussion of the present specificity have been the linked issues of the disintegration of peasantry and the possible dynamics of its stabilisation or even reappearance. During the last generation 'depeasantation' proceeded along two major channels: spontaneous and state-directed. The spread of market relations concerning goods and labour, and the penetration and unification of rural areas by both state bureaucracies and mass media, have played here a major role. Structural aspects of inequality within urban/rural relations, as expressed in the extraction of surplus, cultural hegemony and political domination have been increasingly studied during the last five years. Linked with this is the growing problem of evaluation of the short-term and long-term results of agrarian reforms introduced by numerous governments and aiming at diverse and often contradictory ends such as production increase, providing the needs of industrialisation, social equality, and justice. A 'no specificity' stand makes all those issues theoretically vague, to be referred to only in quantitative terms.

Finally, the issue of the specificity of peasant social structure and its studies is linked to the disciplinary framework of analysis and the way the academic community operates. Through the media of conferences, journals, university departments, and appointment and promotions procedures, disciplinary theoretical 'paradigms' are established and reinforced. These include a variety of theoretical assumptions and ways of questioning as well as basic archetypes of the relevant data (or what is considered to be such data). At least four major disciplines have been involved in the recent studies of peasantry in the Anglo-Saxon countries: economics, sociology, anthropology and history. A possible component of the theoretical difficulties encountered is the fact that in each of those disciplines within the Anglo-Saxon realm, the traditionally established starting point and archetypal data are 'off' the contemporary peasantries as we know them. Be it large scale capital enterprise or a national economy for the economists, a successful capitalist farmer to the rural sociologists, a small tribal community to the anthropologists or societal past to the historians – concepts and theories are badly stretched in encompassing the phenomenon. To an extent difficulties which follow have resulted in attempts to solve such problems by a multi-disciplinary approach, combining for example anthropologists and economists in research and training,[20] which until now did not make much headway. ˙

Where to?

Can one predict, or extrapolate from this, future trends and tendencies described above? There is of course no simple solution there. Should the recent wave of interest in peasantry be simply representative of the severity of a social problem, the issue of peasant poverty and therefore the exposition and analysis of peasantry is probably with us to stay. Should it be treated simply as a fashion, the wave of interest would necessarily be followed by a turning away of its exponents from a studied and trivialised subject to something 'fresh' and 'new'. Both the pressure of social problems and fashionable tendencies play their role, but two other determinants seem more central. Firstly, the political context of the issue, usually not the politics of peasantry but rather the politics of those who try to handle peasants, defined 'the field'. More broadly, that has to do with the relations between the 'third world' and the other two. Secondly, it is the way the issue of specificity of 'the field', which is set within the conceptual realm of academic convention (which calls in turn for further explanation) has been playing a major role.

Whatever the future, the renaissance of this field of study has played a major role in the advance of sociological theory by adding to it comparative understanding, theoretical sophistication and radical political 'punch'. In this sense it has served social scientists well. So well indeed as to obscure at times the fact that half of mankind goes on facing the hardships of temporary peasanthood quite oblivious of the intellectual fashions in a world as remote as the moon, and often as barren.

NOTES

1 C. Wright Mills, 'The cultural apparatus', *Power, Politics and People*, New York, 1963, pp. 4–5.

2 The division suggested follows I. Wallerstein, *The Modern World System*, New York, 1974.

3 For somewhat later examples, see Ngo Vinh Long, *Before the Revolution: the Vietnamese Peasants under the French*, Cambridge, 1973.

4 E.g. H.H. Mann's studies of India gathered in *The Social Framework of Agriculture*, London, 1968.

5 W.I. Thomas and F. Znaniecki, *The Polish Peasant in Europe and America*, New York, 1918. P.A. Sorokin, F.F. Zimmerman and C.J. Golpin, *Systematic Source Book in Rural Sociology*, New York, 1965.

6 E.g. C.M. Arensberg, *The Irish Countryman*, New York, 1937.

7 E.g. R. Firth, *Malay Fishermen: their Peasant Economy*, London, 1946. P. Redfield, *Peasant Society and Culture*, Chicago, 1960.

8 McNamara Washington Address, *World Bank Annual Report*, 1974.

9 Sartre's introduction to F. Fanon, *The Wretched of the Earth*, Harmondsworth, 1967, p. 8.

10 E.g. J.R.B. Lopes, 'Capitalist development and agrarian structure in Brazil', Cebrap, 1976, ms.

11 'UNRISD – Global Two, Summary of conclusions', Geneva, 1973, ms.

12 Proceeding from P. Baran to A. Emmanuel, S. Amin and I. Wallerstein.

13 Barrington Moore, *The Origins of Dictatorship and Democracy*, Harmondsworth, 1966.

14 R. Redfield, *The Little Community*, Chicago, 1965; *Peasant Society and Culture*, Chicago, 1960. R. Redfield and M.B. Singer, 'The cultural role of cities', *Economic Development and Social Change*, 1954, vol. 3.

15 Redfield, *Peasant Society and Culture*, pp. 20, 21.

16 E. Wolf, *Peasants*, New York, 1966.

17 Ibid. E. Wolf, 'Types of Latin American peasantry: a preliminary discussion', *American Anthropologist*, 1955, vol. 57.

18 For elaboration see T. Shanin, 'Peasantry: delineation of sociological concept and a field of study', *European Journal of Sociology*, 1971, 12, 289-300; T. Shanin (ed.), *Peasants and Peasant Societies*, Harmondsworth, 1971.

19 K. Marx, *Grundrisse*, Harmondsworth, 1972, first published in part as *Pre-*

Capitalist Economic Formations, London, 1965. A. Chayanov, *The Theory of Peasant Economy*, New York, 1966.

20 T. Shanin, 'The nature and logic of peasant economy', *Journal of Peasant Studies*, 1973, vol. 1, nos 1 and 2.

PART IV

Anthropology and psychology

MEYER FORTES

Anthropology and the psychological disciplines*

There is a story – not altogether apocryphal – about A.C. Haddon, the
founding father of the British tradition of anthropological field research, which can aptly serve as an introduction to what I want to say.
It is narrated,[1] that when Haddon read the first ethnographic work of a
now famous lady anthropologist, he reacted with incredulity. After a
while, it is said, he remarked that when he organised the Torres Straits
Expedition of 1898, he took out with him three psychologists (W.H.R.
Rivers, C.S. Myers and William McDougall). He did so in the expectation that psychology was the key to understanding the mind and ways
of thought of the native peoples of Australia and New Guinea. (As Mrs.
Hingston-Quiggin notes in her enchanting biography of Haddon.)
Alas however, he went on, he was disappointed in this – as for example
in Rivers's experimental studies of colour discrimination. 'But now', he
concluded, 'I see that I should have taken out not a team of psychologists but a lady novelist.'

Much has happened in the development of both anthropology and
psychology since 1898, not to speak of the efflorescence of the ethnographic novel of the post Second World War vintage in the 'developing'
countries of Asia and Africa. But the dilemma foreshadowed in
Haddon's remarks continues to dog our studies. Thus on one side, in
the interval since, there have grown up vigorous movements rejecting
the relevance of psychological investigations and theory for the analysis
and interpretation of anthropological data, and demonstrating by their
success that significant results can be achieved by embracing these constraints. The triumphs of British socio-structuralist ethnography in the
fifties and sixties are witnesses to this, and the methodological implications were threshed out in the seminal book *Closed Systems and Open
Minds*, edited by Devons and Gluckman.[2] Thus, commenting with
approval on Victor Turner's paper in this symposium, Devons and

* I am indebted to the Leverhulme Trust for a grant towards research and secretarial
assistance which greatly facilitated the preparation of this paper.

Gluckman declare that:[3]

> Turner does not question that psychological drives and dispositions have contributed to these [i.e. Ndembu ritual] developments. What he insists is that a social anthropological analysis of these rites can be carried out independently of the psychological analysis of the same rites by relating them to other facts in the socio-cultural system – the point that Durkheim and many others have emphasised.

Later, they warn against the 'confusion' that can arise from 'undisciplined trespass on fields [such as psychoanalysis] one is not competent to traverse. . . .'[4] And this assertion is supported by contrasting Evans-Pritchard's famous study of Azande witchcraft, first published in 1937,[5] and Kluckhohn's almost simultaneous studies of Navaho witchcraft, first published in 1944.[4] Evans-Pritchard, we are told, 'eschews psychological interpretations' (e.g. reference to a psychological mechanism such as projection) – that is, technically derived, as opposed to common-sense, psychological interpretations – and confines his analysis to the relations of 'modes of thought' and to 'alleged feelings' of envy or hatred, to what Azande state as their beliefs within a 'self sealing and self supporting system' which embraces a 'philosophy of morality as well as a theory of causation'.[7]

Kluckhohn, is, by contrast, criticised in particular for trespassing on the technical psychological field by concerning himself with 'latent functions', such as the ways witchcraft beliefs are supposed (quoting Kluckhohn) to 'allow expression of direct and displaced aggression . . .', or handling anxiety, and in general for assuming without manifest evidence the operation of unconscious mechanisms such as displacement, identification, projection, and so forth.[8]

The main point of this contrast is to claim that Evans-Pritchard is methodologically more correct than Kluckhohn insofar as he sticks to the level of observable data and accepts 'naively' the statements of the Azande themselves about their motives and beliefs, instead of resorting to technical psychological theory to impute to ethnographically manifest actions and statements impulses and motives that are not demonstrable at the level of 'naive' observation.

The methodological dilemma, for that is what it is, that Devons and Gluckman are here attempting to resolve goes back to the beginnings of scientific anthropology and arises not only over the pertinence of technical, as opposed to common-sense psychology, to the tasks of anthropology, but equally in connection with other formally non-anthropological branches of science and scholarship that bear on the same subject matter – e.g. history, economics, linguistics, biology, and geography as well as the various '-isms' currently competing for allegiance amongst us.

In my view the issue is clouded if it is presented in terms of abstract meta-theory or in terms of relations between technically demarcated disciplines. In the context of practice the dilemma disappears and the critical context of practice for the anthropologist is the field situation. The Durkheimian objective of simultaneous description and analysis – of establishing the character and the inter-connections of the observed social and cultural facts without reference to extraneous variables – remains the primary task of anthropological enquiry, but we must never forget that the social and cultural facts identified by our ethnographical techniques are in reality manifestations of complex states of affairs encapsulating a plurality of levels of existence, which can be differentiated by appropriate techniques.

Description *more ethnographico* locates and identifies the institutions, the patterns of thought and of belief and behaviour, the social arrangements and relationships, and so on and so forth, in short the facts of custom and of social structure, which constitute our primary data. Analysis, in contrast, enables us to place particular descriptive facts in contexts of general implication, or to dissolve such facts into constituents and variables of more general range and to identify their modes and mechanisms of combination.

If description gives us the phenotypical constants, analysis enables us to isolate the genotypical variables. But we remain, metaphorically speaking, at a 'horizontal' level of investigation confined to identifying concomitance and consistency, or their contraries, contradiction and conflict, amongst and within the descriptive phenomena, as long as we adhere to the Durkheimian paradigm. To be sure this gives us a representation of structure and it may also reveal some of the conditions that are necessary for the existence of the structure and some of the processes and mechanisms that produce it; and this is of first-rate importance. But its focus is inevitably and primarily on questions of how the system works, rather than on questions of why such institutions, beliefs, patterns of behaviour, etc. occur in it. To answer 'why' type of questions we must seek hypotheses of a causal type to account for the phenotypical state of affairs; and to reach such hypotheses we have to undertake what, again metaphorically speaking, I would call 'vertical' analysis. This, to my mind, necessarily entails consideration of connections at other levels than that of the ethnographically given. And Devons and Gluckman are forced to confront this when they try to argue that Turner's statement that (quoting Turner) 'powerful unconscious wishes of a kind considered illicit by Ndembu are expressed in it [the rite]' admittedly derived as it is from applying psychoanalytic theory to the field data, nevertheless falls within the bounds of psychological naivety.[9]

Answering critics for whom the occurrence in both tropical America and North America of the same group of myths is significant primarily as evidence of the peopling of America by successive waves of emigrants from Asia, Lévi-Strauss[10] remarks: 'En posant ainsi le problème, on méconnaîtrait complètement le sens de notre enterprise. Nous ne cherchons pas le pourquoi de ces resemblances mais le comment.'

This is the crux – whether to confine ourselves rigorously to the 'comment' or to seek answers however inelegantly to the 'pourquoi'. For myself, and I believe for the majority of Anglo-(i.e. socio-) structuralists (as opposed to Gallo- or linguo-structuralists) the lure of the 'pourquoi' is irresistible. This follows long-standing traditional interests reflected, for example, in Frazer's explanation of magical beliefs and practices by recourse to psychological assumptions about the association of ideas and defective primitive logic – which of course continues to flourish in its up-to-date dress of 'metaphor' and 'metonym'. Nor should we forget that Morgan attributed the systems of consanguinity which he analysed in his first great treatise, to underlying and immutable ideas or conceptions 'associated together in such fixed relations as to create a system of consanguinity, resting upon unchangeable necessities'.[11] To invoke property relations as the main force behind the evolution of the family and of the state, as Morgan and later Engels and other writers since have done, is an exercise in the same direction; and so also, at a very different level is Malinowski's theory of culture as an apparatus for satisfying basic human needs rooted ultimately in the biological constitution of mankind.

In the specific case of the relevance of psychological theories and methods for the explanation of anthropological observations the question that, as we all know, has been of perennial concern to anthropologists, is that of the nature of so-called 'primitive thought' in alleged contrast to or comparison with civilised thought. The ghosts of Lévy-Bruhl's hypotheses of pre-logical mentality and of mystical participation still haunt us, and hardly a year goes by without some re-examination of the issues he raised. Field observation convinced Malinowski, and has continually reinforced his conclusion, that pre-literate or pre-scientific, i.e. 'primitive,' peoples perceive the real world more or less as we do and show in their technology, and indeed in all their customary ways, the same logical capacities that modern western man has, the key to the apparent differences lying only in the premises from which they start. It is, therefore, of special interest to consider briefly the findings of the experimental psychologists who have, since the war, been very widely engaged in cross-cultural research on cognition and perception.

From the anthropological point of view, it is very important to note that these studies are, in the words of one authoritative work in this field, 'primarily interested in the study of various cultures in order to test the generality of hypothetical cognitive processes' established by research in western societies.[12] For this task the content of the cognitive activities observable in a particular society is of interest only to the extent that it influences or reflects the process or the capacity. In a sense the cross cultural studies of perception, cognition, and learning, – the range and extent of which can be gauged from Barbara Lloyd's admirable review[13] – mainly by the methods of experimental psychology, can be seen as an extension to the human sphere of the comparative research with animals that goes back to Thorndike, Pavlov, and Köhler. Appropriately enough a prominent topic in these researches concerns the relationship of language to perceptual and cognitive performance. Pursuing this line of enquiry, Cole *et al.* conclude from their experiments with Kpelle children and adults both non-literate and literate, that 'Kpelle [like Americans] know and use taxonomic class relationships to structure their verbal behaviour'[14] with more control among those who had some western-type schooling than with the unschooled[15] and with variations due to age differences.

These and other ingenious experiments lead to conclusions such as the following:

> In particular, we want to emphasise our major conclusion that cultural differences in cognition [e.g. the contrast between the propensity of American school children to follow general schemes, infer rules, and use taxonomic categories in their learning and other cognitive tasks and the more restricted, more concept-based, performance of Kpelle children] reside more in the situations which particular cognitive processes are applied to than in the existence of a process in one cultural group and its absence in another.

Similar conclusions emerge from the extensive cross-cultural research that has been devoted to testing Piaget's theories of congitive development and performance. Barbara Lloyd's analysis of the results of cross-cultural research on 'concrete operational thinking' illustrates their outcome well. Referring to some twelve studies in a range of cultural groups in Africa, New Guinea, and Asia, and including Australian aboriginal groups, she indicates that the cognitive skills which Piaget designates by the term conservation (of substances, of weight, length, and quantity) are universal but that the quantitative and qualitative variations in the ways in which these skills are deployed in different cultural environments depend upon the experiences available to members of the society in question. Thus the order in which different conservation skills appear evidently varies with the cultural experience available to a community, and schooling seems everywhere to foster cognitive performance equal to what is found among, for example, American children.[16]

What then have these researches established? Briefly, and perhaps somewhat crudely stated, it seems to me that what they have demonstrated is that the cognitive and perceptual abilities that have been identified amongst children and adults of western culture in Europe and America are universal human aptitudes and endowments. It has been shown also that if the Piagetian models of the developmental stages and the modes of operation of these abilities are accepted as standard, the divergencies from and approximations to these models that have been observed among subjects of non-European culture are directly attributable to the influence of culture and social organisation and to some extent also of language.

From an anthropological point of view many if not most of the findings reported in these field studies which use the methods of experimental psychology are of value primarily because they confirm conclusions reached by the natural history methods of ethnographic research which approach the same phenotypical data of individual behaviour, thought, and judgment, as evidence of cultural material. This is well brought out in the Cole *et al.* study. Observations they report about the effect of western-type schooling, which equips the recipient with a cultural apparatus that includes mere literacy at one end of the scale but may go as far as the most abstruse mathematics at the other end of the scale, are to the point. Referring to this and related studies Barbara Lloyd notes that 'the abstract thought of formal operations probably depends heavily on Western type schooling' and adds, appropriately, that this is hardly surprising.[17]

The anthropological model is clear. What the experimental psychologist identifies under such rubrics as cognition, perception, learning, and thought, seen from the anthropological angle, are instances of the use of a cultural outfit which the actor has been trained to handle, and can in general be trained to handle, at any rate up to a point, even if parts or all of the outfit are of alien origin. This is possible because the same capacities, propensities, and dispositions, some certainly innate, others acquired in the universal socialisation situations of, for example, mother and child relationships, are common to all humanity. Where differences appear in the deployment of any items of a cultural outfit as between different human groups these are due, not to the absence of the basic and universal human endowments, but to possible quantitative differences in their incidence or to differences in the ways in which they are harnessed to the work of living in society and of employing the cultural equipment at their disposal for dealing with the natural world. In terms of a current cliché, we can conclude that human thought processes are the same for all mankind and that variations in thought performance are due to cultural not natural differences.

To speak of culture in terms of an 'apparatus', or an 'equipment' or in more general terms as a form of 'capital', might seem too narrow and instrumentalist a view. Alternatively I could, as I have done elsewhere, suggest subsuming the phenomenon of custom, which is surely the core of culture, under the more general or at least more tangible category of costume, or dress. The point about these metaphorical descriptions is to emphasise that however diverse and varied the outward and visible manifestations of culture may be, underlying all of them is the same basic human endowment. Nowhere perhaps has this been so well documented as in current studies of cognitive systems, folk taxonomies, and mythology. If there is one thing that Lévi-Strauss has insisted upon, it is surely that the logical procedures reflected in mythical thought are no different from and no less systematic than those that are followed in our science and philosophy, the differences lying not in the way the human mind works but in the material with which it works in different societies.

The field of cognition and perception is not the only psychological speciality in which it has proved to be rewarding to test theories and models derived from research in western societies by means of cross-cultural investigation. Extensive studies have also been made cross-culturally of the emotional and appetitive dispositions and of the factors that enter into the make up of character and personality. These studies are well exemplified in cross-cultural research in psychiatry and in such basic psychiatric disciplines as psychoanalysis. And in my view it is the researches in these fields that are particularly relevant to some of the longest standing problems of anthropology.

To begin with it is valuable to realise, as Kiev's review of the literature shows,[18] that there is now ample evidence to confirm that the main forms of psychiatric disorder identified in western societies also occur in oriental, African, and other non-western societies. There are, as he puts it,[19] 'universal symptom patterns in major psychiatric disorders'. What differs from culture to culture is the 'cultural colouring of beliefs, delusions, and behaviour patterns, as well as differences in the kind, severity, and location of pathogenic factors'. The obvious inference is that the psychiatric evidence supports the conclusion suggested by cross-cultural studies of cognition and perception, namely, that the underlying psychological endowment of mankind in the fields of emotion and personality is the same for all branches of humanity. The same psychopathological disturbances afflict all human races, but what varies is their incidence and the ways in which they are manifested in individual thought and behaviour. Even the forms of psychiatric disturbance that occur idiosyncratically in some societies and not in others, such as the acute and often homicidal mania generally known as the *amok* syndrome, and comparable less violent states of possession elsewhere found, exhibit many features of psychopathology that are common among western patients. Anxiety states, phobias, and other symptoms of psychoneurosis on the one hand, and states of depression, delusions and hallucinatory experiences and similar symptoms of psychosis on the other, are of universal occurrence. What particularly varies cross-culturally is the ways in which psychiatric disturbances are interpreted and dealt with. A condition that a western-trained psychiatrist perceives as a state of depression, an Ashanti diviner diagnoses as an attack by witchcraft. We should realise that what is at issue here is not primarily a conflict between rational scientific theory and primitive superstition but a difference between two models of human nature. And this is where our distinctively anthropological task begins.

This task is to try to understand and as far as possible to explain the uniquely human phenomenon of custom, what Cole *et al.* refer to as the 'contents' of cognition and perception. To make my point clearer let me remind you that the natural science model of human nature, as of course of the human organism, is commonly accepted and believed in by laymen as well as by the experts in our society. It is accepted on trust as authorised and indeed prescribed within our social system. It is customary. Custom, as we all take for granted, is a collective possession; where there is custom, there is society, where there is society, there is custom. The question that I want to put is the following: Granted the uniformity throughout mankind, firstly of man's organic constitution, and secondly of the psychological endowment of capacities and dispositions, in what way if at all can we relate these parameters of individual existence to the collective representations, as Durkheim called them, of custom? More specifically, and here I have in mind the point of view represented by Devons and Gluckman and shared by a majority of so-called functionalist anthropologists, is it either possible, or useful, or necessary to take into account the observations, propositions, and generalisations of the psychological sciences in order to understand and possibly explain – i.e. establish the 'pourquoi' of – the phenomenon of custom?

As I have already noted, attempts in this direction go back to our founding fathers. They continue and proliferate, a notable example being the development and continued vitality of the school of 'culture and personality studies', in the United States, recently authoritatively reviewed in his book on the subject by Robert A. Le Vine.[20] I cite his work in particular because it focusses attention on what is critical for resolving the dilemma I attributed at the outset to the remarks of A.C. Haddon, namely the challenge of the ethnographic field experience. It is there that one realises that custom – whether one thinks of it in terms of code or in terms of patterns of behaviour – has meaning only in the context of the social relationships to which it gives shape and content thus defining their location in the collectivity of the society.

My conviction, that we can make little progress towards fully explaining the 'pourquoi' of custom without recourse to appropriate psychological disciplines, can best, I think, be justified, or at least put to the test, by some account of how this was brought home to me in the course of my own field research.

A few days after arriving in the area of my field work among the Tallensi of northern Ghana, I went round to the house of one of the local head men to introduce myself. While being shown around, I was invited into the main 'living room' of his senior wife. In the corner was a long string net hanging from a rafter. It was filled with neatly packed calabashes. I asked the good lady to show them to me and she courteously unpacked them one by one till she came to the last one at the bottom of the net. This one she pointed out to me was special; it contained six or seven smaller calabashes resting one within the other. This she said was her *kumpio*, her 'death box'. When she died, she explained, all her domestic utensils would be divided up amongst her daughters and daughters in law; but this particular calabash and its contents would go to her firstborn daughter; until then, she added, this daughter would never have been allowed to see the *kumpio*. My field notes tell me that I asked her if this was because she disliked or distrusted her firstborn daughter. My semi-literate interpreter found it difficult to convey the idea to her. However, she understood it well enough to shake her head vigorously in denial. 'We do it' she explained 'because our ancestors did it.' This was my introduction to a complex of customary beliefs and practices the central importance of which in Tallensi kinship and family structure and its religious extension into ancestor worship, in due course became apparent to me. As my stumbling upon it so easily and so early in my novitiate indicates, there is nothing secret or indeed even private about the customary identification of the firstborn – sons as well as daughters. What is at first sight peculiar is the ways in which this status is customarily marked out.

The status of the firstborn is most dramatically displayed in the ritual of 'showing the granary' which terminates the funeral of a man who has left children and thus expunges his earthly existence. In this rite a man's firstborn son dressed in his father's tunic turned inside out and carrying, slung over his left shoulder, a mock bow and quiver made for the funeral, followed by his firstborn sister, is solemnly made to look inside his father's granary which has hitherto been totally prohibited to him. His sister follows suit, and general jubilation ensues. What every-one understands and what the reversed tunic and the inspection of the granary so patently declare is that the son has now taken his father's place, literally stepped into his clothes, thus reversing the generation relationship. The critical feature is that this rite applies strictly only to the firstborn, not to the oldest surviving son and daughter. It is a ques-tion not of inheriting the father's property – to which indeed fathers' brothers have first claim – but of succeeding to paternal status for which being firstborn not merely oldest surviving is the proper qualification. This follows from the fact that it is the firstborn who by the mere fact of birth, creates parenthood irreversibly, once and for all. And it is the ambivalence this generates which as we shall see, underlies the 'syn-drome' of the firstborn.

I borrow this term to indicate that the rite of the granary inspection is really the climax of a lifetime of ritually-imposed avoidance relations between firstborn and parent of the same sex. I have described and dis-cussed these at length elsewhere[21] and therefore refer to them only briefly here. Thus father and firstborn son may never eat out of the same dish lest one accidentally scratch the hand of the other. This would cause one of them to die, whereas the same accident when two brothers or a father and his younger son eat out of the same dish would be harmless. Again, a firstborn may not wear his father's clothes or use any of his tools or implements; and there are other restrictions. Recol-lecting that to eat together among the Tallensi as among most peoples of the world affirms the amity and mutual trust that is the essence of kinship, the implication that, as Tallensi say, 'your firstborn is your enemy' is made plain in these taboos. They say that a man's tools and weapons are imbued with his body dirt and are therefore uniquely representative of his individuality, and that his granary holds his soul. Thus the taboos of the firstborn appear to be quite patently designed to prevent the archetypal son from displacing his father in the latter's lifetime. And parallel restrictions apply to a woman and her firstborn daughter.

What is in issue becomes clear when the son reaches the maturity to marry and become a parent in his turn. Father and firstborn son, mother and firstborn daughter (till she marries), it should be realised, live together in the same homestead, and work together in farming and in the domestic round. At first the taboos serve to keep them out of each other's way at symbolically critical occasions like meal times. But when the son marries and achieves parenthood he must make a separate gateway for himself to his quarters in the homestead, for he and his father may not henceforth meet face to face in the gateway they have previously both used. Tallensi cite this taboo as the key to the whole syndrome. They say that its intention is to prevent a fatal clash between the Destinies of father and son. While the son was growing up, and because he was successfully growing up, his Destiny was growing stronger and stronger, the father's meanwhile beginning to decline. Tallensi fathers say quite bluntly that their firstborn almost from birth desire their death so that they can succeed to their place. It follows logically that the nearer a firstborn gets to full adulthood and parenthood the stronger will be his wish and his claim to oust his father. The imagery of the opposed Destinies, as if they were struggling for a limited fund of well-being, aptly reflects the situation. What is at stake, in fact, is the power and authority, which make up what I have elsewhere[22] called the 'mystical potency' that is vested in the status of fatherhood. It is significant that a man cannot become juridically autonomous, i.e. *sui iuris* – which is also a necessary condition for ritual autonomy– until his father dies. Until then, even if he is himself the father of a large family and economically well-to-do, he is a jural and ritual minor in his father's power.

What is perhaps most important about succeeding to a father's status is that this requires the son to establish his dead father as an ancestor spirit. And it is the same for the mother *mutatis mutandis*. What this amounts to is that the face to face, living parental authority extinguished by death is, so to speak, reinstated at another level, the 'supernatural' level of ancestor worship. Thus the bonds of filial dependence in everyday life are perpetuated at this supernatural level in terms of ritual dependence and the requirements of ritual service.

The fuller implications of this can be made clearer if we look again briefly at the notion of Destiny. The belief that a person's passage through life is governed by his or her Destiny is widespread in West Africa[23]. Tallensi conceive of Destiny as being a choice made by the individual pre-natally. It may be a bad Destiny which manifests itself in continual misfortune and affliction. Thus when Dinkaha's infant daughter died of a wasting disease he himself and her mother were utterly prostrate with grief. Then came the divination to discover the mystical agency responsible for the child's death and it emerged that it was her evil Predestiny. Before she was born she had declared that she did not want a father or a mother or brothers or sisters. So having been brought into the world, she took ill and died. The mother grieved for many days. Dinkaha himself, however, expressed relief at this verdict. In the same way Predestiny is blamed if a woman continually miscarries, if a man continually fails in attempts to marry or to earn his living, and so forth. The significant point is that it is only in retrospect that an evil Predestiny is revealed, in response to what seems like a senseless, premature death, or repeated affliction that has not yielded to other redressive measures or to inexplicable failure to achieve normal goals in life. And the evidence of field observation is that both the alleged victims and those responsible for them get great comfort from the ritual of identifying and coping with evil Predestiny.

But there is another side to Destiny which affects all males, and through them such dependent females as daughters and wives. In this pattern an unusual achievement, an accident or affliction, or a strange coincidence, is interpreted through divination as a sign that a group of ancestors wishes to take over the Destiny of a young man and in return for ritual service from him will foster his development and advance in life. Let me give an example. As a youth Anaaho took to playing the native single string fiddle. He became so adept that he was in constant demand. But his father who, in proper Tallensi style, valued farming above everything, was furious because the boy was neglecting his farm work. So he smashed the fiddle to force the boy to return to his hoeing. Almost simultaneously, the youth was taken ill and his father went off anxiously to consult a diviner. It emerged that the fiddle was ordained by Anaaho's Destiny to be his life task. His illness and the troubles he had got into with his father were signs that a particular group of his ancestors was revealing itself as the guardians of his Destiny. Their command was that Anaaho must make a shrine for them on which to offer sacrifice to them, must give up farming entirely, and devote himself to fiddling. If he refused or was forced to refuse he would surely die; if he submitted he would prosper. The father had no choice but to acquiesce and in the event Anaaho had a long and prosperous career. This is typical, though not all Destiny-ordained careers end up so propitiously.

It will be understood that this is the barest outline of a complex configuration of customary beliefs and ideas that is itself but a part of a very elaborate religious system based on ancestor worship which pervades every corner of Tallensi social life. (But see Newell[24] for parallels from other African societies, from China, Taiwan and Japan.) Certain features distinctive of this religious system are apparent even from my brief sketch of the destiny concept. Firstly, it serves the individual as a means of devolving or projecting the ultimate responsibility for everything that happens to him in the course of his life on to agencies which are perceived to be outside his control by the mundane technological and social processes of ordinary life – not unlike beliefs in witchcraft, or theories of the hereditary determination of intelligence or personality or psychosis in some circles in our own society. And we can see more clearly now how neatly a doctrine of their competing destinies can serve to drain away, so to speak, real and potentially destructive mutual enmity from the relationships of father and son.

Let us consider this a little more fully. Among the Tallensi, as throughout Africa, no person is regarded as fully mature until he marries and becomes a parent. Not only that, but for Tallensi full personhood is only realised by the achievement of ancestorhood.[25] That is why the birth of grandsons is particularly joyously welcomed. Anyhow, it is obvious that parents owe the most decisive change in their lives to their firstborn – who in turn of course owes his very existence to them. And yet it is he who heralds the fate that must inevitably overtake parents: for it is a law of nature that they must sooner or later make way for the next generation, the sibling group founded by the firstborn.

The dilemma, consciously perceived by the Tallensi, is threatening; and it is not extravagant to imagine, as I have already indicated, that there is an underlying ambivalence in the emotions and attitudes of parents, desiring to hold on to their powers and to life itself as long as possible. One can imagine a temptation on the one side to destroy the offspring whose every year of growth brings the time of their extinction nearer, which is however in conflict with the urge on the other side to love and cherish these children who are their sole guarantee of immortality – quite concretely so since it is only through his children that a person can become a commemorated ancestor. Similarly it is easy to imagine equal ambivalence in the emotions and attitudes of the children awaiting the day when they can step into the parents' place. And for both sides focussing this attention on the firstborn is both logical and convenient, serving, metaphorically speaking, as a kind of lightning conductor which draws away the antagonism that is built into the relations of successive generations and enables them to live together in mutual trust. The symbolism of the competing Destinies crystallises in a concrete image the reality that is difficult to conceptualise and even to face openly since it depends upon largely unconscious emotional ambivalence. Again, one can see how the inter-generational taboos tie down concretely, and rationalise in the form of ritually obligatory self-discipline, the latent conflict between the generations.

Here it should be noted that the achievement of ancestorhood is, as we might put it, more a matter of luck or of pure chance than of merit. Tallensi recognise quite explicitly that the achievement of parenthood (like, for instance, survival to old age) is not a reward for good conduct or even for devoted service to the ancestors. It is not always the virtuous, by ordinary mundane standards, whose lives are most successful;

wicked or unscrupulous men sometimes leave many children where up-
right, good men die childless; disease and death often strike the wife or
child of a responsible, provident family head whereas his spendthrift,
improvident brother escapes scot free.

Confrontation with these intractable realities of everyday existence
provides experiential as well as logically-incontrovertible evidence for
the assumption that there are occult[26] powers not susceptible of empirical technological or social control at work in determining the course
and outcome of individual existence. The Tallensi do not have the concept of chance, nor do they accept that luck (*zu-song*, a good head) is
uncaused. To deal with the existential dilemma presented by the un-
predictability and, one might say, injustice of everyday life they fall
back, conceptually and emotionally, on to the doctrine of Destiny and of
the over-riding non-material, non-human powers of the ancestors. At
the level of the action that is necessary if people are to live with these to
them arbitrary constraints, the defences take the form of ritual and
taboo.

It is my argument that this ideology – this system of ideas, beliefs and
practices – is effective for the actors just because the ancestors are so obviously transfigured parent figures; and it is consistent that their most
distinctive characteristic is that they manifest themselves, according to
Tallensi beliefs, predominantly in the afflictions they send to their descendants rather than in the benefits for which they also claim credit.
This reflects the fact, in my view, that it is not the whole parent, who
cherishes as well as chastises, loves as well as disciplines, his or her
offspring, but only the jurally and morally coercive aspect of the parents
that is elevated to ancestorhood. It is symptomatic of the supreme judi-
cial quality of the authority and power vested in the ancestors that it is a
basic religious as well as jural principle that every death must be revealed by divination to be ultimately caused by particular, identified
ancestors. A death not so authorised (for this is what it amounts to) is
not recognised as a normal human death but is comparable to the death
of an animal or is contrary to the nature of man. And it is consistent
with the ideology that every normal death is attributed to ancestral
retribution for ritual negligence or some form of wrongdoing, most
commonly within the field of kinship relations with its all-embracing
norms of prescriptive altruism, of which the victim may not even be
known to have been aware in his or her lifetime. Conversely, it is
believed that life ultimately accrues to the individual through ancestors' gift and watchfulness, in response to service and tendance.

It cannot be overemphasised that in their ordinary life Tallensi are a
realistic and practical people. Living authority is rarely harshly
exercised, indeed parents are noticeably affectionate and tolerant in
their relationships with small children. In real life a father has no
powers of life and death over his children but of course parents are
inevitably the source of discipline, frustration, and what seems to a
small child the arbitrary regulation of their life and control of their

wishes and urges.

The question now is how can we get behind these descriptive data and explain them in terms of a causal and general theory of human behaviour? The problem is the more challenging since, as I have shown elsewhere,[27] the paradigm of inter-generational opposition so graphically displayed by the Tallensi is of very common, if not universal, validity. In different forms of cultural dress it is found throughout Africa, in Polynesia, New Guinea, India, classical China and still further disguised in our own society. And everywhere some form of enforced separation either physically or by religious prescription or apparently inadvertently through educational institutions, age set organisations and so on appears to be required in order to contain the problem. Not everywhere of course, do we find such elaborate ritual provisions for shelving ultimate responsibility from the actor to institutionally established quasi-external agencies as Destiny.

I do not see how we can answer this question without recourse to psychological theory; and for me the obvious and convincing theory is that which is provided by psychoanalysis. Let us consider again the focal and critical relationship of parent and firstborn of the same sex, my paradigm being the relationship of father and firstborn son. I remarked earlier that what is evidently at stake is a resource I have entitled as 'mystical potency'. This is not an ideal concept, I fear, for what I have in mind, but it must suffice. I use it to include the whole gamut of parental power and authority as experienced by the offspring and also as defined in customary law and ideology. It includes the physical and psychological superiority of the parents as manifested, for example, in the control over the material provision of food and shelter and the moral provision of protection. But it refers above all to what, from the filial point of view, is the most mysterious and arbitrary feature of parenthood, their monopoly of procreative right and capacity. The ethnographic evidence, both for the Tallensi and comparatively, to my mind points indisputably to the privileged procreative sexuality of parents as the nucleus of the syndrome. That is why the tension between successive generations symbolically crystallised in the doctrine of the antagonistic Destinies of father and firstborn son is felt to be most dangerous when the son reaches reproductive status, on the threshold of parenthood. One might surmise that a different defensive ideology would have emerged if the Tallensi had the punitive and mutilating initiation rituals through which to gain procreative sexual rights that are found elsewhere.

A pointer to what I am here inferring is the rule, often cited, that the one irreparable breach between father and son occurs if the son commits the unforgivable sin of incest with a wife of his father. Indeed it is enough – since it is taken to imply the wish – for the son to enter the sleeping room and sit on the sleeping mat of the father's wife other than his own mother – and even that would not be permitted for a boy past infancy. And again similar taboos are met with elsewhere in Africa and in other societies. Among the famous Nuer, for example,[28] a marriage is not fully established until the birth of the first child. Indeed a woman lives with her own parents until the firstborn is weaned and only then is the husband allowed to take her home to his own paternal home. Nuer also impose characteristic avoidances on the firstborn. They must never use the spoon of father or mother and a first son must not sleep or sit on his mother's sleeping hide – to do so would make her barren and also injure his father and himself. Indeed Nuer (like a number of other peoples) send a firstborn son away to be brought up by his maternal grandparents explaining that this keeps him from his parents until he is old enough to observe the strict avoidance rules.

Let me recapitulate. The dilemma of parents – and I claim that this is a universal dilemma – is that on the one hand they need children to perpetuate themselves and give them some sort of immortality, the only immortality which is worth having, and which, perhaps, goes down to phylogenetic needs, and therefore they must cherish and properly bring up these children. But on the other hand, they must, from the moment of their children's birth, signalled by the arrival of the firstborn, face the inevitability that they will be ousted and replaced by these children. Cultural ideology may provide various rationalisations such as, for instance, a belief in Destiny to cover up the dilemma. But the ambivalence remains, an ambivalence which is a compromise between a repressed urge to destroy the threatening children and a conscious love for and identification with them. A reversed ambivalence inevitably arises in the children, the filial generation, impelled as they are to fulfil their destiny of replacing the parents as quickly as possible; and the focus of the struggle is the power of, and the right to exercise the procreative capacity that brought them into being. There is, in short, no question in my mind but that the most definitive explanation for this syndrome is to be found in terms of the classical theory of the 'Oedipus complex' and its development through the oedipal phase of filioparental relationships to its eventual replacement by the internalised authority to which Freud gave the name of the 'super-ego'. But there is a significant modification to be taken into account. It is as if the drama originally depicted by Freud as taking place, generation after generation, in the mind and personality of the individual is, in the kind of tribal society I have been describing, thrust out, externalised, into the open of custom and social organisation. But where Freud saw the conflict of successive generations as emanating solely from the aggressive and envious wishes of the filial generation, I see it as engendered by the reciprocal ambivalence precipitated by the crucial dilemma of parenthood.[29] The taboos I have described can be thought of as a culturally authorised and therefore socially controllable mechanism that permits regulated and partially disguised confrontation of the intergenerational ambivalence and so drains away its destructive charge.

Tallensi custom provides the additional backing of what amounts to the externalised 'super-ego', the institutionalised organ of moral and ritual control comprised in their ancestor cult. On the one hand parents derive their authority from their position as agents of the ancestors and on the other they fulfil their responsibilities under the compulsion of their duty to the ancestors. In return, in compensation, as it were, they have the security of the prospect of ancestorhood for themselves. This enables them to tolerate and keep in check their hostile impulses, whether these are consciously felt or not, by the assurance it implies of their being endowed with power and authority forever, even after death, and of having, correspondingly, the perpetual filial servitude of their children.

A number of problems of greater general import arise here. But what I want mainly to bring out is the observation that custom, by reason I think of its consensual, public, collectively authorised and maintained character, serves the purpose of harnessing to legitimate ends human proclivities that can turn into pathological forms where they do not fall within the discipline of custom.

To drive home my argument let me contrast this approach with one that commands widespread enthusiasm in anthropological circles today, being advanced sometimes as showing up the inadequacies of classical functionalism. I refer to the approach that derives with one modification or another from the linguo- (Gallo-) structuralism associated with the work of Professor Lévi-Strauss, and I want to take as my example a brilliant study by one of my former colleagues, Professor J.S. Tambiah. His book on Thai village Buddhism[30] has rightly been hailed as a model of anthropological method. To make my point, I venture to quote *in extenso* an analysis I have myself proposed[31] of a ritual sequence described and discussed by Professor Tambiah. His book, I have argued,

> sticks firmly to the manifest level of cognitive symbolism, broadly along the lines laid down in the linguo-structuralist theory of Lévi-Strauss. Consider, for instance, his account of the entry of a man into monkhood, usually after an earlier period of novicehood. At the village level monkhood is generally a temporary commitment, followed by a return to permanent lay life. Restating the descriptive data in anthropological language he concludes: 'If ordination to monkhood is in religious terms a rite of initiation, in social terms it is distinctly a rite of passage for young men before they marry and set up their own households' (p. 101). 'Why then' he continues 'do youths and young men lead a monastic life as a phase of their lives?' The answer is that this confers merit on their parents. The ordination of a monk is usually sponsored by his parents, and becoming a monk is, Tambiah notes, an expression of 'filial piety'. (pp. 102-3). Entering a monastery signifies obligatory withdrawal from lay life. And this means above all the 'renunciation' (p. 104) or 'suppression' (p. 144) 'of male virility or sexuality and similar attributes of sexual life'. This is dramatised in the ordination

ceremonies, which include a head-shaving ritual interpreted by Tambiah as 'symbolic renunciation of sexuality', thus marking the passage of the ordinand from the lay state to the 'opposed state' of monkhood. Other features of the ritual of ordination are interpreted in the same way, and 'the ritual as a whole' says Tambiah 'states a reciprocal relation between, on the one hand parents and kin and laymen (in general), and, on the other, the monk; it also emphasises the essential features of a monk's life that distinguished it from a layman's' (p. 108).

What then is the nature of this symbiotic reciprocity of relationship (p. 143) between monks and laymen? The monks cook no food for themselves – their food is provided by the villagers as a special merit-making act and is brought to them by unmarried girls who 'can do so without danger because the monk has suppressed himself sexually and is asexual' (p. 144). Other services to satisfy his needs (e.g. clothing) are similarly rendered by the lay public; and here comes an important point. These practical lay activities are regarded as polluting, entered into, Tambiah argues, so that 'the religious specialist can be freed to pursue purity from the world's contaminations'. Thus the 'opposition' of monks and laymen is an opposition also of purity and pollution, the critical feature of which is the opposition between non-productive ritually obligatory celibacy and asceticism, on the one hand, and the productive and procreative lay activities without which the monks themselves could not exist (p. 148-9).

It seems to me that this account of monkhood in a Thai village community takes us no further than the manifest descriptive level, simply restating in anthropological language what the eye sees and what informants tell the inquirer; but psychoanalytically considered these data raise more complex theoretical issues. Why, one might ask, should adolescent boys be willing to renounce their aggression and sexuality in order to confer religious merit on their parents? To answer this question let us assume that the ordination rites represent a symbolical, ritually legitimated working-out of repressed rivalry and mutual hostility of fathers and sons. Could it be then that the ritual Tambiah interprets as the renunciation of sexuality is better understood as expressing filial submission to symbolic castration as preparation for symbolically regressing to the seclusion of infantile innocence and dependence on parents in the monastery, and by this sacrifice winning the merit later to re-enter safely the 'polluting' life of normal, that is of sexually and economically active, adulthood? Is it wildly speculative to interpret the 'filial piety' paraded in the institution of monkhood as a customarily legitimate device for converting repressed filial hostility into socially respectable humility? And it is of interest to learn, in this connection, that the coffin bearers in the cremation ceremonies for a dead man were his sons and a son in law, and that 'they are exposed to the danger that the dead man's *phii* [a kind of spiritual double] may take hold of them or harm them' (p. 182). Again would not the descriptive opposition between purity and pollution make analytical sense, and raise important questions for direct observation, if it is thought of as a phase of infantile sexual innocence and oral dependence on the mother defensively enforced by ambivalent parents, metaphorically speaking a 'back to the womb' phase, in contrast to the parent rejecting stage of sexually active, married adulthood?

Granted that this is all speculation, (but cf. Leach[31] on the connection between head hair and potency, and on the castration symbolism of head shaving) I would nevertheless argue that such an approach opens up questions and suggests hypotheses that do not emerge in the strictly descriptive ethnographic narrative – especially if it is constructed in terms of the intellectualist approach to the study of ritual that is now favoured by many anthropologists (cf. the criticism by Horton[32]).

These speculations are based on hypotheses about certain inevitable and universal features in the relationship of successive generations of parents and children which are derived from psychoanalytic theory, ultimately, but which were impressed on me as a result of my field experience among the Tallensi. In discussing Tambiah's work, I purposely chose to look at a social and religious system that is, descriptively speaking, strikingly different from the African systems I am accustomed to, and that is, moreover, depicted in accordance with a current theoretical position which contrasts with my own. Since formulating my speculations, however, I thought it would be interesting to check on their plausibility from an outside point of view. I did have a chance of outlining them to Professor Tambiah himself and was reassured to hear from him that he thought my speculations were not unreasonable, though he did not have the kind of field data that could be used as a direct check. But observations that do have a bearing on the question were brought to my attention by Professor Melford Spiro. In the course of his exhaustive study of Burmese Buddhism[33] he investigates in considerable detail the 'recruitment structure' of monkhood (ch. 14, p. 320-50). He shows that, despite the obvious economic and status advantages offered by monkhood, 'only a small minority of village boys' choose to enter it (p. 329) which implies that there are selective influences and obstacles of other kinds. He finds that desires to escape from difficulties, responsibilities and personal tragedies are very important. But one of the unconscious factors both of recruitment and of keeping men in the monasteries, one with which the social structure and the customary moral and ritual prescriptions of monkhood seem to be particularly compatible, is what he describes as the need or wish for dependency and complete security (p. 338-43). This is tantamount to a desire for, or at least to a readiness to find satisfaction in, being in the 'structural position' of a young child. 'The monk,' he writes 'is able to reinstate the (real or fancied) blissful period of infancy, in which all needs are anticipated and satisfied by the all-nurturant mother . . .' the monk's permitted regression being symbolised by his very appearance (shaven head etc.) and his ritually prescribed patterns of conduct. It takes hard self-discipline, Spiro shows, for the monks to control their sexual desires, celibacy being the crucial moral requirement of monkhood and the difficulty of to meeting this requirement is the main reason why monks revert to lay life (pp. 366-8). These, and other observations I have not the space to cite here, to my mind lend great plausibility to the interpretation I have suggested for Tambiah's data.

What, then, is the lesson of the Thai example? On the surface, at the manifest, descriptive level, there seems to be nothing in common between the intergenerational avoidance syndrome of the Tallensi and the adolescent withdrawal into monkhood of the Thai villagers. But when we realise that the latter, like the former, is a customary, institutionalised procedure to ensure the containment and to provide a socially legitimate expression of the universal 'oedipal' struggle between parents and children, procreators and procreated, those who have the power and the cultural supremacy and those who must by the inexorable law of life eventually replace them, their common core becomes evident. Starting from the postulate of a common psychological nucleus around which the institutional complexes presented in the ethnography are built up, we are led on to ask questions and propose hypotheses about a people's customs and social system that are not otherwise brought to attention. For the Tallensi, for example, as for a number of other peoples of West Africa, the evidence suggests that there is a direct and reciprocally determinative connection between their customary provision for dealing with the oedipal struggle in the domestic domain and their ancestor cult, on the one hand, and the structure of authority relations in the lineage system, on the other hand. For the Thai villagers, analogously, the way they handle the oedipal confrontation by shifting it to the public ritual arena of the temple correlates well with their disregard of descent in any depth and is consistent with the diffuse pattern of authority in the village polity and the Buddhistic doctrines of morality, human existence and reincarnation, all of which taken together would seem to rule out any form of ancestor worship.

Let me try to sum up briefly the argument I have been presenting. It is my thesis that the situation I have identified as the oedipal struggle or confrontation is an intrinsic, inescapable feature of the filio-parental relationship, through which the succession of the generations is engendered. Since this is the basis of the process of social reproduction on which the continued existence through time of every society ultimately depends, it follows that the oedipal confrontation stands, metaphorically speaking, at the centre of gravity of every social system. But it is a double-sided situation, creative in its reproductive aspect but also potentially disruptive. In consequence, I am suggesting, customary devices are found in many, if not all, human societies (perhaps most explicitly only in those that are relatively stable in structure and homogeneous in culture) for controlling this potentiality. These devices give collective, that is social, recognition to the reality of the oedipal confrontation by affording to it forms of public expression in the symbolic guise of rationalising ideas, beliefs and practices commonly validated by moral and religious sanctions, which legitimation, even if it is painful to individuals, enables it to be absorbed into the reproductive process without danger to society.

I have of course been dealing with a strictly limited field of social structure, and observations appropriate to this field are not necessarily applicable to other contexts of social life. Within this context we could, following conventional ethnographic practice, content ourselves with observing that such customs as the avoidances adhered to by the first-born serve to signify their status in the same way as their prescribed garments signify the status of a chief or a *tendaana*, a man or a woman. This tells us how custom works in a particular social context in a given society. It does not explain why, for instance, the customs I have mentioned take the specific form of obligatory avoidance designated as binding by reason of taboo, or why they have the content they exhibit – relating, for instance, to ways of sharing food or to theories about the make-up of personality. To answer such questions, I am claiming, we must investigate the psychological substructure of the social relations we are concerned with, in this case, of the relations of parents and children; and the key to this lies, in my opinion, in the psychoanalytical theories of filio-parental relations and of what Freud once referred to as 'the anatomy of the mental personality'.[34]

NOTES

1 A. Hingston-Quiggin, *Haddon, the Head Hunter*, Cambridge, 1942.
2 E. Devons and M. Gluckman, Introduction to M. Gluckman (ed.) *Closed Systems and Open Minds*, London, 1964.
3 Ibid., p. 214.
4 Ibid., p. 241.
5 E. E. Evans-Pritchard, *Witchcraft, Oracles and Magic among the Azande*, Oxford, 1937.
6 C. Kluckhohn, *Navaho Witchcraft*, Boston, 1941.
7 Devons and Gluckman, op. cit., pp. 240-4.
8 Ibid., pp. 246-7.
9 Ibid., p. 216.
10 C. Lévi-Strauss, *L'Homme Nu*, Paris, 1971, p. 32.
11 Cf. M. Fortes, *Kinship and the Social Order: The Legacy of L.H. Morgan*, Chicago, 1969.
12 M. Cole *et al.*, *The Cultural Context of Learning and Thinking*, London, 1971.
13 B.S. Lloyd, *Perception and Cognition: A Cross-Cultural Perspective*, Middlesex, 1972.
14 Cole *et al.*, op. cit., p. 90.
15 Ibid., p. 140.

16 Lloyd, op. cit., pp. 126-35.

17 Ibid., p. 137.

18 A. Kiev, *Transcultural Psychiatry*, Middlesex, 1972.

19 Ibid., p. 77.

20 R.A. Le Vine, *Culture, Behaviour and Personality*, London, 1973.

21 M. Fortes, 'The first born', *J. Child Psychol. Psychiat.*, 1974, 15, 81-104.

22 Ibid.

23 Cf. M. Fortes, *Oedipus and Job in West African Religion*, Cambridge, 1959.

24 W.H. Newell (ed.) *Ancestors*, The Hague, 1976.

25 M. Fortes, 'On the concept of the person among the Tallensi', in G. Dieterlen (ed.) *La Notion de Personne en Afrique Noire*, 1973, Colloques Internationaux, no. 544, Centre National de la Recherche Scientifique, Paris.

26 M. Fortes, 'Religious premises and logical technique in divinatory ritual', in *A Discussion on Ritualisation of Behaviour in Animals and Man, Philosoph. Trans. Roy. Soc. London*, 1966, series B, no. 772, vol. 251, 409-22.

27 Fortes, op. cit., 1974.

28 E.E. Evans-Pritchard, *Kinship and Marriage among the Nuer*, Oxford, 1951.

29 Fortes, op. cit., 1974.

30 S.J. Tambiah, *Buddhism and the Spirit Cults in North-East Thailand*, Cambridge, 1971.

31 E.R. Leach, 'Magical hair', *J. Roy. Anth. Inst.*, vol. 88, 2, 147-64.

32 R. Horton, 'Neo-Tylorianism; sound sense or sinister prejudice', *Man*, 1968, N.S., vol. 3, 4, 625-34.

33 M. Spiro, *Buddhism and Society: A Great Tradition and its Burmese Vicissitudes*, London, 1971.

34 S. Freud, *New Introductory Lectures on Psychoanalysis*, translated W.J.H. Sprott, London, 1933.

I. S. KON

Ethnography and psychology

From whichever viewpoint we look at ethnography (ethnology), its foremost social task, its *raison d'être*, is to contribute to the establishment of mutual understanding between peoples, and to the promotion of a meaningful dialogue between them as necessary conditions of international cooperation. An ethnographer may be engaged in the study of cultural symbols, specific forms of clothing, housing, or the customs of an ethnos, but in each of these cases he will be interested to know, in the first instance – how, when, and why did these phenomena emerge, and then – what are their social functions in the system of social relations of the society under investigation and, last but not least – their meaning for individuals as the authors, bearers, and recipients of their influence. The first question necessarily calls for the collaboration of ethnography with history, the second – with sociology, the third – with psychology.

The intensification of international and intercultural contacts, together with the acceleration of social and cultural development and innovation in the time of the scientific and technological revolution, make the 'communicative' aspect of ethnography highly valuable and responsible today.

But as regards the communicative qualities of man and his ability to understand others develop, both in ontogenesis and phylogenesis, there exists a stable correspondence parallel with the evolution of his own self-consciousness. Modern developmental psychology has proved that the attitude of the child towards other people passes through the same principal stages of development as his own self. This development starts in the undifferentiated whole in which 'ego' and 'alter' are merged, a child is as easily psychologically 'infected' from outside, as it will ascribe to others its own motives and feelings. When the incongruity of 'self' and 'the other' is realised, the differences existing between them are brought to light. At this stage 'the other' is conceived as an external being, whose behaviour is explained by the logic of the situation; he may be the object of a more or less conscious manipulation, but his inner feelings and motives remain closed for the child.

According to Hoffman's[1] summary of research findings, children at the age of about one are capable of recognising others as separate physical beings; by the age of about two to three they require a rudimentary knowledge that others have independent feelings of their own; and by the age of about six to nine they begin to realise that people have their own identity beyond the immediate situation. Understanding comes only as a result of assuming the role of 'an other', and in this process the latter is no more an alien or a stranger, but becomes an interlocutor or an 'alter ego'. Subsequently, in the course of such dialogues, the child's self-image becomes more differentiated, comprehensive and stable, and this serves as the starting point for all further communication.

A similar trend can be observed in the development of ethnic self-awareness and even in the science of ethnography itself, with the only difference that egocentrism is replaced by ethnocentrism. The naive ethnocentric assumption that peoples all over the world are similar, or at least, follow a way similar to ours, has been replaced by amazement in the face of the 'strangeness' of alien customs and morals, which become the object of an external classification, alongside with a complete inability to understand their internal coherence. Later on there comes understanding of the structural and functional unity in the life of an ethnos, accompanied by relativism and a stress on the ethno-cultural peculiarities. Finally there emerges the endeavour to explain these peculiarities not only by including them in a specific social and historical context, but also by comprehending the existential meaning of every institution, social norm, standard, etc. The complexity of this task inevitably brings forth a higher level of theoretical and methodological reflection, in which the unconscious ethnocentrism of the researcher as well as the imperfection of his methodological tools may be overcome. The longing for objective knowledge, which does not take any person for a simple echo of one's own self, is combined with disappointment with naturalistic models, regarding others as mere objects, and thus being unable to perceive their subjective selves, and unable to go beyond the saying: 'east is east and west is west . . .'

However, the relation between objects, problems and methods in modern science forms a very complicated pattern which does not and cannot coincide with traditional interdisciplinary boundaries, which have emerged spontaneously and in answer to quite different problems. Alongside 'classical' monodisciplinary topics, the elaboration of which remains fully in the hands of specific scholars and which nobody else would attempt to undertake (either due to their great specificity or to their small attractiveness for others), there emerges a number of marginal fields of study and problems, interdisciplinary by their very nature, which cannot be solved in terms of any single discipline. This gives rise to certain difficulties. Every science is but a game with its own rules which are not to be altered at will nor to be supplemented by others (this being especially true if applied to methodology). But new problems cannot be kept within the limits of old boundaries and traditions. And if we are not carried along by the very procedures of a scientific game, but are keenly interested in the dynamics of a social phenomenon, we must use a new approach to the problem or, unless more elaborate theories are developed, we should at least consider in what ways this problem is conceptualised by neighbouring sciences. The comparison (or, rather, juxtaposition) of approaches seems to be more fruitful than the concern with preserving interdisciplinary boundaries which have long since lost their watchtowers or their guards.

Bearing all this in mind, what should be our conception of the relations between ethnology and psychology? Their connections have always been very close. Bromley[2] justly says that ethnography and psychology are jointly interested in two fields of scientific problems. The first and widest comprises the study of national character, peculiarities of ethnic mentality, the character of the culture derived therefrom, the symbolic world, moral and ethnic norms, and the value orientations of diverse peoples. The features appropriate to ethnic psychology may be expressed immediately in ideological forms (such as art, religion, etc.) or indirectly through specific ways of culture transmission, child rearing and socialisation, sex role differentiation, etc. In the narrow and more specified limits of research we may name the ethnic self-awareness proper, that is, how and in what terms do individuals conceive their ethnic affiliation and the meaning they attach to the idea; the ethnic stereotypes and auto-stereotypes, and their tendencies and mechanisms of transformation under the impact of education, interethnic contacts, the internationalisation of everyday life and means of production.

Each of these problems may be considered on three different levels: first the macrosocial, or sociological (that is, in what ways will certain features and relations be implemented in culture, social structure and modes of life of a nation); secondly the interpersonal, or sociopsychological (in what forms will they be reflected in immediate inter-personal relations and contacts); thirdly the intra-individual, or psychological (their manifestation in the qualities and traits of an individual, in his social attitudes, value orientations, etc.). These aspects may be regarded as mutually complementary yet their study calls for specific research methods and 'belongs' to different branches of science.

In compliance with the existing traditions, ethnography deals chiefly with psychic processes and characteristics implemented and objectified in a certain culture, whereas the manifestation of these ethnocultural features in the individual is the task of psychology. Each of these sciences cannot exist separately or proceed without the aid of the others. Disregarding the ethnocultural differences, the psychologist risks applying some specific characteristics of, say, an American schoolboy to human nature at large (this has often been the case); but the ethnographer, too, cannot explain these differences without making the most of his experience in psychology. Even while studying common problems of ethno-psychology they will use different approaches. The ethnographer is inclined to generalise his findings concerning national character, etc. on the basis of synoptic investigations in the phenomena of culture, language, religion and institutions of socialisation. On the other hand, the psychologist will draw his conclusions from statistical data comprising his experimental study of individuals belonging to various ethnic groups. That also means professional training.

Still, however important their diversity, the two disciplines not only complete one another, but also mutually penetrate one into the other. In our days the psychologists take it for granted that no specific theory can be considered valid or universal without being confirmed by cross-cultural research, and in ethnography more and more importance is ascribed to 'psychological' topics. In a review of 'psychological anthropology', in *The Handbook of Social and Cultural Anthropology*[3] Erica Bourguignon mentions, amongst others, the problems of behavioural evolution, the psychic unity of mankind and the general character of human nature, the comparative study of perception and cognition, personality, child training and socialisation, cultural changes, and cross-cultural statistics. The *Handbook* also contains separate reviews of cognitive anthropology (by Durbin), belief systems (by Black), symbolism in the ritual context (by Munn), cultural psychiatry (by Kennedy), identity, culture, and behaviour (by Robbins).

It remains all but surprising and symptomatic that, among these problems, no mention has been made of 'ethnopsychology'. However widely this term is used, Guillemain, editor of the journal *Ethnopsychologie*, calling it 'too bad', proposes to substitute for it 'differential collective ethology'.[4] Nobody would deny the necessity of studying ethnic peculiarities in behaviour and mentality. But within which theoretical and methodological system should this study be located? Numerous fields of knowledge, the titles of which begin with 'ethno-' (ethnosociology, ethnolinguistics, ethnodemography, ethnogeography, etc.), are theoretically and methodologically the branches of respective fundamental sciences (sociology, linguistics, etc.), the prefix 'ethno-' being used only as a definition of their objects. In fact, for the study of 'psychology of peoples' the traditional methods of psychology are evidently insufficient. Hence the diversity of theoretical and methodological orientations. American cultural anthropology, in the works of Mead, Benedict, Linton, Kardiner and Kluckhohn, stresses the study of psychological types of personality and methods of socialisation, whereas British social anthropology, beginning with Radcliffe-Brown, displays a strong tendency towards the analysis of social structure; the French school, following the example of Durkheim, Lévy-Bruhl and Mauss, points out the importance of the genesis of collective representation, which includes the notion of personality (see, for example, works by Griaule and Leenhardt). This divergence in orientation, though partly obliterated nowadays, is still visibly present.[5]

All these problems are also widely discussed in Soviet science. A number of works have been published during the current decade in the USSR, dealing with general methodological principles of research in

ethnopsychology,[6] national character,[7] correlation of ethnic consciousness and spiritual culture,[8] problems of ethnic self-awareness,[9]
the nature of ethnic stereotypes and prejudice[10] and psychological
aspects of international relations in USSR.[11] Immediately related to
these are the studies in the fields of psycho- and socio-linguistics.

Of course, Soviet and western studies effectively differ in many ways.
Soviet authors are eager to set up ideological boundaries against biologically oriented theories and attempts to reduce the social structure of
a society and even the historical process itself to some universal psychic
factors, as was the case in 'psychological sociology' or in psychoanalysis
in the late nineteenth and early twentieth centuries. The majority of
Soviet publications are closer to philosophy, sociology and culturology
than they are to psychology proper. A few essays approaching these
subjects have been written by psychologists, but they were concerned
not so much with the study of ethno-specific aspects of mental processes,
as with their historical development.[12] Among western publications most acclaimed is the French school of historical psychology
headed by Meyerson, *et al.* Lately several empirical studies on ethnic
attitudes and stereotypes have appeared, based on methods of social
psychology.[13]

Accepting the reality of psychological differences between nations,
Soviet scholars see them as resulting from social and historical
development, and explain them as influenced by a long period of coha-
bitation in common natural environment, with common social activity
and specific channels of communication. The unique features of the
psychic constitution of a nation (national character) and of national
culture do not exclude the fact that all elements of these structures may
be reproducible, or present in many other nations. Any ethno-
psychological trait should be considered as relative, and presuppose
some kind of comparison with other ethnic communities. The firm
stability of certain ethno-psychological qualities does not exclude their
historical variability under the influence of changes in life conditions,
including cross-ethnic contacts. Whether and to what degree the typical features of an ethnos, implemented in its culture, are also dissipated
among the individuals forming this ethnic group, is considered a question open for discussion. Were this question answered positively, one
nevertheless would not but seek the presence of important individual
variations, to which, in a class society, the social class differences are to
be added, which may outweigh the ethnic influences (this being the
major argument against the theory of 'basic personality').

Based on these shared positions, Soviet scholars do, however, have
some divergent ideas. Some authors, while acknowledging the differences between national cultures, are in opposition to such notions as
'national character' or 'national type of mentality' as psychological
phenomena; the respective section of a popular textbook on social
psychology is cautiously entitled not 'National psychology', but
'National features in psychology'.[14] The ethno-specific traits may be

differently reflected in various elements of culture. Although the 'national halo' is implemented in many forms of all arts, its intensity and definition are far from equally expressed. Kagan[15] says that we, for instance, can easily make sense of the difference in the musical orders of Russian and Italian songs, in Ukrainian and Uzbek decorative ornament, in plastic forms of American and Chinese architecture, but there is no such thing as 'Russian drawing', 'German colours', 'Spanish perspective', 'English proportion', 'Georgian composition', and so on. The problem of ethnospecific features implied in unconscious psychic processes has not as yet been fully investigated.

Speaking of collaboration of ethnography and psychology, we have to consider the internal differentiations of both disciplines. The study of national character is closely related to the psychology of personality, whereas the ethnic stereotypes are related to social psychology, and age stratification to the psychology of development. We should also remember that the mutual interaction of ethnography and psychology is never exclusively binary, being always under the influence of certain sociological and historical variables. That is, if the ethnographer is interested in the division of labour between men and women (sex roles), and in the respective stereotypes of an ethnos, he will have to take into account the findings of contemporary psychology in sex differences, as one of the aspects of differential psychology; but in doing so he will also have to make use of the sociological conception of sex role and of concomitant historical data.

The diversity of possible interpretations of any phenomenon in question is evident: we may regard the ritual of initiation (*rite de passage*) either as an element of ethno-specific cultural symbolism, or as a special case of life-span periodisation, or as a social mechanism linking age stratification with inter-generational culture transmission. All this requires not only thorough interdisciplinary knowledge, but also logical lucidity and a systematic approach to the problem.

I would like to illustrate this complexity by one example which, to my mind, is extremely exciting. It is the problem of self, or rather, of self-image. The individual's idea of himself is an important element both of culture and of personality. The self-image may be considered from different points of view. There can be no reasonable activity without some kind of self-awareness. But the self-image has some special aspects too: the psychological differential – it depends on sex, age and individual qualities; the socio-historical element – modern man sees himself differently from a man in the Middle Ages; and the ethno-psychological – the difference between a European and an African, or another self. How can these aspects be coordinated?

Initial investigations of the problem[16] were based on the direct contrast between the integral, autonomous and invisible self of a 'civilised' European and the diffuse, vague self of a 'primitive', with no idea of his own personality, with an identity which is a mere *lien de participation*. But starting with the paper of Mauss,[17] this overall contrast of 'primitive' and 'civilised' selves has given way to comparison of concrete notions of self in various cultures and ethnoses. The historical aspect of this process has been developed by the French school of historical psychology (e.g. Meyerson and Vernant) the principles of which were fully implemented in the papers of the interdisciplinary colloquium on personality problems.[18] The ethnological line of research, less uniform in its theoretical orientation (here I have in mind the influence of psychoanalysis) was represented by the researches of, for example, Griaule, Leenhardt, Dieterlen, Thomas, Benedict, Fortes, Hollowell and Honigmann. The results of this research were reflected in the papers of the Symposium *La Notion de Personne en Afrique Noire*.[19]

These diverse scientific trends do however have a shared tendency to overcome the dangers of evolutionism and Euro-centrism, by limiting their researches with an attempt to reconstruct the system of notions belonging to a specific culture, such as that of ancient Greece or of a distinct ethnos, be it the Bambara, Dogons, or Melanesians. This approach helps to describe individual traits of a given culture and its type of personality, and has some advantages over general philosophic speculations. But do these individual patterns express some general trends and stages in the development of human self-awareness and personality?

In almost every book describing the Japanese personality[20] the authors point to the fact that European culture regards the individual as an autonomous subject of his activities, and underlines the entity, integrity and identity in all manifestations of his self; the splintered image of self, the lack of unity are regarded as abnormal, unwholesome and even pathological. A contrary opinion exists in traditional Japanese culture, where the dependence of the individual on his social group is stressed, and the person is seen instead as a complex system of different 'ranges' of duties and responsibilities: duties towards one's Emperor which are combined in the range of *chu*; duties towards one's parents – the range of *ko*; duties towards people who have done any favour to the person – the range of *giri*; duties of fidelity, loyalty and humanity – the range of *jin*; responsibility to one's own self in the domain of feelings and physical pleasures – the range *ninjo*. Europeans will evaluate a person 'as a whole', believing all his actions in different circumstances to be the external manifestation of his identity. In Japan the value of any person is relative and dependent on the range within which his actions are considered. The Japanese would not name a person good or bad, in general, but they will say that he knows the *jin*, but is ignorant of the *giri*. The European concept explains the actions of men from 'within', assuming that he is doing this or that out of his feelings of gratitude, patriotism, or from mercenary motives, and so on; from the moral aspect, the motive of the action is often considered more important than the deed itself. In Japan one's behaviour is expected to depend on general rules, regulations and moral norms: the person should act in this or that way minding the *chu, ko* or *giri*. It is not so important why the person is doing this or that, but rather whether he is doing the right or wrong thing in the light of the socially approved schedule of duties.

These diversities are interrelated with the system of social and cultural conditions. The traditional Japanese culture was formed under the strong influence of Confucianism, and is not individualistic in its core. The individual is considered, not as an absolute value, but as a cluster of specific duties and responsibilities derived from his belonging to his family or community.

> In traditional Japan, the self-awareness of a Japanese was fused with some conception of expected role behaviour, often idealized in his mind as a set of internalized standards or directives. Accordingly, in psychological terms, his 'ego ideal' was conceptualized as some *particular* form of idealized role behaviour. A Japanese would have felt uncomfortable in thinking of his 'self' as something separable from his role.[21]

Though this contrast of a European with a Japanese seems to be valid and does not arouse any doubts, two questions may still be asked: first, are these differences ethno-specific and characteristic of the Japanese only, or is this type of self-image typical for a certain stage of socio-economic and cultural development? Secondly, how close is the correspondence of cultural symbols implemented in religion and philosophy, with the ideas and behaviour of the individual, and vice versa? In other words, do the Europeans and the Japanese really feel and act in the ways prescribed by their respective traditional models, or, on the contrary, strict and powerful though these symbols might be in theory, are they perhaps not as effective and obvious in every-day practice?

The contrasting of 'polar profiles' allows one to highlight the differences, but one is in danger of overestimating them. However different Japan and Europe may be, the Japanese idea of self is in some aspects similar to the notion of personality existing in medieval Europe.[22] In modern Japan urban youth is becoming ever more egocentric, and lays more value on the motives of personal self-assertion and achievement, which in the past would have been symbolised in terms of familial affiliation or loyalty to one's particular group. The results of mass questionnaires show that the number of Japanese preferring the ideal of 'easy-going life' has increased from 32 per cent in 1953 to 62 per cent in 1973, whereas the number of advocates of the 'moralistic mode of living' has decreased from 39 to 16 per cent.[23]

Nevertheless, certain traditional ethno-psychological features have been preserved in cultural standards as well as in individual minds. Social psychologists[24] engaged in the study of ethnic stereotypes have compared the self-descriptions of six-, ten-, fourteen-year-old children belonging to various ethno-linguistic groups (e.g. Americans, French, Germans, English and French Canadians, Brazilians, Turks, and Lebanese). They were to answer the questions: 'What are you?; What else are you?; Can you think of anything else you are?' The Japanese children were a great contrast to all other children: due to the paucity of their self-descriptions they used far fewer self-characterisations than other children, although the sample included children of nations at a lower stage of socio-economic development than the Japanese. The mass questionnaires also show that 'the pattern of behaviour in social life, whose supporters never assert independence nor approve of it in others and place great importance on personal relations, has remained constant though there were many changes in various other opinions. A sense of the 'individual' is veiled in the mist of a sense of 'group', as it were'.[25] That means that the ethno-psychological differences, whatever their historical sources might be, are very stable and are expressed not only in generalised cultural symbols, but also in the commonplace mind.

But here we run into another difficulty. Ideological forms, be they religion or philosophy, are systemic wholes and this makes their study easier. In the course of ethnological research the degree of clarity and systemic consistency is, as it were, even further increased by the efforts of scholars who place the amorphous (as they see it) data into a strict logically consecutive scheme. But by this process the inconsistency and incongruity immanent in every culture are almost always diminished, and its internal substantive and functional nuances and contradictions are obliterated. (For criticism of statements resulting from the organisation of oral evidence into tables, see Goody.)[26]

Typological procedures and notions (as, for instance, the 'African personality') underline the original, individual character of the subject in question and help to interpret it as a certain whole. But if its implicit frame of reference is not taken into account (for example, that the notion of 'African personality' has meaning only as the antithesis of 'European personality'), one is in danger of overgeneralising and exaggerating ethnospecific traits of an individual, or culture. The conception of man articulated in the belief-systems of a given culture, and the individual self-image revealed by empirical psychology, will never fully coincide.

The comparative and historical studies of the notion of personality are undoubtedly very important and valuable. But modern psychology does not regard the self-image as a mere cognitive construction (a concept, or an idea) but also as a social attitude, or better, as an attitude cluster, in which the cognitive elements (the self-idea, etc.) are tightly connected with emotional (self-evaluation, etc.) and behavioural elements as well. The various elements of this attitude cluster are not formed simultaneously and may have different meanings at different stages of the life cycle, being dependent on the nature of one's personal experience and activities. That is why the comparison of self-images of different individuals should be undertaken not from one aspect alone, but along the lines of various parameters, such as the degree of cognitive complexity, stability, internal coherence, self-consciousness, and self-esteem.

This conceptual framework, with some modifications, may also be applied to ethno-psychology, possibly allowing an increase in the number of cross-cultural comparisons. But we have to remember that analytical reduction of the complex to the simple, of the whole to the combination of qualities and of the structure to its elements, entails the danger of blurring and underrating the qualitative, individual distinctions between cultures.

The typological and statistical methods of approach cannot be reduced one to the other; nor can the culturological and the individual-psychological levels of investigation. And that is why they are always complementary. Both culture and personality can be studied on different levels, and the higher their stage of development is, the greater and more important is the range of individual variations. Psychology helps the ethnologist to understand that the 'pluralisme cohérent'[27] of the African personality, so important on the level of cultural symbolism, does not exclude the awareness by the African of his psychophysiological identity which is a necessary component and condition of any purposeful activity and behavioural continuity.

On the other hand, psychologists found that illiterate peasants from backward regions in Uzbekistan, in the early 1930s, were at a loss when asked to characterise their inner states and qualities, trying instead to describe their actions, or outward circumstances (e.g. naming among their 'foibles', their 'bad neighbours')[28] and will not only be led to interpret these matters as a certain developmental stage of cognitive processes, but will also have to take into account the position of the individual in the traditional culture of his respondents.

The principle of historicism, equally important for ethnography as for psychology, is not synonymous with vulgar evolutionism, but is its opposite, because it conceives the process of historical development to be as divergent as ontogenesis itself. The essence of the problem is not to be reduced to the degree of development of individuality, or even to the value ascribed to it by a given culture. (The desire 'to free a person from his self', typical of the Chinese and Japanese cultural tradition, indicates in fact the existence of this self, a point which should not be overlooked.) It is only the systematic contrasting and comparison of the different types of individual development in ethnosocial environments which will lead to the understanding of the overall regularities in the formation of the human self and self-awareness. And this is a shared problem for psychology and ethnology.

NOTES

1 M.L. Hoffman, 'Developmental synthesis of affect and cognition and its implications for altruistic motivation', *Developmental Psychology*, 1975, vol. 2, no. 5, September, 607-22.

2 Yu.V. Bromley, *Ethnos and Ethnography*, Moscow, 1973 (in Russian).

3 J.J. Honigmann (ed.) *Handbook of Social and Cultural Anthropology*, Chicago, 1973.

4 B. Guillemain, 'World culture and the present age', *Inostrannia Literatura*, no. 1, 1976 (in Russian).

5 J. Lombard, 'L'ethnopsychologie devant le double courant de l'anthropologie', *Ethnopsychologie*, Juin-Septembre, 1974.

6 Bromley, op. cit. I.S. Kon, 'On the problem of national character', *History and Psychology*, Moscow, 1971 (in Russian), and in French translation, 'Le problème du charactère national', *Ethnopsychologie*, Juin-Septembre, 1974. S.I. Korolev, *Problems of Ethnopsychology in the Works of Foreign Authors*, Moscow, 1970 (in Russian). V.F. Porshnev, *Social Psychology and History*, Moscow, 1966 (in Russian).

7 N. Dzhandil'din, *The Nature of National Psychology*, Alma Ata, 1971 (in Russian).

8 K.V. Chistov, 'Ethnic community, ethnic recognition and some problems of intellectual culture', *Sovietskaia Etnografia*, 1972, no. 3 (in Russian).

9 V.I. Kozlov, *The Dynamics of the Populousness of Nations*, Moscow, 1969 (in Russian).

10 I.S. Kon, 'The psychology of prejudice: concerning the roots of ethnic bias', *Novyi Mir*, 1976, no. 9 (in Russian).

11 Yu.V. Arutyunyan (ed.) *The Social and the National*, Moscow, 1973 (in Russian).

12 A.R. Luria, *Concerning the Historical Development of Cognitive Processes*, Moscow, 1974 (in Russian).

13 Arutyunyan, op. cit.

14 G.P. Predvechnii and Y.A. Sherkovin, *Social Psychology: A Brief Outline*, Moscow, 1975 (in Russian).

15 M.S. Kagan, *Lectures on Marxist-Leninist Aesthetics*, Leningrad, 2nd ed. 1971, p. 644.

16 L. Lévy-Bruhl, *L'Ame Primitive*, Paris, 1927.

17 M. Mauss, 'Une categorie de l'esprit humain: la notion de personne, celle de "moi"', *Journal of the Royal Anthropological Institute*, 1938, 263-81, also included in *Sociologie et Anthropologie*, Paris, 1960, pp. 331-62.

18 I. Meyerson, 'Problèmes de personne', *Colloque du Centre de Recherches de Psychologie Comparative*, Paris, 1973.

19 *La Notion de Personne en Afrique Noire*, Colloques Internationaux, Centre National de la Recherche Scientifique, Paris, 1973.

20 R. Benedict, *The Chrysanthemum and the Sword*, Boston, 1946. V. Ovchinnikov, *The Twig of the Sakura*, Moscow, 1971 (in Russian). J. Stoetzel, *La Psychologie Sociale*, Paris, 1963.

21 G.A. De Vos, *Socialization for Achievement: Essays on the Cultural Psychology of the Japanese*, California, 1973/4.

22 A. Gurevich, 'World culture and the present age', *Inostrannia Literatura*, 1976, no. 1 (in Russian).

23 S. Nishira, 'Changed and unchanged characteristics of the Japanese', *Japan Echo*, 1974, vol. 1, no. 2, 21-32.

24 W.E. Lambert and O. Klineberg, *Children's Views of Foreign Peoples*, New York, 1967.

25 Y. Sakamoto, 'A study of the Japanese national character: part 5', *Annals of the Institute of Statistical Mathematics*, suppl. 8, Tokyo, 1975, p.21.

26 J. Goody, 'Civilisation de l'écriture et classification, ou l'art de jouer sur les tableaux', *Actes de la Recherche en Sciences Sociales*, Février, 1976, no. 1, 87-101.

27 L.V. Thomas, 'La pluralism cohérent de la notion de personne en Afrique noire traditionelle', *La Notion de Personne en Afrique Noire*, Colloques Internationaux, Centre National de la Recherche Scientifique, Paris, 1973, pp. 387-420.

28 Luria, op. cit.

PART V

Anthropology and religion

V. BASILOV

The study of religions in Soviet ethnography

The study of religions, which forms an essential part of the history of culture of every nation, is an important field of Soviet ethnography.

In the 1940s and 50s ethnographers concentrated mostly on material culture and social institutions of all kinds, but already in the late 1950s an interest in the problems of religions was revived.

For several decades now extensive investigations of the religious beliefs of the peoples of the world (especially peoples of the USSR) have been carried out by Soviet ethnographers. Rich factual data concerning the traditional religions of the peoples of one-sixth of the world have been accumulated. As a result of this work we now have a detailed and comprehensive picture of the religious traditions of all the peoples of the Soviet Union; and in a number of cases, the specific character of religious beliefs and rites of specified groups within this or that people (ethnos).

The research of Soviet ethnographers into religious phenomena is based on Marxist methodology. This means, above all, that we approach religion from a materialist position, i.e., we seek the 'earthly roots' of religious beliefs. Furthermore, Marxism defines with precision the place of religion among other phenomena connected with human activity: religion is a form of social consciousness. Such a conception of the nature of religion underlies the more elaborate definitions of it, and is shared by all Soviet scholars. It explains the character of the interrelations between religion and other phenomena of social life. It also shows that religion belongs to superstructural phenomena determined by the basis, i.e., the system of the relations of production of people within an economic system.[1] In revealing the social nature of religion Marxism emphasises that religion is only a fantastic (twisted, irrational) reflection of the people's material life which takes the form of images of a supernatural world. Religion develops, like any other kind of ideology, as a result of processes going on in society. Changes in religious beliefs and customs are at best reflections of changes in economic, social or family relations. The history of religion cannot be separated from the history of society.

The above is a general theoretical basis for various specific investigations of Soviet scholars in the sphere of study of religions; it determines the basic differences between our methodological approach and that of non-Marxist trends in western studies of religions, including researches in ethnology.

Of course, we know that western studies of religion are represented by various trends – from the apologetical ones to schools which have developed concepts close to those of Marxism. For instance, statements that religious phenomena are of a social nature, that definite systems of beliefs are socially determined, may be found in the works of western scholars. Thus Smith has said that in totemism a man transfers the features of a social structure to the whole of nature; the same thought had been expressed in different words by Jevons, Frazer and others. Durkheim put forward the more general conception that a deity was a personification, a symbol of society's unity. For Lévy-Bruhl a specific character of the collective ideas was the reason for the peculiarities of a primitive society's beliefs.

But allowing that many of the concrete conclusions reached by these scholars constituted a positive contribution and were carefully substantiated, we nevertheless think that their account of the social roots of religion adds nothing basically new to Marxism. Moreover, the problem of the social nature of religion is accounted for in Marxism with greater accuracy and, in essence, exhaustively. Thus Durkheim defined society as a sum-total of psychic interconnections, and this idealistic position did not allow him to see religion as a phenomenon conditioned by specific features of social life. Furthermore, due to the complicated development of anthropology in western countries, conceptions close to Marxism, worked out by a number of prominent scientists, did not serve as the basis for the study of religion. Suffice it to say that many scholars, trying to locate the social roots of religion, are still ready to invoke Freud's ideas. For instance, Spiro (who, judging by the number of printings of his theoretical work,[2] to some degree reflects the contemporary state of mind of western anthropologists) asserts that Freud is superior as a scientist to Durkheim and declares that Freud's theory explains cross-cultural differences of religious phenomena determined by concrete cultures.

> If personal projective systems, which form the basis for religious belief, are developed in early childhood experiences, it can be deduced that differences in religious beliefs will vary systematically with differences in family (including socialisation) systems which structure these experiences.[3]

Such a use of Freud's conclusions is utterly impossible in the Soviet study of religion. Freud has extended his conclusions based on his study of a specific stratum of a specific society to the whole of humanity. The limitations and anti-historicity of his views are obvious; the notorious

Oedipus complex which Freud believed to be characteristic of all mankind, will serve as a proof of our thesis.[4] Even Freud's admirers make reservations to the effect that Freud's main ideas should not be taken literally. According to Spiro, for instance, in Freud's statement that a child projects his image of father onto the the almighty god, one should see the general theory, indicating the role of the family in the formation of religious views.[5]

Such an 'improvement' of central ideas is in effect a revision of Freud's ideas: Freud deduced religion, first of all, from the unchangeable peculiarities of the psyche. But even when filled with new contents, Freudism admits the social basis of religion only within the narrow limits of the family, or at best in a kin group. But the social essence of religion cannot be identified with the family. It is well known that the family is just one element of society, and not a determinative one, either. On the contrary, the form of the family depends on the character of social relations in general, and changes in family structure have always resulted from changes in socio-economic formations. The concrete analysis of Christianity made by Marx and Engels showed that the character of the whole society and, in particular, the existence of antagonistic classes, was reflected in this particular religious system. This conclusion has been confirmed in many works by Soviet scholars.

In every religious system one can find a number of ideas that reflect the real needs of some classes or of the whole of society. People seek ways to satisfy their requirements, and alongside rational activity they resort to the sphere of religion. So, the origin of Christianity was determined by the need of the society to find a way out of the existing miserable conditions of life. There was no real way out of the situation, and it was substituted by an illusory one – the belief that the God-Saviour would soon come and put an end to that sinful world. As a result of changes in the character of social needs the religious ideas born of these needs change or lose their significance. For instance, the slogan of 'a holy war' against 'the infidel' which reflected the readiness of Arabs for military expansion, very soon lost its importance and in practice did not influence the religious life of the Moslem world.

Characterising the Marxist approach to the study of religion, we must bear in mind that Marxism also takes into consideration the influence which religious ideology, like every superstructural phenomenon, has on its socio-economic base. But the interrelation between the specific features of a religious system and a form of social organisation should not be understood in a straightforward and oversimplified way.[6] Though the evolution of religion is determined by fundamental changes in social life, there is no complete harmony between different stages of development of society and of religion. Suffice it to say that Christianity has been able to survive as a special religious system while societies that created it have passed from slavery through feudalism to capitalism. Of course, Christianity has substantially changed during this period, but its main dogmas, many specific beliefs and rituals have not been lost.

Marxism proceeds from the assumption that social consciousness is more conservative than social being, and that religion is the most conservative form of ideology.

'Religion once formed, always contains traditional material . . .'[7] These and other well-known theses of Marxism form the theoretical and methodological basis for the study of religion in the Soviet Union. As these principles are shared by all social sciences and as ethnographic data are of paramount importance for the study of religion it is hard to distinguish between 'purely' ethnographic works and the works of philosophers, historians and folklorists. It is not that those disciplines study different aspects of the problem and have different tasks, on the contrary, historians and philosophers (such as Franzev, Kryvelev and others) have made extensive use of ethnographic material, and ethnographers (Sternberg, Tokarev and others) have made attempts to classify religions and to analyse the world ethnographic data with a view to eliciting general regularities of religious development (see, for instance, works by Zelenin, Zolotarev and others). The historian Klibanov used ethnographic material collected by him and his colleagues in his own studies of Christian sectarianism. Folklorists who considered folklore as a source for the study of religious beliefs (Propp, Meletinsky and others), resorted to ethnographic data as well. (Incidentally, the connection of the ethnographic study of religions with folklore studies is traditional in Russia, and has its roots in the folklorist Veselovsky's conception of syncretism, which leads one to see poetry, the dance, music and singing as indispensable integral parts of a religious ceremonial act.) The close connection of folklore studies and ethnography is a good basis for a recently-developed tendency towards convergence in the comparative-historical study of ritual folklore.

Thus, the ethnographic investigation of religion can be viewed as a part of the general study of religion. Despite the interweaving of the above-mentioned disciplines, ethnographic studies still have their distinctive feature, namely, attention to the ethnic specifics of religious beliefs and rituals. Thus, the character of the ethnographic study of religions is defined merely by the subject-matter and the tasks of ethnography; we can hardly talk about any distinctive ethnographic approach to the study of religion.

For the ethnographer, religion is an integral part of a people's spiritual culture, closely connected with the other cultural components; that is why monographs, describing the culture of this or that people, usually contain a section on religious beliefs and rites.

Studies of the culture of any people take into consideration its relations with other peoples at different historical stages. Genetic, political or neighbourly links have left their more or less noticeable marks on a people's culture. Hence the close connection of the study of traditional culture with investigations of ethnogenesis and ethnic history of peoples, so characteristic of Soviet ethnography. Religious traditions are also studied with a view to discovering ethnical contacts of a given people. It is known that in spite of the identity of many religious phenomena in the culture of different peoples (resulting from the general regularities of development of societies reflected in the religious ideology), similar forms of religions or cults (like, for instance, agricultural rituals) differ in certain ways, depending on the specific character of a given culture. In the course of cultural contacts, going on for centuries, various cultural elements, including religious traditions originally formed in other ethnic media, are absorbed; as a result the old forms of religious life of a people are changed. Certain characteristics of religious beliefs and rites are a reliable indication of former ethnic contacts; therefore the data on religious beliefs and rituals are extensively used in ethnographic studies for reconstructing the process of formation of an ethnos. In many publications in which religious phenomena are analysed from the viewpoint of religious syncretism, they are likewise considered from the point of view of their ethnical character.[8]

As ethnography studies peoples at all stages of development, ethnographic study of religious beliefs has no chronological boundaries. Ethnographers investigate religion at all stages of its existence – from the inception of the first religious notions to the beliefs of today, when religion as a social phenomenon is falling into decline, and has an ever decreasing influence upon society.

The interest in early (primitive) beliefs is not, as is known, a distinctive part of Soviet ethnography; many western scholars are also engaged in the study of early forms of religion. This is natural; ethnographic material is almost the only source of our knowledge of primitive religions.

Soviet science does not share the view, widespread in the West, that science is unable to understand the mechanism of the inception of religion and its development at early stages. Along with historians and philosophers, Soviet ethnographers take part in investigating the problem of the origin of religion.[9] Since the character of religion is determined by the level of development of a society, we are justified in regarding the religions of peoples observable at the stage of the primitive community as similar to those of early human collectivities, though of course to identify the former with the latter would be a mistake. The study of religious beliefs of the peoples representing various stages of development allows the scholar to establish the historical succession of early forms of religion.

The study of history of religions has always been an important task of ethnography. Already in the nineteenth century, ethnographic material served as a basis for the comparative study of religions and made it possible to understand how religious concepts had evolved since prehistoric times. This approach to religious phenomena, elaborated by evolutionists, is used and enriched by Soviet ethnography. Even in descriptive works, when religious life is regarded as an ethnographic feature of a given people's culture, this approach implies that the information presented may be used to correct the general schemes and concepts of the study of religion.

All this testifies to a certain connection of evolutionism with the traditions of Soviet ethnography. Contrary to certain western trends, Soviet ethnography has never fostered the absolute denial of evolutionism. It is natural for us to refer to fundamental works of prominent representatives of evolutionism, who have done enormous work on the accumulation, classification and analysis of vast factual material and who substantiated a number of conceptions which have furthered the advancement of science, and have been confirmed over and over again.

The shortcomings of evolutionism (a certain schematism, emphasis on the supposed uninterrupted character of development common for all peoples, etc.), which are the reasons for the rejection of evolutionism in the West, should not make us overlook its positive sides. Based on the comparative analysis of exceedingly rich factual data, evolutionism has made a great contribution to the social sciences. Those western scholars who were not satisfied with evolutionism should have directed their criticism to certain oversimplified conceptions, and not to the general idea of discovering regularities in the historical development of mankind as such. Damning evolutionism is a case of throwing out the baby with the bath water.

In their criticism of evolutionism, Soviet scholars proceed from another point of view. Soviet ethnography is based on Marxist philosophy, using the methodological principles of materialist dialectics. Compared with Marxist theory, which gives an account of the driving forces of the social historical process in all their multiformity, the general idea of the cultural evolution of mankind, which has given a name to a whole trend in the social sciences, looks rather feeble. Soviet ethnographers do criticise evolutionism, but at the same time value highly many of its specific conclusions and its material.

Soviet works on the study of religion are at one in striving to reveal the dependence of the character of religious beliefs of a people on their social existence. The acknowledgment of a decisive role for this dependence, following from Marxist methodology, provides a basis for the classification systems of historical forms of religion proposed by Soviet scholars. Thus, the prominent Soviet ethnographer Tokarev believes that 'the social side of religion is . . . the most essential part of it, which should be placed at the basis of any morphological classification of religious phenomena.'[10] In Tokarev's classification the criterion for differentiating between various historical forms of religion is the correspondence of religious phenomena to certain forms of organisation of society and the material needs of its diverse social groups.

It should be noted that Tokarev's classification is not the only one in Soviet ethnography, although its influence upon the interpretation of factual material is visible in a number of concrete investigations. Recently a new classification, based on other principles and concepts, has been proposed by Kryvelev.[11] While Tokarev took as the criterion of

classification the social role of religious phenomena, Kryvelev's classification is based upon the object and character of beliefs. Despite this
difference, however, the thesis of the dependence of the form of religion
upon the level of social development has not been disputed.

The analysis of the social roots of religious ideology and cults is a
major theme in works devoted to the study of concrete forms of religion
and, in particular, those at early stages of its development.

Thus, among early forms of religion, totemism had attracted the
special attention of Soviet ethnographers. Methods of study and criteria were worked out according to which a whole complex of survivals
was connected with totemism; the problem of reflection of the social
structure in totemistic beliefs was also thoughtfully studied. Such investigation of the conditions under which totemism originated made it
possible to consider it the ideology of the clan in the process of formation.[12] These ideas were first formulated by outstanding western
scholars. Soviet scientists have verified their conclusions on specific
materials and have shown the historical development of this form of religion in a more detailed way. Semenov's point of view stands apart; he
thinks that totemism emerged as a social phenomenon, and became a
religion only in the course of time.

The question of the interconnection between religion and social
structure was also studied from the point of view of mythological subjects and personages and beliefs in ghosts which were interpreted as the
survivals of the matriclan system.[13] Some peculiarities of religious
beliefs determined by the patriclan system were also noted.[14]

The connection between mythology and a dual social structure was
traced in a number of works devoted to an analysis of dualistic mythology (i.e. myths with the general plot of the rivalry of two powers).[15]
The interrelation between mythology and initiation ritual was investigated in connection with the analysis of East Slavic fairy tales.[16] A
number of popular mythological subjects have been explained through
an analysis of archaic social institutions.[17]

Ethnographic research into religious beliefs also presupposes the
analysis of the contents of religious notions, with a view to revealing the
specific character of individual phenomena and the nature of their
interrelation with other elements or forms of religion. Tokarev, for
instance, has made an attempt to analyse mythology as a special sphere
of religion.[18] Much attention has been given to magic, which in Soviet
science is not opposed to religion, but is understood as part and parcel
of a religious cult.[19] Among religious-magical beliefs and rituals, Tokarev singled out some distinctive variants of magic (malignant, erotic,
curative), treating them as special forms of religion. Kryvelev extended the concept of magic to cover all religious ritual practice, at the
same time admitting that it is possible to apply this term to the religious
activity not inspired by the beliefs in supernatural beings, but based on
the assumption of the automatic operation of supernatural 'regularities'. Soviet scholars have contributed much to the study of shamanism.

They have gathered unique factual data and drawn a number of fruitful theoretical conclusions on the nature of this religious phenomenon.[20]

When analysing the contents of religious phenomena we take into consideration their historical development, since their contents are not unchangeable – in the course of time new ideas arise and some old ones disappear. Historicism in the study of religion is a prerequisite of Marxist-Leninist methodology.

Soviet ethnographers pay special attention to data which help them to discover the origin and the history of a cult, a ritual or a belief described on the basis of ethnographic material and which, therefore, is chronologically limited. One may argue about the concrete conclusions on the genesis of this or that cult (festival, ceremonial, etc.), but the approach itself in our opinion is necessary and fruitful. We cannot agree with the criticism of our western colleague Gellner,[21] who says that Soviet ethnographers investigate the comet's tail rather than the comet itself. This comparison is picturesque, but erroneous, for a comet doesn't grow from its tail, while every religious phenomenon has been formed on the soil of already existing traditions, and has absorbed and transformed them according to new needs. It is difficult to give a good analysis of a present situation without information about the preceding one. That is why physicians study their patients' anamneses.

The analysis of factual meterial often makes it possible to trace the historical continuity of different forms of religion. Thus, the connection between shamanism and totemism has been shown in several works on shamanism. The study of shamanism has led scholars to interesting conclusions about the evolution of this form of religion (or this form of a religious cult). Thus, Sternberg put forward the idea of sexual selection being an archaic form of the consecration as a shaman.[22] Relatively recently this idea was corroborated on central Asian material. The discovery of shamanism among the Tadjiks is a fact of indisputable theoretical significance, because it provides a new argument for our general conclusion that shamanism was not a local but a widespread phenomenon.[23]

We also have interesting publications devoted to the problems of hunters' cults, of the development of animistic concepts and the traditions of representing spirits (the transition from the zoomorphous to the anthropomorphous images, etc.).[24]

Ethnographers and folklorists studied East Slavic calendar rituals; their connections with the annual agricultural cycle as well as with ancestor worship was brought to light.[25] Ancient production cults have been examined on East Slavonic and Central Asian material.[26] The prehistoric roots of certain beliefs and subjects of 'mature', late religions have been traced. Thus, Bogoraz showed that the myth of the dying and reviving animal precedes historically the myths of the dying and reviving agricultural diety.[27] The image of the Virgin in the Orthodox Church has been examined against the background of a vast amount of material on pre-Christian female deities.[28]

Of all the disciplines studying religions, ethnography has the greatest interest in the phenomena of syncretism, characteristic of the everyday functioning of religion. This peculiarity of ethnographic investigations is determined by the very nature of ethnographic data, secured in close contact by a field researcher with people. It is possible, in the course of ethnographic research, to see the religious life of a people in all aspects – in the sphere of beliefs, in the sphere of rites, in the sphere of everyday behaviour. Ethnography is singled out from sciences studying religion by its own specific source of material. Furthermore, an ethnographer examines religion just in the very form in which it actually exists among people. It means that we are bound to investigate different forms of religion closely interwoven with each other. Methodological orientation to the study of religion as a syncretic phenomenon is inseparable from the research into early forms of religion, which are available for investigation mostly on the basis of their fragments that have survived up to the present. Regligious syncretism is often examined on the basis of material drawn from 'mature' religions, in which there survive many traditions of former religious practices, going back to obscure antiquity.

The problem of everday existence of religion, which in many forms differs from the dogmatic and canonised ideal, has received thorough treatment in Soviet ethnography. In the 1920s and 30s a number of works devoted to 'everyday orthodoxy' came out; in recent years the interest in this problem has revived.[29] In the last decade a number of works have appeared in which the syncretic character of everyday Islam was shown through concrete material dealing with the survivals of pre-Muslim cults which, having been absorbed by Islam, created distinctive everyday religious phenomena among different Muslim peoples.[30] The conclusion has been substantiated in Soviet ethnographic literature that Sufism in its popular forms had absorbed certain pre-Muslim traditions, especially shamanism.

In their striving to deduce general regularities of development of religion from concrete facts, Soviet scholars take into consideration such an important factor as the variation of phenomena of the same type, i.e. their local forms. Marxism asserts the general laws of historical processes common for all peoples, but admits at the same time the rich diversity of the local forms of development of society and culture, acquiring unique features under specific historical conditions. Moreover, cases of the degradation of societies and the subsequent decline of culture are not ignored.

The comparative-typological method is widely used in Soviet ethnography. Thus the comparative-typological study of the West European calendar rituals has begun. In our work on regional historico-ethnographic atlases this method is also applied in the systematisation of material concerning religious beliefs and rituals.

The ethnographic study of traditional religions is closely connected with the analysis of contemporary processes in everyday culture, for archaic beliefs, investigated with ethnographic methods, survive and function in interdependence with other beliefs, cultural elements and social institutions. Only ethnographic researches into the beliefs of today have given us an opportunity to notice that in the course of the general decline of a religion, a whole complex of most archaic ideas keeps its position in the traditional world view more firmly than do many concepts of later forms of religion. Snesarev was the first to discover this in material concerning Uzbeks' beliefs.[31] In their study of contemporary religious beliefs, Soviet ethnographers do not limit their tasks to the problems of archaic phenomena, but also survey the whole contemporary religious situation. Philosophers, sociologists, and historians also investigate the contemporary forms of religion, but at present they are mostly interested in assembling the mass material through questionnaires.[32]

Ethnographic works are based above all on the data acquired by the traditional methods of field investigations: this allows a deeper characterisation of contemporary religious beliefs,[33] and shows their gradual disappearance in socialist society.

While emphasising the unanimity of the methodological basis of ethnographic study of religion in the USSR, we should note, however, that a number of major issues are also widely discussed. Suffice it to say that our scholars disagree on the definition of religion.[34] Marxist general methodological principles are not an obstacle to putting forward new problems and to research in new spheres; and the use of methods and conceptions elaborated by western scholars is not excepted.

NOTES

1 See K. Marx and F. Engels, *Selected Works*, Moscow, 1955, vol. 1, p. 363.

2 M.E. Spiro, 'Religion: problems of definition and explanation', *Anthropological Approaches to the Study of Religion*, London, 1973.

3 Spiro, op. cit. pp. 102-3.

4 For critical comments on the Oedipus complex see V. Propp, *Historical Roots of the Fairy Tale*, Leningrad, 1946; 'Oedipus in the light of folklore', *Transactions of Leningrad University*, 1944, no. 72, Philological Series, issue 9 (both in Russian).

5 Spiro, op. cit., p. 103.

6 See S. Tokarev, *Early Forms of Religion and their Development*, Moscow, 1964, pp. 11-12 (in Russian).

7 K. Marx and F. Engels, *Selected Works*, Moscow, 1970, vol. 3.

8 See, for instance, S. Abramzon, *The Kirghiz and their Ethnogenetic and Historico-Cultural Relations*, Leningrad, 1971, pp. 267-339. V. Dyakonova, *The Tuvinians' Funeral Ritual as an Ethno-Historical Source*, Leningrad, 1975. N. Alexeyev, *Traditional Religious Beliefs of the Yakuts in the 19th and early 20th Centuries*, Novosibirsk, 1975 (all in Russian).

9 See Yu. Semenov, *How Mankind Came into Existence*, Moscow, 1966 (in Russian).

10 Tokarev, op. cit.

11 See I. Kryvelev, *The History of Religions*, Moscow, 1975, vol. 1, p. 10 (in Russian).

12 See A. Zolotarev, *Survivals of Totemism among Siberian Peoples*, Leningrad, 1934. D. Zelenin, 'Ideological transference of man's socio-tribal organisation on wild animals',

Izvestia AN SSSR: Social Sciences Section, 1935, no. 4. S. Tolstov, 'The problems of pre-clan society', *Sovietskaia Etnografia*, 1931, nos. 3-4. L. Sternberg, *Primitive Religion in the Light of Ethnography*, Leningrad, 1936. D. Zelenin, *Totem Trees in the Tales and Rites of European Peoples*, Moscow-Leningrad, 1937. Semenov, op. cit. (all in Russian).

13 N. Dyrenkova, 'The fire cult among the Altaians and the Teleuts', *Collection of Articles of MAE*, Leningrad, 1937, vol. 6. V. Bogoraz-Tan, 'Main types of folklore of Northern Eurasia and North America', *Sovietskyi Folklor*, Moscow-Leningrad, 1935, nos. 4-5. V. Chernetsov, 'Fratrial organisation of the Ob-Ugrian society', *Sovietskaia Etnografia*, 1939, no. 2. V. Chernetsov, 'Vogul tales', *Collection of Folk Tales of the People Mansi (Voguls)*, Leningrad, 1935. V. Bogoraz, *The Chukchi*, Leningrad, 1939, vol. 2. N. Dyrenkova, 'Survivals of the matriclan among the Altaian Turkic peoples', *To the Memory of V.G. Bogoraz*, Moscow, 1937. G. Chursin, *Ethnographic Data on Abkhazia*, Sukhumi, 1957 (all in Russian).

14 L. Potapov, 'The cult of mountains in the Altai', *Sovietskaia Etnografia*, 1946, no. 2. S. Tokarev, 'Survivals of the tribal cult among the Altaians', *Transactions of the Institute of Ethnography of the USSR AS*, Moscow-Leningrad, 1947, vol. 1. A. Zolotarev, *The Olchas' Tribal System and Religion*, Khabarovsk, 1939. A. Anasimov, *Historico-Genetic Study of the Religion of the Evenks and Problems of the Origin of Primitive Beliefs*, Moscow-Leningrad, 1958 (all in Russian).

15 See, for instance, S. Tolstov, *Ancient Khoresm*, Moscow, 1948. A. Zolotarev, *Tribal Society and Primitive Mythology*, Moscow, 1964 (both in Russian).

16 Propp, 1946, op. cit.

17 E. Meletinsky, *The Hero of the Fairy Tale: The Origin of an Image*, Moscow, 1958. E. Meletinsky, *The Origin of the Heroic Epos: Early Forms and Archaic Monuments*, Moscow, 1963 (both in Russian).

18 S. Tokarev, 'What is mythology?', *Problems of the History of Religion and Atheism*, Moscow, 1962, vol. 10. See also O. Freidenberg, *Poetics of Plot and Genre*, Leningrad, 1936. A. Losev, *Antique Mythology*, Moscow, 1957 (all in Russian).

19 E. Kagarov, 'On the problem of classification of folk rites', *Transactions of the USSR AS*, Moscow, 1928, no. 11. E. Kagarov, 'The composition and origin of marriage rites', *Collection of Articles of MAE*, Leningrad, 1929, vol. 8. S. Tokarev, 'The nature and origin of magic', *Transactions of the Institute of Ethnography of the USSR AS*, Moscow, 1959, vol. 51. Semenov, op. cit. (all in Russian).

20 A. Anokhin, 'Data on Shamanism among the Altaians', *Collection of Articles of MAE*, Petrograd, 1924, vol. 4, issue 2. L. Potapov, 'The ritual of the Shaman's tambourine revitalisation among the Turkic tribes of the Altai', *Transactions of the Institute of Ethnography of the USSR AS*, Moscow-Leningrad, 1947, vol. 1. A. Popov, 'Data on the Yakuts' Shamanism: the goddess Ayiysyt cult among the Yakuts', *The Cultures and Written Languages of the East*, Baku, 1928, vol. 3. A. Popov, 'The consecration as a Shaman among the Yakuts of Vilyusk', *Transactions of the Institute of Ethnography of the USSR AS*, 1947, vol. 11. N. Dyrenkova, 'Data on Shamanism among the Teleuts', *Collection of Articles of MAE*, Moscow-Leningrad, 1949, vol. 10. N. Dyrenkova, 'The consecreation as a Shaman as it is understood by the Turkish tribes', *Collection of Articles of MAE*, Leningrad, 1930, vol. 9. E. Prokofyeva, 'The costume of the Selkupian (Ostyak-Samoyedian) Shaman', *Collection of Articles of MAE*, Moscow-Leningrad, 1949, vol. 11 (all in Russian).

21 See E. Gellner, 'The Soviet and the savage', *Current Anthropology*, December 1975, 595.

22 See Sternberg, op. cit.

23 See O. Sukhareva, 'The survivals of demonology and Shamanism among the lowland Tadjiks', *Pre-Islamic Beliefs and Rites in Central Asia*, Moscow, 1975 (in Russian).

24 D. Gulia, *Hunt Deities and Hunter's Language among the Abkhazians*, Sukhumi, 1926. D. Zelenin, 'Taboo words among the peoples of eastern Europe and northern Asia', *Collection of Articles of MAE*, Moscow-Leningrad, 1929, vol. 8. D. Zelenin, *The Ongons' Cult in Siberia*, Moscow-Leningrad, 1936. G. Vasilevich, 'The Evenks' ancient hunting and reindeer breeding rites', *Collection of Articles of MAE*, Moscow-Leningrad, 1957, vol. 17.

A. Anasimov, 'The cult of the bear among the Evenks and the problem of the evolution of totemistic beliefs', *Problems of the History of Religion and Atheism*, Moscow, 1950, and other works by the same author (all in Russian).

25 V. Chicherov, *The Winter Period of the Russian Folk Agricultural Calendar in the 16th-19th Centuries*, Moscow, 1957. V. Propp, *Russian Agricultural Feasts*, Leningrad, 1963 (both in Russian).

26 N. Matorin, *The Christian Orthodox Cult and Production*, Moscow-Leningrad, 1931. O. Sukhareva, 'On the problem of Islamic saint worshipping in Central Asia', *Transactions of the Institute of History and Archaeology: Data on the Archaeology and Ethnography of Uzbekistan*, Tashkent, 1950, vol. 2. O. Sukhareva, 'On the genesis of craftsmen cults among the Tadjiks and Uzbeks', *In Memory of M.S. Andreyev, Transactions of the Academy of Sciences of the Tadjik SSR*, Stalinabad, 1960, vol. 120 (all in Russian).

27 V. Bogoraz, 'The myth of the dying and reviving animal', *Artistic Folklore*, 1926, vol. 1 (in Russian).

28 N. Matorin, *The Female Deity in the Christian Orthodox Cult: Essay on Comparative Mythology*, Moscow, 1931 (in Russian).

29 N. Matorin and A. Nevsky, *Programme for the Study of Everyday Orthodoxy: East European Religious Syncretism*, Leningrad, 1930. N. Nikolsky, *The History of the Russian Church*, Moscow-Leningrad, 1931. S. Tokarev, *Religious Beliefs of the East Slavic Peoples in the 19th and Early 20th Centuries*, Moscow-Leningrad, 1957. G. Nosova, *Survivals of Paganism in Orthodox Christianity*, Moscow 1975 (all in Russian).

30 L. Lavrov, 'The pre-Islamic beliefs of the Adyghe and Karbardians', *Transactions of the Institute of Ethnography of the USSR AS*, 1959, vol. 51. O. Sukhareva, *Islam in Uzbekistan*, Tashkent. G. Snesarev, *The Relicts of Pre-Islamic Beliefs and Rites among the Uzbeks of Khoresm*, Moscow, 1969. V. Basilov, *Saint Worshipping in Islam*, Moscow, 1970. T. Bayalieva, *Pre-Islamic Beliefs and Rites in Central Asia*, Moscow, 1975. T. Bayalieva, *Pre-Islamic Beliefs and their Survivals among the Kirghiz*, Frunse, 1972 (all in Russian).

31 G. Snesarev, 'Some reasons why religious survivals are still preserved in everyday life among the Uzbeks of Koresm', *Sovietskaia Etnografia*, 1957, no. 2 (in Russian).

32 All the necessary information can be found in the series *Problems of Scientific Atheism*, published by the Institute of Scientific Atheism at the Academy of Social Sciences, founded in 1964 (in Russian).

33 For more details see *Concrete Studies of Contemporary Religious Beliefs*, Moscow, 1967 (in Russian).

34 For more details see I. Kryvelev, 'The contents of the concept of religion', *Proceedings of the 7th ICAES*, Moscow, 1970, p. 713 (in Russian).

C. HUMPHREY

Theories of North Asian shamanism

The ancient religious activity of the Mongols and their neighbours, known to us Europeans as shamanism, has no particular name amongst its own followers. The Mongols, even before they were re-converted to Lamaism in the seventeenth century, simply used the term *xara šasin* (black faith), as it were in verbal opposition to *šira šasin* (yellow faith), a popular term for the reformist sect of Tibetan Budd-hism which spread into Mongolia.[1] After the seventeenth century, when shamanism was outlàwed in many of the Mongol princedoms, the lamas and their faithful, although they had names for the great world religions and even for Bon-po and Taoism, called shamanism merely *xagučin ba burugu üzel* (the old and wrong way of seeing things).[2] At the same time, these very lamas used thinly disguised 'shamanist' rituals in their own religious activities. Even among purely shamanist groups such as the north-western Buryat or the Reindeer Tungus it is easy to discover Lamaist deities and cosmological ideas which spread all through Eastern and Central Asia down to India. All this raises the question of whether 'shamanism', which had not even got a name, should be seen as differentiated from Lamaism at all in the Mongolian context. Can we say, in fact, that shamanism is a religion in its own right?

Scholars have put forward many different views on this matter, and it is clear that one of the main reasons for this is the undoubted com-plexity of religious history in Central Asia. The prevalence of nomadic pastoralism in the area, the long-distance trade routes, and early steppe empires all facilitated communication between peoples, and the pres-ence in central Asia at one time or another of all the main world religions (Buddhism, Mohammedanism, Christianity) is only one manifestation of this. I have no wish to suggest that there is a single clear answer to the question of the general nature of shamanism in the Mongol area, and therefore I shall first explain the various directions in which existing theories have pointed, before attempting to put forward some specific conclusions.

Eliade, who has written one of the largest ethnographic compilations on North Asian shamanism, concludes that it is essentially a technique for ecstasy by which men can communicate with the spirits. Although he describes shamanism as 'archaic', by which he means that it pre-dated, in his opinion, the first great expansion of Buddhism through Asia, he does not see it as an autonomous system, nor as a related group of such systems.[3] In his view, the shaman does not create a cosmology but simply uses one – and, as far as one can tell, almost any one.

To Eliade the shaman is essentially a person who is able to put himself into a controlled ecstasy for religious purposes. The original 'archaic' shamanism was centred on a belief in a celestial supreme being and in the possibility of concrete communication (in the person of the shaman) between sky and earth. The present existence of shamans in a great number of societies which do not have such a belief is ascribed by Eliade to the survival of shamanist techniques where the original cosmology has disappeared. Certain basic symbols came to be associated with shamanism through the passage of history – the world tree, the world mountain, the ladder, the bridge, etc., each of these being different manifestations of the single primitive belief in a 'centre of the world', a communication path used by the shaman in his ascent to the sky. The present emphasis in many Siberian shamanist cultures on spirits and spirit-possession are later accretions, perhaps resulting from the spread of Buddhism in Central and North Asia.

Eliade presupposes that 'shamanism' as a phenomenon of ecstatic technique has existed throughout the ages in North Asia; and yet he can give no psychological or physiological description of this technique such as to establish that he is talking about the same thing through history. As we have noted above, the content of the shaman's performance and of 'shamanist' beliefs varies from epoch to epoch and from culture to culture.

Eliade's method, the isolation of elements of belief which are then compared as they occur in different cultures, and the search for 'assimilations', 'borrowings', 'survivals' and 'influences', while fascinating in its permutations of information, has two disadvantages. First, it does not make it possible to study shamanism as it occurs within any one system of thought; it is not apparent whether there are other religious manifestations in which the shaman does not play a part, and the specific contribution of shamanism within this totality is not illuminated. Secondly, although Eliade has a concern with the passage of time, he does not really attempt to give a historical analysis of the development of shamanism. There is no analysis of the social or ideological basis of shamanism, and indeed Eliade's whole enterprise suggests that such a basis would be more or less irrelevant, since in his view shamanism is a single phenomenon which has survived through many and great social changes.

On both of these points, Shirokogoroff's work is an advance on Eliade's (although it was written considerably earlier). Shirokogoroff gives an immensely detailed and comprehensive account of the religious system of the Tungus through history and places shamanism clearly in relation to other beliefs and rituals; an attempt is also made to locate shamanism as a psychological phenomenon within the general 'psycho-mental complex' of the Tungus.[4]

Unlike Eliade, Shirokogoroff sees shamanism as a fairly late phenomenon which was 'stimulated' by the spread of Buddhism. Shamanism was pre-dated by sacrificial cults of offering to the High God or Sky God, and this cult was served by priests with different functions from shamans. The twentieth century shamanism of the Tungus is not concerned with honouring the celestial god, nor with the ancient cult of the dead, but on the other hand it 'has its very profound roots in the social system and psychology of animistic philosophy characteristic of the Tungus and other shamanists. But it is also true that shamanism in its present form is one of the consequences of the intrusion of Buddhism among the North-Asiatic ethnical groups.'[5] Shirokogoroff notes that the word for shaman in Tungus (*saman*) appears to be of foreign origin, and furthermore the phenomenon of shamanism itself has southern elements. It is in the shamanistic cult of spirits rather than the ecstatic ascent to heaven, that we see Lamaist influence on shamanism, and the shaman's spirit-vessels, costume and drum can all be seen as having a southern origin. Ecstatic experience, he held, was basic to the human condition; what changed through history was the interpretation and valuation of it. Among the Tungus the ecstatic ascent to the supreme being in heaven gradually disappeared under the influence of the idea of spirits which came down to possess the shaman. Thus, while religious specialists had existed all along, the shaman's role, according to Shirokogoroff, is specific to the belief in spirits and the experience of possession. He attempted to show with historical material on migrations, etc., how and when shamanism arose among the Tungus. According to him it was quite possible for shamanism to exist alongside continuing celestial cults and also alongside Lamaism. There might even be some intermixture: shamans might be requested to take part in the celestial cults, and lamas might advise people to become shamans, or even take up shamanising for themselves.

Shirokogoroff's description of the psychological and social aspects of shamanism as it functions within the culture of the Tungus is unparalleled in Siberian ethnography, but most scholars find that there is not enough evidence to support his theory that shamanism was 'stimulated by Buddhism'. Apart from anything else, this theory would find difficulty in accounting for the similarities between Tungus shamanism and the shamanism of the peoples of far Northern and Western Siberia where Buddhism can hardly have penetrated as such. Furthermore, Shirokogoroff, like Eliade, gives logical, rather than historical or sociological, reasons for the disappearance of celestial cults and the growing influence of 'active, lower elements', and in this way divorces his theory from social, economic or political realities.

Apart from the early theories such as those of Sternberg[6] and Czaplicka,[7] it is only recently in social anthropology that an attempt has
been made to give a general sociological explanation of shamanism,
and this appears in Lewis's book *Ecstatic Religion.*[8] In most complex
societies, Lewis argues, the form that shamanism, possession, or trance-
states take, is determined by pressure internal to that society. He
suggests that people subject to these pressures, very often the politically
disadvantaged or people whose social role is not highly valued, will be
the people who create ecstatic cults, and in this case the cults will be
'peripheral' and will express the anti-authoritarian views of the members. On the other hand, in a society such as the Tungus, the most
serious pressures are external to society, for example, severe climatic
conditions, lack of food, or prevalence of epidemic diseases. In this case,
shamanism becomes the 'central morality cult' and embodies the main
ideas and values, including political ones, of the society. Shamanism
becomes a means by which the morality of society is activated in relation to individuals and groups.

This is a useful series of generalisations about human society as a
whole, but in relation to this particular culture area it is not very enlightening. In North Asia almost every example of a shamanistic cult
seems to embody features of both 'central morality cults' and 'peripheral cults'. Among the small-scale Tungus, for example, shamanist
spirits concern a far wider range of ideas and values than a 'central morality', if such can be distinguished, and the same is true of the Western
Buryat, as will be shown later. In both of these societies women and
other disadvantaged people can become shamans, and to take the other
case, that of the complex society, the Manchus with their empire maintained a court shaman, surely concerned with 'central morality', until
their downfall in 1911.

It is Soviet scholars who have done the most work and produced the
most interesting ideas about North Asian shamanism. Gumilev[9] criti-
cises Banzarov for seeing shamanism as an original religion emerging
naturally from the worship of the sky, plants, animals and man himself.
The number and qualitative differentiation of the deities found in
shamanism leads Gumilev to suppose that it is not an example of poly-
theism, but syncretism. Why is it, he asks, that the shamans ignore the
sky gods? And how is it that, despite his previous declaration of the
autochthonous character of shamanism, Banzarov ascribes the cult of
fire to Persian Zoroastrianism?

Gumilev himself proposes the following scheme. The early Mongols
did not have shamanism but believed in a single celestial god, and this is
attested by all of the important early writers, Rubruck, Plano Carpini,
Marco Polo and Rashid-ad-din. The blue sky of physical nature was
differentiated by the Mongols from the eternal sky, the latter being a
powerful god who demanded action on the part of his followers. At the
same time, an earth deity called Etügen was worshipped by means of
setting up cairns (*oboga*) on mountain tops, and thus early Mongol re-

ligion was characterised by dualism. The great sky deity Khormusta did not originate in Zoroastrianism, as Banzarov maintained, but in Manichaeism, from the Uighurs. Such creative and providential gods are not compatible with shamanism. Shamanism existed in the context of a cosmology consisting of three 'worlds', the upper, middle, and lower, peopled by human beings in the middle world and their souls (i.e. spirits) in the upper and lower worlds. The shamans were able to effect communication between these worlds, but this was a practice, not a dogma. What had this in common with the ancient Mongol religion?

The ancient Mongol religion died out because the Eastern Tatars took up Mohammedanism and the Mongols took up Buddhism. When these fell into decline there was a flow of shamanist practice which took varied syncretic forms. Gumilev sees the Tungus as the archetypal shamanists, and he holds that the West Siberian Ugrian religions are not really shamanism, but closer in fact to the early Mongol beliefs in an all-powerful sky god.

Gumilev has an extremely wide knowledge of the sources for the ancient Mongol period and earlier, and his article undoubtedly clears some of the confusions stemming from an uncritical acceptance of Banzarov. It is interesting also that he gives an even later date than Shirokogoroff for the origin of shamanism. However, it is worthwhile noting that while it is possible to deny the presence of shamans in the early Mongol period by claiming that the religious specialists mentioned in the sources were other kinds of priests or magicians, it is not possible to ignore the repeated mention of things very like *ongons*, the representations of spirits; this implies that, according to Gumilev, shamanism and *ongons* could exist independently, and this as we shall see is doubtful.

Gumilev is an orientalist rather than an ethnographer, and the Soviet scholars who have been interested in the development of shamanism in society have taken a different approach, although most of their conclusions do not differ substantially from his. Potapov, who has worked extensively on the peoples of the Altai, also maintains that shamanism was not an original, autochthonous religion.[10] According to him, it was preceded at least in the Altai region by a cult of the mountains (which recalls Gumilev's explanation of the worship of Etügen). However, Potapov adds that the cult of mountains was not simply an abstract idea but it was closely linked with the economy and society of a particular historical time: each sacred mountain was situated in the centre of clan territory, whether this was used for hunting or herding, and was the site for the worship of the clan ancestor from whom each living member traced his descent. The existence of a sacred mountain in a particular territory was evidence that this land was in economic use by a particular group. The cult of mountains was generally carried out by elders of the lineage, but in complicated rituals by the shaman since he was the ritual specialist representing the lineage. Potapov claims this cult was essentially pre-shamanist since no representations were made of mountain spirits, while models were made of all other spirits. Here Potapov is saying, unlike Gumilev, that representations (*ongons*) exist together with shamanism, and that one cannot exist without the other.

According to Potapov shamanism arose only with the dissolution of clan-based society in North Asia. Previously the functions of the shaman had been carried out by every member of the clan and it was only when the strict tribal system began to distintegrate that these functions were transferred to a single person. This view is supported by Vainstein who attempts to show in an interesting article entitled 'The Tuvan shaman's drum and the ceremony of its enlivening'[11] that the evolution of shamanism is manifest in the ritual of the consecration of the shaman's drum: in the first section of the rite the shaman-owner-to-be was not allowed to be present, but all of the clansmen acted as though in a trance and struck the drum, handing it from man to man until they passed it to the weakest shaman present; it ended up in the hands of the most powerful shaman among the relatives. The second phase of the rite was conducted by the shaman-owner, alone in a tent, and subsequently no-one apart from him could handle the drum.

Vainstein maintains that this view of the evolution of shamanism is supported by the fact that there are Siberian peoples where the distinte-gration of the clan system has happened more slowly and where there were no professional shamans until recently, the functions of the shaman being performed by many people.[12] Shamanism, he maintains, always existed in a secondary role, but without specialised ministers it went unnoticed by early observers. Only with the development of class society were the old clan cults pushed into oblivion, and single individuals came to take on and elaborate the shaman's role. It is noticeable that the most complex shaman's costume occurs in Southern Siberia, where the influence of class-dominated empires was strong, while moving north-west and north-east, it becomes more and more simplified and finally vanishes.

These are plausible arguments, but unfortunately there is, as yet, little concrete historical material to back them up. It is not clear what, in sociological terms, Vainstein means by 'the disintegration of the clan', since clans in some form or other have been present in the Altai-Tuva-Buryat area virtually until today. If he is implying that clans were previously more communalised and egalitarian in this region, then this remains to be demonstrated, although there is no reason why this should not be so. Vainstein's early historical materials concretely referring to Tuva and the Altai only show that shamanism was not mentioned. In the absence of more data, he tries to show the existence of a series of different existing types of shamanism in Siberia that some of these are 'earlier' in kind than others; the disadvantages of this kind of argument are well known.

All recent Soviet research emphasises the close intertwining of sha-manist, Buddhist, and pre-shamanist elements in the current religious life of North Asian peoples. Zhukovskaya makes the point that Budd-hism itself had undergone a transformation since its early days; the modest cells of ascetic lamas under the guidance of a guru, which at least in legend formed the beginning stages of Buddhism, developed in Tibet into a complex hierarchy of ranks and offices, headed by the Panchen-Lama and the Dalai-Lama.[13] A complex and hierarchical cosmology was elaborated which included large numbers of deities, some of them human beings who had attained holy status. At the same time, the idea emerged that deities could spiritually embody themselves in human vessels, and Tibetan monasteries were frequently headed by such 'gods in disguise'. All of this meant that hierarchical Tibetan so-ciety, which had taken the form of a kingdom since at least the seventh century, assimilated and developed a cosmology which itself closely represented the hierarchical principle.

Zhukovskaya does not mention the fact that the Mongolian region may first have been exposed to Buddhism at a very early period, before the development of the wealthy monasteries and the great teaching sects, when wandering missionaries took the belief along the trade routes to the north of Tibet.[14] She does not even touch upon the taking up of Buddhism by the Mongols during the Yüan Dynasty but confines her study to the later period of the re-penetration of Lamaism into Mongolia in the seventeenth century.

The standard picture of this process is of a distinct, Tibetan form of Lamaism rapidly gaining ground in Mongolia, encouraged by the aristocracy and later by the Manchus; this was opposed by native Mongol shamanism, the religion of the ordinary people, which although it soon gave way to Lamaism was in the end to influence the latter strongly.

But the shamanist elements in Lamaism cannot be attributed en-tirely to the influence of the Mongol 'black faith', since Tibetan Lamaism already been in contact for many centuries with Bon-po. This Tibetan religious system seems to have been closely similar to shaman-ism. There was intense rivalry with Lamaism but by the seventeenth century both systems had acquired some of the typical attributes of the other: Bon-po had acquired monks, monasteries, and holy books, on the model of the Ganjur and Tanjur, while Lamaism had specialists in magic, exorcism, possession, trance and sorcery.

So the Buddhism which reached Mongolia in the seventeenth cen-tury and Buryatia a century later was already to some extent a syncretic religion. Furthermore, all scholars agree that the shamanism which it found in Mongolia cannot have been a 'pure' form, since, quite apart from all the arguments brought forward by Gumilev, etc. it had been preceded only shortly before by the period of Buddhism of the Mongol Empire.

Zhukovskaya observes quite rightly that the key to all of these changes of religion in Mongolia is the development of different forms of society over the period in question. Her view is that shamanism arose with the transmission from a society based on kinship (*rodovoy stroy*) to feudalism. The concentration of religious functions into the hands of one individual, the shaman, was the beginning of this process. But once feudalism had in fact established itself and a class society had developed, shamanism was no longer appropriate. The class of 'exploiters' needed a religion which justified the present state of affairs on earth, and which encouraged the less fortunate to bear their fate patiently in the expectation of a better life hereafter. This function was fulfilled by Buddhism.[15]

This argument is not explained in detail by Zhukovskaya and for it to be fully acceptable we should need to know what exactly were the changes in the society based on clans which turned it into a feudal society and why these should result in the emergence of individual shamans; we should want to know what 'feudalism' means in the context of nomadic pastoralism – it might, for instance, be more enlightening to explore the use of the Marxist types 'military democracy'[16] and the 'asiatic mode of production'[17] for certain periods in central Asian history. This is not the place to explore these questions in full, and I shall simply take it that Zhukovskaya's theory, which tallies in its outlines with that of other Soviet scholars, gives us an adequate explanation in general, if not in particular.

By the nineteenth century, when we begin to have reliable information, shamanism and Buddhism in Buryatia had not only many common ideas, but also numerous common practices. It is not possible to think of them as forming two complementary parts of a single religious system. In this, North Asia appears to be different from South-East Asia, where in Thailand, Burma and Ceylon, Buddhism and 'spirit-cults' have been described as existing side-by-side, with different and complementary religious and social functions.[18] In the South-East Asia case, Buddhism represents an ascetic and holy way of life, usually possible only for short periods of the life-span, directed at obtaining religious merit and a better re-birth; matters of health, material prosperity, fertility and luck in this life are the concern of a variety of other specialists more or less outside Buddhism. But in North Asia, in Lamaist areas, up to forty per cent of the entire male population spent a whole lifetime in the monastery or in orders; a rigorous life spent contemplating philosophical truths and the after-life was not even attempted by the majority of lamas, concubines were regarded as a necessary evil, and high Buddhist ranks were even passed on to natural heirs. Lamaism could fulfil all the needs of this life as well as those of the next, and in this sense there was nothing that a Buryat shaman could do that a lama could not also do: there were lama diviners, lama mediums, lama medicine men, and lama exorcists. Some of the ecstatic/magical practices of the lamas were far beyond the resources of shamans: for example, there was the *tsam*, a huge dance representing the exorcism of the elaborate and terrifying masked figures of demons.

There is no need to assume that the elements of shamanism and

Buddhism which seemed similar by the nineteenth century had a common origin, or even that they were necessarily borrowed from one another. Despite numerous similarities the two implied radically different approaches to morality. However, we can perhaps assume that behind what likenesses there were lay similar social forms.

By the late nineteenth century it was clear that in Mongolia, unlike South-East Asia, shamanism and Buddhism did not exist together harmoniously in the same community. On the contrary, there were areas which were definitely 'Buddhist' and others which were clearly 'shamanist'. In Central and East Mongolia few shamans remained by the beginning of the twentieth century,[19] while, on the other hand, the Western Buryats never took up Buddhism, despite the repeated efforts of lama missionaries and the performance of miracles. The 'Chronicle of the Alar Buryats' tells us what happened in one such case.[20] A temple was built in Alar in 1840 with thirteen lamas and a head-lama (*shiretei*), all of whom were Khori Buryats. The local population was entirely shamanist and was frankly uninterested in the temple, although some people did point out that the *shiretei* was neglecting his vows by keeping concubines. It was decided to replace the *shiretei* with a local man, Choivan Samsonov. Not only did Samsonov keep a 'wife' and rear a family, he knew nothing about Buddhism and soon built special yurts and outhouses for his large collection of shamanist *ongons*. He was succeeded in his old age by his son, Ganzhur Choivanov, the first of the *shireteis* to have a degree from a Buddhist monastery. Choivanov waged an energetic war against the shamanists, but he had no success; the whole idea of making religious merit by sacrificing property to the lamas passed right over the heads of the local Buryats who saw only unnecessary expense for no purpose. In order to avoid his annoying exhortations many of them even asked to be baptised into the Orthodox Church. By the beginning of the twentieth century, the Alar Temple was still small and poor, with twelve lamas, and it was soon closed down.

To these Buryats, Buddhism and Orthodoxy were seen as equivalents, and the decision to join one or other had more to do with politics than religion. Under Russian rule there were definite advantages in being Orthodox.[21] But the conversion was only superficial; many Orthodox Buryats almost never went to church, but had frequent contact with shamans. Side by side with an icon hung rows of shamanist *ongons* in their yurts. St Nicholas himself became the *ongon* of the harvest, bringing luck and prosperity in the crop-agriculture which Buryats associated primarily with the Russian peasant economy.[22]

The two important religion systems for the Buryat were shamanism and Buddhism, and the vital question is – why did the Western Buryat remain shamanist, while the Eastern Buryat took up Buddhism? The answer, I think, can only be given in terms of differences in society. The Western Buryats had a relatively stagnant economy as a result of pressure on land: the growth of the Buryat population, the surrounding forest terrain which made an expansion of herding impossible, and finally the coming of Russian settlers, meant that crop agriculture was greatly increased in the fertile valleys with a consequent lessening in nomadism.[23] The fact that the Western Buryats became attached to particular bits of land whose usufruct was regulated by patrilineal and other kinship links may have encouraged an ancestor-based view of society. An individual's rights to field and pastures were validated by the link he could trace with the commonality of 'original' Buryat users, in other words a link via named and relatively recent ancestors, women as well as men. The different kinds of links employed established a differentiation of rank among land-users. This kind of system was easily represented by shamanism with its multitude of ranked deities,[24] its great emphasis on ancestors as the arbitrary regulators of luck and success, and its professional practitioners tied to clans.

The Eastern Buryats, on the other hand, formed an expanding society based on nomadic herding. Great tracts of pastureland were available to the South and East of the Trans-Baikal steppes, and an expansion in the productivity of herders could result immediately in territorial expansion into North Mongolia, the Aga Steppes, and so on. Crop agriculture was barely practised at all and the use of land was not rigidly prescribed, as among the Western Buryat, by links with previously established ancestors. Eastern Buryats nomadised virtually irrespective of whether neighbours were kin,[25] but nevertheless they had a much more unified and monolithic idea of their society.[26] The eleven Khori lineages of the Eastern Buryat were descended from a common ancestor who belonged to the mythic configuration of people related to Ghengis Khan. Other 'Eastern Buryats' were people of Mongol origin, people who had belonged to some army, guard, or tribe in the Mongol orbit, but who often had forgotten their precise genealogical links with the past. In these circumstances, in which links with recent ancestors were relatively unimportant, it is possible that Lamaism with its universal, non-kin based, professional practitioners and its monolithic hierarchy did correspond more closely than shamanism to the needs and contradictions of Eastern Buryat society. Besides which, it is doubtful whether the Western Buryat economy could have supported a large number of non-productive men living in monasteries, even if such a move towards Lamaism had developed there. As for Zhukovskaya's argument that the Buddhist doctrine of the *karma*, by which individuals can only expect to better their lives in another rebirth, attracted the Mongol and Buryat aristocrats since it justified their privileged position, it is difficult to support this without reservation. Certainly, it was the Mongol feudal lords who encouraged the return of Buddhism in the seventeenth century, and Mongol society was hierarchically divided into classes of state serfs, personal serfs, monastery serfs, free-men, aristocrats and officials. However, the position was not entirely the same among the Eastern Buryats, who still retained a clan-based political system, and therefore this whole question requires further consideration.

In conclusion, the moral and intellectual differences between shamanism and Buddhism did not result in them becoming complementary religious practices which could be employed within one population. Instead, they became separate and even antagonistic in such a way that shamanism predominated in one area, while Buddhism prevailed in another. This was possible because Lamaism contained all the possibilities for ecstatic trance, possession, and curing which were used by the shamans. It is suggested that the development of Lamaism can be correlated with a hierarchical territorially expansive society, while the retention of shamanism is related to a descent-based society in which there is the need to validate land-claims by reference to ancestors. The position was not static and at the beginning of the twentieth century there were regions where Lamaism was gaining ground at the expense of shamanism (e.g. Tunka, Darkhat) and consequently the two did at that point exist within the same population.

NOTES

1 D. Banzarov, 'The black faith, or shamanism among the Mongols', *Collected Works*, Moscow, 1955, pp. 51-2 (in Russian).

2 W. Heissig, 'A Mongolian source to the Lamaist suppression of shamanism in the 17th century: pt 2', *Anthropos*, 1953, 48, 518.

3 M. Eliade, *Shamanism, Achaic Techniques of Ecstacy*, London, 1964, pp. 498-507.

4 S.M. Shirokogoroff, *The Psychomental Complex of the Tungus*, London, 1935.

5 Ibid., p. 130, note 52.

6 L.Ya. Shternberg, *Religion in the Light of Ethnography*, AN SSSR, Leningrad, 1936 (in Russian).

7 M.A. Czaplicka, *Aboriginal Siberia: A Study in Social Anthropology*, Oxford, 1914, pp. 116-291.

8 I.M. Lewis, *Ecstatic Religion: An Anthropological Study of Spirit Possession and Shamanism*, London, 1971, pp. 18-36.

9 L.N. Gumilev, *The Ancient Mongol Religion*, Dokl. Otdel. i. Komissyi Georgr. ob-va SSSR, 5, Leningrad, 1968, pp. 31-8 (in Russian).

10 L.P. Potapov, 'The mountain cult in the Altai', *Sovietskaia Etnografia*, 1946, no. 2, pp. 31-8 (in Russian).

11 S.I. Vainstein, 'The Tuvan (Soyot) shaman's drum and the ceremony of its "enlivening"', in V. Dioszegi (ed.) *Popular Beliefs and Folklore Tradition in Siberia*, The Hague, 1968, pp. 331-8.

12 S.I. Vainstein, 'Shamanism of Touvinians', *7th International Congress of Anthropological and Ethnological Sciences*, Moscow, 1964, p. 13.

13 N.L. Zhukovskaya, 'The influence of Mongol-Buryat shamanism and pre-shamanist beliefs on Lamaism', in G.G. Stratanovich (ed.) *Problemy Etnografii i Etnicheskoy Istorii Narodov Vostochnoy i Yugo-Vostochnoy Azii*, AN SSSR, Moscow, 1968, p. 219 (in Russian).

14 M. Bussagli, *Painting of Central Asia*, translated L. Small, Geneva, 1963, pp. 20-9, for example, describes the spread of Buddhism eastwards along the silk route by tracing early wall paintings dating to the second half of the third century A.D.

15 Zhukovskaya, op. cit., pp. 235-6.

16 G.E. Markov, 'Some problems of social organisation of the nomads of Asia', *Sovietskaia Etnografia*, 1970, no. 6, pp. 74-89 (in Russian).

17 K. Marx, *Pre-Capitalist Economic Formations*, ed. E. Hobsbawm, London, 1964, pp. 33-4, 67-9.

18 E.R. Leach, Pulleyar and the Lord Buddha, an aspect of religious syncretism in Ceylon', *Psychoanalysis and the Psycho-analytical Review*, vol. 49, no. 2. S.J. Tambiah, *Buddhism and the Spirit Cults in North-East Thailand*, Cambridge, 1970.

19 V. Dioszegi, 'Problems of Mongolian shamanism: report of an expedition made in 1960 in Mongolia', *Acta Etnographica* (Budapest), vol. 10, fasc. 1-2, 1961, p. 196.

20 G.N. Rumyantsev, *Chronicle of the Alar Buryat*, 1949, Zapiski NIIKE B-M, 9 (in Russian).

21 I.M. Manzigeev, *The Yangut Buryat Clan*, Ulan-Ude, 1960, p. 202.

22 Ibid., p. 110.

23 N.P. Mangutov, 'Social-economic relations in western Buryatia', *Etnograficheskyi Sbornik*, Ulan-Ude, 1965, 4, p. 111.

24 L. Krader, 'Buryat religion and society', *Southwestern Journal of Anthropology*, 1954, 10, pp. 322-48.

25 I.A. Asalkhanov, 'On Buryat clans in the 19th century', *Etnograficheskyi Sbornik*, Ulan-Ude, 1960, 1, pp. 81-2.

26 B. Rinchen, 'About a Khori Buryat genealogy', *Acta Orientalia* (Hungary), 1965, vol. 18, p. 206, makes an interesting distinction between the written genealogies of the Mongols as opposed to the Buryats. The Mongols called their genealogies *udum sudur* 'chronicle of descent', and these were primarily concerned to show who were the descendants of a given ancestor. The Buryats on the other hand called their genealogies *uy-un-bicig* 'writing of the origin', and the aim here was to find out from whom a living person was descended, who were the ancestors. Rinchen concludes that the *uy-un-bicig* were closer to the shamanist cult of ancestors; they were used by Khori as well as Western Buryat.

PART VI

Concepts and methods

S. ARUTYONOV

Ethnography and linguistics

In this paper I will try to analyse the relationship between ethnography and linguistics. Ethnography studies, describes, and finds general solutions for the ethnically specific and differentiating components of culture (cf. in detail the paper by Bromley in this book). Linguistics is a science which fulfills the same functions for the language or languages as the object of its study. Language is here interpreted in a narrow sense, as definite languages which develop spontaneously in the course of speech activity in human social communities. As far as language in a broader sense is concerned, covering, for example, the languages of mathematical symbolism, we consider them as the object of the general theory of sign systems, of which linguistics is a part.

The problem of the delimitation of ethnography (or cultural anthropology) and linguistics – the problem of the definition of the areas of their common interests, tendencies, and perspectives of their cooperation and interaction – is, of course, topical on the international scale. Nevertheless, in this report I shall proceed mainly from the manner in which this problem is actually handled in the methodology and practice current amongst Soviet scholars, from the point of view of both theoretical considerations and the empirical experience of scientific work. In principle one can hardly dispute the fact that culture in a broader sense also includes language.[1] At the same time the special place of language among the mechanisms of culture as the basic and universal means of communication is also clear. Therefore its study has become the subject of the highly specialised discipline of linguistics which occupies a separate place among the sciences of culture, and differs considerably from the rest of them in method. But it is obvious that linguistics has some areas of contact and that it overlaps with other aspects of the study of culture as interpreted in a more restricted sense. The latter can be labelled as the extralinguistic culture, which also includes its ethnographic aspect. This is already clear from the fact that language, more often than any other cultural factor, serves as the basic factor in ethnogenesis and ethno-differentiation. It is also one of the basic standpoints of formation and preservation of ethnic identity. 'Due to a relative rigidity of every language system, to understand the ethnic identity of the bearers of a language it is sufficient to know only some of its elements, and therefore as a rule there is no need to analyse the system as a whole. '[2] Some exceptions to the rule, and the need to analyse the whole system, however, are often observed in contact zones. Such for instance are the zones of intermediary dialects calling for a study of correlations, coincidence or non-coincidence of dialect barriers with the boundaries of subethnic groups, and especially the zones of formation of mixed so-called creole languages and mass bilingualism. The latter problem is especially topical today and a vast literature is devoted to it.[3]

It is noteworthy that bilingualism is only one of many components of a large and complex problem of study in linguistic situations. This problem consists in the study of correlation in the functions and tendencies of the development of written languages and spoken dialects in homogeneous ethnosocial organisms, as well as different languages in multinational, poly-ethnic countries. The problem is on the border of ethnography and linguistics, and is actively explored by both sides.[4] Possessing an ethnic aspect at all levels, it can in its turn be viewed as part of a broad complex of problems, covered by the notion of social linguistics or linguistic sociology. The interdisciplinary character of this complex is clear from the very duality of these terms.[5] But far from all problems of social linguistics possess an ethnic aspect. In particular it is absent in such problems as language functioning in a society using computers, or the peculiarities of speech in the smallest groups, on the personal and family level. But wherever this ethnic aspect is present, there is the possibility and even the need to include the materials, methods and approach of ethnography in the study of problems under consideration. While the phonetic and grammatical phenomena remain completely in the domain of pure linguistics, and ethnographic materials are mainly utilised only to outline the social background of their functioning, the matter is quite different with lexicography and semasiology. Among the three components of the semantic triangle it is only the denominate which lies in the sphere of a purely linguistic approach, but as soon as its relations with the denotate and significate are concerned, as well as of these two with each other, some degree of ethnic specificity is inevitably present.

Two indispensable prerequisites for any linguistic study are a text (a corpus of texts) and a vocabulary. These prerequisites are granted in languages with a relatively long written record. The situation is different with non-literate languages and ancient texts awaiting decipherment. In the first case a fixation of texts and vocabulary is necessary, in the latter case the vocabulary must be reconstructed. Both tasks are in practice possible only with the invocation of extralinguistic cultural realities. In these cases an introduction of a new language into the scope of linguistics can be done only by a formulation of linguistic tasks within the framework of an ethnological approach and method. Only after this may a study pass into the domain of pure linguistics.

This situation is reflected in the history of practical studies in such languages in the USSR and in the literature devoted to this subject.[6]

It has been said that lexicography as a whole is a part of linguistics, and the one most closely connected with the study of extralinguistic cultural realities. Some areas of lexicography in every language in turn, when concerned with their denotates and designates (significates), comprehend holistic cultural systems, and contribute to the shared heritage of the spiritual culture of the people using this language. The study of such cultural systems, as well as of the corresponding denominational lexical corpuses, in principle implies a complex linguo-ethnographic approach, which is carried out at the overlapping areas of both sciences. Among such systems we can single out first of all various onomastic systems, like toponymy, anthroponymy, zoonymy and so on. A considerable growth of interest in such studies can be observed during the recent decade in the USSR.[7]

'Singling out special onomastic problems from the general sphere of linguistic problems can be explained by the position of proper names in language. Proper names are a part of language, which illustrates a most paradoxical situation, and their analysis will help to originate newer and deeper general linguistic concepts.'[8] So far as ethnologists are concerned, these problems are of interest when related to a number of very specific components of culture, which in some cases bear an ethno-differentiating character, and in others shed new light on the ethnohistory of the people. This may be exemplified by several cases, which do not, however, embrace all problems arising in this field.

Ethnonymy, of course, is directly related to the problems of ethnography, because it reflects ethnic identity as self-consciousness and as the identification of other ethnic groups, stereotypes and autostereotypes, and the ethnic structures and substructures of a society. The anthroponymical model is an important ethno-differentiating index, and its preservation or change may serve as a very reliable indicator of tendencies towards preservation or change in the sphere of ethnic identity. On the other hand, such indicators as specificities of cosmonymical terms often enable us to outline broader areas, which coincide with ancient historico-ethnographic areas, while toponymic data provide a possibility of outlining the regions of ancient substratum ethnic groups, and hence to deepen our understanding of the ethnogenesis of modern populations. A specific group of lexical forms, which is significant as a cultural component, are kinship terms. They form a system, which is actualised not so much in its linguistic, as in its sociocultural and ethnographic aspect. Therefore kinship terms are an object of study not only for linguists, but also by ethnologists. The connections of ethnography and linguistics in this field are numerous. They are not restricted by the fact that the object of study is at the same time both a linguistic and an ethnocultural reality. They are also manifested in the fact that at present kinship systems are investigated by a series of new techniques, especially by the method of component analysis. 'The principles underlying this method, and the main concepts by which it operates [here are meant the notions of denotates, designates, components or differential variables] have been borrowed from the new orientation in linguistics, which studies semantics in the light of sign theory.'[9]

Besides, to avoid the subjectivity and bias originating from attempts to translate the kinship terms of the language under study by kinship terms of the student's own native language, special 'languages' or code systems have been constructed for an adequate representation of these terms and their relations. A number of such codes exists, but some of them, which are the most valid scientifically and are utilised in Soviet scientific practice, have been created on the basis of the concepts and methods of mathematical semiotics, closely connected with linguistics.[10]

I have written above about the delimitation between the spheres of application of linguistic and ethnographic methods, and about the spheres where both these two methods overlap and cooperate. But through the example of kinship terms I have touched upon another aspect of the relationship between ethnography and linguistics.

I am speaking here about the mutual relations of two disciplines, which arise when within one of them certain methods, techniques, concepts and notions are elaborated, which are specifically destined or naturally suited for use in the other discipline, or when methods which developed and were approved in one of these sciences, can be transplanted into the other. A creation of an artificial 'language' (descriptive code) may exemplify the first situation, the transplantation of the method of componential analysis is an example of the second case.

The difference between the lingual and extralingual parts of a culture implies certain consequences, e.g. that in a language we face elements which are essentially much more rigidly organised, systematic, discrete, and hence are more easily available for a dissection into 'emic' units,[11] like phonemes, lexemes, morphemes. This original, initial discreteness is lacking in the extra-linguistic part of culture. Correspondingly, a transplantation of ethnographic methods into linguistics is hardly possible, with the exception, of course, of the techniques of interviewing an informer while studying spoken non-literate languages or dialect peculiarities. But this is already not at the level of scientific methods proper, but rather at the level of 'know-how' or fieldwork techniques. On the contrary, the transplantation into ethnographic practices of a series of methods, previously elaborated and approved in linguistics, has a history of a long standing, as well as certain prospects for the future.

What is already quite conclusive is that each of the two leading methods of any ethnographic study, i.e. the comparative historical method and the structural approach, have initially been developed in the study of language. Furthermore, we may emphasise that one of the main directions in the work of the Soviet ethnographers has always been the study of ethnogenesis and ethnic history. There is no doubt that such an inquiry can only be successful provided that a complex interdisciplinary approach is applied. The study of ethnogenetical problems calls for cooperation by experts in the spheres of language, ethnography, social history, physical anthropology, archaeology and so on. But we may still distinguish between three main aspects of the ethnogenetic process. They are: first, the formation of the language of the people under study, which can be traced back by the methods of historical comparative linguistics; secondly, the formation of their physical type, which can be traced by the methods of physical anthropology (including paleoanthropology); and, thirdly and most important, the formation of a common spiritual and material culture of the people, which is reflected in their shared self-consciousness and identity. The latter is traced by the methods of ethnography, and also of archaeology and social (written) history, when appropriate sources are available. Among these three aspects two, namely the language and the ethnoculture, belong to culture in a broader sense of the word, as a specifically human phenomenon, which can be contrasted with the biological phenomenon of man, reflected in the aspects studied by physical anthropology. This principal difference may help us to understand that physical anthropological concepts and notions, like morphological distances, or metisation, are not usually transplanted into ethnography.

The expression 'metisated culture', which is sometimes met in anthropological literature, would seem unscientific. On the other hand, such notions, elaborated by historical linguistics, as substratum, adstratum, superstratum, not only have entered the practice of ethnography, but have even become fundamental concepts in the ethnographic analysis of ethnogenetic problems.

The main principle of classification accepted in ethnography is the ethnolinguistic principle, which is based on the linguistic classification of the families of languages. Among some other principles of classification we must note first of all the classifications according to economico-cultural types and historico-ethnographic regions. The former has no regular linguistic correlations, but in the latter such can be observed. The sphere of extralinguistic culture, due to its diffused and general penetrability, can accumulate common traits with contacting cultures at a more rapid rate than language does, but in cases when the boundaries of historico-cultural regions remain stable for a long period of time, a tendency can inevitably be observed in such frameworks of a movement towards a formation of linguistic unions as well.

In as much as both language and ethnic culture belong to the class of phenomena which can be differentiated in space, there is a vast field for interaction between ethnogeography and linguogeography. Linguistic and ethnographic maps and atlases can be fully evaluated only by mutual comparison. Both the coincidence and noncoincidence of isopragmae and isoglossae and of their clusters can never be incidental, but always reflect some historical and structural regularities as their particular and concrete manifestation. The study of these regularities creates a number of problems which are common not only to linguogeography and ethnogeography, but also to the whole complex of chorological sciences. Constant work is being done in this direction in the USSR.[12]

Linguistics as a study of spoken languages, as stated above, can be considered a part, but the most elaborate part, of the general semiotics or the theory of sign systems. To a certain extent a sign aspect is present in all components of extralinguistic culture, and many of their manifestations can be also viewed within the framework of concepts of a sign system. Therefore the regularities, notions and principles which are shared by sign systems in general, but have been studied in greatest detail and most completely with respect to spoken languages, can to a certain measure be extended to the study of other cultural aspects, if the latter can be seen within the framework of the concepts of sign systems. This approach has found, probably, its most extreme realisation in the well known hypothesis by Sapir-Whorf, or the theory of linguistic relativity.

According to this theory, the way of life and the whole pattern of culture of every people is highly dependent on the specificity of their language. In Soviet linguistic literature this hypothesis has been criticised for its absolutisation of the role of language as the connecting link between reality and thought.[13] And even more so, from the point of view of ethnography, it seems unreasonable to speak of a such leading, dictatorial role of the lingual part of a culture with respect to its nonlingual parts. At an empirical level one can quote a number of examples in which a relatively rapid change in language did not result in the comparably deep transformation in the area of the extralinguistic culture. Therefore it seems to be more reasonable to suppose that various sign systems, including language, stand in relations of mutual influence and dependency, within the framework of every single ethnically specific culture, but need not always be related hierarchically.

There are attempts to transfer some quantitative methods, elaborated in linguistics, such as lexicostatistics, to the study of material and spiritual culture.[14] They are certainly of some interest, but have not so far been very successful, mainly because ethnography still does not possess a scale of taxonomical levels for the basic cultural units, which could be compared, for instance, with phonemes or lexemes, though some efforts in this direction have already been made. There is a much broader prospect for a creation of models of cultural contacts, using the analogy with the well developed models of language contacts.[15] Indeed, it is quite logical to draw some analogies between the mastering of a new culture and the mastering of a new language, between bilingualism and biculturalism, between the presence of substratum traits in both cases and so on.

On the whole one may conclude that the objects of inquiry of linguistics and ethnography are clearly delineated, and as a rule provide no place for confusion and misunderstanding. On the other hand, these two disciplines are related to each other in two ways: they are components of a broader science of culture, and they possess some notions which are general for the study of sign systems. Therefore their cooperation in the study of complex and border problems and their mutual conceptual and methodical enrichment may be very fruitful.

NOTES*

1 E.S. Markarian, *The Origins of Human Activity and Culture*, Yerevan, 1973, pp. 60, 87. K.R. Megrelidze, *The Basic Problems of Sociology of Thought*, Tbilisi, 1965, p. 120.

2 Yu.V. Bromley, *Ethnos and Ethnography*, Moscow, 1973, p. 222.

3 S.I. Bruk and M.N. Guboglo, 'Bi-lingualism and the rapprochement of nations in the USSR', *Sovietskaia Etnografia*, 1975, no. 4; 'Factors in the diffusion of bi-lingualism amongst the nations of the USSR', *Sovietskaia Etnografia*, 1975, no. 5.

4 *Problems in the Investigation of the Linguistic Situation and of the Language Issue in the Countries of Western and Northern Africa*, Moscow, 1970. N.M. Girenko, 'The ethno-linguistic situation in Zanzibar', *Sovietskaia Etnografia*, 1972, no. 6. *The Socio-Linguistic Problems of Developing Countries*, Moscow, 1975. V.N. Vologdina, 'The linguistic situation in Ghana', *Sovietskaia Etnografia*, 1975, no. 3.

5 *Problems of Social Linguistics*, Leningrad, 1969.

6 Bromley, op. cit., pp. 221-2.

7 E.M. Murzaev, *The Outlines of Toponymy*, Moscow, 1974. V.A. Nikonov, *Introduction to Toponymy*, Moscow, 1965. V.A. Nikonov, *Name and Society*, Moscow, 1974. S.I. Zinin, *Onomastics of the Republics of Central Asia and Kazakhstan*, Tashkent, 1974. A.V. Superanskaya, *A General Theory of Proper Names*, Moscow, 1973.

8 Ibid., p. 5.

9 *The Fifth All-Union Symposium on Cybernetics*, Tbilisi, 1966. M.V. Kriukov, *The Kinship Systems of the Chinese*, Moscow, 1972, p. 24.

10 Yu.I. Levin, 'Concerning the description of the system of kinship terminology', *Sovietskaia Etnografia*, 1970, no. 4.

11 K.L. Pike, 'Etic and emic standpoints for the description of behaviour', *Communication and Culture*, ed. A.G. Smith, New York, 1966, pp. 152-63.

12 *The Problems of Cartography in the Study of Language and Ethnography*, Leningrad, 1974.

13 V.A. Zwegintsev, 'The theoretical linguistic presuppositions of the Sapir-Whorf hypothesis', *Novoe v Lingvistike*, vol. 1, 1960.

14 I. Kwasneiwski, 'Structural and statistical methods', *Sovietskaia Etnografia*, 1964, no. 3.

15 V.Y. Rozentzweig, 'The linguistic approach to the description of cultural contacts', *7th World Congress of Anthropological and Ethnological Sciences*, vol. 5, Moscow, 1970, p. 629.

* All references except no. 11 are in Russian.

V.I. KOZLOV

Ethnography and demography

The ties linking ethnography, the research area that deals with the origin, evolution and interrelations of the world's peoples, with the general and particular elements of their culture and everyday life, and demography, which investigates the regularities in the reproduction of the population, the changes in its age and sex composition, etc. are at present adequately recognised in Soviet literature. The very names of these two research fields testify to those ties by their etymological affinity ('ethnos' translated from Greek bears a meaning almost identical with 'demos').

Until recently, however, these ties had only been recognised by a comparatively small number of scientists. One of the reasons for this was the fact that in the nineteenth and early twentieth centuries, at the time these two research fields were maturing, ethnographers usually concentrated upon culturally and socially backward peoples, and especially upon so-called tribes; demographers, on the other hand, whose studies require statistical data, busied themselves with the population of developed countries. At a later period ethnographers (and first of all Soviet ethnographers) widened their interest to include all the peoples of the world, while demographers extended their studies to the populations of developing countries; the breach between them had, however, already become consecrated by tradition and is only gradually being eliminated. Consequently it was long before many methodological problems having to do with the interrelations between these two fields received due consideration; some of them are still incompletely worked out.

In examining the ties between ethnography and demography it is pertinent to begin with the objects of their studies. The principal objects of ethnographical studies are peoples (ethnoses or ethnic communities) i.e. specific groups formed by people within a particular area; such groups are distinguished by their common language, culture, self-awareness, and certain other traits. The main object of demographical study is a population, i.e. the sum total of human beings as social and biological creatures inhabiting a certain area. In this sense the concept of population is akin to the same word as it is used in physical anthropology and biology; however, the latter presupposes a high degree of isolation of each group. The concept of population in its social sense does not imply such isolation; its investigators may freely change the framework of their study, treating the same people, for example, as belonging to the population of Moscow, of Moscow Oblast', of the European part of the Soviet Union, of Europe as a whole, etc. If the boundaries of such an area coincide with ethnic boundaries (e.g. in studying uni-national states) the objects of study of the two research fields also coincide.

In multi-national states, in areas inhabited by an ethnically mixed population there is, of course, no such coincidence. However, the stability of ethnic communities in comparison, for example, with rapidly changing professional and certain other kinds of social groupings, induced demographers to use the criterion of ethnic (national) affiliation as a group-forming index for measuring such variables as natural increase (birth, death, and marriage rates, etc.) for demographic analysis. In such cases the objects of study of ethnography and demography also coincide; only the issues investigated and the targets of the research differ for the two fields. True, these differences in their targets are not always so great; in some cases they may be organically combined, and this makes possible and necessary the drawing together of the two fields and their fertile cooperation.

In touching briefly upon those of the objectively required conditions for the development of ethnography and demography which help strengthen their mutual ties, we will first of all note their common interest in determining the numerical strength of peoples (ethnoses) and the ethnic composition of countries and regions. Ethnographers need such data because an all-round investigation of ethnic phenomena and ethnic processes is impossible without a detailed analysis of their quantitative characteristics; demographers need them for calculating the basic indices of population reproduction in their ethnic aspect and for carrying out ethnodemographic studies of scientific and practical importance.

The feasibility of cooperation between ethnography and demography in issues of ethnic statistics appears self-evident. Peoples (ethnoses), especially in highly developed class societies, are exceedingly complex social entities; each of them possesses a multitude of specific features which, by the way, gravely hamper the task of elaborating a general scientifically valid definition of the concept of 'a people' and of establishing its basic characteristics. A statistician insufficiently conversant with ethnic issues may easily make the mistake of identifying the ethnic community with the racial, religious, or, for example, a state community; he may mistake a group of kindred ethnoses for a single people or, conversely, a part of an ethnos (one of its ethnographic groups) for the whole. Hence it is ethnography that furnishes demographic statistics with the scientific apparatus needed for registering ethnic affiliation in population censuses, and with a reliable framework for attaching this or that demographic index to particular ethnoses.

Soviet ethnographers actively participate in preparing and carrying out population censuses in the USSR, mainly in elaborating the census programs, formulating questions on ethnos and language, compiling lists of peoples and languages for the final tabulating of the census data, etc.[1] Ethnographers also play an important role in determining the ethnic composition of the population of foreign countries: they work out methods for analysing and correcting materials of the state censuses, for utilising different kinds of indices, including indirect ones, such as religion, citizenship, etc. One of the important problems here is that of the interrelation between the index of national (ethnic) affiliation based upon the people's self-consciousness, and regarded in scientifically organised statistics (such as those of the USSR) as the basic index of ethnicity, and indices of language, (mother tongue, language principally spoken, etc.) which are frequently encountered in censuses. Among works on this subject we will note *Numbers and Distribution of the World's Peoples*, Moscow, 1962, in which the methodology of determining national composition of all the countries of the world is discussed and its detailed description given; this includes data on the numerical strength and geographical distribution of 900 peoples of the world.

Cooperation between ethnography and demography in the study of the trends of change of ethnic and demographic phenomena presents greater complexities, but it is none the less organic. The requirements of ethnography in this respect have been reinforced by those of history, and to a certain extent by those of sociology and other social sciences, owing to the important role played by peoples in historical processes both past and present, as well as by the great social and political importance of the problem of nationality in the life of many societies and in international relations. And one of the major elements in the study of national-ethnic phenomena is the detailed analysis of the numbers of the interacting peoples, the quantitative evaluation of the ethnic (and also linguistic, racial, religious) composition of countries, as well as of their changes in the course of historical evolution due to social-economic and other qualitative changes. We do not here touch upon the cooperation between history and demography, and problems of historical demography arising from the need to evaluate the role of demographic factors in history, and among them quantitative population indices: the numerical strength of past societies. We will only note that quantitative changes in society are not always transformed into qualitative ones or vice versa. Hence in actual social-economic situations the influence of population figures (and indices based upon these, such as density) on a group's evolution have always been of an exceedingly complex and sometimes contradictory character.

Quantitative evaluation of peoples is of particular importance to ethnography, in which they are the main object of study. Its significance lies not only in indicating the size of an ethnic community or the diffusion of a particular language or specific culture elements, etc. The numerical strength of peoples is intimately linked with their ethnic history; it influences this history and itself undergoes changes in the course of historical progress. The formation and evolution of large peoples differs considerably from that of small ethnic communities. Every sharp change in a people's numbers, whether an increase or a decrease, testifies to some change in their condition, mirrors some important stage in their social-economic and cultural development, or such major historical events as famine, war, etc. The quantitative criterion plays an important role in the typology of ethnic communities; it may be of help, for instance, in singling out so-called national minorities and in distinguishing a type of ethnos such as the national (*natsiya*) from earlier, comparatively small tribal and other types of ethnic entities. Interaction between peoples, and the resulting ethnic processes, are also largely determined by the numerical proportion of the contacting groups; thus, it is the minorities that are usually assimilated, and especially those groups that are dispersed in an alien environment.

Changes in the numerical strength of peoples result from two main groups of factors. The first group comprises the characteristic features of their natural reproduction (primarily, the correlation of birth and death rates specific for each ethnos); the second – ethnic processes, i.e. processes of the division or amalgamation of peoples or of their component parts.[3] Obviously, cooperation between ethnography and demography takes place chiefly in the study of those demographic factors which influence the trends in the numerical strength of individual peoples.

The main purpose of demography is, as noted above, the study of regularities and characteristics of population reproduction. As demographic research expanded, however, owing to the aggravation of population problems in many countries in recent decades, it became clear that many demographic problems are still insufficiently studied. Among them are problems in elucidating the ethnic aspects of reproductions – the natality and mortality parameters characteristic of the world's various peoples. Available statistical data show that the birth and death rate coefficients and the natural increase (or decrease) expressed by the difference between them show great fluctuations both historically, at different stages of social-economic and cultural development, and between different population groups (living in different countries or in one and the same country) in each period, within the framework of a single social-economic structure. For instance, it is well-known that the natural increase index among the Yugoslavian Bosnians ('Moslems' as they are called in the population census) is thrice that of the Slovenes; in the Soviet Union it is almost five times higher among the Central Asian peoples than among the Latvians and Estonians, etc. Investigations of such differences have made it clear that the birth rate, which is at present the decisive factor of reproduction, is influenced by a complex set of factors; some of them are fairly closely linked with the ethnic nationality of the population or have a certain correlation with it. Ethnic aspects have also been observed in certain variations of morbidity and mortality. That is why demographers have begun to use groupings by ethnic affiliation more often than before, to investigate ethnic factors at greater depth, to uncover the mechanics of their influence over reproduction, and the level of this influence, and to make use of ethnographic data in such investigations.

Dwelling in somewhat greater detail upon joint ethnographical and demographical studies of the trends in the numerical strength of peoples, we will begin this brief survey with the analysis of natality. It must be noted that birth rates are determined by social-economical, cultural and psychological factors. A certain importance also attaches to physiological factors that influence child-bearing capacity, such as the age of puberty, length of the fertile period, sexual temperament, hereditary fertility (or constitutional bias towards multiple births) or, conversely, obstacles impeding conception or normal pregnancy (such as the difference in the rhesus factor between the parents), etc. Some of these factors are correlated with physical anthropological features and sometimes indirectly with ethnicity. However, the operation of physiological factors is not sharply differentiated between racial and ethnic groups; it is certainly insufficient to explain the existing differences in birth rates between the peoples of the world. Even among single racial groups the differences in the number of children born to people belonging to the same race but to different ethnic and social-cultural groups turn out to be wider than those between people of different anthropological types but of similar social-cultural position and way of life.

Ethnic nationality, as defined by the criterion of ethnic self-consciousness, which some authors include among the principal factors of natality variations,[4] does not in itself, at least in modern times, directly influence the birth rate level, although an indirect influence is fairly often encountered (e.g. when a people is organised into a state and that state carries out a particular population policy). Ethnic self-consciousness, the feeling of devotion to one's own people, may, especially when there is international friction, be expressed by anxiety for natural reproduction, for the numerical growth of this people through the active participation of married couples in child bearing.[5] Such motives for demographic behaviour do not, however, usually arise spontaneously but are inculcated by national propaganda. (A typical instance was the propaganda in Hitlerite Germany which urged 'true Aryans' to raise their birth rate.)

This does not mean that an ethnic aspect of natality does not exist, but only that ethnicity as such provides no answer to the question of why groups belonging to a particular nationality have a certain birth rate and not another. The ethnic aspect of natality results from a multitude of factors connected with the character of economic activities prevailing among particular peoples, their social and family organisation, culture, everyday life traditions, and orientations affecting demographic behaviour. At the same time, it should be borne in mind that ethnic differentials may be a secondary factor in their influence upon birth rates in comparison with others such as education; hence the wide scope of variations of the birth rate indices within one and the same people and, on the other hand, the occasional great similarity between different peoples. In the USSR, for example, spatial differences in reproduction types do not coincide with ethnic boundaries (all the peoples of Central Asia have approximately the same high birth rates).

A survey of those cultural and psychological natality factors most closely linked with ethnic identity[6] is best begun with the traditional attitude towards marriage. The high birth rates observed at present among many peoples, particularly in developing countries, are in great measure due to the traditions of early marriages prevailing in these countries. In conformity with these traditions, efforts are made to get a girl married almost as soon as she reaches puberty. Early marriage may adversely influence women's health; at the same time they may considerably increase reproduction owing to the longer duration of marital sexual relations. Traditions of early marriage are usually combined with the fullest possible inclusion of all nubile women in marital sexual relations; female celibacy in such societies is rare; when it does occur it is usually connected with religious prohibitions (such as the condemnation of the re-marriage of widows by Hinduism).

The basic unit of reproduction is the family; there is a certain correlation between the forms in which families are organised and birth rate levels. Many peoples indubitably owe their high nuptiality and reproduction rates, at least partially, to the prevalence of joint or extended families whose members aid one another with work in child rearing. The fall in the birth rate in many economically developed countries is certainly connected with the loss of the extended family tradition, with the 'autonomy' of married couples arising from urbanisation, the growth of education, and so on. In speaking of the demographic impact of family organisation forms the dual role of polygamy should be noted: on the one hand it somewhat decreases reproductivity owing to the lower incidence of sexual intercourse and larger period of post-birth abstinence; on the other, it may (especially where there have been losses in the number of males) heighten the marriage rates and thus somewhat raise the overall birth rate.

A very important natality factor is the tradition of bearing many children. Such traditions doubtlessly first arose in primitive society as a natural reaction against the prevailing exceedingly high mortality. They were largely retained and consolidated in the early class structures of agrarian societies. At present children are considered among many peoples as the highest good; childless families are pitied and socially condemned. One important stimulus of a high number of births, especially among peoples of developing countries, is the high infant mortality and the consequent danger that if the children are few, none of them will survive to the adult stage and there will be nobody to take care of their old parents. Among peoples with strong patriarchal traditions particular significance is attached to the birth of sons who will preserve the clan, or family.

The tradition of many children is fortified among many peoples by religious norms. Not infrequently religion also influences the birth rate level through orientations determining the age of marriage, marriage generally, forms of the family, and sexual relations. Confining the discussion to four major religions – Buddhism, Christianity, Hinduism and Islam – we may note that the two latter exert a strong direct positive influence over reproduction by encouraging early marriage and the bearing of many children (especially sons). As for Buddhism and Christianity, their influence in this respect is less clearly defined: on the one hand, the major branches of these religions condemn the use of contraceptives and abortions, thus furthering higher birth rates; on the other, they encourage 'mortification of the flesh', celibacy, monasticism, etc.

The social position of women is also a considerable natality factor. The social and domestic inequality of women, stemming from the survival of patriarchal traditions or from religious teachings (for most religions assign a humble place to women) certainly hinders birth control, and conduces to a high number of births, which raises the status of a woman in the family and in society. As this situation changes with social-economic and cultural progress, women acquire a stronger concern for birth control than men, since bearing a smaller number of children permits them to escape from the narrow circle of domestic interests and to become men's equals in the sphere of production and social life. Under these new conditions women may expand birth control in order to overcome the residue of their inequality.

Turning to factors of mortality, we must note that the results achieved in recent decades in overcoming its various causes (primarily disease) and the fall in the death rates in many former colonies almost to their level in developed countries, have, as it were, relegated its investigation to a secondary plane in comparison with birth rate studies.[9] (It is significant that in a survey of this subject – B. Benjamin, *Social and Economic Factors Affecting Mortality*, The Hague, 1965 – essentially no cultural mortality factor is examined other than smoking.) Nevertheless, this aspect of reproduction also deserves the greatest attention. Analysis of mortality has particular significance for historical-demographic studies, since for thousands of years, practically up to the twentieth century, it was mortality that determined the principal differences in reproduction, the features of the population trends peculiar to various peoples.

Unlike natality, mortality is strongly influenced by biological factors, including ecological and anthropological ones. In the course of thousands of years, people forming ethnoses lived in certain natural environments and adapted themselves biologically; this found its reflection in the origin and perpetuation of racial variations. Hence, there are the differences in the morbidity and mortality of racial (and partially the coinciding ethnic) groups of migrants to regions with conditions to which they were unaccustomed. Thus the greater incidence of respiratory diseases among the Negro populations in temperate countries (such as the USA) is due in part to certain physical anthropological traits (particularly their wide nostrils which led to better thermoregulation in the tropics but were of little use under temperatures below freezing point). Each ethnic territory, being geographically localised, differs in its natural environment from those inhabited by other peoples. Thus an adverse influence of environmental factors (climate, radiation, etc.) may have a localised ethnic aspect. The role of certain genetically transmitted diseases should be touched upon: owing to the universal prevalence of ethnically homogeneous marriages these may acquire an ethnic aspect; their injurious influence may be reinforced by traditions of cross-cousin marriages between blood relations.

An ethnic aspect of mortality was very apparent in wars. These sometimes changed the whole course of natural reproduction and the trends in the numerical strength of peoples. Such an ethnic aspect was clearly apparent in primitive communities and in early class societies, where military conflicts between individual tribes and peoples were predominant.[7] A nationally selective character was also nurtured by many modern wars, e.g. wars between national states, wars of national liberation, and a number of colonial wars. In the two world wars their effect upon the change in the numerous strength of peoples varied greatly: e.g. the losses of the Dutch in the Second World War were much smaller than those of the Byelorussians, approximately their equal in numbers. The losses sustained by certain peoples as a result of genocide resemble military losses in their violence: sufficiently characteristic are the slaughter of the Armenians in Turkey in 1915 and the extermination of Jews and Slavs by the Nazis in occupied Europe.

The specificity of morbidity and the level of mortality are strongly influenced by the way of life, in the broad sense of the word, i.e. including the types of economic activity which determine man's relations with the social and natural environment. The Javanese rice-grower, for instance, differs sharply in this regard from the Turkman sheep raiser, the Icelandic fisherman and the Welsh miner. Among ethnically differentiated factors of morbidity and mortality are popular traditions regarding the work regime, the daily routine, the diet, etc., as well as certain rituals. In many cases they lead to ethnic variations in mortality by sex and age. Thus the predominance of males in a number of Asiatic countries (India, Pakistan, etc.) is due primarily to the traditional disdain for women: new-born girls get less care, worse clothes and food, seldom receive medical aid in case of sickness, etc. All this, as well as hard work, early marriage, frequent pregnancies and child-bearing under unsanitary conditions has led to higher female mortality.

Morbidity and mortality among women and children are greatly affected by customs connected with pregnancy (such as various food restrictions for pregnant women) and child-birth (e.g. traditional methods of aid at delivery) and with infant care. In this respect customs of infant feeding are of importance, such as the duration of lactation, which varies among different peoples from a few months to three years and more. For instance, in investigating the differences in infant mortality between the peoples of pre-revolutionary Russia, the extremely high infant mortality among the Russians was shown to be correlated with their widespread custom of giving the baby, almost from the first days of its life, besides mother's milk, chewed bread, buckwheat gruel, etc. Among the Tatars and the Bashkirs, whose life conditions were no better, but who traditionally fed babies only at the breast, infant mortality was much lower.

In higher age groups mortality also shows a certain correlation with peculiarities of diet. Traditional food regulations, methods of cooking and consumption may play an important role in originating a number of gastric and other diseases including cancer. It is sufficient to mention the cancer-inducing effect of very hot dishes, of various smoked foods, etc. Moreover food traditions are so enduring that people are apt to reject new and better products even when suffering from food shortage (in India, for instance, many Hindus still reject meat, as well as fish from 'sacred' rivers); often food is cooked by methods under which its nutritious value seriously deteriorates.

Morbidity and mortality are seriously affected by the use of various foodstuffs used as stimulants, primarily alcoholic beverages. The traditional type of such beverages and the amount consumed varies greatly between different peoples. For instance some peoples include grape wines or beer in their daily diet, among others they are only consumed upon ceremonial occasions, etc. Very variegated and no less widely diffused are other stimulants, especially smoking of different types, from the comparatively weak tobacco up to such strong drugs as opium and hashish. The harm done by stimulants to the nervous system is aggravated by their injurious effect upon other organs and, besides this, by the cancer-inducing properties of many drugs, especially in cases of abuse. It is well-known, for instance, that tobacco-smoking leads to cancer of the lungs, of the oral cavity or the nasopharynx; studies of such diseases in India have shown that they are especially prone to attack adherents of traditional smoking methods (the hookah, smoking with the burning end inside the mouth, etc.). Bethel-chewing is prevalent among many peoples from the earliest times. Bethel, which is usually mixed with lime, as well as oral irritants, as it is in Central Asia (a mixture of tobacco, ashes, lime and cotton oil) may also lead to cancer of the mouth cavity or the gullet.

In concluding this brief survey of morbidity and mortality factors differentiated by culture and ethnos, I would underline certain links some of them have with religious teachings; this is particularly apparent in cases where contiguous peoples belong to different religions. Some examples, such as the influence of religion over the depressed domestic and social status of women were adduced above. In addition we will mention the existence in various religions of rituals and rules (baptism and the sacrament among Christians; ablution among Moslems and their pilgrimages to holy places, etc.) which have not infrequently caused widespread epidemics. The comparatively few healthy religious rules, such as (in Islam) the inclusion of ablutions in the number of actions welcome to Allah, take a secondary place in comparison with the mass of harmful rituals and teachings, e.g. exhausting fasts, and food restrictions. Such a negative role of religions, and their, on the whole, adverse influence over health, is due to their attitude towards life on earth as a temporary episode, to disease as the just punishment for people's sins, to suffering and privation as a sure path to eternal bliss in the hereafter. Consequently the struggle against religion may become an important part of the struggle for human health and happiness.

The organic links between ethnography and demography are expressed in the emergence on the boundary between these two sciences, of the new scientific discipline, ethnodemography. The intermediate position of this discipline may be seen in the two-fold character of its studies: on the ethnographical side they include trends in the numerical strength of peoples (i.e. of the principal object of ethnographical research), as well as of ethnographic, racial and religious groups; on the demographical side, the ethnic aspects of population reproduction processes and the influence of various ethnic factors over this process. The further development of ethnic demography may favourably influence the progress of both ethnography and demography. It may also greatly promote the complex study of important nationality and population problems.

NOTES

1 See S.I. Brook and V.I. Kozlov, 'Questions on ethnic nationality and language in the forthcoming population census', *Vestnik Statistiki*, 1968, no. 3 (in Russian).

2 See V.I. Kozlov, 'Demography and the system of historical sciences', in *The Place of Demography in the System of Sciences*, Moscow, 1975 (in Russian).

3 V.I. Kozlov, *Trends in Numerical Strength of Peoples: Methodology of Research and Principal Factors*, Moscow, 1969 (in Russian).

4 B.C. Urlanis, *Birth Rates and Life Expectancy in the USSR*, Moscow, 1963, p. 49 (in Russian).

5 P.N. Ritchey, 'The effect of minority group status on fertility: a re-examination of concepts', *Population Studies*, 1975, vol. 27, no. 2.

6 F. Lorimer, *Culture and Human Fertility*, Paris, 1954. Moni Nag, *Factors Affecting Human Fertility in Non-Industrial Societies: a Cross-Cultural Study*, New Haven, 1962.

7 W.T. Divale, *Warfare in Primitive Societies*, Santa Barbara, 1973.

J. POUILLON

Structure and structuralism

My aim in this short contribution is not to offer a systematic and exhaustive account of structuralism, nor to justify it theoretically, but simply to make its rationale understood. Since this can be achieved in many ways, from different points of view, I have to make a choice and to limit myself.

'Structure' is a word that can be used trivially and without special import, or conversely it can have an aroma – whether pleasing or aggravating – of esoterism. It is part of ordinary language and is included in every dictionary – which, incidentally, is not the case with 'structuralism'. It refers to the way in which the parts of a whole are organised, and applies to quite diverse orders of reality: spatial, as when one talks of the structure of a building; or temporal or linear, as when, for example, one speaks of the structure of a speech. These two examples show that the realities in question can be mental as well as social or material. Using the very terms of this definition, one can describe structuralism as a way of discovering the internal pattern of the reality under consideration. However this does not tell us much: everyone agrees that no reality whatever can be completely amorphous, and that coming to know it is consequently a matter of finding out how its elements are combined; in that sense everyone is a structuralist. But is that sense the right one? If everyone is a structuralist, no one is a structuralist, and why is there so much fuss, unless indeed structuralism needs a different and more precise definition? This tends to show that one can talk of structure without being a structuralist and that the word 'structure' as it is currently used does not imply the 'structuralist' method in the more specific sense which I shall attempt to define. Hence the idea that the method can only be understood in contrast to the current use of the word.

In practice, the current use amounts to making this word synonymous with organisation or pattern. Any structural reality – whether material or social, and of course here we shall stick to the latter – is a complex of elements that have established stable relationships amongst themselves; the network of these relationships is like the framework of the complex, it is its structure. In this perspective, structure is an empirical, visible aspect of reality which makes it possible to identify and classify an object, and this is no doubt useful. But, as such, structure is not explanatory; it is, on the contrary, explained by the very elements of which it is the combination, and which ensure its reality. These elements have their own meaning; it is their features that determine the different complexes to which they can belong, and these complexes can be compared and classified according to which elements are or are not present in them. The current use of the word 'structure' is therefore based on two implicit postulates: that elements have an intrinsic meaning, independent of the structures to which they belong, and that these structures are considered as belonging or not belonging to the same family, according to their similarities, that is according to the nature of their constituents.

It is precisely these two postulates that are rejected by structuralism which can be defined on the basis of this rejection. Contradicting the first postulate, structuralism makes it a principle that the meaning of an element is always a function of its place in the complex i.e. the relationships that link and oppose it to the other elements. The very notion of an element is itself relative to the whole, from which the element is extracted as a result of a partitioning that alone gives meaning both to the whole and to the parts. A type of behaviour can be an element in a system of attitudes, a term in a kinship terminology, a sequence in a myth. In all such cases it exists only in relationship to other elements. For kinship terms, this principle is obvious; its practical import comes out more forcefully when it is applied to the analyses of myth. Myths have often been characterised in terms of themes. Often these themes were merely striking and recurrent episodes, which were assumed to have the same meaning in whatever narrative they occurred. They thus served as a basis for the classification of the narrative. On the other hand, for structural analysis – and this is what makes it into an analysis – 'the significance of what seems given as [for instance] cannibalistic conduct is always contingent upon a context which alone can determine its real meaning,' and not upon a 'thematic approach, whose domain would extend to the series of myths and narratives where, in a more or less episodic fashion, the theme of cannibalism is present' (Marcel Detienne, *Dyonisos mis à mort*, Paris, 1977). It is true that in the *Mythologiques*, sets of myths are found which seem to share one simple motif: for example the origin myths of the cooking fire in *The Raw and the Cooked*. But it is enough to read these myths to ascertain that their unity is in no way based on the recurrence of the same episode, the same sequence: in terms of a narrative analysis, they can be completely different. The Bororo reference myth belongs to that set; and yet, should one choose to characterise it on the basis of what it tells, one would rather call it an origin myth of wind and storms. On what basis, then, can one class these myths together?

It is by rejecting the second postulate that the answer to the question is found. The rejection of the first postulate led to concentration not on the terms but on the relations between them, it is necessary to go further and concentrate on the way in which these relations are themselves correlated. It would indeed be useless to consider a relation in isolation: it would amount to treating it as an element at another level, and once more the set of terms and relations would appear to be the outcome of a summation. Relations must also be given a positional value arising from the system they constitute. In what way is this system explanatory? Precisely because it is defined as a set of correlations, and structural analysis aims at bringing out their rule(s). These rules not only account for the specific configuration from which they have been deduced, but also, and above all, for diverse ways in which this configuration could have been actualised. For this reason, to compare two sets is not so much a question of finding out whether they are alike or to what extent they differ; it is more a question of finding out whether they involve the same rules, whether the one can be considered as a transformation of the other. Thus the same structure can be materialised in quite different forms, and the recurrence of similar elements by no means warrants structural identity.

Let us take, to summarise what has been said, the case of what Lévi-Strauss calls the 'atom of kinship' (*Structural Anthropology*, 1958). It is based on four terms: brother, sister, father, son – where the brother and sister are also the mother's brother and the mother of the son, respectively; it links together ties of consanguinity, of affinity, and of descent. The terms are defined in relationship to each other, and similarly the three types of ties cannot be conceived of in isolation, since each one is a condition of the others. If the avuncular tie raises a problem, it is not, therefore, because it could fail to be present; then one would need to explain why in some cases it would be an addition to the other two. The avuncular tie cannot be missing since it is in the first place a relationship between brothers-in-law and as such a condition of the alliance on which kinship is based; thus the only problem is that of the various values that the relationship between the uncle and nephew may assume. From a structuralist point of view these values do not define the relationship in isolation from the others; they vary along with those taken on by the other relationships, according to a law of correlation which defines the structure as such: the relationship between uncle and nephew is to the relationship between brother and sister as the relationship between father and son is to that between husband and wife. The structure is that very correlation; it is not constituted by one or another of its possible patterns, for instance the pattern in which the avuncular relationship is positive, the sibling relationship negative, while the father-son relationship is negative and the husband-wife relationship positive. Otherwise there would be as many structures as there are patterns, as is implied by the ordinary use of the word. On the contrary, structure is what is invariable behind this variability. Yet one must definitely not mistake this last opposition for a new form of the dis-

tinction between reality and appearance. Singling out the same structure in different complexes does not cancel their reality or differences
since it is precisely the latter that makes the discovery possible; there is
no privileged materialisation of a structure compared to which the
others would turn out to be secondary. For instance there is no 'good'
version of a myth, if only because structural analysis developed precisely in an attempt to solve the problem raised by the plurality of
versions – whether of a myth, an institution, or a type of social
organisation. Let me add that the variability of a system is of course not
unbounded, and that there is not one but several structures in any
domain. In other words, analysis aims as much at determining the internal structure of a complex as at specifying the boundaries of the
family to which this complex belongs, according to its structure.

Thus the key notion is that of transformation. 'There is a very close
relation between the notion of transformation and that of structure . . .
an arrangement is structured only if it meets two conditions: it is a
system governed by an internal cohesion; and this cohesion, which
cannot be perceived when a system is observed in isolation, is brought
out by the study of the transformations, with the help of which similar
features are found in apparently different systems.' (Lévi-Strauss, *Structural Anthropology*, 1973, ch. 1.) I consider that the use of the word
'apparently' is unnecessary: systems do differ. What he means, it seems
to me, is that appearances, i.e. the manifestation of differences between
systems, make one suppose that they are unrelated. I would add that
even when systems resemble each other, this resemblance does not constitute their common structure. For instance, where social organisation
is concerned, structure is not a typical organisation that could be more
or less faithfully 'printed', to use a photographic analogy, in so many
copies; nor is it a schema that could be abstracted from several similar
organisations. Its definition depends on the way the following problem
is solved: how, among several organisations assumed to belong to the
same family, could one conceive of a connection which would be more
than a blurred reproduction, and one which could bring these organisations together as a group, irrespective of their manifest similarities or
differences? Each organisation is a given pattern of terms and relations
between terms, and is the outcome of their interdependence. But interdependence does not mean regular, permanent association; it also
presupposes interdependence of the terms or relations: they can be
associated in one place, and kept apart or linked otherwise elsewhere. A
term has no meaning other than a positional one, which is not to say
that it can occupy only one position. To understand this variability, one
must be able to show that the various configurations considered have
among themselves relationships of transformations such that each is a
variant of the others; jointly they form a group, the structure of which is
the rule of these transformations. This is why we cannot uncover the
structure of a reality taken in isolation: structuralism consists in considering, in principle, any reality as a case for which, as in grammar,

one must discover the declension rule.

This was the problem I was faced with in Chad. (It might have been more convincing to take as an example Lévi-Strauss' analyses of marriage exchange or of American Indian mythologies rather than a personal investigation which was left unfinished – I have been unable to return since 1967. In doing so, however, I hope to show the general value of the method.) In the area in which I was working, there are some fifteen localised groups (numbering in all about 100,000 people), speaking different languages and probably of very diverse origins. These groups are nevertheless known under the general name 'Hadjeraï' which simply refers to their land (the area is mountainous and the word means 'mountain-people') and does not imply any sociopolitical unity: each group has a name of its own and encompasses a few traditionally autonomous villages; common clanship across villages (and inside the same group) has no other consequence than marriage prohibitions, and no trans-village organisation can be detected. The villages' internal organisation varies from one group to another, so that whether it makes sense to claim to study 'the Hadjeraï' is open to question. However, that they constitute a culturally definable group is first shown by the remarkable identity of beliefs present in all these groups; and also and above all by the fact that the variability of social systems exhibited, upon analysis, a single structure, the states of which can be inferred from each other, once several principles present everywhere have been disclosed: at the level of beliefs, unity through recurrence; at the level of social organisation, unity of a combinatory system. The hypothesis of such a system can be put forward as soon as one notices that variations concerned the devolution of chieftainships as well as the distribution and hierarchy of titles and functions that were actually the same everywhere, the title being accurately translatable from one language to another. What varies is the relationship between the titles, their partial fusion or their complete dissociation, and above all the attribution of political power, linked here to one title, there to another. In short, it was as if the Hadjeraï shared the same conceptual lexicon but were using it to build different sentences, the common grammar of which it would be our task to discover.

Some villages are clearly built according to a manifest opposition – as well as a complementarity – between clan(s) 'of the earth' and clan(s) of the chiefship, the former being in charge of the rituals required for the prosperity of a village, whose chief and officers are chosen from among the latter. (I am here expressing, in a simplified manner, what is in fact a more complex opposition; it actually involves different stresses in a power that is two-faced: a religious dignitary is also a clan or lineage leader, while the village chief is also in charge of the rites for his clan of origin.) This opposition is put forward as being between natives and immigrants, with religious competence characteristic of the former, and power belonging to the latter. Village organisation would thus be the outcome of an historical process – there is no doubt that villages are composed of various elements, and that clans which inhabit them are of diverse origins – and, what is more, it could presuppose a former organisation, that of the village prior to immigration, where religious and political powers would have been but one. At first sight it seems that this interpretation could not be valid, either for those villages where all the clans claim to be autochthonous, or for those where, on the other hand, all clans acknowledge having come from outside. But one quickly becomes aware that in the first case some natives are, so to speak, more so than others, and in the second case the order of arrival makes it possible to oppose first-comers to late-comers, as natives to immigrants. Should one conclude that in all cases it is the process of settlement that has caused a division of society – and a fundamental division – since it would determine the distribution of offices in a way that would itself vary according to the degree of heterogeneity of the people? Should one assume an initial homogeneity only broken up by history? The analysis of rituals and foundation myths suggests, on the contrary, that even before the arrival of immigrants in an allegedly homogeneous village, religious competence and political power were already distinct, and that the former was based on a greater familiarity with the powers of the earth and of the mountain, which determine the fate of humanity; in other words, it was based on an assertion of an accentuated autochthony. This distinction is therefore primary, it is the structural *a priori* of the system, and provides the model of the distinction which subsequently opposes the original inhabitants to the newcomers. The first distinction makes the second conceivable, and provides the means of integrating immigrants, whose arrival has no other effect than a displacement and down-grading of power without change of structure. Thus the second distinction does not change the opposition-complementarity which is always present, but which is, on each occasion, the result of the specific history of each group, differently expressed; it informs the variable, but always correlated, relations between the various positions of authority.

Thus the Hadjeraï case illustrates the relationship between history and structure. (I could only present it briefly here. For a more complex presentation, see my book, *Fétiches sans fétichisme*, Paris, 1975.) Structure digests events, and imposes its own direction on them for as long as it can – and this may last a long time (when it does it is precisely what one calls a 'history'). Otherwise, under the impact of events, structure explodes and everything is rearranged, 'changing the course of history', or giving a specific history a new direction. This is probably what happened to the Hadjeraï with the troubles that Chad has undergone during the last ten years.

And yet, some may object, if structure 'cannot be perceived when a system is observed in isolation', how can one make the structural analysis of a given society? This objection is based on a misunderstanding: social structure is easily talked about as if there were only one for each society, when in fact any society 'covers a set of structures corresponding to various types of order' (Lévi-Strauss, *Structural Anthropology*, 1958, ch. 15): kinship, social organisation . . . each of which is to be studied according to the method described. Obviously it is because they interact, because they fit together that a society exists. But this fitting together is neither automatic nor predetermined. It would be so only if one postulated a perfect homology between structures. This is what functionalism does: functionalism does not consist in talking of function – one can think of function without being a functionalist, just as using the word structure is not enough to define structuralism; but it consists in granting a privilege to one of the several structural levels so as to bring back to it all the other levels, according to the assumed homology. There is undoubtedly a relationship between structural levels: morphisms but not homomorphisms. These levels 'can very well be – and often are – in contradiction to each other, but the modalities according to which they contradict themselves all belong to one group' (Lévi-Strauss, op. cit., ch. 16), which, incidentally, shows that structuralism is not tied to the static view of an harmonious social order. If it is possible to formulate the 'total model of a given society', it will not necessarily be a model in equilibrium.

To talk of a total model in no way means that an exhaustive knowledge of the societies studied by anthropologists can be achieved. The model considered is that of the transformations that would make it possible to move from one level to another and thereby to uncover the specific character of a society, whose various structures can nevertheless be found in many other societies. Indeed 'our ultimate aim is not so much to know what each society we study is in itself as to discover the ways in which societies differ from each other.' (Lévi-Strauss, op. cit.) It is precisely for that purpose, in order to throw light on 'those differential gaps [which] are the proper subject-matter of ethnology' (ibid.), that structuralism was developed. In short, the structuralist aim is to work out a system of differences that does not lead either to their simple juxtaposition or to their artificial effacement.

To conclude, let us go back to the ordinary use of the word 'structure'. Never mind, in the end, if this use continues to survive, not only outside structuralism but also among those who claim to adhere to it, Lévi-Strauss included. It is indeed handy and in agreement with etymology to call structure any consistent arrangement, any built-up system that can be identified within a complex set. What structuralism offers is less the singling out of a new reality than a new point of view on a kind of reality that was never ignored. One does not have to be a structuralist to acknowledge that a kinship terminology, social institutions, or a set of religious beliefs have the character of a system. And yet, rather than limiting oneself to describing such systems in order to establish a taxonomy based on their external similarities, the structuralist contribution has been to ask what makes a system a system, what rule governs its internal relations, what defines its possible transformations and may enable it to be brought together with other systems, even though perhaps no taxonomy would put them under the same heading. In other words, structuralists look for the structuring factor behind the structured set; and even behind that which fails to reach a precise and stable structure, but develops (to quote Lévi-Strauss) in a 'nebulous' fashion, as for example the world of myth. This is why, just as many talk of structure without being structuralists, one could almost – despite having little taste for paradox – be a structuralist and never use the word 'structure'.